Reg Pascoe

The Vet They Called God

Published by PascoeInk

PO Box 56,
Greenslopes QLD 4120

website - azpascoe.com

Copyright © AZ Pascoe 2022

The moral right of the author has been asserted in accordance with the Copyright Amendment (Moral Rights) Act 2000.

All rights reserved. Except as permitted under the Australian Copyright Act 1968 (for example, fair dealing for the purposes of study, research, criticism or review) no part of this publication may be reproduced, stored in a retrieval system, or transmitted in any form or by any means, electronic, mechanical, photocopying, recording or otherwise, without the written permission of the publisher.

 A catalogue record for this work is available from the National Library of Australia

https://www.nla.gov.au/collections

Title:	Reg Pascoe
Subtitle:	The Vet They Called God
Author:	Pascoe, AZ (1991–)
ISBNs:	9780645426304 (hardback)
	9780645426335 (paperback)
	9780645426311 (ebook – epub)
	9780645426328 (ebook – Kindle)
Subjects:	**BIOGRAPHY & AUTOBIOGRAPHY**/ Medical *(incl. Patients)*; **HISTORY**/Australia & New Zealand **MEDICAL**/Veterinary Medicine/Equine

The author has made every effort to ensure that the information in this book was correct at the time of publication. However, the author and publisher accept no liability for any loss, damage or disruption incurred by the reader or any other person arising from any action taken or not taken based on the content of this book. The author recommends seeking third party advice and considering all options prior to making any decision or taking action in regard to the content of this book.

Cover photograph of Dr Reg Pascoe with the some of the famous Nonda camp draft mares at Dr David and Heather Pascoe's Plaintree Farms at Wellcamp on the Darling Downs in Queensland. Photograph is (C) Copyright Heather Brown Pascoe. Reproduction is expressly forbidden.

Cover design and layout by Sarah Davies at www.instagram.com/lemon.design.studios

Photo collection supplied by the Pascoe family.

Reg Pascoe

The Vet They Called God

AZ Pascoe

for Grandad and Grandma

'You never have bad days unless you fail to learn something new and useful to take with you into tomorrow.'

– Reg Pascoe

Contents

Preface	xi
Introduction	xv
Part I — The Boy from the Bush	
1 An Unexpected Letter	1
2 A Wonderful and Very Frightening Expedition	21
3 Oakey's New Vet	45
Part II — A Leader in his Field	
4 The Oakey Veterinary Hospital Begins	65
5 An International Journey	85
Part III —Contributions to Veterinary Science	
6 Equine Medicine and Science	100
7 Growing Professional Veterinary Bodies	144
8 Publications and Symposia: the Sharing of Knowledge	189
Part IV — Contributions to the Australian Veterinary Industry	
9 A Vet and a Businessman: Provet	205
10 A National Veterinary Exam	229
11 The OVH Equine Teaching Unit	240
Part V — Going to Work for God	
12 Reg and the OVH in the 1970s	267
13 Reg and the OVH in the 1980s	287
14 Reg and the OVH in the 1990s	313
Part VI — Winding Down	
15 Retirement	343
16 A Lasting Legacy	358
Afterword	371
Acknowledgements	375
About the Author	381
Glossary	382
Endnotes	383

Preface

It is both the easiest and the hardest thing to write a book about someone you love. The easiest, of course, because you *care* so much: you would do almost anything to honour their memory and to craft a book worthy of who they were. And inevitably it is the hardest, for precisely the same reasons. I tried to distance myself as I wrote this book: I wanted the incredible things that my grandfather Reg Pascoe did to speak for themselves and on their own merit, rather than through the rose-tinted glasses of someone who loved him. Even writing this preface, referring to him as 'Reg' seems to come easier than Grandad. It can be challenging to navigate that space between a (mostly) objective biographer and the person I have been for far longer: a granddaughter who admired and adored her grandfather.

Who was Reg Pascoe to me? I spent most of my life knowing in a rather vague way that Grandad was 'someone' in the horse world. I can still remember meeting a boy in Grade 4 and telling him my full name. 'Pascoe?' he asked. 'As in, *Reg Pascoe*?' (Unsurprisingly, he and his family were involved with horses.) It was an inkling of a world beyond my comprehension, but other than an intermittent haughty feeling about my grandad's acclaim, to me he was just Grandad Reg.

My memories of Grandad are deeply tied to the small Queensland town of Oakey near Toowoomba and specifically to the Oakey Veterinary Hospital: in my child's mind, they were a package deal. Knowing what I know now about the intricate link between the two, this simple fact is beautifully, wonderfully fitting. I grew up in Brisbane, so we often visited Oakey in the school holidays, or Grandad and Grandma came down for Christmas and other holidays. They never missed an important event in my life and provided a safe and steady point of continuity of which many would be envious; it is only as I have grown older that I have been able to recognise just how precious such a gift is.

I have two particularly clear and treasured memories whenever I think of Grandad. One is of him at my graduation from the Royal Military College, Duntroon in December 2011. He sat at the long table and drank port and chortled, merrier with every sip and looking like he was having the time of his life. I remember how he and Grandma came up to pin my new rank on my shoulders, and the gentleness with which they did so.

The other memory is of the final time I saw him. My now husband and I were a few short weeks away from moving to the US for two and a half years. I had recently dreamt up the nebulous idea of writing the book you now hold and fumblingly proposed it to Grandad – which, of course, he received with his usual cool composure, leaving me unsure whether he thought it was a good idea or not. But this memory is simple: I remember how he hugged me goodbye for what neither of us could know would be the last time. He held me close and tight like I was precious to him.

2015. The author, second from left, with Reg and Joy and her eldest brother, Elliot Pascoe.

Settled overseas, I focused full-time on study and my fledgling project languished. In part, I was reticent to push. Grandad was private, and wrangling information from him wasn't always easy. It was also hard having such conversations from a distance because there was a kind of forced feeling to the discussion; trying to make sure I got what I needed, rather than the organic development of sitting with someone and gradually wending your way through the tale. This owes something to my 'interview technique', which is not my strong suit: I found interviewing people to be cumbersome and awkward, never quite sure of where to put my feet. Yet Grandad's assistance, even if at times it felt reluctant, was a vital part of my 'plan', such as it was. I intended to write his biography. I did not intend to do so without him here.

Grandad's death was one of the hardest experiences of my life. I say that with the honest admission that I in no way claim to have had a special relationship above or beyond any of my siblings or cousins; neither Grandad nor Grandma ever played favourites. I just loved him, very deeply, and felt loved by him in return. It was an easy, simple kind of love, though the word itself didn't get said often; that wasn't really his way. I just knew his love in the way he hugged me.

Sometimes it takes a disaster for us to realise just how wrong we've been going about things and what our choices have cost us: all that I lost, in being slow and awkward and reticent. And so, as cold as it sounds, in the immediate aftermath of his death, one of the biggest questions in my mind was: *How will I write his biography now?* It was my only clear path to remembering him, to treasuring who he was. It was – *is* – my passion.

I spent hours trawling the National Library of Australia's *Trove* database to clarify timelines and questions of fact; to augment my understanding of Australian geography, politics and history; and to situate my grandfather's life within the development of Australia and her beloved horse industry. I spent hours interviewing veterinarians, horse breeders and authors around the world to uncover his many variegated layers.

Yet for all my discomfort with interviewing, the conversations that I have had with those wonderful sixty-odd people who helped me write this book are memories I will treasure forever. There are few things as challenging as losing someone you love, so it seems only fair that there are few things as joyful as hearing the stories others have of that person – particularly when it is clear that they too love the person you have lost.

I hope that in reading this book you will learn something of Reg Pascoe as a vet and as a man – for, despite the book's title, the latter is every bit as important as the former, if not more so. I believe Reg lived a life of honour and integrity, of enthusiasm and joy, of passion and service and dedication to something beyond himself. I believe there are lessons there for all of us and I hope that not only will you find his life interesting, but that some of those lessons will resonate with you as deeply as they have with me. The death of someone we love is inevitably coloured by the fear that they will be forgotten – this book, a tribute to my grandad, is my effort to ensure Reg Pascoe never can be.

Introduction

'Don't look now … but God's in the front row.'

For decades, these were words to strike fear into any presenter's heart; regardless of experience, most veterinarians heard that warning and a frisson of fear rippled through them. Collars were tugged, sweat beaded on brows, throats were cleared, notes were given one last skim. Perhaps a hope and a prayer were sent skywards. Anyone who had witnessed it before knew the presentation about to begin might be a hairy one. With his grey brows beetled over his spectacles, Dr Reg Pascoe was sitting in the front row – and he was listening carefully.

This scene, or something like it, played out countless times during Reg's long and storied career. For over fifty years, he was a linchpin of the Australian horse industry, and this was never more obvious than during veterinary conferences. Reg was a fierce policeman of scientific standards. With little time for egotism or self-aggrandisement, he was scathing of those who succumbed to such traits rather than advancing the truth or the good of the profession. His determination, his tireless work ethic, and his fierce passion made him a legend. His colleagues called him 'God.' But was that just a funny nickname? And what does it say about such a man, and what they give to those around them?

These sorts of questions fuelled this book.

I grew up in my grandfather's shadow, but it was only in my early twenties that I realised I knew almost nothing about him. It is one thing to live near a legend, and another thing entirely to understand what that legend means. All I knew was he must have done *something* interesting to acquire such a nickname.

During the writing, I was lucky enough to interview around sixty of his friends and colleagues. What emerged was a picture of a man who rose to the highest echelons of his profession and dominated it for decades; an expert not merely in one aspect of equine science, but in many; and similarly skilled and knowledgeable in small animal medicine and teaching. Reg both directly and indirectly influenced hundreds, if not thousands, of Australian vets. And he was renowned internationally.

His career was marked by feats that were not only rare, but vital to Australia's horse and veterinary industries. Far more valuable than his professional accomplishments, however, was his character. The deeper I delved, the more I found a story worth telling – not because of that original intriguing premise of a vet so damn good they called him God, but because of the man behind that nickname, and the qualities that made him unique.

Vets are of most interest to other vets. But Reg Pascoe was so much more than just a vet. His life spanned countless seismic technological and social changes. This provided opportunities – which he gladly pursued – but it also brought challenges. He was a man who embraced change and innovation – from using an ice chest as a child to readily wielding a smartphone in his final years. He also keenly observed the shift from community to the individual – a move that has so challenged our societies over the past century.

Reg saw that to live well was to live for something *bigger* than himself. He learnt this as a child of the Great Depression, witnessing firsthand the misery and struggle of so many around him. He came from little: a modest teaching and farming family on Queensland's Darling Downs, with no money to splash around and little expectation that he'd excel. But when the opportunity came, he didn't hesitate. He poured himself heart and soul into his profession, and once he got there, he poured some more to make himself the best he could.

Throughout his long career, he never hoarded his knowledge: he regularly spoke at national and international conferences; he published prolifically; and he freely shared his expertise with others. *This* is what made Reg remarkable. This is what made him 'God.' His dedication to the betterment of those around him is the reason he was so important. His ethos and character provide invaluable lessons for us all. He dealt with life's vicissitudes with a simple stoicism, accepting, if necessary, the things he could not change, but fighting like hell to make better those that he could.

Australians have always hungered for stories of the lives and accomplishments of great people who have fought to achieve success and, in doing so, shaped our nation. There can be no doubt that Dr Reg Pascoe did all this and more.

Part I —
The Boy from the Bush

1
An Unexpected Letter

It was a clear, serene day in late 1946, the Queensland summer sun a brilliant white orb in an endless blue sky. A young man wandered down to the front of his family's property, as he had countless times before, to check for the mail. He opened the mailbox to find a letter addressed to Mr R. R. Pascoe. His pulse quickened and his fingers were clumsy as he tore open the envelope. Inside was a letter offering a Commonwealth government scholarship for tertiary study. His heart leapt. It seemed like a sign. It seemed like, somewhere, the door he had thought locked and barred was being flung open for him.

Some weeks earlier, the same seventeen-year-old had sat in an interview with the Toowoomba City Council's chief engineer for a sought-after training position. Peering over his desk, the chief engineer saw a tall, quiet young man with dark hair and a serious demeanour. He had won the engineering cadetship upon his recent graduation from high school and was already an excellent candidate. By the end of the interview, he received the job offer that he'd come to secure.

But things were more complex than at first they seemed.

'Why do you want to be an engineer?' the chief engineer asked.

The young man was stumped. 'I didn't have a bloody clue,' he confessed later. What did he know? That both the teacher's training scholarship and the forestry scholarship he'd been offered upon graduation didn't appeal. Nor did his father's offer to come and work on the family dairy farm. *I don't want that*, he thought to himself. At just a few months past his seventeenth birthday, he wasn't interested in anything in particular, or thinking of his life ahead ... but he knew he wanted to do almost anything but sit on the farm.

Unperturbed by his visitor's ambivalence, the chief engineer coaxed the conversation along, listening closely to what the young man said. The answer was soon self-evident. 'You can forget about doing engineering,' he declared bluntly. 'It won't suit you. You ought to see if you can get in and study about animals.'

The young man was dubious. He had never even considered it because he knew there were few such options available to him. His family was poor, barely scraping together enough to pay the rates, and university was as remote a possibility as tap dancing on the moon. He thanked the older man for his time and advice and left.

The young man – Reg Pascoe – came home with more questions than he'd left with. It was true, as the chief engineer had said, that he loved animals: he had ever since childhood, when he'd roamed over every inch of the family property, cradling his beloved rooster. The cost of studying veterinary science, however, meant such a career was out of the question.

Now, weeks later, the impossible was somehow made intoxicatingly possible by the letter in his hand: perhaps this was the moment, holding the tangible opportunity to become a vet, that Reg realised it was precisely what he wanted. But the Repatriation Department for Returned Servicemen postmark clearly indicated a mistake had been made. His father confirmed Reg's suspicions. 'That's not really yours,' Vyvyan Pascoe told his son. 'It should have gone to another R. R. Pascoe: a schoolteacher up in Pittsworth.' The other R. R. Pascoe was a returned Second World War veteran. It was bitterly disappointing, but there was only one thing to do: head in and see 'the mob' who'd misaddressed the fateful letter and tell them about the error.

Several days later, Reg was received by a government official who may have been sympathetic to his plight at having been given the golden ticket to university only to immediately lose it.

'What's the family income look like?' he asked.

'None,' Reg replied. 'We've barely enough to pay the rates.'

It seemed to satisfy the official and he suggested Reg apply for a Commonwealth 'hardship' scholarship through the social security branch. The same hard-earnt grades from Toowoomba Grammar which had gained Reg the two scholarships he'd earlier rejected, coupled with the family's financial straits, might secure for him what he wanted. This time, when the much-hoped-for letter appeared in the mailbox, it was no accident. Reg Pascoe was going to the University of Queensland to study veterinary science.

Unwittingly, the perceptive chief engineer had set the young man's feet on a path that would take him to places beyond anything he ever could have imagined when he sat down for his interview.

Insensible to his looming destiny, Reginald Roland Roessler Pascoe left the letterbox with his UQ hardship scholarship clutched in his hand and strolled back up to the main building of Schoenberg, the family property on the outskirts of Harlaxton, one of Toowoomba's smaller, poorer northern suburbs. In a nod to his mother's German heritage, 'mountain view' got its name for its scenic position on the edge of Queensland's Great Dividing Range. It had been Reg's whole world since his birth on 13 July 1929. That same German heritage meant he inherited his mother's family name, Roessler. Therein lay a remarkable coincidence for the future that awaited him: originating from Middle High German, 'Ross' and its derivatives is a metonymic occupational name for a 'breeder or keeper of horses.'

Reg came from a large family and, although unusual almost a century later, its composition was not uncommon at the time. His mother, Milly Roessler, was the second wife of Vyvyan Pascoe, a rural schoolteacher who had originally been married to Lily Roessler – Milly's younger sister. Vyvyan and Lily's three children – Edwin, Roess and Corinne – had been left motherless after her unexpected death from pneumonia in 1922 when Edwin was only seven. Vyvyan married Milly two years later; she was thirty-four. Milly had helped care for Edwin, Roess and Corinne for most of their lives and the children already viewed her as another mother. The curtain ring that Vyvyan put on her left hand in place of a wedding ring (a move for which Reg later described his father as 'a bit of an old stinker') simply made the fact official. When Milly's father died in June of the same year and left her Schoenberg (as well as a property at Tallai, in the Gold Coast Hinterland), it was to this property that the family moved.

Schoenberg's single original dwelling with its primitive cellar was hardly suitable for a large, busy family. Vyvyan's older brother, Ted, came to the rescue. A skilled carpenter, he built Vyvyan and Milly a typical 'Queenslander' with four bedrooms to accommodate not only

Vyvyan, Milly and the eldest three Pascoe children, but also Milly's mother Adelaide, who lived with them until her death in 1943.

A young Reg playing out the back of Schoenberg.

Milly and Vyvyan had two children together. Their daughter Adelaide died of pneumonia at just a year old but three years later in 1929, Reg was born. He was the youngest of the four children by a country mile: his brothers, Edwin and Roess, and sister Corrine were fourteen, twelve and ten years older respectively. This age difference was a defining feature of Reg's youth. He recalled Corinne playing her seniority trump card whenever she needed to. 'Well,' she would say, 'I'm ten years older than you are, so what would you know?' It was an argument with little hope of rebuttal. The age gap also meant that Reg spent a lot of time alone: Schoenberg was a large property near a small town and there were no nearby neighbours' children to play with.

Milly must have realised this and did her best to compensate for it. With the other children off at school and despite the distinct scarcity of storybooks in the 1930s, she often read to her little son of a morning. Reg adored her. Milly taught him to lip-read, a skill she used herself, for she had been born deaf. Thanks to this hearing impairment (and perhaps her associated use of an ear trumpet), Reg thought her shy, though her disability appears to have had little other effect on her life – she was an eloquent speaker and Reg doubted many people would have been able to tell she was deaf.

Milly was also a talented watercolourist and won a school scholarship to study painting in Paris in her youth. Her father refused to let her go. Perhaps he was concerned for her safety: a young woman, travelling by sea, living alone. Paris at the beginning of the twentieth century was a global creative centre, widely seen as a 'frivolous, carefree and optimistic place to be' – hardly words to reassure a father worried about his child's physical and moral safety.

Fundamentally, however, it is impossible to discount the role that Milly's gender and disability would have played in her father's decision: he likely felt that the daughter of a respectable businessman had no place traipsing across the world to study art in a foreign, morally questionable city ... And so, like countless other women throughout the twentieth century, Milly's ideas and dreams were subservient to the desires of her family. It's likely that after her father's decision and as a young, disabled and unmarried woman she remained in her parents' home until her marriage to Vyvyan sixteen years later.

She continued to paint throughout her life, but certainly after her marriage this free time was limited. Her artistic soul was subordinate to the demands of a busy and simple life, characterised by early mornings of milking cows and the challenges of raising four children. It was a hard existence made harder given few of the big city technological advances were available. Like most others in the area, the family used an ice chest which was topped up every Monday. For many years, the property's only water source was a well with a pump – when Vyvyan later tried to sink a bore to access groundwater, he got about 12 metres down without finding anything before calling it quits. Milly worked hard. She was often the first one in the yard to milk the cows and would grouse about Corinne's tendency to, like Vyvyan, stay up reading late into the night and then struggle to rise the following morning.

As his mother was usually busy, Reg spent much of his free time wandering the family property with his greatest friend and prized pet, an Australorp rooster named Cocky. Where other small children clung to pups, dolls, or teddies, Reg clung to Cocky, and the bird rewarded the little boy's devotion with remarkable resilience.

Cocky's survival would not have been so extraordinary were it not for the tragedies that plagued other local poultry. The Pascoe family kept hens for eggs and, like most of the area, Schoenberg was prey to attack by both foxes and quolls. These 'native cats', as quolls were colloquially known, are a carnivorous marsupial: the spotted-tail quoll targets homes and farms in search of the poultry they were once famed for massacring. The Pascoes were no exception; on more than one occasion, Vyvyan emerged in the morning to discover the family's entire flock slaughtered.

Finally, fed up, he set to work. Later, Reg became adept at woodwork but, he remarked dryly, 'I must have inherited that from someone else.' Vyvyan's chicken coop was made of four wooden posts crowned by half a metal tank, rounded off with split timber slabs around the sides and some chicken wire to hold it all together. It was ugly, but Vyvyan was triumphant. 'That'll stop that cat from getting in!' he declared.

The quoll didn't get the message. Undeterred, and leaving no discernible evidence of how it had done so, it repeated its massacre that night. Yet one feathered friend routinely dodged the hungry beast: no one knew where he wandered off to, but somehow Reg's rooster Cocky emerged unharmed every morning.

Schoenberg was full of wonders, and perhaps it was from this childhood spent roaming the natural world that Reg's love of animals, his passion for gardening and his renowned manual dexterity were born. Certainly, it introduced him to growing fruit and vegetables that was to become a mainstay of his adult life.

Late 1930s. Reg as a boy, standing on the grounds of Schoenberg.

Schoenberg had a citrus orchard which had been planted by Milly's father, John Roessler. He was a railway surveyor and had actively searched for parcels of land that he thought would support productive orchards. The Pascoe family, like many in the region, supplemented their diet with home-grown produce. To the north of the house lay the vegetable garden; there, a young Reg often 'helped' Grandma Roessler, washing the dirt from freshly harvested radishes and eating them still warm from the ground. Flowers didn't fare as well and Reg's best efforts to bolster Vyvyan's rose growing began and ended inauspiciously. Vyvyan returned home one day to discover that Reg had enthusiastically uprooted several prized roses and decapitated a few others. 'It didn't get me any brownie points,' Reg remembered. Vyvyan was furious, smacking Reg and sending the boy off with a sore rear as a reminder to be more careful.

Fortunately, there were plenty of other things to keep Reg

occupied. A Moreton Bay fig, planted in 1888, towered over the garden. Among its vast network of low, spreading limbs, Reg climbed to his heart's content; when he grew bored of that, he might take himself off to wander around the bush, seeking the mandarins and oranges that grew in the bottom orchard. A leisurely stroll typically yielded a hearty serving of the fruit and Reg would stuff his shirt full before finding a spot in the sun. There he would feast until he was full before returning to the house and struggling to explain to his mother why he didn't want any lunch; as he remembered, 'I was a loner ... and that usually got me into trouble.'

If his weeks were characterised by solitude, weekends brought a particular prize. Both of his brothers, Edwin and Roess, had left home for further study when Reg was very young, beckoned by the wide world awaiting them after school and beyond Schoenberg, but they often returned once the week was done. The trips home meant they could get their washing done and enjoy some of Milly's home cooking. The visits left a deep impression on Reg, who idolised his brothers.

A schoolteacher like his father, Roess was usually exhausted by the time he got home. He wrote letters to his little brother during the week, but when at Schoenberg he wanted nothing more than to sleep and recover. Reg had other ideas. Full almost to bursting with the stories that young boys carry within, he would clamber into the bed to snuggle in next to his brother. Into Roess's drowsy ear, Reg would pour all the tales of his intrepid adventures. Roess endured with admirable forbearance, but eventually the young man's patience would be exhausted and he would kick his little brother out. Evicted but undaunted, Reg went off to await his next opportunity to repeat the ritual.

For the first five years of Reg's life, Schoenberg and his family were his entire world, and he explored it with all the joy and vigour of a small boy discovering new wonders. In 1936 at the age of six, he started at Wilsonton State School, where his father Vyvyan was a teacher. Vyvyan had begun working as a 'pupil teacher' at the age of sixteen in 1901 – under an apprenticeship scheme that was common for teachers across Australia – at Harlaxton State School, where his father was head teacher. Edward Pascoe, or 'the Boss', was renowned in the region; local stories held that letters addressed simply to 'the Boss, Toowoomba' were dutifully delivered.

In the twenty-eight years before Reg was born, Vyvyan taught at seven different schools across the Darlings Downs region. A man ahead of his time, he believed in the education of women and devoted himself to the development of every student in his charge. Wilsonton, like many schools across rural Queensland, was small: when Vyvyan was appointed, he was the only teacher. His energetic campaigning for the school's development, however, saw another teacher added in 1934, and a third, two years later. By the time Reg began, Vyvyan had started a social committee and presided as its inaugural chair. He was an energetic and enthusiastic advocate for the community and the children he served and dedicated much of his own time to developing the school's facilities and services.

While he may have lacked the manual skills required to build chicken coops, Vyvyan was a consummate sportsman. Just like his father, he was a good cricketer, and played tennis with his cousin Stella every Thursday afternoon. Encouraging organised sports at Wilsonton, he strove to inspire his students – not least his youngest son – and supervised the school's sporting endeavours, accompanying the boys' teams to their matches. He even composed the 'Wilsonton School War Cry' for the students to sing before competing.

However, Vyvyan's years at Wilsonton were coloured by the broader context within which they occurred: the Great Depression had begun in 1929 and its effects were widely felt. Queensland had experienced a rollercoaster ride throughout the 1920s due to intermittent periods of extreme drought. After the First World War, economic instability made it hard to access developmental finance and as the Depression spread its insidious tendrils throughout the country, Queensland found itself sliding into hardship earlier than the other states and territories. States characterised by large, urban-based manufacturing centres (like New South Wales and Victoria) suffered the most. But while Queensland's underdeveloped manufacturing sector occasioned one of the lowest unemployment rates in the country, over 30% of the workforce was unemployed by 1931. National unemployment peaked at 32 per cent in 1932 and throughout the 1930s the nation struggled to regain its feet.

'Men without work' was the norm. As the typical strongholds of 'masculine' employment like manufacturing and building crumbled, women-dominated sectors – such as household work, office work, hospitality and clothing manufacturing – remained more stable. Contributing to women's higher employment rates was the fact that their wages were lower than men's: many employers sought ways to reduce costs and remain in business. Women often became the sole breadwinners in a society where masculine identity was predicated on a man's ability to provide. Countless families found themselves floundering.

The national tolerance for immigration plummeted as Australians, fighting to stay afloat, became more isolationist and increasingly hostile to any 'outsider' who might 'steal' Australian jobs. It was an attitude that cast a long shadow. By 1932, over 60,000 Australians – men, women and children – were dependent on the meagre state-based sustenance payment known as the 'susso', which provided only enough to purchase the bare minimum. Queensland was the only state which from 1929 had an unemployment relief scheme controlled by the government, yet people everywhere struggled. Countless men left home and travelled across Australia in search of work and the country was rife with such 'swaggies.'

In 1932 a five-hectare site dubbed 'The Eagle's Nest Camp' was established on the edge of the Great Dividing Range. Constructed with the encouragement of a local doctor, it provided itinerant men with a place to sleep and grow their own food. The camp housed and fed unemployed men for the next eight years. In its first fourteen months alone, over 600 men passed through its doors. The local community supported the venture: the Toowoomba Girl Guides donated a tent, the matron of St Andrews Hospital gathered and distributed clothing and bedding, while the public and local businessmen donated tea, sugar and meat.

Perhaps there was a sense of relief that these hungry, homeless men were housed away from the town; regardless, these efforts exemplified a common attitude that it was the responsibility of social groups and the broader community to care for those less fortunate. Reg was exposed to the privations brought about by the Depression from his earliest years and would have witnessed how the local community responded to such challenges. It was a simple, profound lesson, and one he could not help but absorb.

Despite the community's generosity of spirit, many poor children went hungry. The schoolyard was a particularly tough. Impoverished children, clad in ill-fitting hand-me-downs, were often bullied by their better dressed peers. Some avoided school entirely to escape this harassment, spending their days hiding in an old quarry nearby. Others gazed longingly at their friends' lunches. Vyvyan, wandering among his students at lunchtime, began collecting unwanted food from those fortunate enough to have it. Under the pretext that these leftovers were fodder 'for the ducks' – a friendly pair of birds who ran snail patrol in the garden – he passed it instead onto those students who had little.

Australia has never suffered another severe depression, but Reg's attitude towards giving back to his community – whether at a local, state, or national level – was firmly ingrained.

When the Second World War broke out in September 1939, Vyvyan was transferred to the position of headmaster at Oakey State School and Reg's time at Wilsonton came to an end. Milly, still caring for her mother, Grandma Roessler, at Schoenberg, was less than thrilled at the idea of moving 30 kilometres away from the family home. The distance – and petrol rationing across the country due to the war effort – meant a daily commute was out of the question. So Vyvyan decided he would live in the Oakey schoolhouse during the school week, supported by an ice chest stocked with Milly's home-cooked, ready-to-reheat meals, while the rest of the family remained at Schoenberg.

With Vyvyan gone and no other way to get to school, Reg transferred to Harlaxton State. Only about a mile from Schoenberg, he walked every morning to the nearby rail bridge at Munro Street to catch the bus, an unexpectedly fraught journey. Magpies nesting in the vicinity of the stop attacked with impunity. Boarding the bus was no safer: Reg's classmates found in him the perfect target, bullying him relentlessly, spurred on by cutting comments from his teacher, who once snidely reminded Reg, 'You're not the teacher's pet in this school.' Reg quickly grew to hate Harlaxton and, with no real talent for handling the problem, started wagging. Frequently developing a 'sickness' on his morning walk to bus, he returned to Schoenberg wearing his most pathetic face, complete with crocodile tears.

'Mum, of course, got sucked in,' he remembered wryly later in life. Unable to bear her son's distress, Milly promised he wouldn't have to go to Harlaxton anymore. His unhappiness was even enough to overcome Vyvyan's earlier reluctance for him to attend Oakey State and his father suggested he stay with him during the week. Reg jumped at the chance.

There, in the headmaster's smart, little four-roomed cottage with a toilet in the backyard, removed from the schoolyard harassment, Reg thrived. His weekday life followed a simple, easy routine. He was in charge of breakfast: Weet-Bix with milk, toast and a cup of tea. Afterwards, Reg climbed to the schoolhouse verandah. Like many rural Queensland schools at the time, the Oakey schoolhouse was raised on eight-foot wooden stumps with stairs at the front and the back. They had a short break for morning tea, or 'little lunch', which was typically a piece of fruit, then for lunch at 12.30 p.m., Reg made sandwiches.

Small but distinctive moments marked Reg's memories of his childhood schooling. The horse-drawn OK Pie Cart came on a Tuesday, a much-anticipated lunch or dinnertime treat. Between the mid-1930s to the late 1950s, the OK Pie Cart man would bake his wares at home, load them into the cart's wood-fired oven and deliver the delicious hot pies around the Toowoomba area.

Every Thursday brought 'the rural school', another of Reg's favourite weekly interludes. This manual training block on the grounds was run by a builder and a saddler employed by the Department of Education to teach the students trade skills. The children learnt woodwork, leatherwork and domestic science and it was here that Reg first encountered what were to become some of his most enduring and well-loved hobbies. Arriving in Oakey in 1939 as a Grade 4 student, he took up woodworking for four hours in the morning, then in Grade 5, began leatherwork of a Thursday afternoon as well.

That year, 1940, the Second World War took its first steps into the Pascoe family's lives. Roess, having been a cadet while at Toowoomba Grammar School, enlisted in the Royal Australian Air

Force (RAAF) as an aircraftman; the next year, Edwin followed his younger brother's footsteps.

Meanwhile, war evacuations from Brisbane meant more students were sent to rural areas, including Oakey. Despite the war, Reg's years in Oakey were among the simplest and most idyllic of his life. Unlike at Harlaxton, he was no longer bullied; he enjoyed living with his father during the week and energetically pursued woodworking, his schoolwork and varying sports under Vyvyan's watchful and encouraging eye.

After school, Reg often played with the next-door neighbour's boisterous German shepherd, Trouble, kicking a soccer ball for the exuberant pup to retrieve until one or both grew bored of the game. For the most part, these were enjoyable encounters – the unwitting beginning of what, for Reg, was to be a lifetime of staunch friendship with canine companions. But the aptly named Trouble had two unfortunate tendencies. The first was a habit of chewing the life out of the ball every time he retrieved it and repeatedly puncturing the bladder; the second was becoming overexcited. The combination lent itself to disaster. During one afternoon's game, Trouble got so excited he lunged for the ball and missed it entirely, latching onto Reg's leg instead. Reg summed up what was doubtless a very painful experience in his characteristically laconic fashion. 'It wasn't very funny.'

Sitting down together in the evenings, Reg recalled frequently sharing a dinner of tomato soup with his father – doubtless an easy option, both for Milly to send and for Vyvyan and Reg to reheat. Later, in 1941, limited accommodation in town meant another teacher and his wife came to live in the other half of the schoolhouse, bringing with them a refrigerator – a 'great change' from the ice chest, improving the quality of their meals. But the best night of the week was a Thursday when father and son ate in the dining room of the Royal Hotel. The next day they headed home for the weekend – dirty washing and empty dishes in tow.

Reg's final year at Oakey State School was 1942. On 27 May, a telegram arrived: Roess, training as an RAAF pilot in England, had been involved in a catastrophic accident involving another aircraft. He died at the scene. Reg was only thirteen. This theft of a brother he adored was the first major loss of his young life and it left deep and enduring scars. He never discussed Roess's death with his own family and rarely even referred to Roess's existence. All he could find to say about his brother's unexpected, accidental death was that 'things sort of went downhill' afterwards.

At the end of the year, Reg started high school at Toowoomba Grammar. About twelve months later, Vyvyan, still reeling from the death of Roess and now bereft of Reg's company, decided he'd had enough. He resigned from the headmaster's position at Oakey and returned to Schoenberg.

Back in Harlaxton, Vyvyan turned his attention to the family milk run, an activity that combined his own lifelong passion with the entrepreneurial spirit of his eldest son, Edwin. Despite being the son of a teacher, as a young man Vyvyan had dreamt of building his own herd, and began dairying almost twenty years earlier while he was the head teacher of the Marburg Rural School. Dairying soon became a fundamental aspect of Schoenberg life, with every Pascoe playing a part. Vyvyan dubbed his new enterprise 'Helston', after the Pascoes' ancestral home in Cornwall in England, and energetically began to seek out stock. His verve, however, outweighed his ability and his knowledge, and the results showed it.

'The stud breeders,' Reg remarked later, 'probably used to rub their hands together when they saw him coming, because it gave them a chance to offload their not-so-good cows.' Vyvyan's enthusiasm netted him a herd of big-uddered Jerseys with a relatively low milk yield. What they did produce was high in butterfat and, at least initially, deemed of too poor a milk–fat ratio for drinking. Instead, for many years much of the product went to the Toowoomba Butter Factory, making for the family a 'pretty low-key, miserable sideline.'

Edwin created the milk run in the late 1930s, just before the war. This wasn't his first innovative business venture. After finishing school in 1932, he cannily identified a gap in the market for the long journey from Brisbane to Toowoomba and devised a small transport business. Rail stretched the distance between the two cities, but the 1930s train commute saw the geographically shortest leg of the journey from Helidon to Toowoomba end up just as long as the rest of the trip. The twenty-minute road transit by car was much quicker, and purchasing a seven-seater Studebaker limousine, Edwin began running a service.

For a while, it worked just as he had planned, but it wasn't long before others cottoned onto the idea. A bus company put a route in and in the late 1930s, the commissioner for railways capitalised on a 'quicker service than travelling the whole journey by train' when he announced a coordinated rail–road facility. Even early on, Edwin couldn't compete: the buses' greater size meant more passengers and lower fares. He found himself out on his ear. Undeterred, he started up a similar service in Dalby. It worked well for a few years, yet before long that too was undermined.

However, his entrepreneurial streak was far from exhausted.

He next conceived the local Pascoe milk run, selling the family's product around the streets of Toowoomba. The milk which had previously furnished the Toowoomba Butter Factory had so much cream it was almost too rich to drink – but customers loved it. It sold well and, in time, the family built up quite an extensive run. But Edwin, who had enlisted in September 1941, was gone flying in war zones around the world, wherever the RAAF needed him. When Vyvyan returned home in late 1943, his son was on a six-week deployment to Papua New Guinea flying Dakotas with No. 36 Squadron. He was in one of the earliest aircraft detachments conveying troops and freight to the forward bases, flying supply drops over difficult terrain in treacherous weather conditions.

In Edwin's absence, and while Vyvyan had been living in Oakey, the responsibility for maintaining the family business must have fallen to Corrine and Milly. Reg remembered his father joining Corrine on deliveries after their move home and, given Reg's recollection of Milly being the first in the yard of a morning to milk the cows, it seems likely that the two women had simply dusted off their hands and gotten the work done while men were away. But Vyvyan soon found himself with more on his hands than simply delivering milk.

The Toowoomba market was a cut-throat business. With suppliers vying to undercut the competition and steal customers, different factions would travel miles just to deliver a pint. It wasn't uncommon to see two or three different vendors in the one street. It was a messy situation, one the vendors themselves admitted was an inefficient use of resources, and so the idea of 'milk zoning' was introduced, having already been floated around various parts of the country struggling to deal with supply during the war.

To facilitate the zoning, every vendor submitted an account of their current run, detailing the amount and frequency of milk delivered. Vyvyan was asked to draw a map dividing Toowoomba into gallon equivalents to be allocated to milk suppliers. It was tricky, as some vendors were bigger, producing more milk than others daily, and different areas of Toowoomba had differing requirements: some took up to a gallon, others as little as half a pint. (One imperial gallon equals 4.55 litres, while an imperial pint is equal to just over half a litre.) Many vendors started delivery between 4 and 5 a.m. to fulfil their obligations. The idea of zoning wasn't popular, as it tended to restrict each vendor's potential for customer growth, and Reg later recalled that in the end everyone involved was 'half happy.'

While Vyvyan navigated the challenges of the milk run, Reg entered a completely different world to the one he'd known in Oakey. The first few months of 1943 at Toowoomba Grammar were 'very new and a bit strange': coming from the small premises of his state school, the 50-acre expanse of Toowoomba Grammar must have seemed enormous. The grounds included two ovals, three tennis courts, a rifle range and large swimming baths. It was 5 miles (or 8 kilometres) from Schoenberg, so Reg rose early every day and helped with the milking before riding his bike to school, a cut lunch in his bag.

School started at 9 a.m. and finished at 4.30 p.m. with a class of roughly thirty students in Reg's form, 3B. It was an unfamiliar experience for most of them, initially called only by their surname, but eventually doling out various nicknames to one another. After the first week, new boys were divvied up into one of four houses. Reg joined Taylor House. Toowoomba Grammar's participation in inter-school competitions as 'one of the nine great public schools of Queensland' meant all boys were strongly encouraged to participate.

Fortunately for Reg, this was an arena he knew well. Cricketing ran in the family – Vyvyan had played for Toowoomba against an English team in 1910 – and under his father's watchful coaching eye, Reg had played in the Oakey state school team. He also enjoyed soccer and discovered the sweet taste of sporting triumph when he won the 100-yard dash in Grade 7.

Toowoomba Grammar's endeavours, however, were something else altogether. The inter-house competitions provided a willing pool of talent for the higher-level inter-school events, fielding cricket, football and swimming teams. 'Swimming' in 1943 meant venturing into the old bore-filled pool: not only was it unchlorinated, it was also unheated and a perpetual murky green. Nevertheless, Reg was comfortable in the water and he gained his bronze medal for still-water lifesaving at the much cleaner Queens Park municipal swimming baths.

Meanwhile, his brothers' legacies had left their indelible mark. Outside the classroom, Reg joined Toowoomba Grammar's cadet corps. Established in 1892, the corps was likely subject to the vast organisational growth experienced in 'school branch' cadet groups throughout Australia. Particularly after 1941, the effects of the Second World War coupled with enthusiastic public-school involvement saw cadet numbers increase exponentially: by 1945, there were over 22,000 cadets nationwide, up from 4200 in 1939. Toowoomba Grammar boys were instructed by Australian Army Reserve warrant officers and had the opportunity to go on cadet camps every second year. Reg missed his first one, but he was able to attend the second, travelling from Toowoomba via train to the permanent camp established in Tweed Heads/Coolangatta.

During the 1943 Easter break, Reg and a friend went on a long hike together. Over the main railway line they walked, then down to the creek running north from Swanson's rail bridge. The fierce heat of the day drove them into the water for a swim before they ate their lunch and trekked back. Arriving at Schoenberg exhausted, they ate dinner then collapsed into bed.

On Monday morning Reg awoke with a fever that grew steadily worse. Having lost Lily, Vyvyan's younger brother Kenneth, and their first child Adelaide to pneumonia, it seemed best to err on the side of caution. Vyvyan and Milly took their son to Mylo Private Hospital that day.

Reg wasn't happy. The first night, he tried to abscond out a window and was grabbed just in time by the on-duty nurse. The matron rang Vyvyan: it might be best, she suggested, if Vyvyan slept in Reg's room while he was in hospital.

The following night, Reg tried escaping again.

'Where do you think you're going?' came Vyvyan's voice from a dark corner of the room.

Reg paused. 'Nowhere, Dad.' He hopped meekly back into bed. The reasons for his desire to escape aren't clear; perhaps he found the hospital confining and unfamiliar – it's uncertain whether he had previously spent much time, if any, sleeping anywhere other than at home either in Schoenberg or Oakey, with his parents close by. Perhaps he was so ill that reason deserted him and running home just seemed sensible, though whether he was in fact sick with pneumonia or simply exhausted from overexertion is also unknown.

Regardless, he was confined to Mylo for four days. Afterwards, he found himself banned from playing sport or any other serious physical exertion (including riding to school) for the rest of the first term and much of the second. It must have been chafing, to be so imprisoned, but Reg stoically bore his sentence. With the physical resilience that was to become one of his trademarks he abandoned the daily school bus journey in third term and, the picture of good spirits once more, returned to cycling to school.

His studies at Toowoomba Grammar consisted of English, French, arithmetic, algebra, geometry, physics, chemistry and bookkeeping in his junior years; senior years saw the curriculum whittled down to just English, maths I, maths II, physics and chemistry. And though later in life he was wont to say, 'Was I academically bright? Probably not', he clearly did well enough to secure the teacher's training scholarship and forestry scholarship – whether he wanted them or not.

At the end of Reg's senior year, as he mulled over the question of what to do after school, the Pascoe family property at Tallai suffered a string of minor disasters. Like Schoenberg, the land on the Upper Nerang River in the Gold Coast Hinterland had devolved to Milly upon her father's death in 1924 and, like Schoenberg, John Roessler had established it as a multi-harvest property. A canny businessman, he had been one of the original pioneers of Toowoomba, a farmer and a surveyor who surveyed all the railway lines around the city.

More notably, he and his brother Henry had established

themselves as successful businessmen and the family had owned various orchards across the Range. Roessler's 'Jams and Pickles' became well known in the region, and with a vineyard at Lyra (a few miles out of Stanthorpe), the family also established their name as winemakers in Toowoomba and surrounding areas. The Gold Coast property produced bananas, pawpaws and potatoes, but it was Tallai's timber – used to create railway sleepers – that provided most of the earnings.

Despite these other, more reliable sources of income, Vyvyan's love of dairying had seen him establish a dairy at Tallai in addition to his Schoenberg venture, a decision only possible because of the presence of a sharefarmer on the property. Visits to Tallai throughout Reg's childhood necessitated the family leaving Toowoomba at four in the morning. Though the road to Southport was all bitumen, it was unpaved after turning off the highway towards the property and driving along the bumpy road with the sunlight flashing in between the trees inevitably made Reg 'bloomin' carsick.'

Not long after he finished his final year of school, the sharefarmer – whom Reg recalled had repeatedly proven himself a pain in the neck – up and vanished, leaving the house a mess and no one to take care of Tallai. Vyvyan and Reg headed down to tidy up. They had a bumper crop of potatoes that year, but most were unharvested and had been left lying all over the ground. Vyvyan imagined father and son could go down and pick them all up; *a crazy idea*, Reg thought, and, sure enough, they arrived to find the summer heat had turned most of the crop green and inedible.

To make things worse, torrential rain flooded the local creek, and though Reg found some good in the deluge by catching some catfish, the weather greatly hampered their visit. To make the daily cream delivery, Vyvyan and Reg had to cross the Nerang River, which they did in a two-wheeled spring cart. These horse-drawn carts were a common sight on dairy farms in the first half of the twentieth century, with their five-foot diameter wheels that were meant to keep driver and merchandise high and dry during water crossings. Swollen with the recent rains, the Nerang River was, fortunately, still manageable in the cart – until one of the two chains connecting horse and cart broke. For Reg and Vyvyan, watching river water lap threateningly at the cart's sides, that lone remaining chain must have seemed far less reassuring than it had only seconds ago. Though they escaped unharmed, it wasn't a surprise that Reg was less than enthused about working on the farm after school.

Not long after came the interview with the Toowoomba City Council, then the misdirected mail and the subsequent arrival of the Commonwealth hardship scholarship. Reg turned towards the newly opened door and went through eagerly, though he could not have known what lay on the other side.

2
A Wonderful and Very Frightening Expedition

As Reg prepared to head to university in 1947, the most pressing matter was where he would live. His five-year scholarship paid his tuition fees for his Bachelor of Veterinary Science at the University of Queensland and provided a generous living allowance of £420 per annum (roughly $29,000 in 2020). The only stipulation was that after graduating, he repay the loan in full – both tuition and stipend – once his taxable income exceeded £20,000 a year. Fortunately, for reasons that remain unclear, the repayment scheme never eventuated.

The living allowance was intended to cover room and board but securing these proved difficult. Roess, while studying at UQ a decade earlier, had found a room at King's College in Kangaroo Point, where it had predominantly boarded theology students. But King's had struggled to stay open throughout the Second World War, suffering a repeat of the declining enrolments experienced by both the university and the college during the Great War. And, unfortunately for Reg, college accommodation was scarce as college buildings were being erected on campus at the new St Lucia location. He submitted an application that put his name on a waiting list, but he was never to reside at King's.

The Pascoes cast about for other options. Vyvyan's younger brother, Rex, lived in Camp Hill, a scant 8 kilometres from the Brisbane CBD. Rex and his wife Olive had no children of their own and this might have made them nervous about the prospect of providing a home for their nephew. In the end they grudgingly agreed, but it didn't last long. Perhaps their initial concerns never abated, but for whatever reason, halfway through his first year of study Reg moved to stay with family friends of Milly's, the Blunts.

Both Aunty Bess and Uncle Bert (addressed by a familial honorific as was common in the day) were educators. Having many years previously been the head teacher of Charlton, in 1947 Uncle Bert was now the head teacher at Ithaca State School, while Aunty Bess had played a crucial role in opening and presiding over the Ashgrove Kindergarten in 1930.

Reg yet again found himself surrounded by friends and mentors who both embodied and valued the twin pursuits of learning and teaching. These passions served him well in the five study-intensive years to come; more vitally, they entwined themselves within his DNA to become a part of his own ethos. And this love of learning was about to be tested, as he and thirty-two intrepid classmates embarked upon the wonderful and frightening expedition into higher learning for which Reg recalled, 'most, if not all, of them were ill-prepared.'

Reg's first year BVSc class at UQ sounds small by twenty-first century university standards but it was large for UQ; the institution had suffered a downswing in enrolments during and immediately following the war. Roughly a third of the class was returned servicemen who had only recently finished their final stint in high school, in accordance with the Commonwealth protocol that required them to complete Grade 12 before tertiary study. They were, Reg thought, at a big disadvantage. Perhaps he believed the time they had spent away from formal education made it more difficult for them to re-establish the cognitive framework necessary to successful learning; perhaps he was considering the effect the Second World War had on their mental and physical health. Regardless, the validity of his assessment seemed to be upheld by the facts: many of these returned servicemen, along with the only woman enrolled in the course, wouldn't survive the first year. Over two-thirds of the initial thirty-three students would leave or founder before graduation day – veterinary science at UQ in the late 1940s was characterised by a high attrition rate that, for Reg's class, wouldn't slow until fourth year.

One surviving alumnus claims this attrition rate was the result of the university's strict standards: 'In those days, they didn't hesitate to fail you if you weren't up to scratch.' But the case is more complex, not least because the same veterinarian also affirmed, 'I didn't think the veterinary degree we finished up with was worth a drink of cold water ... because of the quality of instruction and the fact that we didn't get through enough work.' It's a bold claim in direct contradiction to his assertion of the university's fastidious criteria for success. It was repudiated both by Reg's subsequent successes and the reminiscences of other alumni.

It is, however, undeniable that aspects of UQ's veterinary school were lacking, and this was symptomatic of a larger issue. UQ was still in its infancy and the infrastructure necessary to support its students over the full span of their degree was still in development. The veterinary faculty had opened in 1936 before being subsequently closed in 1942 due to the war; it reopened in 1945 with a grand total of six students. Like many institutions across the country, the school suffered from a dearth of qualified instructors. This was in part due to effects of the war: there had inevitably been casualties sustained among the numerous staff and students, and the school's closure had necessarily driven other vets to different universities. Further, the accepted practice of sending Queensland vet students south to the University of Sydney to complete their fourth- and fifth-year studies not only meant graduates were more likely to remain there after graduation, but also that UQ was inherently less well-resourced than it might otherwise have been.

The class started their studies in haphazard circumstances. Beyond merely the increased numbers of returned servicemen in their peer group, the Second World War had other far-reaching effects. The redistribution of public monies, commandeering of various facilities and construction of temporary buildings for war usage, as well as the university's staggered move to the St Lucia campus, meant classes were strewn like breadcrumbs throughout Brisbane and the surrounding suburbs. Later, when the St Lucia campus was fully operational, a ferry service conveyed students across the river, but fortunately for Reg, such expeditions were unnecessary. Instead, he commuted by tram every morning – first from his aunt and uncle's house in Camp Hill and later from the Blunts' – to George Street in Brisbane City, from where he was able to walk to his classes.

Near Parliament House sat one of the temporary buildings that remained after the war, which housed the students' chemistry practicals. There, the lecturer known as 'Swoose' enforced a stringent watch over the lab's Bunsen burners. Named for his swan-like dressing and grooming habits and 'his measured, toe-out' goose-like strut around the classroom, Swoose possessed a (perhaps not unjustified) phobia of unattended Bunsen burners. Regardless of whether they were in use or not, he obsessively turned them off if he thought them unwatched.

Bunsen burners are a chemistry lab staple. Used for heating solutions, they're turned on and off by way of a stopcock that controls the flow of gas to the flame. During one of Swoose's brief absences from the room, the students used one Bunsen burner to heat the brass stopcock of another, then left the newly heated burner sitting alone and alight. They intently awaited the lecturer's return, eyes fixed on the bait they'd so carefully laid. And, as they'd intended, Swoose spotted the unattended burner as soon as he entered the room.

'Like a homing pigeon he ... eagerly advanced to do his bit for university finances by turning it off,' Reg recalled. As he grabbed the stopcock, 'his fingers sizzled and some smoke was reported from the immediate area of the tap. His face and body language gave naught away, but with slow and steady gait, he returned to his office. He had bandaged fingers for several weeks.' Perhaps it wasn't surprising that 'many of the group got SUPs' – supplementary exams which provided a (failing) student the chance to achieve a passing grade. It seemed, Reg remembered some fifty years later, they were a group of slow learners.

Whether Reg meant academically or more practically, his assessment is supported by other tales of class antics, which were more often than not to their academic detriment. Like Swoose before him, their physics lecturer discovered his students had keen noses for weakness and they joyfully seized upon news of his morbid fear of dogs. At the university's original home in Old Government House, where the physics lecture theatre typically housed both physics and biology lectures, the students laid their next trap. Once or twice a year, the lecturer shuffled into class to find a huge black Labrador tied to the lectern, sending him bolting right back out the door. It earnt the students a good laugh and a free lecture period, much to their delight – although, at the end of term, many also had SUPs for physics. Their professor, however, died before the year ended and those who had been allocated SUPs were granted a pass.

Biology completed the curriculum's basic science subjects, and the thirty-three incipient veterinary students were lumped in with their science and physiotherapy peers (which incidentally meant a far greater proportion of female students). If anyone held hopes that this subject might prove friendlier to the veterinary students, those dreams were quickly dashed; Reg thought it a great subject, but it proved tough for all concerned. Many had previously only had minimal or poor-quality exposure to the subject, as biology wasn't well taught in many secondary schools post-war. To their lecturer, world-renowned biologist Professor Ernie Goddard, Reg thought that the class must have seemed a sorry lot.

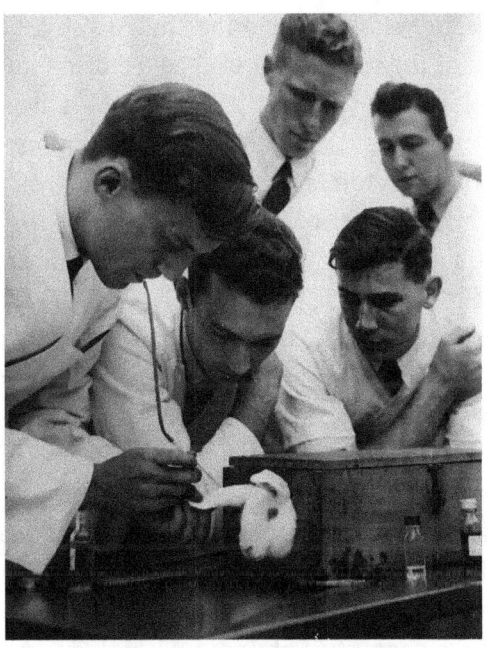

Reg (front right) and classmates drawing samples from a restrained rabbit, possibly as part of an experiment.

The sense of being underprepared and overwhelmed wasn't helped by Professor Goddard's disconcerting habit of abandoning his lectern during classes and roaming the room. He lectured as he did so, pausing every now and then to sit on someone's desk. Transfixing them with his baleful blue eyes, he would demand of his target, 'Do you understand?' Invariably the only response was a painful silence that seemed to stretch on forever; though logically Reg 'knew it was only ten to fifteen seconds ... it felt like ten to fifteen minutes.' It was no surprise to see SUPs all round for much of the class at term's end.

The final subject in first year was zootechny, which today is usually called animal husbandry: the scientific art of maintaining and improving animals under domestication, including breed, genetics, nutrition and housing. Taught out at the Animal Research Institute (ARI) in the southern Brisbane suburb of Yeerongpilly, it was run by an ex-serviceman called Robbie Burns who had served in New Guinea as a major in a horse unit. Appointed UQ's acting lecturer-in-charge of veterinary science the previous year, 1946, Robbie quickly became a central figure in the students' lives, overseeing the first three years of their course as well as lecturing in zootechny and later pharmacology. He was, one of Reg's cohort averred, 'really the "father" of the vet school' and though he was more aloof with the students than other lecturers, Reg credited him with doing 'sterling work in nurturing the veterinary course' in these early years.

It was the coursework, however, which truly endeared zootechny to the students. 'Brother, what a relief to be actually doing something useful!' Reg remembered. The one afternoon a week in which the class travelled by council bus from George Street to Yeerongpilly for two hours of practical work on cattle or horses was a welcome break from the classroom for everyone. There were far fewer SUPs given out in zootechny than in other first-year subjects, so it seemed Reg wasn't the only one who found it more stimulating and relevant than the rest of the syllabus. But after managing to pass all his term one exams, he found his third term finals sobering. Despite scoring a credit in zootechny, he received SUPs for chemistry, physics and biology, managing to pass biology and gaining a concessional pass for chemistry due to his strong results in zootechny. The learning curve from high school had been steep. By the end of 1947, only four students in the class had managed an outright pass across the course curriculum, and many of the remainder relied on SUPs to make the grade and continue their studies.

By the start of 1948, Reg's class had been whittled down to twelve out of the original thirty-three. The curriculum broadened considerably, with biochemistry, pastoral botany, zootechny II, veterinary anatomy I and pharmacology added.

Pharmacology lectures were held at UQ's medical school in the inner Brisbane suburb of Herston, with the small group of vets clustered together among sixty to seventy medical students. The lectures were taught by a 'very intense medico' who had a habit of posing a question to the class at large without warning and then singling out students to answer. The questions were focused on dosages and side effects of drugs relating to humans, and the second-year vet students were 'pretty clueless.' Somehow, they managed to escape the professor's notice for five lectures, but during the sixth, his pointing finger landed on one of the veterinary cohort, Doug Brown, and demanded he explain the effects of digitalis. Digitalis is a drug derived from the dried leaves of a foxglove plant and used to treat certain heart conditions. Its use was almost unheard of in veterinary medicine at the time. Baffled, Doug replied, 'Please sir, we're vet students, not medical students.' The professor exploded, Reg recalled, declaring he wouldn't lower himself to lecture veterinary students, then 'stormed out of the room and that was that.' The subject was moved to Yeerongpilly, where Robbie Burns took up the slack, lecturing on drugs, usages, reactions and outcomes.

A locally-practising vet named Arch McDowall taught anatomy during second and third years, one of a rotating roster of eight to ten external guest lecturers in addition to the three permanent lecturers. His method was simple: the students were split into group of four to six to pore over the anatomy manuals for dogs and horses. The class seemed to bear him no ill will for this seemingly lackadaisical approach to lecturing. Reg noted they were 'a happy group and aimed to please everyone.'

Unfortunately for Arch McDowall, he was slated to be on the receiving end of such congenial efforts. Noticing that he appeared to be a 'little below par with 'flu', one of the students lit upon the brilliant idea of whipping up a rejuvenating brew, specifically using Arch's 'pewter tea pot, of which he was extraordinarily proud' by heating it on a gas ring. The results were catastrophic. Reg noted that at least 'his increased blood pressure did seem to improve him a little.'

Perhaps the class had learnt something following the numerous SUPs and mass student exodus of the year before; with the exception of Arch McDowall's unlucky teapot, there were far fewer hijinks in second year and beyond. Amid the considerable challenge that the second-year curriculum posed, their small class size meant a great camaraderie developed. Reg became lifelong friends with his classmate Stan Knott. They spent much of their time together, travelling into the ARI at Yeerongpilly early to tutor one another and spending their free time poring over the most recently released veterinary journals and research studies. Stan recalled the 'academic slaughter' continued throughout 1948 and by the end of the year another four students had dropped out, leaving just eight.

As part of his study requirements, Reg spent a week of his long Christmas break that year on a stud Jersey dairy farm at Devon Park near Oakey, where his proximity to Toowoomba allowed him to stay at home in Schoenberg. He helped with the milking morning and night, fed and reared the calves, made up feed for the bails, and generally pitched in however he could.

On another occasion, he spent time at Warwick Vet Clinic which, having been opened by Scotch McLellan in 1949, was the second-oldest practice in Queensland. These experiences stood Reg in good stead, both while studying and beyond, as was doubtless the intent behind the university's mandate that vet students spend a portion of every holiday break doing practical placements.

Returning for their third year in Brisbane at the beginning of 1949, the class found that the vet school had vacated the ARI and another temporary building had been added at Yeerongpilly. A new barrage of learning commenced. In addition to the increasingly advanced iterations of their earlier classes – including zootechny III and veterinary anatomy II – the students started learning pathology and immunology. Pathology was taught by the newly appointed part-time lecturer ROC King (affectionately dubbed Rocky), who also ran a private practice in Ipswich and seemed to find it difficult managing these competing demands on his time. When he did turn up for his lecture – which wasn't guaranteed – he was invariably late; sometimes, the class spent the hour-long period simply waiting for Rocky at the bus stop. If he hadn't turned up by the end of the period, they would catch the next bus home.

The class spent a week working in sheep husbandry at Gatton Agricultural College, about an hour outside Brisbane, to increase their clinical exposure. Students sheared sheep and became acquainted with livestock classification and general handling protocols, including the castration of lambs, trimming of over-grown hooves, docking of tails and testing for worms and flystrike, a condition induced by blowfly larvae which is fatal if untreated. They were given the chance to observe 'mulesing', a process which had been developed roughly twenty years earlier and rapidly became routine procedure for sheep husbandry in Australia. This surgery – which cuts flaps of skin from around the lamb's tail and breech (the back and top of the hind legs, beneath the tail) – is designed to minimise the risk of flystrike. Despite the work, the students found 'there was not enough to keep us busy' and were reprimanded by university staff for being disruptive because they spent some of their free time riding their bikes where they weren't supposed to: through the shearing shed and drafting yards.

The class yet again found the academic rigours of third year taking a toll on the cohort. By the time they went on Christmas holidays, their numbers had been whittled down to seven, less than a quarter of the original class.

As the 1949 university year ended, the students began planning their forthcoming move from Brisbane to Sydney for the next two years of their study. Before that had to be dealt with, however, the end-of-year break furnished an opportunity for yet more valuable 'real world' experience.

Stan Knott's brother, Charlie, a well-known North Queensland doctor with a medical practice in Cairns, organised for Reg and Stan to spend three to four weeks at Gunnawarra Station in North Queensland, about 50 miles south of Mount Garnet. The large, million-acre cattle property lay near the Gulf Country – the low-lying land bordering the Gulf of Carpentaria that stretches across north-west Queensland and the Northern Territory's north-east. Laced with numerous river distributaries, the Gulf Country provides a prime area for the breeding and fattening of cattle and the station was awash with wild pigs, brumby mobs, horned Shorthorn cattle, and numerous lagoon swamps, a favourite spot for the pigs.

Reg and Stan often camped outside in their swags. On the first night, they heard the plaintive childlike cry of a curlew and froze. The sounds quickly became more familiar and the chorusing of dingoes and howling of curlews formed an eerie lullaby as they fell asleep.

At Gunnawarra, the two friends were swept up in the various physically demanding station activities, playing their part in the routine mustering, branding and castrating of cattle. The station had several vehicles, each equipped with a high-powered rifle with which all hands were under instructions to shoot any brumbies seen on the property – regarded as vermin – but the two young men also spent much time on horseback. Fortunately, Reg was a competent horseman.

On a previous visit to Schoenberg to muster cattle, he had found a very quiet horse for the less-experienced Stan to ride and taken upon himself the feisty remaining animal. It had fought and bucked, but 'the man from Harlaxton never shifted in his seat.' It had left Stan with a great story to tell their friends and the feat was repeated at Gunnawarra. Needing some mustering done that was too good for the young ringers (the station hands skilled at roping and handling cattle), the head stockman asked Reg to mount up on a feisty 'buckjumper' to do the work, perhaps wondering if the young man would struggle – only to find that he rode the horse to a standstill.

Reg and Stan rode with a group from the station and a staff cook to Native Wells, one of the property's outstations. The building was about eight feet off the ground and had no verandah railing to prevent mishaps which meant, inevitably, there was one. An old, bearded prospector turned up to have dinner with the group and toppled over the edge in the middle of the night. The man was badly hurt and Reg and Stan joined the station owner in fixing a bed in the tray of a ute to drive him to the Mt Garnet hospital. It was after dawn by the time they arrived back at Native Wells. Pragmatically, Stan remembered it as a good learning experience for both him and Reg, allowing them some insight into human anaesthetics and surgical techniques.

'The man from Harlaxton never shifted in his seat': Reg on horseback with whip and rifle during his university years, possibly at Gunnawarra.

Returning home from his time in the Gulf Country, Reg prepared to move south in January 1950. He had booked his new accommodation in Redfern in Sydney's inner city and had his bags packed when he received a telegram: the UQ Veterinary School was reopening at Yeerongpilly in its fullest capacity. There would be no transfer to Sydney, marking the first time Queensland BVSc students had been able to complete their degree in their home state. Queensland's intentions to provide a five-year course had been established some years earlier (as early, in fact, as 1947 – the same year that pioneering class had first dipped their uncertain toes into the fast-running river of tertiary education), yet it came mostly as a surprise to the students. The university's plans for the extension of current structures and the provision of new ones to accommodate the fourth-year teaching requirements were approved in October 1949. A small animal clinic, pharmacy, lecture rooms and theatres, and bacteria laboratory expanded the facilities, while the staff was augmented with more professors and lecturers.

Reg's cohort directly benefited from these changes and it was a great relief to know they didn't have to move to Sydney. The UQ

Veterinary School provided a clinical service in the local area and students assisted their professors throughout their studies, an arrangement which meant students 'became adept in the practical application of all aspects of veterinary science.' It stands to reason that exposure and opportunities within the clinic were commensurate with students' experience and Reg later said his class had been very fortunate to be the senior vet students at UQ for three years running. Combined with the semi-rural nature of Yeerongpilly in the 1940s and 1950s, their seniority meant they had significant exposure to large animals, with which they became quite proficient in handling; particularly, Stan Knott recalled, horses.

This wasn't unusual. In the post-war period, most veterinary schools worldwide still emphasised large domestic animals such as horses, cattle, sheep, pigs and goats over the study of small companion animals. With the benefit of hindsight, such a focus seems illogical – in 2011, veterinary services for companion animals comprised roughly 83 per cent of total industry revenue. Even among rural practitioners, companion animals accounted for a staggering 70 per cent of most clinics' income in 2003, increasingly essential to such practices' survival.

Although the overwhelming focus of today's vets is small animals, it's a relatively new phenomenon. Historically, the centrality of large animals in maintaining industrial power conveyed horses and cattle with significant economic value that justified the expensive treatment. In the early twentieth century, some vets began to specialise in small animals (specifically dogs), but the effects of the First World War were disastrous for these individuals. 'Pets came to be seen as an irresponsible waste of resources during a national emergency' while large animal vets experienced a resurgence due to the importance of horses in the war. Despite economic hardship, there is evidence that British vets increasingly treated small animals during the interwar period. More commonly, however, the growing prosperity and urbanisation experienced around the globe after the Second World War are credited with precipitating the shift of veterinary focus from large animals and livestock to companion animals.

The transition was still in its infancy during the late 1940s when Reg was studying and may also have been more gradual in Australia than other developed nations. An historical economic dependence on agriculture since European colonisation had entrenched large animal husbandry as a crucial facet of Australian life and culture; while there was explosive growth in Australia's mineral exploitation and industrial activity after the Second World War, this process would also have been nascent in the late 1940s.

The result was a UQ Bachelor of Veterinary Science with an emphasis on large animals such as those typically seen in a country practice – a focus which not only played to Reg's strengths (a familiarity with farm animals) but was to prove invaluable in his future. The small class size allowed significant personal attention from staff, with whom the students developed close relationships, and provided the opportunity for far greater exposure to hands-on experience with various aspects of their coursework. Their fourth and fifth years of study were, in these senses, unique.

At the start of 1950, the stalwart seven who had survived third year prepared to commence UQ's inaugural fourth-year course, for which they were joined by a Sydneysider named David Tennent. A returned serviceman, he had been shot down over Yugoslavia during the war and sheltered by Yugoslavian resistance fighters, and he now migrated north from the University of Sydney to take the class number up to eight.

It was to be their final reconfiguration and the eight students plunged headfirst into the broad swathe of fourth-year studies – including the dizzying worlds of bacteriology, parasitology, surgery and medicine. Stan Knott wryly recalled the very successful clinic developed at the school where students learnt 'the mysteries of large animal rectal examinations.'

Robbie Burns now managed the class's surgical education, where their small numbers conferred another advantage: in Sydney, the corresponding 1951 cohort was seventy-three students strong. UQ's aspiring vets performed large animal surgeries outside on the grass, so their exposure was likely somewhat more rustic than that of Sydney students. Under Robbie's tutelage – characterised by his frequent reminders about the close relationship between safe, competent restraint and successful surgery – they acquired a solid grounding in equine restraint.

Reg (far right) and his classmates receiving a lesson on treating hoof conditions on a horse that is being carefully and properly restrained.

Robbie introduced an ambulatory clinic that offered travelling veterinary services, affording students interaction with the wider community and experience with a greater range of cases. With similar intent, he insisted they accompany him to local horse races to swab the winners.

Some days, the unintentional lessons were more quotidian, though still important: Robbie's failed attempt to wriggle through a slippery barbed-wire fence one day left his expensive trousers ruined and reinforced that a vet's clothing needed to be appropriate (and hardy!). Other lessons were less amusing. Though Reg and Stan considered themselves adept at 'bacto', they were left feeling cheated when they racked up subpar performances in an exam which, Stan lamented, wasn't actually about the details they'd devoted so much time to mastering.

Reg discovered another love during this time. 'I badly wanted to buy a motorbike,' he remembered, but his mother Milly hated them and when she found out he planned to buy a second-hand machine, she stepped in. If he could not be deterred, then at least it shouldn't be something for which they had little to no quality assurance; Reg would be far safer, she argued, on something more mechanically sound. She and Vyvyan footed the bill for a new, two-cylinder Ariel, which Reg repaid after graduating.

The bike was a boon to Reg and Stan, proving the ideal mode of transport to and from Yeerongpilly, and removing the necessity faced by other students to thumb a ride or catch the bus, as Reg had done in earlier years. Reg provided the bike, Stan supplied the petrol, and the freedom offered by their new wheels was exhilarating – especially during one commute, when a truck failed to stop in time and ploughed into the back of the bike, where Stan was riding pillion. Thankfully, neither man nor machine was seriously damaged, though the same couldn't be said of the truck driver's ears. Stan and Reg, more than a little shaken by the experience, heaped abuse on him while waiting for the light to change.

Reg with one of his later motorbikes, a Mercedes fondly dubbed 'Gert.'

As fourth year progressed, the students' learning experiences grew both increasingly diverse and complex. Dr Tom Ewer, a 1937 University of Sydney graduate who had recently completed a doctorate at Cambridge, was announced as chair in animal husbandry in January 1950. Assuming his post in August, he taught the class animal nutrition and history of science and subsequently played a vital role both in Reg's study and in the UQ Veterinary School.

Ewer was an equine vet and Reg credited him with having 'the most influence on the direction I decided to take.' During the breeding season, Reg recalled the class trailing Ewer, 'palpating each mare after he had examined her and absorbing his description of what was happening with her uterus and ovaries.' The procedure required Reg to insert his gloved arm into the mare's rectum to feel through the rectal wall for the changes in the horse's reproductive tract that Ewer described to him. At the time this was the main technique for determining equine pregnancy. Reg's peers were less keen on horses and Reg gained 'plenty of hands-on pregnancy and follicle-testing experience' under Ewer's tutelage.

Ewer was crucial to the ongoing development of UQ's veterinary school in the 1950s. Despite the extensions built prior to his arrival, his initial impression of the facilities was one of consternation: the veterinary school, he said, was little more than a 'miserable collection of wooden huts on the outskirts of Brisbane.' This disparaging assessment likely resulted, at least in part, from the striking contrast between UQ's facilities and those at the universities of Sydney and Cambridge.

Established in 1209, the University of Cambridge is among the oldest in the world and in the post-war period, like many other institutions globally, was rapidly growing. Cambridge town boasted its own airport in a borough with a population of roughly 91,000 in 1951, the same year it was chartered as a city. In contrast, the whole of the greater Brisbane area had a population of around 111,000 in 1954, while Yeerongpilly (which likely fell within the census area of either Yeronga or Marooka) had a peak population of no more than 4300 in 1947 and 12,000 in 1954.

Having studied among Cambridge's imposing stone buildings and lived in Cambridge town, Tom Ewer's move to Yeerongpilly must have seemed like flying from the future into the past – a rural, backwater past in a small country town and its paltry excuse for a veterinary school. The makeshift facilities doubtless hindered the quality of instruction, which was inevitably poorer than Ewer was accustomed to.

Alongside Professor John Francis, who was appointed to the faculty in 1952, Ewer fought hard for the funding needed to expand its facilities and research capabilities. Together they precipitated the development of the Pinjarra Hills Farm research facility, the new vet school at St Lucia, and associated research laboratories. The addition of further faculty members continued this widespread development, including the parasitology department (Professor John Sprent) and the animal husbandry department (Professor Des Dowling).

Looking back on this period fifty years later, Reg noted that the transition to a five-year UQ veterinary course and the concomitant gathering of such intelligent, driven and enthusiastic vets appeared to have 'been the entry into a golden age for the Queensland school and faculty of veterinary science.' Such an evolution was representative of a broader attitudinal change towards tertiary education which became particularly pervasive after the Second World War. There had been strong bipartisan support for increasing Commonwealth involvement in tertiary education after 1939, initially with the focus on bolstering key study areas (that is, those related to Australia's war efforts, particularly science and engineering).

When the Curtin Labor government came into power in late 1941, however, this shifted to more widespread support for tertiary students across a variety of faculties. From these foundations, the 1945 implementation of the Commonwealth Post War Reconstruction Scheme had far-reaching implications, increasing the number of students and helping them get there through the same kind of financial assistance Reg received.

The scheme established widespread expectations that the Commonwealth meaningfully (financially) contribute to tertiary education. As a result, the federal government substantially invested in state education systems – the vastly improved buildings, equipment, staffing and research opportunities achieved by Tom Ewer, John Francis and their peers at UQ were among its direct results over the coming decades.

The students were expected to spend time among the wider

agricultural and veterinary community to gain practical experience as well as some insight into how the industries worked and a vet's role within them. Every student had to spend a fortnight each with a private practitioner and a government veterinary officer; Reg ticked both boxes in Toowoomba. He recalled that he 'was fortunate to see one of the outbreaks of pleuropneumonia in cattle at Gowrie Junction, where more than thirty cows died of the disease.' Described as 'one of the three great cattle plagues of history', (the other two being foot-and-mouth disease and rinderpest), pleuropneumonia was the subject of a national eradication program and had already been eliminated in New South Wales in the early 1940s. Reg's 'good luck' lay in observing the disease first-hand prior to its eradication, exposure which proved invaluable.

While his studies were consuming, Reg took what opportunities he could to enjoy his freedom with his friends. In March 1950, his classmate Doug Brown proposed a weekend bike trip down the coast. There was an ulterior motive; Doug wanted to meet up with a young woman named Muriel who was holidaying at the well-known Greenmount Guest House in Coolangatta with her friends Kath and Joy.

Meeting on the beach, the group spent a pleasant day together. Something about Muriel's friend Joy, a quiet young woman with a beautiful smile, caught Reg and held him fast. When, later, they walked over some precarious rocks, he reached out to gently take her hand. As he supported her over that uneven ground, he left Joy with two enduring thoughts. The first was the strength in his arm, that power so carefully deployed to ensure she didn't fall. The second was his young, clean-shaven face and strong, straight teeth. There was something good and trustworthy about him which Joy could not forget.

When the day ended, she thought that was the end of the story. But Reg, confiding in Stan that he found Joy very attractive, kept in touch. They came from very different backgrounds. She was a city girl, having grown up in suburban Taringa with her parents and younger brother; he was a country boy. Furthermore, Reg had been encouraged to pursue his veterinary school desires after graduating, while Joy's dreams of studying physiotherapy had been quelled by her father's insistence that she follow in his footsteps and receive clerical training at Stott's Business College. When Reg and Joy met, she was working full-time as a clerk typist at Bearing Service Company in Brisbane. Typical of the times, Reg had a lot of freedom after graduating. For Joy, the trip to Coolangatta was the first time she'd been allowed to holiday without her family.

A young Reg and Joy laughing together on a later holiday excursion to Kirra Beach, Queensland.

Her parents expressly forbade her to ride on Reg's motorbike, so the young couple caught buses or shelled out for taxis, walking or bike-riding through the suburbs, except for those occasions when Reg borrowed Vyvyan's Prefect ute. Joy was rather shy and her Uncle Jim had advised on more than one occasion not to go for 'the good-looking ones' who were 'not always reliable.' But if reliability was the point of concern, Reg quickly allayed the family's fears. Joy visited Reg in Toowoomba and, as her father had lost an eye to a pea rifle accident in his youth and her family had never owned a car, Reg taught her to drive.

Later that year, Reg and his sister Corrinne drove down from Toowoomba to the O'Connor Boathouse in Brisbane where they celebrated Joy's twenty-first birthday with her friends from work and the local Methodist church. Reg invited Joy to the occasional vet school function, where her presence became so well-accepted that the following year, one of Reg's professors passed by their table and inquired, 'I say, are you two married yet?'

Reg, Joy, Joan, and Stan Knott enjoying themselves at a vet school function in 1952.

But for all the happiness and possibility that 1950 brought, it also delivered an enormous blow. About halfway through his fourth year,

Reg's eldest brother Edwin died in a tragic accident. Edwin had flown numerous dangerous missions over Papua New Guinea throughout the Second World War and survived the wartime perils that had took his younger brother, Roess. Returning home, he continued to expand the Pascoe family milk run, satisfying his yearning for flight by amassing over 1500 flying hours and becoming president of the Toowoomba Soaring Club, where he volunteered to train aspiring RAAF pilots. But while out with a trainee on 13 August 1950, Edwin was killed in a tragic glider accident at the Oakey aerodrome, leaving behind a wife and nine young children. He was just thirty-five.

Reg immediately returned to Schoenberg. He must have felt helpless as he sat next to his grieving parents and his sister, doing his best to comfort them in the face of this second, insurmountable loss. The members of the Soaring Club chipped in both practically and financially; along with neighbours and friends, they helped run Edwin's 20-acre family farm and managed the milk run in the days following his death. Six carried his coffin at the funeral later that week.

Reg never spoke of his bereavement following Edwin's death, though two of his sons later bore forms of their uncles' names. The tragedy reverberated throughout the family in other ways; Milly developed an abiding horror at the thought of losing Reg in an aircraft accident, and for the remainder of her life, Reg and Joy never told her of his travel in small, non-commercial planes to visit distant cattle stations until he had safely returned.

In 1951, the fifth and final year of the class's BVSc, pastoral botany, animal husbandry and meat inspection were added to the curriculum. The new lecturer, Eric Reid, conducted the meat inspection classes while wearing a trademark felt hat. He finished each lecture with a Bible verse: *sufficient unto the day is the evil thereof*. The aphorism urged the students to focus on the present and not waste time worrying about the challenges of tomorrow – perhaps an attempt to keep them grounded in the face of an onerous workload.

The pastoral botany professor, Selwyn Everest, returned Reg to his roots when he took the class to the Darling Downs for three days. Though another valuable experience, they were plagued by increasingly inclement weather, with the rain getting heavier and heavier as the excursion went along. This, however, did furnish yet another useful, if inadvertent, lesson about choosing where to sleep in the field: Reg and Stan woke one morning and peered from the safety of the covered university truck to see Tom Ewer wringing water out of his sports coat.

'Tall, imposing and personable', the dean of the vet school was 'very keen on research', Stan recalled. Accordingly, the fifth-year zootechny project required the students to spend a month in the town of Gatton, between Ipswich and Toowoomba, developing a short-term project. Reg's classmates thought the relocation was because the vet school found themselves short of teachers at the end of first term. Conveniently, Gatton wasn't far from Toowoomba and so Reg, Stan and Doug Byrnes stayed at Schoenberg, where Vyvyan and Milly made them very welcome. The three young men accepted an offer from the Gatton students to visit various studs throughout the Darling Downs and enjoyed both the freedom and the welcome change of scenery.

The eight students were divided into two groups to examine the effects of different food sources on growth and development in calves and piglets. They were almost completely unsupervised and since feedings, weighing and general observations only partially occupied them – and as they were highly mobile with four motorbikes between them – they were granted permission by Dr Neil Brittan, the principal of Gatton Agricultural College, to visit a few dairy farms.

On the odd occasion, the eight students would 'descend on an amazed dairy farmer', trying to work out any and all of his livestock's problems. Their success rate was good and it wasn't long, Stan remembered, before the college 'was grumbling that [they] had started up a viable practice.' With the students providing a legitimate, useful and gratis service, their return to Brisbane meant the college was left to handle local expectations that the pro bono work continue.

Reg wryly described their 'little group [as] ... scientists at heart', and that year provided excellent fodder for continuing to develop these skills. Another experiment arose. Imperial Chemical Industries, a British chemical giant based in London producing paints and speciality chemicals, began trialling a new intravenous anaesthetic in horses. The drug was a 'weird mix originally designed for cattle', which possessed the 'consistency and colour of watery yoghurt.' They were all keen for the experience – but Reg and three other students were allocated external tasks, taking them away from 'this seriously scientific adventure, much to [their] disappointment.' They returned in the early evening to a silent, seemingly deserted vet school and, with no way to find their peers, Reg's group headed home.

Unbeknown to them, their classmates sat inside with the test subject, for whom they were solely responsible; when Reg and his three fellow inadvertent truants arrived back at Yeerongpilly the following morning, they found four 'rather worn out' friends and an incredibly docile horse. It remained anaesthetised for over *seven hours* – testament to the power of the drug, it seemed – before becoming electrified. The animal 'charged around an acre paddock for another two hours ... exercising all present ... before he sobered up.' Someone decided it best the product wasn't registered for use in horses.

Budding scientists, the students were also good sportsmen and decided to turn the bitumen road in the middle of the school into a cricket pitch. With buildings conveniently dotted all around to stop the ball, it offered the class a bit of fun ... until Reg hit a master stroke right through Robbie Burns's office door where the lecturer was indulging in his lunchtime snooze. Awakened by the smashing of glass, Robbie was, Reg thought, 'unusually agitated over such a great cricket stroke.' He rewarded the daring sportsmen with the task of administering medications to the school's horses. This was usually facilitated by a gag or a balling gun (an applicator that allows a vet to keep their hand out of an animal's mouth), but Robbie's directions were clear: the students were to 'handball' the drugs into the horses' mouths using pieces of pumpkin – *without* any additional equipment. Fortunately, no fingers were lost and, somehow, the students made it through to graduation intact.

The Veterinary Association arranged a celebratory evening to commemorate the landmark occasion of the first graduates from the new UQ Veterinary School. Reg was awarded the surgery prize and, in a joint prize with fellow student Ray Clem, also received the university medal – a fitting end to a period in their friendship that, ever after, Ray would recall as a 'great rivalry.'[1]

Eight firework rockets were arranged to symbolise 'launching' the new graduates into the profession – but when seven rockets were successfully set off, one remained. Ray was found sleeping on the pharmacy table and the other students generously lit the wayward firework which, unlike the rest, 'had a mind of its own and roared across the darkened internal garden, narrowly missing the dean!'

1951. UQ's inaugural BVSc graduating class.
Rear: SG Knott, AA Seawright, RR Clem, J McD Beams, DD Tennent, DH Brown.
Front: RR Pascoe, R Millar MRCVS, Professor TK Ewer BVSc PhD, RHG Burns BVSc, D Byrne

The joys and challenges of the adventures and innocuous mishaps while studying formed the basis of Reg's lifelong professional philosophy. 'If you are going to be kind to animals, *be safe* in what you do,' he reminded a class of graduating vets in the early 2000s. 'Don't get into positions from which you cannot retrieve your personal safety and dignity at the end – not of the day, but of the moment, because a vet's day really never ends, and so there are both better and worse events awaiting who knows when.'

Reg Pascoe's own 'day' had just begun.

3
Oakey's New Vet

Back home in Schoenberg, his Veterinary Registration Certificate 186 in his pocket, Reg began a small mixed practice on the wide front porch – one of only five private practices in Queensland outside the Brisbane metropolitan area.

The graduating class of 1951 was a professional rarity. There were no more than ten university-qualified practitioners in Queensland and, thirty years later, Reg recalled that they were vastly outnumbered by 'quack vets.' The term referred to practitioners without formal training, who often had practical experience but whose skills, methods and general ability were unregulated.

Most farming communities, particularly in rural Queensland, had never seen a qualified veterinarian before. Reg and his peers were therefore regarded as somewhat of 'a curiosity', their 'theoretical training' seeming to hold little weight against the practical knowledge and expertise of the heralded 'bush vet.'[2] Doubtless, Reg's use of the phrase 'quack vets' revealed his frustration: to have spent years studying, only to have those credentials disdained, must have been galling.

Perhaps those communities believed, having managed well enough without qualified veterinarians for decades, there was no need for such interference now. The atmosphere must have been unwelcoming and, at times, intimidating. Certainly, in the early days, Reg's dairy farmer clients were resistant to new ideas and struggled to accept an 'outsider' investigating problems like mastitis (a painful inflammation of the mammary gland or udder) and abortion. There was, Reg mused, 'almost a social stigma attached to the presence of such diseases on a dairy farm', as if they were an indictment of the farmer, rather than a normal part of animal husbandry.

Perhaps Reg seemed to them like a book-learned but practically inexperienced interloper, preaching about matters of which he was ignorant. The challenge in confronting such attitudes must have been immense, but Reg was undeterred. He had been well-schooled in the values of client service, professionalism and ongoing development; these tenets were the foundation of his practice and the means by which, he maintained, the veterinary profession 'would be raised above the level of the "cow leech" and the "horse doctor."' Professionalism in all aspects of his practice was paramount to achieving and maintaining respect.

His first job arrived in March of 1952: a buck goat with a calculus (a hard mass formed by minerals within the body, such as gall or kidney stones in humans) in his urethral process, the most common site of obstruction in sheep and goats. Now, Reg discovered, his 'surgical prowess was severely challenged. I could see the calculus, I could feel the calculus ... but I could not shift it.' He selected one of his most reliable instruments – a pair of scissors – and snipped off the process.

It was only later he discovered that his decision might not have been ideal: he hadn't realised the strange, curly appendage was important, perhaps even essential, during mating. Thankfully, the error proved inconsequential; ten months later in what must have been a welcome piece of news, the grateful owner told Reg that the buck had added several new kids to his flock. This situation illustrated the ways in which his theoretical experience fell short of more practical exposure and highlighted just how much there still was to learn.

Reg might have remained on Schoenberg's verandah treating troublesome buck goats forever, but that would never have satisfied him. Instead, he took two steps in 1952 that fundamentally changed both his life and his career. The first was his successful application for a tuberculosis testing contract with the Queensland Department of Primary Industries (DPI). The timing was ideal. Though states and territories began introducing independent TB control programs in the early 1900s, the initiatives had greatly expanded following the Second World War due to an improved test and an increased number of veterinarians. It was hoped that contracted vets would educate local farmers about scientific methods for improving herd health and that these ideas would progressively pervade and advance the industry.

The scheme provided Reg with an invaluable opportunity to build relationships (and trust) with local dairy farmers and beef cattle owners. Although it absorbed much of his time, it also provided a 'low but very reliable income for many years' that served as the practice's financial mainstay. Simultaneously, Reg continued treating small animals and developing a private local client base.

The second big event that year was Reg's marriage to Joy. Their tender romance was the key unfinished puzzle piece in his life, and Reg spent much of his free time with the lovely young woman who had so captured his heart. He sold his motorbike to repay Vyvyan and Milly and bought himself a small Austin A40, regularly travelling to Brisbane to visit Joy and continue teaching her how to drive. He approached Joy's father, Harold, to ask for her hand and received her parents' blessings.

Having set upon August for the wedding there was one last crucial piece of administration to be dealt with – Joy's driving licence – and she duly arranged a lunch-hour test at the Roma Street police station in Brisbane's CBD. Reg thought he'd taught her everything she needed to know but as he waited outside the station, he was more confident in her abilities than she was. She came back and told him she'd failed.

Waiting to start the ordeal, she'd been plagued by nerves. It was one thing to sit next to *Reg* and drive, another entirely to be scrutinised by a stranger. And not just any stranger: when a burly policeman plopped himself into the passenger seat, the butterflies in her stomach began doing triple somersaults. Joy took a deep breath and put the car into gear, but it didn't move. The policeman reached across and turned on the ignition. It was hardly a promising beginning and her nerves skyrocketed at this first, simple mistake.

They drove out to Spring Hill, where Joy easily navigated the narrow streets, but when she began reversing towards a telephone pole, the copper ordered her back to the station. He was kind, Joy remembered, gently suggesting to Reg that more practice was needed. The young man took it to heart. They filled most of that weekend with hill starts and reversing and with Reg's tutelage, Joy adeptly passed her next test.

The couple was married at Joy's local Taringa Methodist Church on 9 August 1952.

Reg and Joy's wedding day. From left: Vyvyan, Milly, Reg, Joy, Helen and Harold.

A few days later, the new Mr and Mrs Reginald Pascoe set off for Katoomba, in New South Wales's scenic Blue Mountains, on their honeymoon. It was a long trip – more than twelve hours – and no doubt they were grateful to share the driving.

A few hours out from Katoomba, the weather turned drizzly. Joy was at the wheel when, rounding a corner, the car skidded across the road and into a guidepost. Thankfully, no one was hurt. Later, they were told the camber on that particular corner was bad in wet weather and had caused more than one casualty. Reg and Joy were lucky to escape with only minor damage to the car. They were, however, more than a little shaken.

Joy was relieved that Reg 'very kindly, did not criticise' as together they headed to a nearby farmhouse to call the NRMA. They were towed into Orange and told the car could be repaired late the following day. Once their accommodation was sorted, and eager to learn about the local area, Reg contacted a local vet by the name of John Springhall. Reg and Joy spent the rest of that 'fearfully cold, wet night' cosy before John's kerosene fire heater, devouring homemade melted cheese on toast while being thoroughly entertained by the Army Reserve colonel's lively conversation.

John later became a staff member at the UQ Veterinary School; noting the intimate nature of veterinary science at the time, there's little doubt he and Reg met again, but it's unlikely those subsequent meetings could have bettered this fortuitous and enjoyable first encounter that Joy remembered so fondly.

Even at the outset, Reg's passion for his work was already a major factor in his personal life. Joy recalled that 'his thirst for knowledge was ever present.' He had capitalised on their impromptu stay in Orange to connect with John Springhall, but he and Joy had already designed their honeymoon to incorporate another opportunity. After a week in Katoomba, they headed down to Sydney so Reg could attend the Australian New Zealand Association for the Advancement of Science (ANZAS) conference – the first of many such events over the coming decades.

The newlyweds then returned to the Darling Downs. Reg's recently awarded DPI contract stipulated that he must live within the area – in his case, in Oakey – and so the couple stayed with Milly and Vyvyan at Schoenberg as they searched for their first home.

Cattle were the dominant business in the region, which was an extensive dairying district in the 1950s. Under the Queensland state government's scheme to eradicate tuberculosis, roughly 36,000 head fell under Reg's remit. There were only two small racing stables and a very small broodmare farm, but as Reg was the only vet around and keen to build his practice he added these clients to his books too.

The site of Reg's simple, idyllic childhood saw him step off on a new journey with his wife, and that small town was to be his home and his professional kingdom for the remainder of his life. It was a strangely apt coincidence: Oakey's sole claim to fame in 1952 was as the home of the Australian thoroughbred, Bernborough, who raced from 1942–46. Remembered as one of Queensland's greatest racehorses, Bernborough revolutionised Australian racing and brought the word 'Oakey' to the nation's lips. The parallel is striking: nowhere else in the country could have served as a more fitting domain.

Housing prospects, however, were thin on the ground. Some homes, poorly situated for drainage, had pools of stagnating water in the backyard after recent downpours; others had no sink in the kitchen, requiring occupants to fill buckets from an outdoor rainwater tank. But luck was with Reg and Joy. They found and arranged to buy a three-bedroom house on Cory Street, which not only had dry yards and a sink, but both rain- *and* town-water taps in the kitchen – though the wood stove was rather daunting to a green, 'city girl' like Joy. They were just down the road from the livestock sale yards, where pigs and calves were sold on Tuesdays and cattle on Thursdays.

Pooling their resources – including monetary wedding presents, money from Joy's twenty-first birthday and their respective savings – and helped by their families, Reg and Joy furnished the house as best they could. Vyvyan and Milly donated an old cedar table, which Joy deftly turned into a bedroom dresser by adding a skirt that matched the bedroom curtains and allowed shoes to be hidden underneath. Stan Knott's father made them a cane chair, and Joy commissioned her uncle to make a dining table with chairs and a sideboard. Having three bedrooms allowed them, while they were still getting settled, to convert one into an office-cum-surgery for small animal treatment. Later they divided the house's long, brick garage into a car and workbench area, a small 'laundry' section near the outdoor washing copper and an L-shaped surgery that Reg augmented with a concrete extension in his 'spare' time.

The surgery was necessarily basic, but it had the essentials and Reg made whatever he could to defray his expenses. The plate glass shelf of the single long cabinet held his instruments; the cupboards below, various paraphernalia. A glass-fronted cabinet contained drugs and consumables, prepared by Reg on the garage workbench, and he had a local engineer make a wheeled operating table, topped by a stainless-steel slab with a central drain and a basin underneath to catch fluids.

Like many junior veterinarians' wives at the time, Joy became Reg's 'right-hand man.' The education she'd reluctantly undertaken at Stott's Business College proved invaluable in her administrative management of the budding practice, but her ready willingness as Reg's vet nurse spoke volumes of the passion for learning and science that had precipitated her interest in physiotherapy.

She learnt to give anaesthetic to the small animals, mostly cats and dogs, brought in for spaying or neutering. It was a primitive operation: two rubber tubes – one ending in a drawstring-tightened canvas mask, the other in a hand pump – ran from a small jar of ether with a screw-top lid. Cats were swaddled in a towel and Reg controlled larger dogs while Joy fitted the mask to the animal's face and started pumping ether until Reg determined the creature sufficiently sedated to be rolled onto its back and each leg quickly secured to the operating table's uprights. The animal pinned, Joy returned to managing the anaesthetic for the surgery's duration, keeping a weather eye on the jar of ether to make sure it didn't tip over as Reg completed the operation.

As the practice grew, Reg divided the backyard to create a small pen for the livestock he treated in addition to cattle and companion animals. Joy's attempts to maintain a garden suffered during what she dubbed 'kindness to sheep week', when the oblivious woolly beasts crushed her rose bushes in search of shade. Despite his early mishap with the buck, there were plenty of goats to treat too. Later, the practice added a boarding service for dogs, and Reg travelled to a few small equine clients across the district.

But under the DPI's tuberculosis programme, cattle were the first order of business, and it was within the programme's requirements that the majority of Reg's contact with local cattle farmers occurred. The practical application of tuberculosis testing remains much the same today as it was in the 1950s. Over two days, animals are injected with two different kinds of tuberculin, a 'safe' manufactured derivative of the bovine tuberculosis bacterium. Seventy-two hours later, the vet returns to measure and compare the animal's reactions.

Thursdays and Fridays became Reg and Joy's 'injection days', when they visited the next farm on the list. There, Reg proceeded to inject every animal and tag their upper ear with an aluminium label which repeatedly proved difficult to read. Each animal had to have its own certificate with the farmer's name and address and the date of inspection, as well as a long list of the animal's details, including sex, age, breed, description and name. The last was a tall order: few farmers went to the effort of naming every animal in their large herds, and most were christened on injection day with whatever name popped into Reg and the owner's heads. Of course, the real challenge came three days later – when the owner had to try to recall which cow was which.

The days were long and hard. If Reg and Joy had a good run, and depending on the farm setup, they could process 400 to 500 cattle at a time. The dairy farms' rudimentary facilities weren't designed to have people clambering in and out of pens to squint at cattle tags and there were various farmyard dramas: Reg thought it 'quite exciting to have a long-horned old Ayrshire with about two feet of very sharp horn fencing with you while you read the tag.' Some years later, a new farmer to the district who had some prior experience with TB testing suggested a different way of doing business. Rather than climbing up over each bail partition to read the tag number, the farmer's previous vet had strolled down the front of each row of cows – the farmer would then open the door and the vet would read the number. Reg was all for making the job easier.

It worked surprisingly well and was far quicker, and Reg was feeling rather pleased by the time they reached the last three cows – 'the suspicious animals who don't want to enter the bails anyway.' The first two cows were fine, but the third had been waiting, 'knowing bad things were happening all around her.' The door opened and Reg appeared, but no sooner had he grabbed a horn and her ear to read the tag than she bolted, keen to head down the paddock and join her mates for breakfast. Grimly determined, Reg hung on and managed to get the number – but 'had to walk 50 yards back' to the bails, where the farmer covered his mouth to hide his mirth. 'You know,' he said to Reg, 'my previous vet had the same thing happen to him, but you beat him by nearly 30 yards before you let go.'

Another morning, Reg visited a farm that needed 150 milking cows and two bulls tested, and a young thoroughbred colt gelded. There had been 50 millimetres of rain the day before and the yards were soggy underfoot: the driest end was more than a foot underwater. *Best to geld the colt first*, Reg thought. The farmer, a large strong man who weighed in at over 100 kilograms, agreed. But when Reg suggested tying the young horse to a post, the owner demurred. 'I'll just hang onto him,' he said.

Reg didn't argue, simply slipped a bag of chloroform over the horse's nose. The colt seemed to like it, Reg thought, 'even whinnying a little for more.' Then he bolted. Twenty feet of rope travelled through the astounded farmer's hands until the large knot at the end arrived in his grip … but rather than let go, he held on. Reg watched in awe as the farmer's '130 kilograms took off in an arc on the end of the rope and splat into the mud and water at the end of the yard.' Fortunately, after taking a few more wobbly paces, the chloroform belatedly kicked in and the horse went down too. Reg trussed the colt, hosed him down, dried him off and finished the business of gelding him while the owner complained about getting water in his boots.

The cows were no trouble, and with the two bulls still to go, Reg suggested separating the flighty young two-year-old from the others in case he got antsy. Working with the farmer, the men trapped the older bull and a couple of cows in the bails and left the end bail empty, into which they coerced the younger animal. Luckily, though rather vocal about being tagged, he didn't put up too much of a show and the job was quickly done.

The old bull, however, hadn't been idle while the men were otherwise occupied. Escaping the bails, he noted the open door to the milk room and decided to have a look around. Reg and the farmer, realising the door to the road was open and the danger posed to the bull, leapt into action. 'With a yell and a flourish, the outside door was slammed in his face.' Crisis averted, the men breathed a sigh of relief.

The bull, unfazed at being thwarted, turned to walk out the way he came in ... but as Reg dryly recorded, 'fate is always lurking.' While turning, the bull somehow 'shoved his bum onto the exhaust pipe of the milk fridge engine' and with a thunderous bellow, leapt away from the pain – taking the full, 400-gallon (1500-litre) milk vat right off its stand and zipping across the yard.

An injured bull wasn't a great outcome ... but it was far better than being hurt or killed by a passing truck; securing the exits became a high priority afterwards.

Reg stood and watched, wide-eyed, at the destruction his ostensibly routine visit had wrought on the property. 'I'd better be getting to the next farm,' he said, beating a hasty retreat. 'They don't like having the cows standing around waiting.'

On the weekends, Reg and Joy knuckled down on administration, spending their Saturdays and Sundays furiously writing out all required certificates in triplicate – one for the farmer, one for the DPI office in Toowoomba and the third for their own records – and enlisting any visitors into their Herculean effort. The following Monday, Reg returned to the farmer to read the TB test, sign the pile of certificates, and arrange for the removal of any beasts showing evidence of reaction to the injection.

Not surprisingly, the Toowoomba arm of the DPI quickly found storage to be a problem as thousands of tuberculosis certificates inundated their office. Reg, realising the questionable sustainability of this method, created a single master document for each farm; chronicling all the required information for every tested animal and created in triplicate for dissemination as before, the idea was soon adopted for widespread use for the remainder of the eradication programme.

As Reg grew his practice, Joy supported him wholeheartedly. Theirs was a beautiful, tender and enduring partnership – Joy was irrefutably the love of Reg's life. Though his 'really soft side' was rarely on display, when it was, it emerged in the smallest, most subtle of ways. 'The thing that struck me,' one of Reg's vets remembered decades later, 'was the love that he had for Joy and the respect that he had for her all the time ... he was just always kind and always wanted to hold her hand ... the love that they had was amazing.'[3]

Their family grew. John was born 29 June 1953 and Joy moved to solely home-based work, handling phone calls and dealing with those drop-in clients looking to leave a pet for surgery, pay an account, or arrange for Reg to visit their farm. The effect of her absence would have been keenly felt by Reg, who likely had to juggle more moving pieces without Joy's quick and ready assistance.

Reg feeding John breakfast in the kitchen at Cory Street.

The arrangement caused a few other hiccoughs too – Joy's habit of putting her freshly washed hair in rollers or clips and wearing shorts in the summer disconcerted some clients, who sensitively averted their eyes while talking to her. At other times, she had to wield all her persuasive skills to overcome clients' reluctance to thoroughly describe the 'delicate' nature of a cow or bull's symptoms so she could obtain the information Reg needed to assess the problem. Confronted with urgent calls from farmers needing Reg's help, Joy was unruffled; her experiences accompanying him on TB testing visits over the past year proved invaluable, providing her with a sound knowledge of the local area.

Upon receiving a call from a client in search of Reg, Joy would work out the timeframe for his journey to the caller from his current position. Like many rural areas throughout Queensland and Australia at the time, Oakey was connected by use of a 'party line' telephone. This meant that multiple phones in the area shared the same local loop circuit – if anyone else on the party line was using the phone, others could pick up and listen in – with calls coordinated through a switchboard. It was with the assistance of these ever-helpful local telephone operators that Joy could get in touch with other families and clients to find Reg. Luckily, they often had a good idea whether he had passed or was on his way, and though challenging, this method of passing messages worked.

During this time, John was Joy's constant companion. Much like in Reg's childhood, and in Joy's own, there was little in the way of books to read to young children – 'rag books with simple pictures such as a boat, bat/ball, house, ice cream, car that occupied the eight pages' were the norm and soon 'became very boring to both reader and child.' In the face of such a shortfall, Joy's mother suggested saving the sturdy covers of the record books used for TB testing. From these, Grandma Lingard made four 'books' to read to John, cutting out relevant pictures of everyday items from magazines and pasting them onto numerous covers, which she then bound into makeshift books. It was an ingenious solution; beyond quickly, cheaply and easily providing the little boy with simple picture books, such actions also demonstrated the prevailing attitude of resilience and adaptability that, by necessity, characterised the lives of many – particularly wives and mothers in rural areas, more isolated than their urban and suburban counterparts.

Reg and John with a joey in the backyard of their Cory Street home.

Consumed by the busy TB eradication scheme and their new son, 1953 was soon over. A new thoroughbred farm was established the following year and Reg began to offer the first routine three-days-per-week ovarian palpation service to breeders, using rectal examination to physically inspect mares' reproductive organs and determine whether they were fertile.

With the increase in both general and equine practice, the year was a particularly challenging one in terms of travel. The nearest client was as close as 8 kilometres, others were up to 144 kilometres away, and travel time ate into Reg's clinical and personal life. He imagined creating an expansive, well-equipped veterinary facility to which large animals could be brought for treatment.

That same year, 1954, a young fourth-year student veterinarian by the name of David 'DJ' Laws came to Oakey for the external practical placement required by UQ. He had asked a fifth-year student for recommendations and the older student, having spent time the previous year with Reg during his own placement, extolled the practical aspects of veterinary science that he'd learnt. Such facets of the work, DJ felt, weren't always available at the veterinary school in their dealings with large animals. The prospect appealed and he spent a fortnight of his vacation staying at Cory Street and assisting Reg.

In 1955, Reg and Joy welcomed their second son, David. John was becoming more mobile and at some point a border collie named Lassie wandered in and decided to stay, then later added a litter of puppies to the tumult. The already-busy household began to bulge at the seams. In the backyard, boarding dogs shared space with sheep and goats receiving treatment, as well as a small vegetable garden and a wood heap: there wasn't much room left for two little boys to play.

As the region began to accept the competent young vet thrust into their midst, the practice steadily expanded, and Reg concurrently began serving as both a guest lecturer and external examiner for the UQ Veterinary School. When DJ returned to spend a few weeks of his university vacation at Cory Street, Reg recognised the need for a permanent second set of hands in the field and offered the younger man a job.

The transition to a two-veterinarian operation meant Reg had slightly more free time in 1956, which inevitably saw him find a new project. Across the road from Cory Street a man had started to build himself a caravan but hadn't gotten very far and, deciding it would be great for taking holidays at the beach with the boys, Reg and Joy bought it. The project offered both a chance to do the manual crafting that Reg relished so much, and an opportunity to turn that craftsmanship into a gift: taking new family adventures together. Together, Reg and DJ made the two-wheeled plywood caravan functional and comfortable; they finished by the end of 1956 and DJ used it for his honeymoon the following year. Reg and Joy meanwhile packed their two little sons in for holidays at the Burleigh Heads foreshore and in Mooloolaba on Queensland's Sunshine Coast. But these were smaller slivers of the larger whole, which was inevitably dominated by work.

Recalling this period, Reg noted that 'dairy cattle practitioners were often found wanting during the first few months after graduation.' Whether he included himself in that statement, there can be little doubt these early years were challenging and the local farmers remained uncertain about their new vet for some time. Decades later, Reg often regaled junior vets with a favourite story about one client's view of a vet's usefulness. When confronted with the loss of livestock, a farmer eyeballed Reg and said, 'You know, before you came, we used to lose a cow and that was it. Now we have to spend ten dollars and *still* lose the cow.'[4] It was a perception made more prevalent by Reg's role in the DPI's tuberculosis eradication programme: any animal who returned a positive test had to be culled from the herd and humanely euthanised. Inevitably, Reg would be the bearer of the bad news.

Despite these difficulties, Reg was driven and meticulous, and these traits allowed him to build trust in the region (which is likely the reason DJ didn't recall the same atmosphere of general wariness that Reg remembered encountering in 1952). The mandatory DPI programme meant the region's cattle farmers had no choice about Reg conducting TB testing on their livestock: the contract gave him an inviolable right to treat their herds. It was an invaluable opportunity to build relationships and Reg did so with quiet dedication and professionalism.

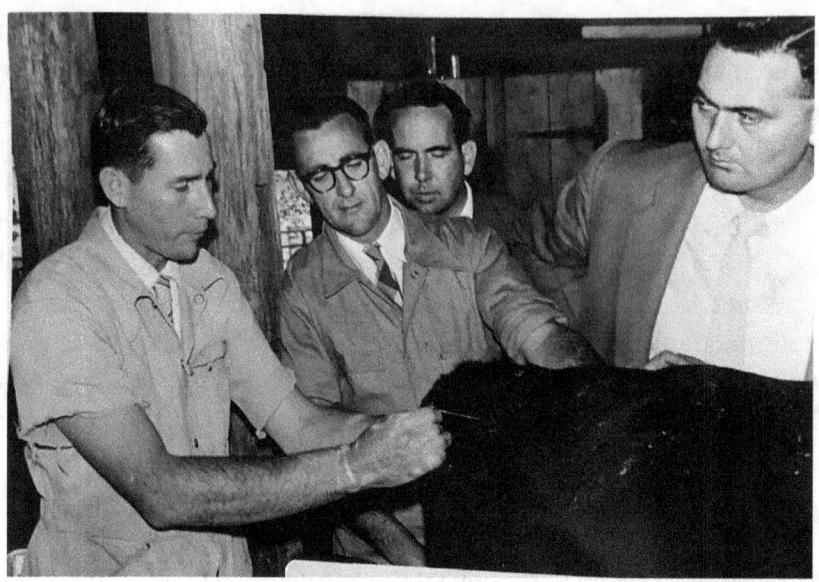

Reg as a young veterinarian, treating a cow, likely as part of the DPI tuberculosis testing contract.

Alan Jones, the well-known conservative Australian radio broadcaster, grew up on a dairy farm near Oakey and attended Toowoomba Grammar School as a boarder during his high school years. He was in his early teens when Reg began working with the local dairy farmers. As the young vet's reputation grew, Jones could 'remember people speaking of him with a sense of reverence as if he was occupying some arcane world of scholarship which was completely unfamiliar to farmers at the time.'[5]

But while Reg was certainly committed to the advent of science in his work and used it to great effect for his clients' benefit, this was not the primary reason behind his growing reputation. He was forthright, hardworking and unrelentingly devoted to the animals in his care: from the beginning, he was on call twenty-four hours a day, seven days a week. What was most telling of the community's increased faith in vets, was not a single event, or even a clearly defined moment of transition. It was that when farmers *did* have a choice about whether to call a vet – say a cow was having trouble calving, or a horse had a bad case of colic – they rang Reg. To this young man's professionalism and sense of honour, the local community responded with the highest mark of esteem: their faith in his ability at the very moment when everything, it seemed, had gone wrong.

Part II — A Leader in his Field

4
The Oakey Veterinary Hospital Begins

The year 1957 was a landmark one in the Pascoe household. Though cattle work remained the practice's backbone, Reg became 'modestly' engaged in Toowoomba's horse racing industry, taking on a Toowoomba stable with 250–300 racing thoroughbreds. The increased workload brought with it increased travel and Reg's plan for a central clinical location to which clients could travel with their animals, large or small, took its first steps towards reality.

Using money they'd saved from the DPI's tuberculosis eradication programme, Joy and Reg purchased twelve and a half acres of a dry, hilly farm paddock on Hamlyn Road, on the outskirts of Oakey. Reg's stipulations were simple. He chose the land for 'good drainage, access to the Warrego Highway, [its location] close to public utilities, yet isolated from the community as far as noise, odours and privacy were concerned.' It was also devoid of any infrastructure, unfenced and had no water supply.

The Oakey Veterinary Hospital (OVH) was born.

From 1957 to 1959, Reg and Joy worked hard to transform their uninspiring plot into home and practice, drilling a 280-metre-deep bore to negate the lack of town water supply (which was of a poor quality anyway) and fencing the block. Though the stony terrain was challenging, they dug post holes and threaded barbed-wire strands through ironbark posts. With John and David on the back seat of Reg's DeSoto and strands of barbed wire attached to the tow bar, Joy drove slowly forward to pull the wires through the current post until Reg yelled, 'Stop!' and finished threading that section of fence. They'd then move onto the next. This technique served as a perfect microcosm of Reg and Joy's life together – they were a strong team, growing more intertwined as time went on.

The hillside was bulldozed, and plans made to accommodate a house on the upper slope just below the ridgetop, and a shed further down. They'd move into the shed as soon as it could be made habitable, and both live and practise from it as the house was built.

Reg, Joy, and John enjoying the sunshine (and some comics) in the backyard of Cory Street.

In October 1959, they sold their Cory Street home and moved into a rental property nearby; fortunately, Reg's surgery in the Cory Street garage remained available for their use. A few weeks after the move, Joy gave birth to a third son, Roess. Unlike with John and David's births, their rental property meant Joy's mother was unable to stay and help and so a juggling act began in earnest. With John at school and David at home, Joy handled the addition of baby Roess while continuing to monitor the practice calls and accounts.

Their rental brought other challenges too. An extended dry spell, typical of the region, meant the house's new tank remained empty. With no rainwater for washing up, Joy was forced to use the hard town water, boiling dirty nappies on the one-plate electric stove – a situation which horrified the visiting sister from Oakey's Maternal and Child Welfare Clinic. Luckily it was a brief arrangement. With help from Joy's younger brother Don who travelled from Brisbane most weekends, Reg could concentrate on building the shed and by mid-December they moved to the new property on Hamlyn Road.

However, the shed wasn't quite finished. Neither the single 'front' door, nor any of the three sets of large wooden double doors had been hung; where window louvres were to be installed, huge wounds gaped in the building's outer cladding.

'Lady, you should write a book,' remarked the Postmaster General's linesman to Joy from beneath the brim of his rakishly tilted, work-stained felt hat as he surveyed her new living quarters and went to work installing the telephone.

'Yes,' she answered, holding Roess as she watched the man. 'Probably the only difference between my great-grandmother's shed and mine is the cement floor.' As they spoke, Reg and Joy's scanty furniture was being loaded into a removal truck. Upon arrival it would be arranged within the 12 x 4.6 metre shed to create two bedrooms and a multipurpose space which functioned not only as kitchen and dining room but living area and office as well. Milly's donated one-plate electric stove served as the only cooking method, giving Joy another challenge to overcome in the event of visitors, as Vyvyan and Milly occasionally drove from Schoenberg to Oakey for dinner.

There was no bathroom. Instead, outside under a grand old eucalyptus and a 2000-gallon rainwater tank, Reg built a slatted wooden bench to hold Milly's old iron washtubs. Using water heated inside in kerosene tins, these washtubs served for both bathing and washing clothes, though Roess had his own little baby bath. The toilet was rustic too. A three-sided structure, the curtain tacked along the front had an unfortunate habit of blowing open in the wind; rather embarrassing when building began higher up the slope. A jerry-built shower was prone to the same troubles.

Still, it was close to Christmas and Joy was a firm believer in festivity. Despite her desire for one while growing up, her family had never had a live Christmas tree. The year she turned nineteen, her father had bought her a small, artificial tree in a red wooden pot. That Christmas of 1959, in the small spartan shed on Hamlyn Road, Joy's parents – visiting for Christmas as was their habit – entered through the single blue door, only for Harold to exclaim to his wife, 'Look darling, Joydie has her Christmas tree up!' It became a Pascoe family staple, the gradually accumulated decorations – from plastic bells to Christmas card cut-outs – telling their own story over the years. Though the branches are a little bent, today they remain green and well-covered; each year the tree is presented for the family, and after Christmas is done, it is wrapped up again still fully dressed and put away until next year.

Post-Christmas, life continued as usual – as much as anything could be usual. Having consulted a Brisbane architect for help with the floor plan, two local builders began erecting Reg and Joy's new family home. Fortunately, at six, John was going to primary school, but there was no kindergarten in the area for David, and missing his playmates from Cory Street, he took to trailing after the long-suffering builders. They gave him sawn-off bits of wood to play with and kept him out of harm's way, though he didn't always appreciate their efforts.

'I'm not going to eat any more of his sandwiches,' an angry David declared one day. He had stormed back to the shed after being reprimanded by one of the builders for getting in their way. On another occasion, the determined young boy told his mother that he'd walk back to Cory Street (almost 3 kilometres away) to play with his friend – or better still, walk to Nanny's in Brisbane.

'I really wished we had a kindergarten, then,' Joy said. (Later, she and some friends would strive to have one built for the area.) David seemed 'a bit lost' as Joy both cared for a new baby in 'less than desirable surroundings', and kept up with the practice's office work. Meanwhile, Reg and DJ carried on working out of the original surgery at Cory Street, with David intermittently accompanying his father. These idyllic childhood memories remained with him, as did the love of veterinary science – and the wealth of scientific knowledge he accumulated by osmosis.

As the months passed, the weather grew colder and the uninsulated, rather draughty shed grew frigid. Joy's mother, Helen, loaned the young couple a kerosene heater; it was an almost hopeless task, but Joy persisted. She positioned the heater close to baby Roess, who, after awakening in the meshed cage-cot Reg had made for John and had in turn housed both older boys, spent his days either in a playpen on a rug on the concrete floor or in the pram. As winter hooked its claws firmly into Oakey, Joy asked Reg if they could move into a recently vacated house nearby.

'No,' Reg told her unequivocally. 'We can't keep shifting.' Out on call every day, it was difficult for him appreciate just how cold the shed was.

As their new home gradually grew from nothing upon the hill behind them, the Pascoe family endured. Every day upon arrival at the site, the builders 'knocked, peered in to see if we were frozen', then bid Joy and the boys good morning before connecting their tools (the shed being the property's sole source of power). They worked hard and by August 1960, with builders, painters and plumbers still labouring, the family was finally able to leave the shed behind and move into a mostly complete part of the house.

Since they'd vacated Cory Street the previous October, the family had kept their noses to the grindstone. Baby Roess had suffered a bout of bronchitis while the family rented, while both John and David caught chicken pox during their eight-month stint in the shed. Reg inadvertently found out he was allergic to penicillin and was left prostrate on one of the boy's beds, and Joy spent eight months checking the building's bare rafters every night on the lookout for mice, rats and snakes, noting wryly that their 'primitive accommodation would not be allowed in today's rules and regulations ... but we survived.'

Moving into the house proper meant the surgery could also relocate to Hamlyn Road: a dividing wall was erected in the shed and the walls lined with tarred paper to improve its appearance before the surgery furnishings and equipment were installed. The other half of the shed became Reg's workshop. Those skilled hands were to find enduring employment and creativity in woodworking in that shed – starting with the new home's kitchen cupboards, which Reg crafted from a Bunya pine that he and Vyvyan felled together at Schoenberg.

Nonetheless, the challenges of country life persisted. With Roess in a cot in a corner of the bedroom, Reg and Joy spent some months sleeping on a mattress on the floor. Reg had dismantled their timber bed for the move and discovered seven red-back spiders hiding in cavities at the foot and the head. Putting it back together again moved down the priority list for a while. Their new 'open-plan' pantry was easy to access but 'certainly did not keep mice out', and the split level meant that Joy, between tending to her sons and answering the telephone in the downstairs office, endlessly ran up and down the internal stairs Reg had built.

Her work was essential. The difficulty in attempting to record the scope of Joy and Reg's partnership – as often occurs when speaking of the wives of powerful, successful men – is that such attempts often tend to relegate wives to a supporting role that understates their influence and importance. Certainly, in her unfailing devotion to captaining their busy family life, Joy provided a domestic support to Reg that it would be hard to match; but to categorise her in this manner overlooks the crucial role she played in Reg's career. If Reg was a great success, then there is no doubt Joy was integral to that success: as one friend recalled, 'everybody called him "the rock", but she was the glue that held it all together.'[6]

As the practice grew, Joy offered compassionate and unwavering support to Oakey Veterinary Hospital's (OVH) staff and their families, bringing a gentle kind-heartedness that could sometimes slip from Reg's priorities list. Andrew Dart, one of Reg's vets, recalled, 'Quite often, if Reg had done something wrong, Joy would chastise him and tell him to pull himself together. She was an incredible individual but yet incredibly compassionate too. When Reg was being really hard on me, she could see that he just needed to back off a little bit. She was always there, and I often chatted with Joy for half an hour here and there and had a cup of tea with her and she was really very compassionate.'

No one was more capable of managing a man who could be mercurial when angered. Another of Reg's vets, Max Wilson, noted, 'They were very close … but by Jove, he put her through her paces sometimes when she came down and things weren't exactly how he thought they should be – [like if] she'd made a mistake in writing up one of his papers. And we'd all shrink away and hide, but underneath it all, we all always knew who the boss of the place was, and that was Joy.'

Reg and Joy at the beach together in the early 1950s. From the start, they were a strong team, complementing each other and always finding time to laugh together.

It would be simplistic to portray Joy as merely a quiet, retiring foil for her husband: despite their differences, they were perfectly matched. Joy held her own in every way and her opinions and quiet counsel meaningfully shaped Reg's path for over sixty years. One friend recalled Reg telling him about a day when 'Joy summoned him up to the house from the practice to have a cup of tea and [told him] that he needed to pay attention – which, of course, he did ... Joy pointed out some of his flaws and [emphasised] what was happening at that time of life and that he needed to pay more attention to family.' Reg shared this story openly.

There are countless instances where the spouse of a successful and renowned professional has co-opted that acclaim in some way or another, wielding their partner's clout as their own weapon. That was never Joy's way. They were inseparable and frequently travelled together when Reg attended conferences and meetings, both around the country and often around the world. Yet despite her desire to help, she felt neither the need nor the want to encroach upon Reg's professional life; she had her own interests, not least of which was her active role in the community – and their rambunctious sons. Joy was constancy and safety in their household, providing a warm, caring and encouraging home: she was the fundamental thread tying their family tapestry together.

At times, that role called for steely nerves.

'One afternoon,' Joy recalled, 'holding Roess and phoning our neighbour from the downstairs office wall phone ... I saw a brown snake. Although Reg had shown me how to use the gun, I had trouble shooting because I seemed unable to look straight down the barrel, but was, however, instructed never to take my eyes off the snake. This I did until Colin Werth, a farmer and scout leader, kindly arrived from his farm across the highway, and despatched same.' Joy handled the situation with her characteristic poise; like many of the challenges she'd faced since leaving the city for the country, she rose to the occasion.

In August 1961, the family's twelve-month anniversary in the new house was celebrated with the addition of Reg and Joy's fourth and final son, Andrew.

'I don't recall the older boys being excited about the prospect of another playmate,' Joy said, 'except that it had to be a boy.' Reg's woodworking skill again came to the fore as he almost singlehandedly furnished the children's rooms, making two new beds for his youngest sons, a set of shelves for John and David's bedroom, and later, a wardrobe with two sliding drawers.

The wildness of the block remained a point of concern for Joy throughout 1962 and 1963: though John and David were now both at school, Roess was increasing mobile. With the death of Lassie, the family bought a golden Labrador puppy they called Goldie. Goldie became Roess's shadow as he roamed the block, exploring long-grassed paddocks without fear for the snakes that may lurk there. The duo's recurrent failure to come when called caused Joy some anxiety, especially considering the home's isolated spot near the highway.

On one such occasion, Joy called, scanned the paddock, and even drove down to the side road in search of her son and Goldie, but they were nowhere to be found. She headed home to call Reg but as she reached the house, she heard the phone ringing. Heart in her throat, she raced to answer it.

'Hello?'

'Hello, Mrs Pascoe, this is Mrs Buckley. There's a small child and a yaller dog near the cows' water trough across the road from here. Could they belong to you?'

Relief swept over her. 'Yes, thank you, Mrs Buckley. I've been searching for them.' The adventurous pair had wandered far from their own paddock into the Buckleys' dry cow paddock, trudging up over the hill behind the Pascoes' house and down the other side again to the trough.

Reg was present in his family's lives, though, inevitably, his heavy caseload and external commitments meant he missed some things. Andrew didn't remember Reg ever attending one of his sporting matches, but he does recall other little rituals. Once a year, the family spent a few weeks holidaying down the coast and Andrew recalled staying at the White Dolphin near the waterfront at Currumbin. Each day was gloriously the same: long hours on the beach, swimming and body surfing. Despite his landlocked childhood, Reg loved the ocean.

The four Pascoe boys with Goldie at Tugun for a family beach holiday. From left: John, Andrew, David, and Roess.

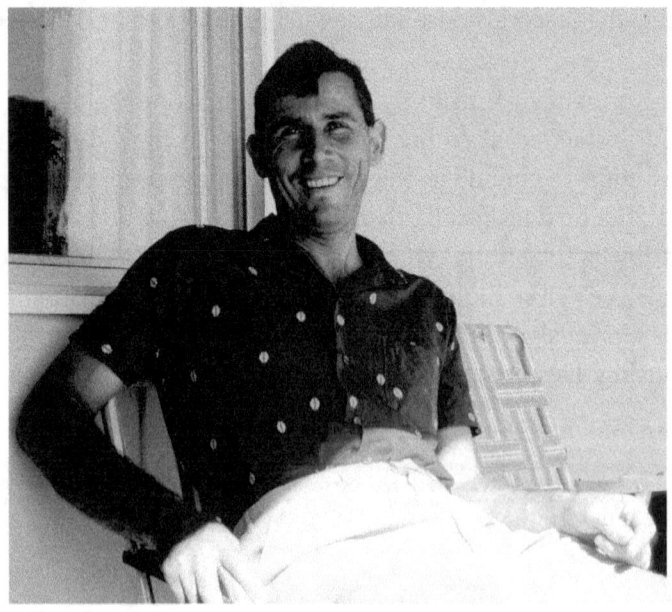

Reg at Caloundra, enjoying a family holiday at the beach.

At home on Saturday nights, the boys would gather around their father to watch *Dr Who* on the two-channel, black-and-white TV. Weekends brought the televised horse races, which Reg always wanted to watch closely – invariably one client or another had a runner. He picked winners with startling accuracy.

'Dad, why don't you bet?' Andrew would ask, awed, as another of Reg's picks soared over the finish line.

'It'd be unethical,' Reg said simply, and that was that.

Naturally enough, the Pascoe boys grew up surrounded by animals. There were dogs, of course; first Lassie, the surprise Cory Street arrival; and later Goldie, the golden Labrador, each of whom also had litters of puppies on at least one occasion.

Joy leading John on Prince.

There was the family pony, Prince, who preceded a horse named Gypsy and then later a beautiful golden palomino stallion that Reg called Flash. Much as Schoenberg had seemed full of wonder for Reg as a child, parts of the boys' Oakey childhoods were similarly magical – Reg's horsemanship became one of Andrew's favourite memories. Reg and Flash formed a strong bond and the clever stallion learnt funny tricks, like carrying Reg up and down the stairs near the woodshed or flying around the bitumen near the surgery as Reg cracked his mammoth stockwhip overhead so that it sounded like thunder. 'To me,' Andrew remembered, 'he was like a horse whisperer.'

Horses were everywhere, an inevitable and vital part of the boys' upbringing, and Andrew witnessed countless surgeries as a child. He remembered watching his father scrub up while he stood off to one side, out of the way but close enough to get a good look at the sometimes-gory work.

But the most notable animal in the Pascoe family was a sulphur-crested cockatoo called Cocky. In the mid-1960s, Reg was handling the mare run for a client named Bruce who had a farm out near Cambooya and an ongoing problem with birds on his property. Or to be more accurate, an ongoing problem with *one* bird: a cockatoo with a mischievous streak a mile wide. Reg was familiar with the problem: the bird frequently played with the two-way whip aerial on the car when Reg visited. If surgical tubing was left lying around, the bird couldn't stop himself from playing with that too, or he might have a go at the tyres while Reg was otherwise occupied. Nothing was safe.

One morning, Reg arrived to check Bruce's mares and found his client almost incandescent with rage. 'I'll shoot that bloody bird!' Bruce cried. 'He's gone and pulled up all my wife's vegetable seedlings. He's ringbarking the roses too and clucking at the mares to stir them up in the yard!'

'You can't shoot him, Bruce,' Reg said laconically, but with an undeniable ring of authority in his voice. 'That bird's got too much character. If you like, I'll take him home – my boys like birds.'

And he did. Whether his name was a tribute to Reg's childhood friend and constant companion is uncertain, but this Cocky, too, adored Reg, who cared for and often conversed with him. Joy was unperturbed by the new addition; her father had loved birds and bred canaries during her childhood, building cages underneath the family home to house his little flock. Cocky came to roost in Oakey in a cage from Schoenberg donated by Vyvyan – one that proved more reliable and longer-lasting that Vyvyan's early henhouse – and the feisty bird established himself as an immovable thread in the family tapestry. He learnt to imitate Roess and Andrew's laughter as they played on the back lawn after school and Joy's father Harold would visit and whistle 'Pop Goes the Weasel', to which Cocky learnt to squawk and dance around the cage. He was a remarkably sanguine fellow: when other birds wriggled beneath the metal cage walls to join him, Cocky tolerated their presence without any noticeable concern.

As OVH continued to grow, so did the Oakey community. A colleague of Reg's remarked that 'a real estate guide in Oakey ... told Reg that his business was flourishing because people wanted to buy horse properties to be served by Reg's practice. Thus Reg's practice, as it was building up, was able to broadcast for people to [further develop] the equine thoroughbred industry, breeding in particular' in rural Queensland.[7]

The small town's infrastructure doubtless benefited from the growth of both OVH and the thoroughbred profile of the Darling Downs. Where Reg had once had to transfer to Toowoomba Grammar from Oakey State School, Oakey State High School was opened in 1964 in time for John to start two years later, and his younger brothers followed suit. Similarly, where Reg's introduction to swimming had been in an old, murky bore-filled pool, his sons were the beneficiaries of the Jondaryan Shire Council's 50-metre swimming pool in 1967.

Throughout this time, the equine aspect of the Oakey Veterinary Hospital grew steadily. Reg's clientele increased to a total of three horse farms, with approximately 300 mares and seven stallions. Though these additional clients were welcome and demonstrated Reg's growing tendency towards equine veterinary science, cattle work remained the linchpin of OVH's clinical commitments. Reg went on to practise across the full spectrum of thoroughbred husbandry, but he remained involved and up to date in all aspects of OVH's veterinary care.

One of the biggest challenges for a vet – beyond the fact that, unlike in human medicine, the patient can't verbally describe what's wrong – is that the vet is only called when someone realises there's a problem. Often, by the time a client rings, it's too late and the vet is confronted with a scene that's likely only half the story, if that. The vet must piece together the situation, both interrogating what appears before them in the present and asking the right questions to determine what happened in the past. Integrating these different but vitally connected components is crucial to addressing the problem – and this was where Reg excelled.

Arriving when everyone was panicking, Reg was adept at analysing the situation and then assembling all the facts to give a diagnosis. One long-time client referred to this as 'horsemanship.' Reg understood implicitly that 'the horse will always telegraph what he's going to do before he does it.' Knowing that the onus remained on the human to observe, correctly interpret the signals and react accordingly, Reg watched carefully and read the signs as only a horseman can. He was 'always interested in … what [the horse] was doing' in the lead-up to the owner calling OVH, and what actions had already been taken.

Such deductions could save lives. In 1995, a chestnut gelding called Dan arrived at OVH with head and throat swelling that was slowly suffocating him. After staff inserted a tube into his windpipe to allow him to breathe, careful investigation revealed Dan's owners had only recently moved to a new property in Mt Kynoch with a large avocado tree. Avocados can be toxic to horses, affecting the heart muscle, and without that information, Dan likely would have died. Careful analysis enabled Reg to react and save Dan's life.

Afterwards, his work done, Reg followed up with his clients, wanting to know about the horse's recovery. Here too he broke the mould, tracking horses to observe how they responded to his treatment. He was helped by his close and long-standing relationships with many studs, and later through his establishment of a dedicated equine care facility. The cooperation of the studs was vital and in turn precipitated his vast knowledge of pathology and treatment methods recorded in the papers and textbooks which chronicled his investigative research work.

One such crucial partner was Eureka, the McAlpines' family-run stud in Cambooya, roughly thirty minutes' drive south-west of Toowoomba. Eureka was among Reg's first horse clients. At that time, the stud was under the management of Andrew McAlpine, who had established it in 1935. His son Colin took over in 1960. Reg was older than Colin, but they had gone to school together at Toowoomba Grammar and knew of one another. Whether this influenced Reg's hiring is hard to say, but it was more likely a coincidence – vets in the area were few and far between. Happily, it was a good fit, instituting a long and mutually beneficial relationship. In Colin McAlpine, Reg found a kindred spirit: a stud owner who was as passionate as he was about improving breeding practices and producing the best possible horses. Not only that, his views during their long association, particularly regarding the issues plaguing Australia's horse industry and their possible solutions, were often well-aligned with Reg's own.

As Scott McAlpine, Colin's son and current owner of Eureka, recalled, 'They were eccentrics ... [they] came together ... to take the industry to a different level.' But their formidable partnership and long friendship was not without its moments of discord. At Reg's public memorial in 2017, Scott remembered the relationship as 'a clash of the Titans.' 'Reg was pretty forceful, direct and he had his own mind ... If he didn't like it, he told you so.' He and Colin were cut from the same cloth. Both dedicated, passionate and stubborn, there was inevitable conflict from time to time. These moments, however, did not diminish their respect for one another; above all, their relationship was founded on their shared desire to excel and a reciprocal understanding of the other's role in achieving excellence, both for the horse and for the stud.

Reg and Colin pursued the ideal method for breeding horses to get mares in foal as easily and successfully as possible. With this aim in mind, Reg learnt as much as he could about equine reproductive science. Eureka's success as one of Queensland's leading studs, Scott noted, 'was a combination of [Colin's] horsemanship and [Reg's] veterinary science.'

The valuable scientific understanding Reg brought to the partnership took time to develop. Though the UQ Veterinary School – and particularly Dr Tom Ewer with his equine background – had given Reg a firm foundation in large animal treatment, the nature of ongoing scientific discovery and the possibility for innovation meant there was still much to learn. Reg invariably would have blundered, especially in that first decade following graduation: every professional life is littered with mistakes. What defines success, however, is how people learn from those mistakes and implement the lessons. Throughout those early years there was a 'steep learning curve that Reg had to go through without much mentorship. He had to think on his feet and develop reasons for failure of surgical techniques and procedures and then set out to find solutions.'[8]

Many years later, one of Reg's junior vets would recount visiting a client, an older man who had known Reg in his early days. 'Oh,' the client said, 'little Reg Pascoe? I remember him when he was a young fellow. He wanted to be a horse vet, but he didn't know too much about horses. He was out there looking at a horse and he touched it in the wrong way so that it kicked and knocked all of my shoeing gear over. There were shoeing nails all over the yard – so I made little Reg pick up every one of those nails.' Reg's response to hearing this tale was succinct. 'That's a load of bullshit.' But whether it's true or not, Reg agreed with the basics: when mistakes were made, you did your best to clean them up and learn from them. He was also not above admitting when he was wrong.

Scott recalled one occasion when a Eureka foal got sick. Feeling the condition was becoming serious, Colin called Reg, who assessed the situation in his characteristically blunt way.

'It'll be dead in the morning,' he said.

Colin thought about this. 'No, it won't be.'

'I'll be back in the morning and it'll be dead,' Reg said. 'If I do come back in the morning and it's not dead, I'll eat my words.' And with that, he headed home for the night. He came back in the morning to find the foal still clinging to life and, words duly eaten, went to work with Colin to save its life.

'I think Reg and Father had a great association because of that early altercation,' Scott remembered. '… they worked out that the both of them had the same amount of input into the welfare of the horse.' They could both 'eat humble pie if they were wrong', and as a result the two determined and dedicated men formed a symbiotic relationship that enabled them to put aside everything else as they worked together to find an answer.

At no point was Reg's approach easy; his was a hard-earnt success.

'He drained himself until he did find out what the problem was,' Scott recalled. 'He didn't pass it off and go, "Oh, someone else will do it. Someone else can work it out." *He* worked it out.'

As OVH continued to develop, various veterinary students completed their required university placements there. Reg and DJ worked out of the half-shed allocated for surgery while construction of the practice proper progressed further down the hill. Limited finance meant progress was slow and so dairy cattle medicine continued as the main source of income, bolstered by pig practice and small animals, while horse work persisted on the practice's fringes.

By the early 1960s, however, Reg was becoming more and more interested in equine medicine, and there was much to be done. Veterinarian Bill Howey, who had trained and worked under the eminent Murray Bain in Scone and taken over the practice after Bain's untimely death, noted some decades later that 'prior to the 1960s horse practice had long languished for many decades in the arcane world of whimsical ephemora [sic] ... [with] a practiced mystery.'

Horses were used in all arenas of life without much knowledge about the animal or the more scientific aspects of their care. A New South Wales veterinarian named Taylor who began practising in Wollongong in 1940 chronicled his professional involvement with pit ponies, which remained a mainstay of Australian (and international) coal mining throughout much of the twentieth century. This legacy extended much further than many might imagine: 'The last pit ponies used in Australia, Wharrier and Mr Ed of the Collinsville Coal's No. 2 Mine in Queensland, were finally retired in 1990 after many years' service.' The management and treatment of these animals provides insight into both the scepticism faced by many veterinarians of the era, and also into the most common early treatment methods in the country, many of which were rudimentary at best.

Pit ponies were handled by 'practical horsemen who fed, broke in, handled and attended to sick and injured horses ... They had no training but long experience.' Much like Reg's experience in Oakey a decade later, Taylor discovered that initially these horsemen 'were not very responsive to a young University-trained Vet, who naturally they thought was going to take over their jobs.' As time passed and the value of a trained vet became evident, camaraderie and trust developed.

Taylor noted two key points of interest in the treatment of the pit ponies. The first was that, prior to his arrival, 'there were no anaesthetics used on horses. Major operations like eye removal, castration, suturing massive wounds, removal of tumours, were performed with a nose or ear twitch which caused local pain, enough hopefully to allow the surgery to proceed.' A 'twitch' refers to a small rope noose attached to a stick which is placed around the upper lip or ear of a horse, applying pressure to subdue the animal for a period.

The true mechanism for using a twitch remains unclear. Distraction, pain, decreased sensitivity, or a combination thereof have all been theorised as the means by which it works; many also claim the horse experiences an endorphin release due to nerve stimulation. Regardless, the horse entered a trance-like state in which painful operations were undertaken or, as was common since the mid-twentieth century, an anaesthetic was administered. (A 2016 study indicated that the use of an ear twitch, unlike a lip twitch, functions primarily through fear or pain and evokes a physiological stress response; lip twitches are seen as more humane and these days many people avoid using ear twitches at all.)

The second point Taylor noted was that, 'There were no antibiotics or antibacterials used to control or prevent infections and no pain killing drugs. Spiderwebs (plenty around horse stables) were used to control bleeding from wounds.' Spiderwebs, rich in the coagulant vitamin K and with inherent antibacterial properties, would be gathered to cover the injury – a method which has origins dating back to Ancient Greece where spider silk was commonly used to staunch soldiers' wounds (and is still used in some cultures to treat minor lacerations). Taylor further noted, 'The common colic cure was a bottle of stale beer or a drench of bitter aloes [a purgative made of aloe leaves]. Of course, they had no idea of the different causes of colic pain and where the apparent pain originated.' It was a field within which there was vast scope for education and development, which needed to be directed towards improving conditions and providing what treatment was best for the horse.

From this previously-untended pasture emerged in 'the

enlightened '60s' a crop of 'a few real scientists [who] began to fully examine "what makes a horse good" and what "makes a good horse."' Much of this drive was happening elsewhere in Australia – particularly in the south, and most notably in some of the more forward-thinking and scientifically-advanced New South Wales clinics such as the practice at Scone. Hidden away in a small rural corner of Queensland, Reg was far removed from these hubs of progress.

In 1964, a young man named Paul Green spent a fortnight of his UQ placement working with Reg and DJ. Paul had grown up on a farm and the idea of working in a large animal practice was appealing. For Reg and DJ, both with young children and looking forward to taking a little more time off over the school holidays, another set of hands was welcome. At the end of that year, Paul joined the practice and, like DJ before him, lived with Reg and Joy for the first six weeks or so. He saw the job as a steppingstone. 'Like most students at the time,' he said, 'I thought, I'll stay in this job for a couple of years and maybe do the big overseas trip to England.'

His rationale was understandable. Paul arrived soon after the first building of the Oakey Veterinary Hospital was completed: constructed of cavity concrete block, the new 6 x 12 metre facility comprised an office, a small animal surgery, a consulting room, a pharmacy, a small laboratory and kennels. There was a lot crammed into what was a small space and it wasn't particularly exciting for an aspiring young vet at the start of their career. Paul could hardly be condemned for noting that, despite the new building, OVH really 'wasn't on par with most of the other practices at that time.'

Fortunately, despite being in the early stages of development, the practice offered him a valuable opportunity: he was interested in cattle, while Reg and DJ were clearly increasingly invested in OVH's fledgling equine practice, and so a natural division of labour presented itself. This remained important, even as over the next three years, OVH gradually shifted more towards horses. This change was almost a necessity: cattle work dwindled as Queensland's DPI tuberculosis and brucellosis programmes tapered off to facilitate the transition from voluntary, state-based initiatives to a national elimination campaign in 1970. Regular visits to cattle properties dropped off, coinciding with a general decline in the dairy cattle industry and a beef cattle slump during the late 1960s.

During this period, the practice continued with ante-mortem inspections of cattle at Oakey Abattoir and enjoyed an increase in equine workload. For Reg, the latter clearly had his heart. Almost twenty years later, he recorded that, 'With the passage of time and the downward trends of the dairying industry, further interests were developed. I have always been deeply interested in horse work and with the gradual emergence of new horse breeding farms and the slowly increasing interest of property owners in both racing and breeding of horses, more and more of the practice was devoted to horse practice. This was fairly equally divided between breeding farms and racing stables.' (Small animal practice remained essential; OVH was renowned for its horse work, but cats and dogs, goats and pigs, and even snakes and other less-dangerous local wildlife were also treated.)

By the mid-1960s, Reg was the chief vet for the major Queensland studs. It was an unofficial position, but as Scott McAlpine pointed out, the role gave Reg 'access to all the different problems that could occur and that gave him more challenges ... the more horses, the more studs, the more experience and the more different things you find.' But doing so took up a lot of time, and DJ and Paul were crucial in ensuring that OVH ran smoothly. Reg's reputation continued to grow and alongside it an increasing demand for his time and expertise, not just in the clinic, but out where the breeders needed him – on their studs.

5
An International Journey

From the very beginning, Reg wanted creativity to flourish at the Oakey Veterinary Hospital, but this often meant balancing differing objectives. The clinic had to be fit for its core purpose: the adroit and efficient care of both large and small animals. But it also had to remain flexible enough to both incorporate the technological and scientific advances occurring within the industry and permit Reg's own investigations and innovations.

Achieving this required a multifaceted approach made possible largely due to his tenacity. The path he had chosen and his own exacting standards demanded considerable time, energy, money and conviction. This was evident in his own continued academic and scientific edification; his search for international best practices to integrate into OVH; and his adherence to a gruelling work schedule.

A typical week incorporated at least several hours of professional development outside of his clinical hours. He pored over scientific journals and considered the implications of his own practical work while managing both the practice and a growing family. In 1967 he completed a Master of Veterinary Science with a thesis on hypomagnesaemia in dairy cows (a condition where a cow's output of magnesium in milk is greater than their dietary intake).

At the same time, he continued with the clinical work brought on by the increase in equine clients, particularly in the breeding season which, in Australia, runs from September through to late November. Eureka was always the first stud on Reg's roster and that meant arriving at around 4.30 a.m. Scott McAlpine recalled the challenge of getting everything ready for those visits. 'I used to muster the mares in the morning before the sun came up. I would be riding out in the paddock in the dark and I'd be going, "What the bloody hell am I doing this for?"'

The schedule was rarely interrupted. On one occasion, the Darling Downs suffered an unusual spate of rain that left the region sodden. 'We needed him desperately to get here,' Scott recalled, 'but he didn't turn up.' And in the days before mobile phones, there was no way of finding Reg. Sure enough, without any fanfare, he eventually walked in the gate. The Eureka crew was stunned. 'What are you doing walking?' they asked.

Reg, ever laconic, replied, 'Well, trying to get here. So far now, all I've done is been swimming.' Driving the back roads, he'd tried to follow the road – but found himself in a creek instead. His car got stuck and seeing no other option, he pulled himself free and waded through the water to reach the stud. What struck Scott, more than anything else, was Reg's attitude. 'Anybody else would be swearing their head off, but he treated it as if it was entertaining.'

Reg speaking with one of his early horse clients. The wry caption was added by family for Reg's 60th birthday.

The early starts, long days and mentally and physically intensive work must have taxed him, but he viewed it as neither a burden nor a trial. It energised him, it enthused him and it ignited his curiosity, driving him to learn more. Such traits were invaluable: as the horse industry, particularly in Queensland, continued to grow, it became increasingly important to understand why horses were breaking down. Reg began to specialise in bone surgery, everything from fixing bone chips to a disease called OCD (osteochondritis dissecans), a joint condition which typically presents in young, growing horses as lesions in their joint cartilage and bones. Many such lesions heal of their own accord, but those that don't risk leaving a horse with permanent problems – problems which could both inhibit the animal's quality of life and prove costly to a stud looking to sell their yearlings at market.

Reg willingly stepped into this lacuna and those pre-dawn visits to Eureka allowed him to be home by mid-afternoon to start work on the day's surgeries. The hospital's equipment was still modest at this stage: the second-hand mobile X-ray machine had a faulty timer meaning scans had to be manually developed, and his tools comprised a collection of cheaply bought but good quality second-hand human surgical instruments.

Today, modern technologies such as ultrasound help studs determine whether a mare is fertile without manual examination, but Reg and veterinarians of his ilk were reliant on their sense of touch. During the oestrous (heat) cycle, one of the thousands of follicles in a mare's ovaries will begin to develop; inserting their hand into the mare's rectum, veterinarians could palpate the follicle and determine when the mare would be most fertile. The procedure would then be repeated to determine if she was pregnant.

The working timeframe for detecting pregnancy had previously been forty-five days. Advancing equine knowledge saw this decrease to around thirty days, at which point most vets could tell if the mare was pregnant. To do so any earlier, however, the vet had to have both sensitive fingers and a well-developed awareness of equine reproduction. Reg and 'his magic fingers'[9] were routinely able to determine pregnancy early in the cycle. His 'feeling test' meant his diagnoses were superior to many other vets.'

Such knowledge is important for stud owners. The earlier they can determine if a mare has conceived, the earlier the mare can, if necessary, be recovered. Today, technological advances mean these determinations can be made within a few weeks of covering the mare, but prior to such technology, Reg's skills were a stud owner's best bet.

By 1967, the Oakey Veterinary Hospital trio's work covered ten horse farms with approximately 600 mares. But the practice hadn't yet developed into what Reg envisioned: a fully equipped equine veterinary surgery that would negate the need to travel to horse farms and facilitate the ongoing expansion of the practice's equine work. There was a clear gap and the national, and particularly state, levels of advanced equine veterinary knowledge were sadly lacking. Reg knew that if he wanted to learn from and expand on the best the veterinary world could offer, he needed to look beyond our shores.

As 1968 dawned, Reg and Joy took a twelve-week, intercontinental trip. From Brisbane, via Sydney, they travelled first to England to visit universities in Bristol and Cambridge and practices at Lambourn and Newmarket. From there, they went to Kildare in Ireland, then onto the US – to Davis in California, and Lexington in Kentucky. Reg planned to visit twelve large animal veterinary establishments that comprised the world's premier equine practitioners and equine research centres. He'd observe the methods used in breeding and surgical techniques and evaluate best-practice equipment and hospital designs.

With four boisterous sons at home, however, the couple needed a lot of outside help for such a long trip. John was almost fifteen, but both Roess and Andrew were still in primary school, and Andrew was just six. Insisting they would care for the boys, Joy's parents urged her to accompany Reg. Her father Harold took three weeks' holiday, but Joy was concerned: her mother wasn't well and her parents didn't own a car. Friends, family and the local community pulled together to help. Joy's aunt (her mother's eldest sister) visited on several occasions, while Reg's niece came to stay with the boys for a while. The grocer delivered and so did the fruiterer. A kindly friend agreed to do the cleaning and ironing and provide some company for Joy's mother, as well as offering a car should one be needed. The older boys rode their bikes, but Reg and Joy's neighbour took Roess and Andrew to school and, since the man was also the scout master, ferried all four boys to scouts and cubs too. Ensconced in the Oakey community, the Pascoe children were in safe hands.

While the trip was for work, it didn't mean there was no time for fun. From Sydney, Reg and Joy flew to Hong Kong and spent their two-day layover being shepherded around by a friend of a friend, who introduced them to the delights of bespoke fashion. It was thrilling to choose clothing and have it made especially for them, and so quickly! As well as shirts, a suit and matching dress shoes, Reg bought a stylish, black-trimmed maroon tuxedo. More than forty years later, Joy still had one of the two dresses she'd had made hanging in their wardrobe.

Arriving in London, Reg and Joy hired a car and drove the 100-odd kilometres north to Newmarket, in Suffolk. Newmarket is widely considered the birthplace and traditional home of thoroughbred horse racing. In 2021 it was slated as a future UNESCO World Heritage site. During Reg and Joy's visit in 1968, it was home to two of England's leading equine practices, as well as the Animal Health Trust (AHT), a veterinary and scientific research charity renowned at the time for its equine work. (Due to a lack of funding the Trust was forced to close in mid-2020 after more than seventy-five years in operation.)

Reg divided his time between the two equine practices and the AHT, spending long days observing and discussing breeding and surgical techniques. A newly graduated British vet called Leo Jeffcott was working at the AHT's Equine Research Station as the centre's assistant pathologist; more than fifty years later, his recollection of his first meeting with Reg remained sharp. When Reg entered the room, Leo was examining an aborted foetus, absorbed and intrigued by what he'd found: the foetus was undersized and exhibited an evident lesion on the placenta – an example of fungal placentitis (an infectious disease which causes abortions in mares). He was feeling rather self-satisfied with his deductions, so it must have been a bombshell when, after they were introduced, Reg glanced at Leo's work and said, quite offhandedly, 'Oh yes, I've seen lots of those. I know exactly what all that's about.' Momentarily chagrined at having his balloon burst, Leo gathered himself and proceeded to pick Reg's brain.

During their time in Newmarket, Reg and Joy stayed at Byculla, a residence reserved for directors of the UK's Thoroughbred Breeders' Association. Mrs Brown, Byculla's warm and friendly housekeeper, took Joy under her wing, and the two sometimes sat together in the kitchen downstairs, chatting as Mrs Brown worked. When the directors dropped by for lunch or dinner, Mrs Brown's meals were conveyed from kitchen to dining room via a dumbwaiter. These visits were dominated by lengthy conversations between Reg and the directors about horse breeding dynasties. Joy ate her lunch and listened as the men chatted, their enthusiasm for the topic seemingly inexhaustible. 'To me, a horse has a head, tail, and four legs – but I marvelled at the breadth of their knowledge,' she later recalled.

Reg also spent time in Lambourn in Hungerford. After Newmarket, the village of Lambourn is England's second-largest centre for racehorse training: roughly 110 kilometres west of London, it lies in the heart of Lambourn Valley, a region more commonly known as the 'Valley of the Racehorse' due to its proliferation of training centres and studs.

In between Reg's work, he and Joy seized the opportunity to embark upon any and all adventures they could share. Joy fondly remembered 'an expensive, entertaining and energetic weekend in Paris', including an evening at the renowned Folies Bergère. Famed for its grand and elaborate spectacles featuring beautiful, young, near-nude women as well as singers, acrobats and dramatic sketches, in 1968, the Folies was in its ninety-ninth year of operation. They climbed the Eiffel Tower and strolled through the Louvre; boated around the Île de la Cité, the island considered the epicentre of Paris and home to the historic Notre Dame cathedral; and promenaded along the Champs-Élysées, often touted as the 'most beautiful street in the world.'

Days earlier, as they had flown over the Channel, Joy had reflected on the armada that had crossed that same stretch of water in 1940 evacuating almost 350,000 Allied troops from the French port of Dunkirk. Now, at the Champs-Élysées' eastern end, they walked the cobblestones of the Place de la Concorde surrounded by buildings marked with bullet holes, a visible reminder of the lasting impressions left behind by the tragedies of the Second World War.

Later, Reg and Joy wandered along a narrow street near their hotel to investigate a small store which sold jewellery and an array of china. At the time, Joy was collecting Limoges pieces, a hard-paste porcelain produced in factories in and around the city of the same name. Joy resurrected her schoolgirl French and bought a miniature coffee set on a tray, though she later remarked wryly that the gentleman behind the counter probably spoke fluent English.

Of course, the main reason for their travels was never far from Reg's mind. He had intended to visit France anyway, drawn by his interest in a French vet called Edouard Pouret, known for his surgical abilities when treating horses with 'roarer' problems (an abnormal respiratory noise during exercise), but was told instead to head to Ireland to see cousins Stan and Maxie Cosgrove. The Irishmen, Reg learnt, had work for him to do.

Reg and Joy flew into Dublin and hired a car, driving west to County Kildare where they checked into their cosy accommodation in the village of Maynooth, a short drive from Moyglare Stud in County Meath. Six years earlier, a Swiss billionaire called Walter Haefner had bought an old dairy farm and turned it into a stud, hiring Stan Cosgrove as the vet. In time, the two men turned Moyglare 'into one of the most successful and respected bloodstock operations in the world.'

Who were these men and why does it matter that Reg sought them out? Reg and Stan Cosgrove were about the same age (Reg was thirty-nine that year, Cosgrove forty-one) and, though Moyglare had only been in operation for six years, Cosgrove was already well-established as a pre-eminent equine vet. He was an innovator and lateral thinker. Keenly involved in the development of Ireland's equine industry and the UK veterinary scene more broadly, he co-founded Ireland's famed Racing Academy and Centre for Education; was a founding member of the Irish Thoroughbred Breeders' Association; a steward of the Turf Club; and one of only two Irishmen (the first being his cousin, Maxie Cosgrove) to serve as president of the British Equine Veterinarians Association (BEVA). He blazed new paths in colic and equine orthopaedic surgery – specialities which came to the fore when, in the mid- to late-1970s along with two other vets, he established the Troytown Veterinary Hospital in County Kildare. The clinic specialised in treating racehorses and rapidly became internationally respected. When Stan Cosgrove died in 2019, tributes poured in from around the world.

Like, as the old saying goes, attracts like.

For both Reg and Stan, their more notable successes occurred after they met in 1968, but this does not detract from the significance of their meeting. Both were plunging headlong down the path of discovery to which their passions had led them, pushing the very limits of what they knew.

Reg and Joy took time to enjoy the cultural offerings that surrounded them during their time in Ireland, frequenting a local pub and travelling around the area. Joy bought pieces of Irish linen to make dresses for her mother and herself; a mistake, she recalled, for the lovely fabric 'crushed if you looked at it.' As they explored County Meath, the couple noted the sprawling stretches of peat marshes that cover up to one-sixth of Ireland and have, for over a millennium, provided a valuable fuel source, and marvelled at an ancient round tower nearby. There are sixty-five such towers scattered across Ireland's verdant, rolling hills. The imposing stone structures are in varying states of repair, remarkable given scholars believe they were constructed between the seventh and tenth centuries. Noting its proximity to the university town of Maynooth in County Kildare, it seems likely that this tower was Taghadoe Round Tower – part of a monastic settlement that dates back to the sixth century and is one of Maynooth's oldest surviving monuments.

At the end of their time in Kildare, Reg and Joy drove across the country to Ireland's west coast. Nearing Galway, they turned south for Shannon Airport to bid adieu to the Emerald Isle, watching through car windows as the light played over the gently wind-ruffled waters of Galway Bay.

They then flew across the North Atlantic to the US, arriving in Lexington in Kentucky. Often called the 'horse capital of the world', in 2019 the region boasted some 450 horse farms. Lexington is home to Keeneland, the largest and most prominent thoroughbred auction house in the world and is also the 1917 birthplace of Man o' War, America's most famous thoroughbred. More crucially, Lexington possesses arguably the finest equine care facilities in the world, including the Hagyard Equine Medical Institute and the University of Kentucky's Gluck Equine Research Centre. When Reg visited in 1968, the former was nearing its centenary; the latter had not yet been established.

Reg headed to the University of Kentucky and spent several days with two equine pathologists in the Vet School's faculty: Dr James Rooney and Dr Milton E. Prickett. Information on Prickett is scarce, but Rooney, at the time of his death in 2008, was one of the world's leading experts on equine anatomy, pathology and biomechanics. Like Stan Cosgrove, Rooney was two years older than Reg, and like these other two men, his most remarkable career successes occurred after 1968. That year was, in fact, the final year of Rooney's first stint at the University of Kentucky. He went to Newmarket, where he established the Equine Research Station's first pathology programme and served at its acting director. Later, after returning to the University of Kentucky in 1983, he chaired the university's veterinary science department from 1987 until 1989 and in this capacity was the inaugural director of the Gluck Equine Research Centre. Describing Rooney's effect in 2008, a fellow University of Kentucky professor remarked, '[Rooney], probably more than anyone else, was able to explain why lameness occurs in horses.'

Much of Reg's work had centred on equine reproduction services for the studs on the Darling Downs, but he was intrigued by all things to do with horses. Rooney, with his interest and expertise in equine research, in disease and in biomechanics, doubtless facilitated Reg's journey down another avenue.

Kentucky was also the professional stomping ground of an equine vet by the name of Dr Delano Proctor. Unlike Rooney and Prickett, Proctor's career focused on the provision of veterinary and surgical services for several of Kentucky's most prestigious stables – in this sense, his work was at least ostensibly more closely aligned with Reg's. Accompanying Proctor on his rounds doubtless provided Reg with valuable exposure not only to possibly unfamiliar clinical cases, but also to the career of a successful equine vet and surgeon. Moreover, Proctor maintained an esteemed clinical practice in Kentucky (and was later certified as a specialist equine surgeon by the American College of Veterinary Surgeons) while simultaneously participating in state and national veterinary organisations. Throughout his career, he advocated for improved communication within the profession, and between vets and the public. Reg, as we shall later see, was similarly enthused about, and devoted to, these complementary professional endeavours.

From Kentucky, Reg and Joy flew to the US's west coast. They stayed in the college town of Davis, home to one of the University of California's nine campuses, to visit the team working at UC Davis's Veterinary Medical Teaching Hospital. Chief among these was Dr John Hughes, who by 1968 had been a member of the faculty for over a decade. Of especial interest was Hughes's work in equine reproduction. He was one of the charter members of the American College of Theriogenologists (ACT) in 1971. (The ACT chose the term 'theriogenology' to represent their primary focus through the constituent parts of 'therio' [animal] + 'gen' [genesis, referencing birth and reproduction] + 'ology' [the study of].)

In 1973 Hughes established the Centre for Equine Health (CEH) within the UC Davis School of Veterinary Medicine, transforming it from a concept to an international leader. He was a gifted teacher and an exemplar in his profession; his scientific knowledge was legendary and he demanded students adhere to the same high standards he expected of himself.

Reg shared many traits with the equine vets with whom he spent his time – whether this is because he sought to emulate their qualities, or whether it was more a case of the consolidation of his own interests is impossible to know ... But as will become obvious, Reg and John Hughes had a lot in common.

Hughes organised for Reg and Joy to visit his mother in Merced, in the San Joaquin Valley, roughly two hours south of Davis. It was the end of spring and from Merced Reg and Joy drove to Yosemite National Park, where life was in full bloom. Over fifty years later, the mountains' majesty still resonated deeply with Joy. She recalled the feeling, in the shadows of those soaring peaks, that she was merely 'a small scrap of humanity.' The surroundings promised the chance for wonderful photos, which Reg, with his passion for photography, capitalised on. As they wandered through the park, Joy carried Reg's camera while he toted his other lens.

If there were ever any doubts as to Reg's care for his equipment or his love of his camera, they are dispelled by Joy's memories of that day. Yosemite is known for its countless waterfalls, which vary in size from the minute to the colossal – the largest, Yosemite Falls, is one of the world's tallest, soaring to a height of almost 740 metres. The nearby terrain is inevitably wet and greasy underfoot. As Reg and Joy strolled along, Joy stepped onto a wet rock and started to slip – behind her, Reg called out in dismay, 'Mind my camera!' Fortunately, both Joy and the camera emerged unscathed.

When the couple returned to Davis, they received a message to ring home: Joy's mother had fallen and hurt herself. She told the Pascoe boys not to tell their parents for fearing of ruining their trip, but John saw little sense in that and headed down to the telephone at the hospital immediately.

Reg and Joy were on the next Qantas flight home.

Though slightly truncated, Reg later recorded that the overseas 'trip was highly informative.' The knowledge he acquired underpinned the development of the Oakey Veterinary Hospital – not only regarding surgical technology and methods, but also in conceiving an ideal hospital layout. At the back of Reg's mind was the need for flexibility in design. Horses are large animals, their care needs unique, and treatment facilities must be commensurately tailored.

The inevitable limitations of time and money necessitated staged growth, and each phase had to be designed to accommodate subsequent developments, adding layers of complexity to an already intricate task. Late in 1968, the first iteration of the desired equine hospital became a reality: a cavity concrete block was added to the pre-existing structures, incorporating a new professional office, pharmacy and toilet block, as well as a small animal operating theatre.

A common scrub and instrument storage room linked to an operating theatre, which was complemented by a large, padded recovery room and four stables with five outside yards and a new autopsy area. Within this L-shaped facility, the walls were steel rod- and concrete-filled for additional strength wherever horse contact might be expected to occur. Oakey Veterinary Hospital now provided the only large animal hospital in Queensland and from within its still-small sphere of influence set about revolutionising Australia's horse industry.

Employing local engineer Lloyd Iland for its construction, Reg designed an operating table, recording that it was 'a combination of all the good points I had observed in my overseas visits. Due to cost, some [features] had to be modified, but this [did not] detract from its simplicity and extreme easiness of use.' It was an extraordinary innovation: a 2 x 1.5 metre stainless steel slab fixed to a hydraulic, ram-mounted steel sub-frame. Mobile and manoeuvrable, the table could carry up to five tons and used removable plates to fix anaesthetised horses in position.

When Reg and Lloyd were finished, they had developed an operating apparatus that rapidly became central to the Oakey Veterinary Hospital's daily practice.

Most equine surgeries use hoists. The horse is typically anaesthetised while standing and staff ensure it isn't hurt when, insensate, it crumples to the floor. From that side-lying position, veterinary staff secure the horse, usually by means of ties around the hooves, and hoist it into the air to be swung over to lie on its back on the operating table. Reg's elegant design meant that the sedated animal was immobilised and secured to the table by use of multiple ties while still standing. Once the anaesthetic had taken effect, the table was electronically tilted from vertical to horizontal and adjusted to the required operating height.

After the operation, the table – equipped with steel castor wheels that enabled it to be removed from the sub-frame – could be wheeled into the adjacent padded recovery room. Here, the final brilliant design element became apparent: the floor featured a sunken pit of the same dimensions as the operating table. Once the table, complete with the still-insensible horse attached, was emplaced, the recovery room floor became completely flat. Unstrapped and left alone, the horse could regain equilibrium and reorient itself with a greatly reduced risk of injury.

It was this sequence of events, designed to both simplify and expedite surgery and protect the horse, that was most remarkable. Even today, horses have a greater risk of dying during surgery than other animals – a study in the early 2000s determined that even normal, healthy animals undergoing routine procedures perish at a rate of approximately 1 per cent, staggering when compared to humans (~0.001 per cent) and small companion animals (~0.07 per cent). This rate has not changed much in the past fifty years, though the causes of fatalities have changed with ongoing surgical advances (particularly in the kind of anaesthetic used). A 2020 study of more than 1100 horses over a four-year period showed that recovery from anaesthetic remained the riskiest phase of the process and the phase where 92 per cent of complications occurred.

OVH's streamlined method of handling insensate animals throughout surgery – only two or three people were necessary to get most horses onto the table and later to move them into the recovery room – mitigated the risk of injury by simplifying a complex process and reducing the possible points of human error. It may also have hastened the surgery generally. This was important because horses don't tolerate having their cardiovascular and respiratory functions depressed – an inevitable aspect of sedation – and this, in addition to their size, makes them poor candidates for spending a long time sedated on the operating table. One equine surgeon noted in 2020 that the length of time a horse is under general anaesthetic is correlated to an increase in mortality rates. Being quick, efficient and allowing the animal somewhere safe and controlled to recover were crucial factors in maximising chances of recovery.

On 22 March 1969, the revolutionary operating table was put into practice. Within a few years it had seen close to 150 surgeries and, by 1984, that number had climbed to more than 2000 – mostly horses, but also some bulls. Its success was notable enough that, in 1977, Reg acted as a consultant for both Murdoch University in Western Australia and the University of Florida as these institutions designed and built their own tables.

Other equipment advances were instituted concurrently or in close succession: a new equine anaesthetic machine and a Stephen's circle anaesthetic machine with an in-circle vaporizer for foals and small animals were added and remained in use for the next thirty years. New instruments were purchased and Reg concentrated on stocking the best quality irrespective of the cost. UQ students continued coming to OVH to complete their clinical exposure, carrying on what had begun fifteen years earlier with DJ Laws's visit in 1954. Reg's active mentorship of junior veterinarians, particularly Queensland graduates, became even further entrenched as a cornerstone of his professional ethos.

And quietly, inexhaustibly, he was, as we shall soon see, pursuing both his own ongoing education and investigation into a wide range of aspects of equine medicine. In every sense, he was laying the groundwork for what he intended OVH to be, who he saw himself as a veterinarian, and what he hoped and would fight for veterinary science to become.

Part III —Contributions to Veterinary Science

6
Equine Medicine and Science

During a career spanning more than half a century, Reg Pascoe was a vital and influential force in the advance of equine medicine both in Australia and overseas. His enduring influence resulted from the irrepressible combination of unyielding curiosity, passion for education, and a sincere, bone-deep conviction of the individual's responsibility to use their skills in service of the collective. Though this combination manifested differently across different arenas in his life, the fundamentals always remained the same.

Reg's deliberate cultivation of an environment of professional curiosity at OVH enabled him to investigate both general recurrent conditions and specific individual cases that aroused his interest. He remarked that from his earliest days in practice he 'was keen to investigate problems occurring in the area.' Originally, such investigation focused on cattle; later 'as dairy cattle practice decreased and horse practice increased, the emphasis of work changed markedly to all aspects of horse work.' This professional environment promoted similar exploration by OVH's other vets, which Reg openly encouraged and facilitated; he both co-authored papers with, and provided advisory guidance to, other vets conducting clinical research. Through these various investigations, Reg was fundamental both in discovering the causes and impacts of several equine diseases, and in pioneering treatments and technologies which are now crucial to conventional daily veterinary practice.

Reg's numerous clinical discoveries occasioned advancements in equine medicine that continue to reverberate to this day. He possessed a wealth of practical experience across a wide range of medicine, a multidisciplinary mastery unusual for the time; today, such extensive knowledge is unheard of. It was made possible in part because veterinary science in Australia – and specifically in Queensland – was in its infancy during the early decades of his career. The number of equine vets today, in conjunction with the profession's development over the past sixty years, precludes such diverse expertise.

Reg's ability to pursue a range of interests was helped by a unique professional situation: one of only a few vets in rural Queensland, his clinical exposure was broad, and working on the Darling Downs, Queensland's cradle for thoroughbred studs, provided distinctive opportunities, even if the isolation and distance from clients outside of the region sometimes brought its challenges. As OVH grew, Reg commanded a large, well-constructed and well-equipped facility that allowed horses to be brought for treatment and then remain for ongoing monitoring. This saw what he described as 'a large surgical through-put of horses' that provided him with the opportunity for 'research studies extending into viral, reproductive, surgery and skin disorders.'

The rationale behind anyone's life choices is rarely straightforward and attempting to define a single, simple reason for Reg's decades-long dedication would likely be reductive and inaccurate. There is, however, a tale frequently retold by friends and colleagues that summarises his beliefs. Speaking to a small group one day, Reg reminded them what he considered their true purpose to be. 'We must not forget why we're all here,' he said, 'and that's for the horse and the majesty of the horse.' It was a philosophy of respect and compassion that shaped everything he did – as one OVH employee said, he 'would attempt anything to try and fix those horses. They were his pride and joy.'[10]

Some of Reg's innovative ideas were less deserving of accolade than others – a few were even rather mundane. Oakey during the summer is a haven for flies; they breed and live and die in their thousands. Masters of squeezing into the smallest of spaces, in a workplace characterised by blood and other bodily fluids, they're a horrendous plague. As one OVH vet recalled, Reg 'used to take the bandages off the horses that had cut their legs. He'd have these horrible bandages with pus all over them, and [he] used to plant them all around the building and around the compound area.' He wasn't concerned about what clients might think. He covered the bandages in a fly-killing powder and sat back to let them do their work; the 'bandages attracted the flies; the flies would eat the poison.'[11] It was a pedestrian solution but its ease and effectiveness spoke volumes for Reg's approach to solving problems: think outside the box, but don't turn your nose up at simple, practical solutions.

This same philosophy made other, more remarkable endeavours possible. Reg pursued several treatment options that were rare, particularly in Australia – such as equine amputation – and was fundamental in pioneering technology and techniques, such as ultrasound and arthroscopy, that are now routine practice. Not all animals can be saved; Reg, of anyone, knew this ... but he also didn't believe in leaving the boundaries of the possible untested.

Equine Viral Disease Investigations

Reg's investigations into viral diseases produced some of the most scientifically important outcomes of his career. This work was a continuation of his early interest in clinical conditions and their accepted treatment methods which had originated in the 1950s during the years of working mostly with cattle. From what he termed 'these early, rather primitive attempts' sprang his ongoing interest in determining 'the causal organisms in acute clinical cases.' As time passed and new graduates joined the practice, he was able to convert this interest into investigative clinical research. His efforts were limited by the lack of broader scientific support: the University of Queensland's virology lab only began virological investigation in 1962 and so Reg completed most of the laboratory work for his master's degree in the OVH lab.

As OVH's equine workload increased throughout the 1960s, his interest in virological investigation developed 'because of the high prevalence of colds, coughs and loss of form.' He observed how often cold-type illnesses occurred in young horses when they first entered training; even if recurring in later periods, it was typically only serious at the start, upon a horse's first exposure to the stable environment. The situation intrigued Reg.

The UQ virology lab had previously focused on bovine virus

studies but in 1967, a recent graduate named Trevor Bagust became interested in equine herpesviruses alongside his research on bovine herpesviruses. This enabled Reg to have equine viruses tested and cultured through the UQ virology lab and, working together, the two men achieved the first isolation of equine herpesvirus (EHV) in Queensland in 1968.

Herpesviruses are members of a large family of DNA called *herpesviridae* that infect both humans and other animals; the virus strain that Reg and Trevor Bagust isolated in 1968 is related to herpes simplex 1 (which gives people cold sores) and varicella zoster (which produces chickenpox and shingles). There are over 100 different strains of herpesvirus and as of 2020, nine strains have been identified as affecting horses. EHV1, EHV3 and EHV4 are the most common while EHV1 and EHV4 are the most dangerous.

Until 1981, the EHV1 and EHV4 strains were thought to be subtypes of the same EHV strain, with subtype 1 referred to as 'equine abortion virus' and subtype 2 as 'equine rhinopneumonitis virus.' It wasn't until 1988 that EHV1 subtype 1 and EHV1 subtype 2 were designated EHV1 and EHV4 respectively by the International Committee for Taxonomy of Viruses.

This is important because Reg's description of his isolation of EHV1 relates to the presentation of *respiratory illness* in young horses and must therefore, in modern parlance, more accurately be referred to as EHV4. A handbook released by the American Association of Equine Practitioners in 2017 reinforces this, noting that 'equine herpes viral respiratory disease is usually caused by EHV-4 and is most commonly seen in weaned foals and yearlings, often in autumn and winter. Older horses are more likely than younger ones to transmit the virus without showing signs of infection.' The description aligns with Reg's account of the EHV strain he isolated with Trevor Bagust in 1968.

This success galvanised him to re-examine 'stored deep frozen specimens which I had collected the previous year from a suspected case of coital exanthema (ECE).' Coital exanthema is a highly infectious venereal disease characterised by raised lesions, ulcers and pustules on a horse's external genitalia. While it is known nowadays to be non-invasive and relatively benign, in the late 1960s there were fears that ECE may have long-term repercussions for fertility. Despite a 1961 paper hypothesising that ECE resulted from a bacterial infection, there was also no confirmed causal agent for the disease. Reg's interest was inevitable.

The deep-frozen samples that he returned to in 1968 had been preserved from two of three separate Darling Downs studs outbreaks between 1962 and 1967. Aided by UQ Veterinary School's Dr Peter Spradbrow, Trevor Bagust once more conducted the laboratory work in support of Reg's clinical observations and samples. The three men made a crucial discovery. Equine coital exanthema, they proposed, was caused by another equine herpesvirus strain and alongside concurrent findings in the US and Canada, the trio provided 'the first report of the viral aetiology of coital exanthema published in world literature.'

Over the next several years, Reg continued his investigation of ECE, conducting experiments in cooperation with local studs and publishing papers that demonstrated the disease did not prevent conception nor cause spontaneous abortions. He was quickly acknowledged as an expert in the area. The panel coordinating the inaugural International Symposium on Equine Reproduction (ISER) in 1975 asked him to contribute a paper on ECE, while the editors of the *Merck Veterinary Manual* requested that he contribute a section on ECE for their fifth edition, published in 1979.

This work simultaneously occasioned Reg's investigation into another equine viral disease, specifically one that he'd noticed treating Arabian horses. Though thoroughbred studs predominated on the Downs, Reg's long-standing interest in Arabians precipitated his recurring concerns about the tendency for Arab foals to contract severe respiratory infections. The publication of other papers on adenovirus in 1969 and 1970 led Reg to approach the virology laboratory with a new proposition: he would swab and take samples from a group of Arab mares and foals for the lab's analysis. The collaboration led to the isolation of two strains of adenovirus and, as Reg noted in his doctoral submission, provided the 'first isolation and identification of this virus in Australia.'

Equine Dermatology – Rain Scald and Fungal Infections

Rather than in a linear progression, Reg's specialties typically originated and were pursued concurrently. As he noted in his 1982 doctoral submission, his mid-1960s 'interest in virological investigation ... led to the isolation of coital exanthema virus, and due to the skin manifestation of this disease, stimulated my interest in dermatological conditions in horses.' As a boy, he'd loved playing in Schoenberg's enormous Moreton Bay fig tree and, like the spreading branches of that old tree, each of his professional interests fostered the next, forming an intricate and expansive network of expertise.

His investigations of the skin lesions associated with coital exanthema led him to realise there was a notable 'paucity of sound descriptions of dermatological conditions.' This was increasingly evident when considering a recurring skin condition dubbed 'rain scald': a bacterial infection which causes matted scabs over a horse's back, rump and lower limbs. Reg was well-acquainted with the condition, having repeatedly observed it on the Downs. Many vets suggested the scabs were a form of sunburn and what few studies had been done, Reg noted, 'implied it was a disease of little significance.'

In 1966, parts of the Darling Downs experienced a particularly wet June and July; after the weather eased, rain scald broke out across the region. As the instances mounted, Reg noticed that the younger mares were the worst affected – the old mares showed fewer effects and typically recovered quicker. His curiosity piqued, over the coming months Reg recorded seventy rain scald cases of varying severity across five different thoroughbred studs and two training stables within roughly a 150-kilometre radius. A second outbreak affected almost 280 horses over 1970–71.

Two papers analysing these outbreaks were published in 1971 and 1972; the latter, in which Reg was aided by scientists at the Animal Research Institute at Yeerongpilly, allowed him to isolate the bacteria responsible. Simultaneously, and in contravention of earlier findings, he demonstrated the seriousness of the disease: severe instances were 'capable of causing lameness in both paddock and racing horses due to lower leg lesions.'

Reg noted that rain scald was also responsible for related conditions such as 'greasy heel' (an inflammatory condition of the skin of a horse's lower limbs) and 'aphis' (lesions on the face). He initiated new treatment methods, using antibiotics through direct application to the affected area or intravenously, and saw a remarkable success rate.

The lack of information both in Australia and internationally further stimulated Reg's interest. Once more he had found a significant lacuna in veterinary knowledge and he rapidly established himself as a leading authority. Clinical exposure facilitated his exploration and he quickly realised that his 'routine stable work indicated a fairly high percentage of dermatological problems.'

He began investigating mycotic diseases (ailments caused by fungi), specifically the superficial fungal infections confined to the skin, and focused on two of the three major groups of types of fungus, exploring under what conditions horses showed symptoms of ringworm, and the difference in physical manifestations. Throughout the 1970s and early 1980s, he examined almost 4000 horses, producing three papers in seven years. There emerged a clear and important difference between how racehorses got ringworm and how non-racehorses did: two infective agents were at work. From this work, Reg also isolated two previously unidentified unique dermatophytes.

As his investigations into mycosis continued, Reg explored the mechanisms behind the spread of the common training stable problem known as 'girth itch.' Girth itch is the colloquial term for a fungal infection which occurs around a horse's torso along the belly towards the front legs, near the 'armpits', and which takes its name from the girth of a saddle – the band which fastens around a horse's belly to keep the saddle in place. At the time of Reg's investigations, he noted that 'the mode of spread of girth itch ... was always a great puzzle to owners and trainers.' His research not only formed the basis for his fellowship thesis for the Royal College of Veterinary Surgeons, but later highlighted both the highly infectious nature of the ailment and the common vehicles for spreading infection – saddle girths, grooming brushes and riders' boots. Even saddles stored for long periods of time between use, such as those kept for riding young or unbroken horses, showed enduring evidence of the dermatophyte: one saddle girth retained the fungal culprit for a whole year.

Mid-1970s. In amidst this busy workload, there was still always time for family. Holidaying together in Girraween National Park in New South Wales. From left: David, Reg, Roess, Andrew, and Joy.

Just as importantly, Reg spent time exploring the usefulness of the many treatments. His found that two of the most common drugs for treating ringworm had a lower efficacy than other options and that other frequently used treatments were ineffective, some even serving to spread the infection or damage the horse's skin. Whether he realised it at the time or not, Reg's position as a practising clinician allowed him to bring a unique and valuable perspective. He recognised that scientific concerns (such as, in this instance, the degree of efficacy of a treatment method) had to be balanced against the needs of the client – finding the most effective ointment was irrelevant if the treatment's cost or associated care method made it impractical for owners, especially those who had numerous horses needing treatment. Reg even suggested that those horses being treated with less-effective solutions be given a simple 'scratch test' to check if further medication was needed.

The Caslick's Procedure

As equine reproduction matured from a small part of Reg's work into what he termed 'a total commitment', foremost among his concerns was 'the use, misuse and lack of use of "Caslick's operation."' Pioneered by American veterinarian E. A. Caslick and first recorded in 1937, a 'Caslick' is a surgical procedure that aims to improve equine fertility by addressing compromised vulvar function.

To understand this treatment a basic grasp of horse anatomy (which is not entirely dissimilar to a human's) is required. The equine reproductive tract is divided into two structural groups: inner and outer. Comprising the uterus, fallopian tubes and ovaries, the inner tract's condition is central to the mare's fertility, but is also susceptible to infection from environmental contaminants, particularly airborne contaminants. The outer tract comprising the vulva, vagina and cervix is nature's answer to this hazard, designed to protect the inner tract by means of an anatomical barrier – primarily, the vulva – and the barrier's effectiveness relies on the vulvar lips remaining closed. Ideally, muscle tone and anatomic structure ensure this occurs, but numerous factors can compromise this barrier, including advanced age, poor general physical condition, foaling injury, or poor conformation (a horse's general structure which is often discussed for its impact on athletic ability). Hypotonic (poor muscle tone) or gaping vulvar lips mean a mare is liable to experience pneumovagina, or vaginal 'windsucking', which inevitably introduces contaminants to the reproductive tract. Whether they are bacterial, fungal, or viral, such contaminants can cause infections which can damage a mare's fertility or, if she is in foal, cause deformity or miscarriage.

The link between vulvar integrity and fertility was not Caslick's original focus. Observing how standard treatment of genital infections introduced air into mares' reproductive tracts, Caslick recognised the negative effects outweighed any benefits. A decade later, he advanced his hypothesis and pioneered a procedure that surgically closed the upper two-thirds of a mare's vulva, restoring the barrier function.

Reg noted in 1982 that when he began investigating Caslick's procedure a decade earlier, there were papers published on the procedure's successful application and sound technical descriptions of the surgery, but 'its use or non-use were largely a matter of personal experience. For this reason, I decided to try to establish a scientific basis for the operation.' Reg could see that the ambiguous and inevitably subjective assessments being used as the basis for performing a Caslick meant a high likelihood that vets were getting it wrong: the margin for human error was inescapable. What was needed, he thought, was a set of reliable, *quantifiable* parameters to determine suitable conditions for the surgery. This was particularly relevant in those cases where the condition resulted from poor conformation – broodmares could appear to be otherwise in good health without having suffered any inciting incidents and yet be 'poor breeders', their repeated uterine infections resulting in either an inability to conceive, or recurrent involuntary abortions. Similarly, a mare could exhibit none of the classical signs of pneumovagina and yet suffer from those issues associated with the condition. Failure to recognise a mare's predisposition to these risks meant risking the mare's ongoing health, including the possibility that she might conceive only to miscarry or deliver an unhealthy foal. It made sense to act pre-emptively, and rigorous diagnosis criteria was the obvious answer.

In 1979, Reg published two papers that drew upon his clinical examinations of over 9000 thoroughbred, standardbred and Arabian mares on South-East Queensland studs between 1966 and 1977 to advance a new method for determining a mare's Caslick suitability. He proposed 'the Caslick index': a mathematical formula which quantified the relationship between the length of the vulva (in centimetres) and the angle of declination (in degrees) to produce a score between 0–200. To ensure consistency in the measurements, Reg invented a stainless-steel measuring device that he named a 'vulvometer.' He described the device as comprising 'a half protractor (0–90 degrees), an arm calibrated in centimetres and pointer attached to and pivoted at the base of the protractor, which had a spirit level fixed to its upper edge.'

Reg's creation of the Caslick index and the vulvometer by which to determine it, was a watershed moment for veterinary science. Both are straightforward, practical tools that, as of 2020, remain valuable when assessing broodmares. These findings were probably Reg's most significant discovery in equine reproductive medicine and, along with his other efforts, they improved the fertility of mares on the Downs at a crucial juncture for Queensland's breeding industry. A fellow Queensland vet noted in 2020 that increased Caslick use in Queensland from the late 1970s was likely attributable to Reg's findings, which helped to make Caslicks an almost-ubiquitous procedure for broodmares. The result was greatly improved fertility in Queensland and throughout Australia.

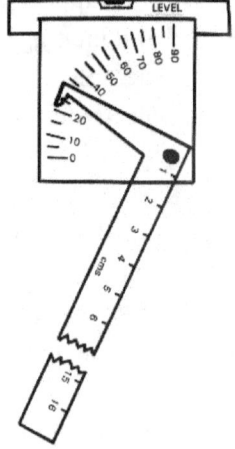

Diagram of a Vulvometer.

Equine Amputation

In the late 1970s, a little campdraft mare arrived at OVH with a catastrophic front leg injury. Campdrafting is a unique Australian sport that's a bit like American stock horse events such as cutting. Entering a corral, or 'camp', where six to eight cattle are penned, a lone rider isolates one steer or heifer from the group and performs a series of manoeuvres which demonstrate both the rider's horsemanship and their control of the chosen animal. Horse and rider work intimately together and build strong bonds. As with any livestock, lineage and demonstrated potential mean campdraft horses range in price: in February 2020, a two-year-old quarter horse stallion sold for over $100,000 in New South Wales. The injured campdraft mare brought to Reg wasn't particularly valuable – at least not in dollar signs – but her owners adored her.

There was a common refrain in Queensland (and further afield) at the time: if anyone had anything wrong with their horses, they'd 'take it to Pascoe.' The mare's owners had done just that, but as Reg examined the injury and tried every possible standard treatment option, he began to realise the leg couldn't be saved.

Prior to the 1970s, euthanising a horse was the routine answer to severe leg injuries; today, lower limb injuries continue to play a major role in the number of horses euthanised both on the racetrack and off. Of course, there are other options: the horse might be immobilised until the injury heals, or the affected limb amputated and the horse rehabilitated. But these options are typically seen as unfeasible. While the bones of their lower limbs are relatively light and fragile, horses are heavy and not well-suited to immobility; splints, casts, and even the use of slings tend to be impractical.

Amputation has been practised on both large and small animals for hundreds if not thousands of years but successful equine amputation and rehabilitation remains uncommon even today. This is partly due to expense. In 1996 a 'successful amputation, complete with fitting a prosthesis, [ran to] between [USD]$10,000 and $15,000 [AUD$15,000–$23,000].' The cost has not changed much in almost thirty years. The other concern is temperament: high-strung horses are unlikely to remain sedate enough throughout the recovery process to ensure success. And, of course, if amputation *is* feasible, noting the concerns above, a horse fitted with a prosthetic leg will require special care for the rest of its life. (A 2018 article noted that there have been only seventy cases, worldwide, of successful horse prostheses.)

Reg knew all this and the challenges of successful lower-limb amputation couldn't have been a surprise to him, but he had the unconquerable habit of seeing a problem and confronting it with all the knowledge and skill he had at his disposal. He amputated the little campdraft mare's foreleg just above the knee then, working with a local craftsman, had a fibreglass artificial leg made.

A challenging period followed. 'It was a long and tedious process,' Louise Winkel, Reg's vet nurse at the time, remembered. 'I'm sure at times [the owner] wished we hadn't done it and I'm sure at times *we* wished we hadn't done it.'

The prosthesis material was hard to work with: fibreglass surfaces are typically covered in microscopic splinters that, needle-like, can inflame the skin. Where the mare was protected by means of the dressing on the amputation site, OVH staff initially handled the prosthesis with their bare hands. Then, as the mare healed and the foreleg stump swelled and changed shape more than once, there were countless adjustments to the prosthesis; new moulds were made over the ensuing months to protect and keep the mare comfortable.

A 2010 study of the short- and long-term complications associated with equine amputation noted that the timing of the surgery was a key factor in the horse's prognosis. Too soon after injury and the horse might not yet have adjusted to a non-functioning leg and redistributed their weight, leading to increased pressure on the newly fitted prosthesis. Too late and the horse's sole reliance on the front or hind uninjured leg could result in new pathologies, such as laminitis (inflammation of the sensitive tissues inside the hoof wall).

The same study observed that it was the collapse of the supporting structures in the *opposing* limb that often proved the main reason for euthanasia after an amputation. Simultaneously, vets must be vigilant for the adverse effects which can result from extended use of nonsteroidal anti-inflammatory drugs (NSAIDs) for pain relief, including renal failure and gastrointestinal ulcers. Finally, the site of injury added further complexity. The little campdraft mare's foreleg was wounded, and as one expert noted in 2003, 'horses seem to handle hind limb amputation better than forelimb amputation, possibly due to weight distribution and the constant twisting load placed on the front end that is not imposed on the rear.'

Reg had taken on a big job, made more tricky for the rarity of such procedures at the time. While the first clinically documented prosthetic device was developed by a Washington State University vet called Dr Lavon Koger in the 1960s, the procedure remained uncommon enough that his protégé, American equine orthopaedic expert Dr Barrie Grant, was referred to as 'one of the pioneers in the field' in 1996. Reg had met Grant in 1968 when he visited UC Davis during his three-month overseas study trip; at the time, Grant had recently graduated with his Doctor of Veterinary Medicine (or DVM, equivalent to the Australian Bachelor of Veterinary Science, BVSc) in 1967 and commenced his internship and residency at Davis.

By 1985, he was head of the equine section of Washington State University's Veterinary Clinic when he managed the hind-hoof amputation, prosthesis-fitting and rehabilitation of a high-profile stallion called Boitron. It was a well-publicised case. Grant worked with an eighteen-person team (a mix of veterinary professionals and senior equine medicine students) and 'an instrument maker in the mechanical engineering shops at WSU' to design a prosthesis for the champion stallion. The process required additional surgery and numerous failures before finally reaching a unique and expensive solution: the USD$1000 prosthesis included a shock absorber from the steering component of a motorcycle!

Noting Grant's experience in the field, his 1985 remark that he knew of only two horses with artificial hind legs indicates that equine prostheses – and successful equine amputation in general – were rare. And, though the exact timing of Reg's treatment of the little campdraft mare is uncertain, it certainly occurred prior to Boitron's injury. Louise Winkel remarked that the amputation performed at OVH 'was the first time it'd ever been done' and while this might not be entirely accurate, it is representative of the general awareness of such surgeries and may well have been true within the late 1970s Australian veterinary scene.

Whether Reg had heard of Grant's earlier successes is uncertain though not unlikely given his perpetual interest in advancements around the globe. What *is* known is that although it was a long and arduous undertaking, Reg's own endeavour was a triumph. If the measure of success is a horse's ability to thrive and return to some degree of 'normalcy' following a procedure, then the plucky little campdraft mare more than fit the bill. She adapted to bearing much of her bodyweight on her three remaining legs, allowing the prosthetic foreleg to be left off for stretches of time. This helped with healing and inadvertently became somewhat of a habit, so that after returning home, she often plodded around her paddock on three legs. Sometime down the track, she produced a healthy foal. It was a great outcome for a surgery and treatment trajectory with which Reg had no practical experience. Compared with Grant's treatment of the famed Boitron, Reg's success was arguably more remarkable given he was in rural Queensland.

Skin Grafts

Throughout the 1970s, Reg experimented with equine skin grafts. He never published on the subject, so there is only anecdotal evidence of this professional interest, but as Louise Winkel recalled, 'Reg was always doing things that were a little different.' A large number of surgical cases came through the doors of OVH and given his ongoing interest in dermatology, he likely saw the potential for using skin grafts as an extension of this work.

The origins of skin grafting stretch back to the 1950s through to the 1970s – a period during which UK vet Derek Knottenbelt noted, 'Reg was at his most vibrant. His interest in everything surgical was legendary even then.' The following tale, a recollection of Louise Winkel's, provides further context for Reg's interest.

A mare was brought into OVH one day with barbed wire wrapped around her leg. The damage had caused the proliferation of 'proud flesh': a normal granulation tissue that overgrows wound edges, preventing the wound from healing correctly and is more common in horses than other animal species. 'The boss,' Louise Winkel recalled, 'operated on her and pulled all the barbed wire out; it was quite spectacular.'

Reg would have recognised that the proud flesh itself posed a challenge. The best way of treating it is prevention: suturing a wound immediately or as soon as possible after it occurs, termed 'primary closure.' When primary closure doesn't occur, the wound is left open to allow for 'second intention' healing – by granulation, contraction and epithelialisation (the growth of new skin cells across the open area). It is the failure of this process that causes the formation of proud flesh, which must then be surgically removed in order for the wound to heal. But what if suturing isn't possible?

Horses' lower legs are more prone to proud flesh than other areas because of their composition: comprised mainly of bone, ligaments and tendons, the lack of underlying soft tissue such as fat and muscle means greater tension in the skin's surface and less available loose skin to pull together. With suturing not possible – and the greater surface tension making it more difficult for new skin to grow – such lower limb wounds are often slow to heal, increasing the risk of proud flesh.

This challenging situation is exacerbated by the amount of *movement* in these areas: wounds on the lower legs, such as on joints (the knee, hock, or fetlock), or over areas with lots of flexing and contracting connective tissue (along the cannon bone with its superficial tendons for flexing and extending the foot), are in constant motion that tears apart the new tissue and further slows the healing process. Skin grafting offers a solution. Today, the efficacy of grafts is widely acknowledged; a 2015 article noted, 'In horses, skin grafts are most often used for limb wounds where primary closure [suturing] is not possible or second intention healing is delayed or not occurring.'

But Reg was operating in a different climate. He had come of age professionally in a world characterised by a prevailing and dismissive attitude that Derek Knottenbelt summarised as, 'horses don't heal.' (He would know: at the time of writing, Derek Knottenbelt is one of the world's leading authorities on equine wound healing, having written the seminal text on the matter, *The Handbook of Equine Wound Management*.) There was little wider appreciation for the development of wound healing techniques. This goes some way to explaining the dearth of scientific papers on skin grafting in the 1960s and 1970s – something that makes it difficult to identify the instigator of contemporary equine skin grafting. What is certain is that while Reg was not the first, he was among the early pioneers. And, crucially, as Derek noted, '[Reg] certainly developed the technical aspects of it with the best them!'

Using a 'punch' biopsy tool, Reg took skin-deep samples from the horse's neck and planted them in the open wound area, repeating the process numerous times to encourage the graft to take. He was enthusiastic about the possibilities, as always and, along with his OVH vets, tried different methods across numerous cases. But success was variable and the results were not stellar. Perhaps this accounts both for Reg's decision not to write academically on the topic and the general lack of publications on skin grafting during the period. Derek proffered an alternate explanation, noting that, by virtue of Reg's reputation and the profession's acknowledgement of his expertise and 'relevance to our everyday lives in practice', Reg actively drove forward the use of skin grafts. There is, he pointed out, a flaw in presupposing academic publication as the only avenue by which Reg shaped the landscape of equine veterinary science. 'Overall, his presentations in conferences were the forum where he put out his ideas. I think whilst he did publish a lot, his main forum was when there were people present with whom he could discuss difficult issues and new techniques.'

Reg's desire to broaden his own knowledge continued to lead him to these borders. He would have been the first to note that every success was occasioned by countless failures, yet his pursuit of improved treatment methods never ceased.

Pioneering Equine Reproduction in Australia

Speaking about veterinary–client relations in an address to the 2004 UQ Veterinary Science graduating class, Reg urged his audience, 'Remember, if you are asked a question, find time to answer it.' His advice illustrated his philosophies to not only pursue his own learning or even a dedication to innovation, but to advocate for the vet's responsibility to his or her clients. New technologies always piqued his interest, and never more so than when they directly related to one of his core responsibilities on the Darling Downs: developing improved reproduction processes for Queensland studs.

The year 1982 dawned a bright and promising one for Australian veterinary science. It was characteristically busy for Reg: he had received a grant from the Queensland Equine Research Foundation to acquire an early ultrasound scanner and incorporate it into routine broodmare examinations. In France two years earlier, an enterprising veterinarian called Eric Palmer performed the first equine reproductive ultrasound when he borrowed an Aloka scanner from his obstetrician father and inserted the probe into a mare's rectum. Palmer's approach was a logical progression: use of the 'transrectal route' was well-established. The publication of his 1980 paper (co-authored with French vet, Marc-Antoine Driancourt) was a watershed moment that triggered a cascade of ultrasound-focused research around the world. Reg would have followed these developments with interest and they doubtless influenced his own explorations.

Reg and second-eldest son, David, scrubbing up at OVH together.

At the same time, Reg and Joy's second son, David, was pursuing further study in the US. Having graduated from the University of Queensland with a BVSc in 1977, David moved to California in 1979 to become a Resident in Equine Reproduction at the School of Veterinary Medicine at Davis, where he spent the next seven years completing a residency and a PhD. His exposure to the cutting-edge developments occurring at Davis precipitated his own interest in ultrasound, leading to later research breakthroughs. His experiences inevitably filtered back to OVH.

Reg began thinking more and more about the possibilities of ultrasound, specifically in relation to twin pregnancy. In a 1979 paper, he'd discussed treating twin pregnancy using prostaglandin –

a group of compounds in the body which have hormone-like effects, most notably the induction of labour. Twins have historically been the single most biggest cause of abortion in thoroughbreds, which are more prone to twin pregnancies than other breeds due to the greater frequency of double ovulation. Regardless of breed, twin pregnancies generally 'terminate in early foetal resorption or loss, late term abortions, or the birth of small growth retarded foals.' It's rare for twins to be carried to term, and their spontaneous late-term abortion can seriously damage a mare's reproductive tracts, complicating rebreeding.

In the unlikely instance of twins being carried to term, most mares will deliver two stillborn foals, but if both are born alive, their foaling is riskier and more complicated. Combined, twins' birth weight is typically equal to that of one normal, single foal – and if they survive, these newborns will never catch up to other foals in weight and size. For many twin foals, their 'long-term survival necessitates expensive sophisticated critical care.'

It's a heartbreaking situation, one described in the horse industry as 'a disaster [that] should be avoided at all costs.' Financially, of course, there are consequences: it would be disingenuous to not acknowledge how valuable a foal is, and an unmanaged twin pregnancy is an expensive situation with little to no hope of positive return for the owner. More crucially, those who breed and treat horses care deeply for the strong, noble and beautiful animals. When asked in a 1986 newspaper article why he did what he did, Reg replied, 'I guess I just like horses. And the people who own them.' And, like Reg, 'horse people' are both passionate and compassionate: the sight of a mare or a sickly, undersized foal needlessly suffering is abhorrent.

Considering the financial and emotional costs, the widespread practice of aborting one of the foals in a twin pregnancy is a logical one. And the higher incidence of twins in thoroughbreds would have been of considerable interest to Reg. His biggest clients in the Darling Downs were thoroughbred breeders for whom the late detection of a twin pregnancy had serious repercussions. Reg had built a large part of his professional repute on his ability to detect conception through rectal palpation at very early stages of pregnancy – but ultrasound offered an even earlier, and more exact, confirmation.

There was a third influence in Reg's ultrasound journey. Beyond David's experiences at Davis or even the influence of Palmer and Driancourt's landmark 1980 paper, Reg's experimentation came about, at least in part, via human medicine. Though the species being scanned was different, the evolution of ultrasound use at OVH was an inadvertently fitting continuation of the pioneering work done by Australian scientists in the preceding decade. These scientists, in achieving a technical breakthrough in 1969 called 'grey scale ultrasound', produced much clearer and more detailed images. Forty years later, ultrasound is a ubiquitous tool in human medicine, but it's also among the contemporary veterinarian's most important pieces of equipment.

But back in the early 1980s, ultrasound for all species was still in its infancy. Use of the technology in Australia had begun some twenty years earlier, with the 1959 establishment of an Ultrasound Research Section within the Commonwealth Acoustic Laboratories. Later renamed the Ultrasonics Institute (UI), the institute rapidly garnered recognition as one of the leading research groups in the world. Unlike other similar organisations, the UI was predominantly manned and 'projects initiated by a nucleus of engineers and physicists rather than clinicians ... [with] technical advances the heart of the Institute's work.' Although technical staff collaborated closely with clinicians in Sydney teaching hospitals, the institute's focus on technological advancement – as opposed to a single specific practical application – was a subtle but vital distinction that enabled the UI's broadscale investigation of ultrasound's possibilities without being restricted to focusing on a single medical field. The resulting advancements could be applied to multiple medical disciplines and, as time went on, tailored according to specific needs.

By 1976, the institute had put into circulation a machine called the UI Octoson. As the name implies, it featured eight probes or 'transducers', the electronic devices which convert energy from one form into another. In ultrasound, the transducer is both emitter and receiver, producing 'sound waves that bounce off body tissues and make echoes' which it then receives and sends to a monitor to create an image. The Octoson's eight transducers were on a single circular arm; mechanically linked, they scanned simultaneously but served as independent transmitters and receivers which operated in longitudinal, transverse and oblique planes. When used to scan pregnant women, the Octoson was encased in a water bath beneath a 'waterbed' on which the woman lay prone. It was this device which UQ possessed from sometime in the late 1970s.

In 1981, Reg and Joy's third son, Roess, was in his fifth year studying medicine at UQ. Like his brothers before him, Roess boarded at King's College during the week, but returned home to Oakey most weekends, working around the property to help support himself. His studies invariably cropped up in conversation. By this point, UQ had owned the Octoson for some years, but medical students' experience with the device, and ultrasound more broadly, was non-existent. This reluctance to teach ultrasound in the early 1980s was doubtless due to UQ's use of the device for research purposes – and no doubt also the hefty $100,000 price tag (almost $650,000 in 2020). It was important, however, to provide some broad-brush familiarisation and Roess and his cohort received a brief overview during a radiology lecture. This precipitated a discussion about the technology around the dinner table in Oakey that weekend and it became clear that collaboration in the Pascoe family was not limited to the vets.

Speaking with his father left Roess afire with enthusiasm. It was unorthodox for a lowly medical student to encroach, uninvited, on a lecturer's time, but Roess approached the head of the Department of Radio-Diagnosis, a British professor of radiology by the name of Dr Hiram Baddeley. Roess explained Reg's desire to further explore the use of ultrasound in equine medicine by trialling the technology on pregnant mares and suggested that it was an experiment worthy of UQ's involvement. 'I had to get [Baddeley] to understand that I wasn't just talking about some country vet. This was a guy who'd done some stuff.'

The proposition may have seemed bizarre to Baddeley, but the idea of expanding the use of ultrasound beyond human medicine was tantalising. What Roess described offered the opportunity to continue testing the technology and see how its general principles might be adapted. He had Baddeley's interest and the wheels were set in motion.

By this stage, Reg's relationship with UQ was well-established. He was already a widely renowned veterinarian, a valuable alumnus, and in the preceding quarter-century he had supported the UQ Veterinary School as a guest lecturer and external examiner. Doubtless, his long-standing relationship with the university – though external to the Medical School – played some role in the ultrasound partnership. As the Head of Department, Baddeley's name is inscribed on the UQ research contract and it was most likely Baddeley who evaluated the project and deemed the concept interesting enough to warrant the university's investment.

A radiologist called Mark Benson worked most closely with Reg. Like Baddeley, Mark is a British doctor. He moved to Australia in 1979 to work at UQ as a senior lecturer, bringing with him what he modestly described as 'a reasonable amount of ultrasound experience.' Together with his wife, Mark (and possibly Baddeley) drove to Oakey to meet Reg and discuss the architecture of the 'experiment.' Bringing one of UQ's small, suitcase-sized ultrasound machines, Mark spent between two to four sessions guiding Reg in its use.

As with manual palpation, the ultrasound of mares is conducted trans-rectally and Mark recalled 'putting on the long white glove ... to try and keep some of the muck out from your armpits.' Once Reg inserted the transducer head into the mare's rectum and began scanning, Mark advised him how to position the probe, describing how increasing or decreasing signal volume or changing signal pattern affected the scan's quality. Their experiment brought together two distinct skills in pursuit of one goal. Mark contributed an understanding of, and wealth of practical experience with, ultrasound that Reg lacked; yet its successful application relied on Reg's expertise with the equine reproductive system, which enabled him to translate Mark's explanation of the visual data to correspond with the biological structures with which he was so familiar. Reg was utterly absorbed. As he began to grasp the new technology's intricacies and it transformed from a mystery into a useable tool, a smile spread across his face.

Almost forty years later, OVH veterinarian Max Wilson still remembered the thrill of seeing the first identifiable image resolve upon the scanner's screen. This moment of revelation was 'mind-blowing', particularly for Reg. For more than two decades, he'd manually palpated mares but, as Max pointed out, 'good and all as

Reg was, it had always previously been impossible to diagnose twins until almost thirty days when it was very difficult (if not impossible) to reduce them.' Ultrasound enabled detection at fourteen to sixteen days' gestation, at which point the vet could carefully 'squeeze' one follicle and destroy it to ensure the safe maturation of the other foetus. Reg quickly perfected the technique.

In 1982, the International Symposium on Equine Reproduction (ISER) in Sydney featured developments relating to ultrasound, led by British veterinarian 'Twink' Allen. Eric Palmer had demonstrated his methods to Twink soon after his own 1980 Aloka scanner experiment, and Twink had arranged the purchase of an identical machine for the National Stud at Newmarket. When the more moveable and agile Fisher scanner was developed in Scotland, Twink brought both this device and his understanding of equine ultrasound to Australia. At the Sydney Vet School, he and a colleague demonstrated the scanner to several equine stud vets – including Reg.

Between Twink's demonstration of the newer Fisher scanner, David's work in the US, and Reg's own experiments with UQ's machine the year before, he was convinced of the emerging technology's importance in equine reproductive science. He secured a QERF grant to purchase a Fisher scanner for OVH – just how he did so is somewhat murky, and the nature of this murkiness warrants a brief detour. Why? Because, as Joy recalled in 2020, Reg acquired the scanner because he 'persuaded Russ Hinze, as Minister for Racing, to donate the probe from the QERF funds.' Max Wilson also noted Hinze's involvement, remarking that the grant came 'from Russ Hinze and part of the deal was that I had to undertake more study with it [the ultrasound scanner] and present some papers.'

Reg's acquaintance with Russ Hinze – the infamous Queensland politician whose multiple portfolios in the 1980s earnt him the moniker 'Minister for Everything' – was clearly important. Yet the precise nature of the association, and what role it played in the grant process, is unclear. The two men came, ostensibly, from similar backgrounds. A decade older than Reg, Hinze was the son of a dairy farmer and had been born in the then-rural region of Oxenford. Although now a suburb of the City of Gold Coast – and in 2020 best known for the gargantuan attractions of Warner Bros. Movie World and Wet'n'Wild – Oxenford only underwent residential development in the 1980s; prior to this, it was a rural area, with dairy farming the livelihood for many local families. Hinze was a dairy farmer himself prior to entering politics. After his death in 1991, Queensland Labor Premier Wayne Goss remembered him as 'forthright' – a descriptor few would hesitate to ascribe to Reg too.

Yet that's where the similarities end. Hinze's father was a 'farmer of some influence' and the family owned the Oxenford Hotel. In other words, Hinze was well-accustomed to both money and power, two vital themes which underpinned his political life. In the 1987 Commission of Inquiry into Possible Illegal Activities and Associated Police Misconduct in Queensland (more commonly known as The Fitzgerald Inquiry), he was identified as corrupt, but he died in 1991 before facing court.

Hinze had little respect for Reg's vocation, at least outwardly. When the Minister for Racing arrived by helicopter with great commotion at a large race day in Toowoomba in the early 1980s, Joy recalled that his speech wasn't very complimentary to vets. Hinze recognised Reg that day, so clearly the two men were familiar with one another. As this book examines in detail later, Reg had already performed several high-profile consultancy roles for the federal government by this point and was active within various state-level equine and veterinary organisations. He was also, inevitably, well-known in the Queensland racing industry, in which Hinze was deeply invested both politically and personally. Hinze owned over 150 racehorses (some identified this, in the Minister for Racing, as a conflict of interests; he averred it was, instead, a *convergence* of interests').

Yet, as one public servant recalled, 'if you asked for his assistance in helping your shire out, or resolving a local government problem, Russ Hinze would fix it ... if Russ Hinze gave you his word on something it would get done with no further follow up of the minister ever needed.' It was, and remains, a rare trait and one Reg would have respected. Whatever he thought of Hinze's methods or conduct, Reg undoubtedly recognised the value in a minister who was passionate about racing and, just as vitally, in a man who followed through on his promises. Pragmatic to the bone as he was, Reg's 'persuasion' of Russ Hinze to provide the funding for the Fisher scanner demonstrated his ability to put aside personal judgement to achieve a goal, particularly when it was an important one.

The development of equine reproductive ultrasound, Reg recorded, was 'one of the greatest advancements in public relations between veterinarians and stud masters in the breed industry this century, as it focused attention on the scan screen and removed so many of the doubts about the pregnancy test that embryonic abortion engendered. In our practice, [the addition of the ultrasound machine] also meant the introduction of improved covered examination areas on the farms and more importantly, the use of crushes (stocks) greatly improved the safety for veterinarians.'

The modifications Reg referred to were necessary to use the scanner with any degree of efficiency: the Fisher was a huge, heavy machine and removing it from the car at each stud was fraught with risk and guaranteed to waste valuable time. Instead, Reg had studs create a space for mare examinations which included the installation of a 'crush.' Also known in North America as a 'squeeze chute' or 'stock', a crush is a strongly built stall designed to hold horses and cattle still while they are examined or treated, reducing danger to both human and livestock. The addition of this structure to local studs meant Reg could reverse up to the stocks and use the Fisher scanner from the boot without having to remove it from the car.

The addition of the Fisher precipitated other changes too such as a revision of OVH's fee structure. Reg was charging clients $10 for a palpation at the time (which in 2020 equated to just under $40) but told the practice's accounts manager, Shirl, to charge $12 for an ultrasound scan. Misunderstanding him, Shirl billed clients *$22*. Most clients were unperturbed, thanks to the newness of the technology and Reg's dominance of the equine reproductive market, which meant they had little point of comparison. Only one client complained – Reg's old friend Col McAlpine from Eureka. Col ended up paying $12, but the fee stayed at $22 for everyone else.

As ultrasound attracted more and more interest, the technology continued to develop. Machines have progressively become smaller and more portable, including battery-powered models with smaller probes that are yet more powerful and provide greater range for improved adaptability. Reg ensured OVH remained abreast of these changes. In 1986, four years after the initial grant-funded purchase of the Fisher prototype, OVH bought several of the newer models for the practice's three full-time equine reproduction vets. The Aloka 120 scanners were smaller and portable, a big improvement over the much-larger Fisher device that Reg had described as 'clumsy', and their acquisition enhanced the clinic's reputation as equine reproduction specialists.

David Pascoe remarked in a 1996 news article that Reg conducted 'groundbreaking and pioneering work in horse reproduction in the 1970s' and this is certainly true; however, his exploratory work into ultrasound in the early 1980s was just as important. He was among the first Australian vets to experiment with ultrasound's potential and his work laid a valuable foundation for ongoing development both at OVH and beyond. In 1985, in conjunction with a US-based vet, Reg and David refined the syllabus of the Sydney Post-Graduate Foundation ultrasound workshop, speaking together on the technology's application.

With David's return to Australia in 1985 and knowing that his son's passion lay in equine reproduction, Reg shifted his clinical focus to surgery. David was subsequently awarded a Fellowship in Animal Reproduction specialising in Equine Reproduction from the Australian College of Veterinary Surgeons in 1988. The following year, he became both a Registered Specialist in Equine Reproduction through the ACVS and an OVH partner. Reg ceded the reins of control to David in this area, but retained a keen interest in equine reproduction. The mainstay of his clinical work for decades, Reg's expertise was extremely valuable.

David was predominantly responsible for the succession of equine reproductive specialists who travelled to live and work in Oakey over the coming decade and more, but Reg's influence was undeniable – pursuing the individuals he thought best-suited to joining the OVH team was an endeavour in which David followed in his father's footsteps. These vets often came at David's invitation, but Reg remained OVH's leader and director, and in conjunction with his breadth and depth of veterinary knowledge, this meant he had a lasting influence on all OVH veterinarians' lives and careers.

The world-renowned British expert in equine reproduction Jonathan Pycock was finishing a PhD in mare infertility in the late

1980s when he attended the Newmarket conference and met David Pascoe. As the pair chatted, David asked whether Jonathan would be interested in coming to Australia for a breeding season. The proposition was intriguing. A relatively recent graduate, Jonathan had heard of the Pascoe practice and as he drew close to the end of his PhD, here was a unique opportunity to get some practical experience.

Jonathan recalled in 2019 that it seemed to him that Reg and David 'wanted somebody that had a degree or clinical skill but hadn't necessarily done several years working in a practice situation.' He fit the bill perfectly; that he'd recently completed his PhD must have 'made me a more attractive proposition to employ.' The PhD was evidence of his keen interest in continued learning and a willingness to explore new ideas – a strong drawcard. David was particularly keen; he'd seen Jonathan's presentations and read his papers and sensed the eager young Brit would be a valuable addition.

Reg followed up the verbal invitation with a letter and, echoing David's sentiments, offered Jonathan a job at OVH for five months over the 1989 breeding season. Not long after the letter arrived, Jonathan touched down in Australia in August 1989. Thirty years later, he wryly described himself as having 'been quite a protected English boy up to that stage' and both the country and Reg came as a bit of a culture shock. In turn, he surprised Reg more than he knew.

On the day of his arrival, Reg and Joy travelled together from Oakey to Brisbane's International Airport. They sat, waiting, while passengers disembarked. A young man emerged from customs clearance looking somewhat scruffy and holding a windsurf board.

'Well, that's not him,' Reg said to Joy. The young man sat down and got comfortable, pulling out a book, and Reg couldn't resist another little quip, 'At least he's got his book the right way up.' The rest of the arrivals gradually dispersed and only the young man, book and board to hand, remained. Reg and Joy swallowed their surprise, gathered Jonathan up and took him home.

If his appearance at the airport was unexpected, it was nothing compared to what he was about to encounter. Coming from England's autumn made the Queensland spring heat a shock, and Reg wasn't interested in pandering to anyone who found it hard to acclimatise. Driving together one day early in Jonathan's stay, the oppressive temperatures got the better of the younger man; as the car's sweltering heat closed in on him like a great, suffocating fist, he voiced the frustration he'd been bottling up. When he'd finished, Reg pointed to the handle that wound the window down. There would be little sympathy for Jonathan's climate woes.

Reg and Joy hosted Jonathan for the first month of his visit. The brief tenancy gave the two men a chance to become acquainted outside the practice and they struck up an amiable, relaxed friendship. Jonathan had always thought himself an early riser, but was in awe of Reg's routine 3.30 a.m. starts. In the dark stillness of pre-dawn, the creaking of Reg's sock-clad feet padding around the house woke the young Brit and made sense of the household's nine o'clock bedtime.

Much of Jonathan's role comprised working at Murray and Betty-Ann Wise's Bahram Stud Farm. Reg's forty-year friendship with Murray had long offered a safe proving ground for OVH's junior vets: both David Pascoe and Glen Laws, DJ's son, completed work experience there, providing Murray a unique perspective on Reg's hard but fair leadership. 'He made men out of them,' Murray once said. But Reg's actions were neither arbitrary nor unjustly harsh; he sought to instil a strong work ethic, a passion for veterinary science and a commitment to professional mastery. 'If you worked and respected him, he'd look after you. He was a great man. I've met about five outstanding men in my life and he's certainly one of them.'

Their association began in the early 1970s, when renowned thoroughbred stud Gainsborough Lodge was at its zenith. Gainsborough Lodge was the passion project of an entrepreneur called Alfred Grant. In the late 1960s, having built a substantial fortune through various agricultural endeavours and property development, Grant dreamt of 'establishing one of the finest horse studs in the country.' He sunk millions into the creation of a dual-location stud on the outskirts of Toowoomba and by 1974, it 'was the largest and possibly best-equipped stud in the southern hemisphere with an airstrip, a horse hospital and an all-weather training track alongside architecturally designed breeding barns and training stables. In 1976, Grant sold more than one hundred yearlings.'

Gainsborough was a huge business and Reg was the chief vet. He was likely involved from the stud's earliest days; it's also likely that a large portion of his early investigations in equine medicine, particularly reproduction, occurred there.

Murray Wise started working at Gainsborough as a general hand in the early 1970s and worked his way up to manager before leaving to open Bahram. He and Reg worked closely together and a strong friendship, based on mutual respect, quickly grew. Murray trusted Reg implicitly and relied upon his professional judgement, deeming his expertise superior to most other vets', especially when the stakes were high, such as during the 'Magic Millions.'

The Magic Millions describes itself as Australia's premier thoroughbred sales company and holds its famous eponymous flagship event on the Gold Coast every January – an extravaganza which in 2020 ran to twelve days, featuring a carnival, race day and yearling sale. As the name suggests, millions of dollars change hands both in racing purses and the purchase of some of Australia's finest young horses. The associated pressure of the event for breeders and stud managers is intense and when one of Murray's horses got sick one year, everyone was understandably worried. The event has its own team of skilled vets on staff to inspect horses prior to racing or sale, but knowing Reg was there was enough for Murray to ask the vet to hand over the case: as far as he was concerned, there was no one better.

When Murray and his wife, Betty-Ann, established their stud at Westbrook, Reg handled their work. It began as a small operation, comprising only a 'little rail behind a box bay' where Reg examined the mares, but Bahram benefitted from Reg's tenacity as surely as any other stud on the Darling Downs. His research efforts – facilitated through his work at Gainsborough and his strong cooperative relationships with other horse farms – were crucial to the unceasing pursuit of success. As Murray recalled, Reg 'had so many different innovations for getting mares in foal ... He was light years ahead of everyone.'

What remained uppermost in Murray's mind was Reg's use of placental assessment to guide his recommendations for rebreeding. Every mare's placenta was examined post-delivery; if it weighed more than 12 pounds (roughly 5.4 kilograms), Reg wouldn't allow the mare to be serviced on her foaling heat. The term 'foaling heat' refers to a mare's first oestrus or 'heat' after delivering her foal. It usually begins between six to eight days post-partum, and most studs capitalise on this oestrus to get the mare in foal again. This 'foal heat breeding' is designed to accommodate the restrictions of the official thoroughbred breeding season to ensure foals are born at the optimal time.

Foaling date matters; in fact, it's of crucial importance. In Australia, every horse's 'official' birthday is the first of August, regardless of their actual date of birth. (In the northern hemisphere, where the breeding season runs from February to July, the official thoroughbred birthday is the first of January). Foals born earlier in the season will be more mature than their peers when it comes to their official first birthday and these older foals typically cope better with the demands of racing when the two-year-old racing season begins. Racing younger, potentially smaller foals not only leads to poorer performance (affecting the foal's market value), but also brings a greater risk of injury. A breeder wanting to ensure their foals are born at the 'right' time will use foal heat breeding to keep successive delivery dates as close together as possible.

The alternative is to wait until the mare's second oestrus, usually thirty days from foaling. This delays the mare's delivery date for her subsequent foal by a month but over time and successive deliveries, her foaling date will become too late in the season. This will eventually require the owner to leave the mare unbred for a year to bring her next delivery back within the season window. It's a decision which has ramifications for a breeder and so being able to accurately determine a mare's suitability for foal heat breeding is important. Even more crucially, the placenta weight provides a vital indicator of 'infectious and non-infectious agents that may affect foal mortality.'

Recognising and accurately interpreting these signs allows owners and vets to identify at-risk foals and implement preventative or remedial treatments to save the newborn. And, of course, placental analysis extends far beyond simply weight: even the seemingly simple task of ensuring the whole placenta has been delivered is vital. Regardless of animal species, placental retention (where part or all of the placenta remains in the uterus) poses a serious risk to the mother and can lead to infection. Detailed examination of the mare's placenta provides the vet fundamental data to ensure a healthy mare and foal.

But was Reg really revolutionary in his approach? Placental examination began in Venice, Italy in 1598, almost four centuries before Reg treated mares at Gainsborough Lodge, however the practice has 'a long but discontinuous history.' It may have originated in the late sixteenth century, but interest waned for the most part until the late 1800s, almost three centuries later. Yet again attention petered out. The renewed recognition can be traced to a 1952 paper published in a British scientific journal but even then, the profession's interest was gradual. Much of the contemporary literature on the subject stems from the early-mid 1970s onwards and while Reg may not have invented the concept, his awareness and application of the technique around the same time – and possibly earlier – suggests that he was again operating at the forefront of contemporary knowledge.

He continually sought excellence for the region's horse farms. Breeders work very hard to make their studs a success; Scott McAlpine wryly noted, 'It's a seven-day-a-week, twenty-eight-hours-a-day [job]: not twenty-four, because it never stops ... But that's what we do. We work all day, and we stay up [night] after night to get our foals on the ground and make sure we're doing a good job.' Doubtless, the shared sense of purpose underpinned these deep and lasting friendships.

When Jonathan Pycock arrived at Bahram for the 1989 breeding season, Murray and Betty-Ann welcomed him warmly. It was clear to Jonathan that Reg was held in 'a tremendous respect both among vets and among his clients.' The Wises were no exception. Their ready acceptance of Jonathan exemplified the trust that the OVH partners had built within the community over the years: clients knew that a vet sent to them could be relied upon to do the right thing. It was a responsibility of which OVH vets could not help but be aware, and one which they took seriously.

On Jonathan's first day out at Bahram, he got ready to scan a mare while Murray watched and the mare's foal lingered nearby. It's common practice to leave foals un-haltered when treating their mothers: if the mare is haltered and lead away, the foal will follow and, once she comes to a stop, the foal will stay near its mother. Jonathan prepared his equipment and inserted the probe to begin scanning, hands steady despite the first-day jitters. It was a simple enough process and a procedure with which he was familiar, though the location was new, and he probably felt Reg's eyes boring into him as he worked, even from the distance of OVH. The ultrasound scanner he was holding was also new, the foal was untethered, and as Jonathan concentrated on the display, the foal, thrilled at her unusual freedom, kicked up her heels and began running around the stocks. She dashed past Jonathan and her neat little hooves caught the cable that connects the body of the scanner to the transducer, yanking it free and sending the scanner clattering to the hard concrete floor.

Jonathan went pale.

'Oh god,' he said to Murray, visions of his future dancing before his eyes as he picked the machine up. 'I have to go back and tell Reg.' He'd only just arrived and now he might have broken a very expensive piece of equipment. Thankfully, the machine was (mostly) in one piece, but there were some wobbly parts that definitely weren't wobbly before.

'He thought he'd get killed,' Murray recalled, chortling at the memory of the young man's horror. Jonathan's mind worked quickly. If he could fix the hopefully only cosmetic damage before Reg found out – well, then, there was no *real* reason for Reg to know, was there? All he needed was someone to help him tighten up the connections and tape the machine in any rickety spots. He packed up the scanner and swung out of Bahram. Pulling into the OVH carpark not long after, he slunk into the clinic. He avoided Reg long enough to collar Glen Laws with a plea for help; together, they 'managed to fix the machine pretty quickly albeit with a bit of insulating tape over it like a large band-aid.' Reg appeared in the doorway as Glen and Jonathan completed the last of their emergency surgery.

'What are you doing back so soon?' Reg asked Jonathan, his formidable grey brows beetling at the sight of his newest vet in the clinic, rather than out handling Murray's mares.

'Nothing serious,' Jonathan said breezily, though his heart must have been galloping. 'I just forgot something – but here! See? I have it now.' He ran past Reg out to the car and powered away from OVH, sending a silent prayer skyward that the scanner would perform smoothly. It did. The relief must have been heady as he and Murray had a good laugh about the whole debacle – but they never did tell Reg.

At the end of the 1989 breeding season, Reg and David asked Jonathan to come back the following year. It was a good sign, Jonathan figured. 'I couldn't have been too bad.' In fact, he was flattered, later remarking, 'Among the accolades I have been fortunate to achieve, being asked to go back to work for the Aussie luminary remains right up there.'

Jonathon's two breeding seasons while at OVH were crucial formative experiences, not only shaping his early career, but also providing him with an advantage in the UK upon his return. Working with Australian studs entailed handling a far greater number of horses than he'd been used to in the UK; busy days on the Downs meant examining in excess of a hundred mares. Then there was the technical side of the work: the OVH approach to equine reproduction seemed more advanced than what was being done in the UK. There were several techniques used in Oakey that Jonathon hadn't previously encountered, and where common UK practice typically began scanning mares from around day seventeen, OVH started scanning by day fourteen. Earlier scanning and more regular examinations allowed OVH to better monitor mares' fertility prior to insemination, facilitating more targeted (and thus more effective) insemination, while earlier conception checks meant it was possible to recover mares sooner if they had failed to conceive.

The other crucial facet of Jonathon's experience in Australia, of course, was Reg. Jonathon worked most closely with David – the lead veterinarian handling the practice's reproductive clients – but he spent a commensurate amount of time with Reg, and their interactions left an indelible mark. Jonathon credited Reg as a major influence in his later and notable professional success. For a vet, the breeding season comprises long, hard days: during Jonathon's seasons at OVH, Mondays, Wednesdays and Fridays were the busiest for stud work, rising early and returning between 4 and 5 p.m. Tuesdays and Thursdays were slightly less frenetic, and the day's visits might be complete by 2 p.m. With his primary responsibilities fulfilled, he took the opportunity to head into the practice where he spent countless hours observing Reg at work. No matter what task was at hand, Reg would discuss what he was doing. For Jonathon, these conversations were priceless. Reg 'had a lot to give ... he was obviously a very clever chap anyway, but he had come across so many things.' He possessed 'a tremendous insight' and his stories didn't just centre on unusual veterinary cases.

Another OVH vet recalled that 'a lot of times while [Reg] was in surgery he would just be talking through about what was going on and trying to be logical.'[12] Doing so enthused the vets who worked with him: through his willingness to discuss different views and ideas he taught them *how* to think not just *what* to think. This approach made Reg's formidable mind easily accessible, allowing insight into his problem-solving in action.

Respecting others' processes and giving them the space to work through their ideas was a mainstay of Reg's career. As Jonathon Pycock remarked, 'You always felt Reg listened to your opinion about something when you were discussing it.' Reg's enthusiasm for teaching was self-evident, though he 'expected people to work really hard, if you were prepared to work hard, he would give you the benefit of his time.' And Reg's time was a gift, for it comprised his incredible range of both knowledge and practical experience. Such professional expertise, Jonathon noted, was rare in those days and even rarer today; in the contemporary profession, vets are increasingly specialised and there is nothing comparable to 'Reg's depth of knowledge across equine subjects.' This wide-ranging interest, combined with Reg's attention to detail and his ability to observe and interrogate clinical signs to unravel a problem, made him unique. As Jonathon once said, excluding visionary UK vet Peter Rossdale, he has never come across anyone he would equate with Reg Pascoe.

Arthroscopy in Equine Surgery

A fairly new technique for joint evaluation, arthroscopy is used across both human medicine and veterinary science. Via a small incision in the skin, a narrow, rigid camera on a tube called an endoscope is inserted to enable the examination of the internal structures of a joint. Nowadays, human arthroscopic surgery is one of the most common orthopaedic procedures in the world. The technique was first recorded in 1912 but only became common for humans in the 1950s and 1960s.

Equine arthroscopic surgery was developed in the 1970s, spearheaded by a New Zealand vet called Wayne McIlwraith who was completing a large animal surgical residency at Indiana's Purdue University. In 1976, after attending a medical conference on arthroscopy of the human knee, McIlwraith began developing the technique in horses, providing courses at Colorado State University from 1983. The following year, he published the first edition of his landmark textbook, *Diagnostic and Surgical Arthroscopy in the Horse*, republished in 2014 in a fourth edition.

Reg was a long way from Colorado but he recorded that in 1984, the 'introduction of arthroscopy to equine surgery increased the range of very successful surgical cases which were less invasive and a less dangerous approach to joint repair.' Here, too, he was at the forefront. The University of Sydney, considered 'the most advanced of the Australian University Equine Centres' at the time, does not appear to have been using arthroscopy at this point. Andrew Dart, who joined OVH in 1986 after a year-long residency at the university, noted, 'I would be confident [Reg] would have been the first or one of the first surgeons to be using this technology in Australasia.'

Arthroscopy revolutionised the treatment of joint injuries. Surgery on horses' knees often required the removal of fragments of bone that had chipped away from the joint and were aggravating the soft tissue, causing swelling and pain. 'Before arthroscopic surgery,' Scotty McAlpine recalled, vets 'made the incision, they found the chip and they took it out with pliers.' This brute-force method caused greater trauma to the joint, meaning more pain and longer convalescence and, worse, that an expensive racehorse may not fully recover. Arthroscopy was more precise and gentler on the joint tissue, meaning less damage in the process and a quicker, less painful recovery.

Reg taught himself arthroscopy using cadaver limbs before attempting the procedure on a live patient. By the time Andrew Dart joined OVH in 1986, Reg was routinely using arthroscopy on thoroughbred racehorses, though without the later ubiquitous use of a video camera and display monitor. In those early days, Reg looked through a lens into the joint. He told a reporter in 1986 that OVH's most common surgery was on the knee, and this hadn't changed over a decade later. A 1999 newspaper article recorded his comments that the 'biggest percentage of horses we operate on are thoroughbreds. In this field, the most common type of surgery is the removal of bone chips and operating to correct breathing problems.' OVH later added a full arthroscopic surgical suite, completed in 1992 and thankfully, Reg noted, with the 'welcome addition of a video camera and monitor.'

As he had after the other emergence of other procedures, Reg studied the new apparatus until its use was as easy as breathing. Then, he shared it. His friend Bruce Pott recalled Reg's willingness to travel to Bruce's Townsville clinic, allowing Bruce to offer North Queensland clients the option to have an equine specialist treat their horse. The pair collaborated in solving problems and Bruce observed new techniques that might otherwise have been inaccessible. Watching Reg operate enabled Bruce to develop the technique in his own time and, as Reg once had, he used cadaver legs that he kept in the freezer. Eventually he bought his own machine.

Like ultrasound, arthroscopy has become a crucial tool in the veterinarian's toolbox and Reg's work played a role in the technology's inception in Australia. His introduction and championing of the technique from the early 1980s was a crucial part of his ongoing commitment to keeping up with new technologies and working at the vanguard of veterinary science in Australasia.

Equine Euthanasia

Reg was pragmatic: if it was simple and it worked, there was no need to complicate it. This was true in every facet of his life and it extended to a task that many find the most distasteful and distressing: euthanasia. Vets love animals and are passionate about saving them, but they also understand the effects of pain, disease and injury. Euthanasia is never a desirable option, but it is *an* option and one that vets must evaluate the necessity for and, when required, perform with care.

There are a variety of methods for euthanising a horse, a process which, due to their size, is more complex than humanely putting to sleep smaller companion animals such as cats and dogs. In 2021, one of the most common approaches is to sedate the horse before injecting it with drugs that depress the central nervous system; the combination of barbiturates and anaesthetics are administered in large enough quantity to quickly put the horse to sleep. There are times, however, when this method isn't feasible. There may be no vet nearby (procurement of these drugs is limited to licensed professionals), or no way of safely disposing of the remains, which are usually cremated to prevent poisoning the ground or other animals. The horse may be in shock, which impairs blood circulation and thus drug efficacy, or their distress may make it impossible to give an injection quickly and effectively. In such instances, it's essential to humanely euthanise the horse as soon as possible to spare it further pain.

There are two methods, both of which can be confronting. Exsanguination or 'bleeding out' is horrific to consider, but horses are typically rendered unconscious, after which death is quick and painless. Alternatively, and though it may seem counterintuitive, shooting a horse in the head is one of the kindest methods. Similarly quick and painless when done correctly, it's also the safest and surest option because it doesn't require close contact with the horse, which allows the quick euthanasia of skittish or little-handled horses. For these reasons and others, OVH always performed euthanasia by gunshot.

A US vet called Dorraine Waldow, who spent time in Oakey during the mid-1990s, recalled her first experiences using gunshot. Juxtaposed with the challenging and at times conceivably dangerous alternative of trying to pharmaceutically euthanise a horse as she had back home, Dorraine said 'the practicality of shooting horses ... was unbelievable ... When a horse is throwing itself on the ground, to try to inject 100ccs of thick fluid into his jugular vein is really hard.' Injection in these circumstances might not only be difficult but dangerous to the vet; other sources point out that such situations also delay death, prolonging the horse's suffering.

Reg recognised the necessity of skilful euthanasia by gunshot. Accuracy was vital to ensure the horse didn't suffer, and speed was necessary to minimise its anxiety; Reg ensured he was quick and that he never missed, and he impressed upon his staff the humane need for both.

'You have to show me where to shoot and how to do this,' Dorraine said to Reg, the first time she was faced with a horse that had to be euthanised.

'This is the way you do it,' Reg said, walking over and pulling the pistol from his pocket. Dorraine was standing near the horse as Reg placed the pistol muzzle on the horse's forehead. 'Right here,' he said, 'like this,' and pulled the trigger. The horse dropped immediately by Dorraine's feet, a sharp, clear memory she never forgot. 'It was always sad that the horse was being euthanised,' she remembered, 'but [shooting them is] so fast and so efficient.'

Fostering Vet–Farrier Relationships

Reg's career was characterised by a remarkable prescience. This foresight spoke to his emotional and intellectual investment in his field. His role in integrating farriers into routine veterinary medicine exemplifies his ability to anticipate and even precipitate the future trajectory of veterinary science. In simple terms, a farrier is someone who shoes horses. It's likely that in Reg's early career this description would have been considered apt; today, it's widely accepted that it does little justice to 'highly skilled equine hoof-care professionals.'

In contemporary veterinary science, there are few vets worth their salt who don't work in close conjunction with a trusted farrier when handling cases of lameness. Vet conferences will regularly include farriers in the program. There are now equine podiatry clinics, and at some universities there are in-house farriers who work with veterinarians to address hoof and lower limb issues. But what is nowadays so routine as to barely rate a mention was once rare.

Reg's interest in the treatment of horse lameness began around the time he presented a lecture in 1977 on 'The treatment of hoof abnormalities, contracted hooves, hoof cracks and the use of acrylics in hoof repair.' It was not until roughly ten years later, however, that he began to actively bridge the gap between vets and farriers. As his exposure to different instances of lameness and lower limb complaints grew, he realised that as much as 90 per cent of the lameness cases originated from the lower leg and were intricately tied to the hoof. Poor hoof health, hoof care practices and the skills of the farrier shoeing the horse were all implicated: good shoeing practices meant sound (or at least sounder) horses. Surgical expertise could only do so much if the horse was not being shod correctly. By the late 1980s, Reg was convinced how important correct shoeing was as a method of reducing and treating lameness – and the associated requirement for a close working relationship between vets and farriers.

The farrier industry in Australia was, and remains, unregulated, and this gives rise to countless different paths to finding work, and countless variations in quality. The industry in the 1980s and 1990s was characterised by wide discrepancy in standards and was populated by farriers whose training ranged from formal apprenticeships with a master craftsman to next to nothing at all. It was likely the reason for the disconnect between farriers and vets: certainly, the two professions kept their distance, invariably to the horse's detriment. Reg saw the cost. The accepted approach of treating the horse in-clinic and sending it home with instructions to be conveyed to the farrier – either by the owner or by the vet at another time – meant messages got mixed and treatment didn't always accord to what was needed. A closer working relationship between vet and farrier would produce far better results.

Arriving at UC Davis in mid-1988, Andrew Dart saw evidence of this kind of vet–farrier association and thinks that 'perhaps that was where Reg got a little bit of the idea.' The truth is more convoluted. John Pascoe's work at UC Davis, combined with Reg's own dedication to remaining abreast of current veterinary developments meant that any hint of such collaboration at Davis would have registered on Reg's radar. There were, however, events closer to home which likely played a bigger part in the process.

A skilled horseman, trainer and farrier called Keith Swan was working in Ipswich in the 1980s. He had attended Oklahoma's Farrier's College in 1976 and subsequently began teaching shoeing principles to both farriers and laypeople. He had 'no particular formal training even in farriery but because of his intelligence and his enthusiasm, made himself into an eminent farrier.' In 1986, he began working with a Queensland veterinarian by the name of Chris Pollitt who had a keen interest in equine hoof issues. The two men coordinated the first Australian vet–farrier conference during the earlier years of their relationship, a choice which saw 'many veterinarians in the district [scold Chris] for even ever considering inviting farriers under the same roof, into the same auditorium as qualified veterinarians; they would not attend, and they thought it was a retrograde step. But Reg was all for it.'

The conference was a success, though Reg disagreed with Chris's opinion on a possible cause of cases of club foot in foals. Reg, Chris remembered, 'could be a wonderful warm, friendly individual and at the other side, he could be an acerbic, critical, unsmiling, intimidating presence. And I think that latter was always what he wanted to project towards me.'

Yet it was Chris's work with Keith Swan that seems to have brought Reg and Keith into contact. If Reg needed to connect with a great farrier to improve the integration of farriery and veterinary science, he found that person in Keith Swan. Keith's own expertise remains legend in the industry – what Keith '[didn't] know about a horse's hoof is not worth knowing' – and so he was the perfect partner for Reg's newest endeavour. That Keith was to a large extent self-taught and had forged his own success through the combination of his intelligence and drive to excel, gained Reg's respect and provided a firm foundation for their friendship.

Reg and Keith formed a strong, 'brotherly sort of partnership' and their collaboration quickly became routine. Working at Oakey between 1986 and 1988, Andrew Dart recalled having one and sometimes two days a week reserved exclusively for horses with hoof problems. These were the days when Keith would come to OVH to work with Reg on sticky problems. To Dart, Reg and Keith's partnership in the mid-1980s was 'the first time that anyone I was aware of in the world' was exploring the benefits of vets working closely with farriers. Given Chris Pollitt's role, this assessment isn't entirely accurate, but Reg's partnership with Keith spanned a longer period and the treatment advances that they made together were important.

Bruce Donaldson worked as Keith's apprentice from March 1988, accompanying him on a visit to OVH every Tuesday. Every horse presenting with foot issues would be X-rayed and treated as Reg thought necessary before he consulted with Keith and Bruce, who shod the horses based on Reg's assessment. The benefits of working in close partnership with Keith – an experienced professional whose values and attitudes aligned with Reg's own – spoke for themselves.

Reg's path to advancing the cause lay in education: in 1992 and 1994, he presented papers with Keith espousing the importance of vet–farrier relationships at UQ and at Murdoch University in Western Australia. At the same time, Reg became involved with the Queensland branch of the Australian Farriers and Blacksmiths Association, serving as its patron from 1994 until 2012. His impact there was so marked, and the donation of his time so beneficial, that in 1996 the association established the annual Reg Pascoe Farrier Improvement Award. The prize is awarded to a junior farrier who is pursuing skill development through attending clinics and competitions.

Fighting Botulism in Horses

As one of his vets recalled, Reg 'was always ahead of the game.'[13] It's an accurate statement: Reg seemed to have an uncanny skill for perceiving gaps before – or independent of – others in his field. Once he had identified a deficiency, he set about finding a solution and would stay invested for as long as it took – decades, if necessary. Perhaps nowhere was this more evident than in his efforts to tackle botulism and his crucial role in the first successful use of an antitoxin in Toowoomba in 1987.

Botulism is a rare but often lethal form of poisoning, which horses typically contract by ingesting contaminated food or water, or by absorption through wound sites. Produced by a bacterial organism and presenting in seven known strains (types A through to G), botulism toxin is the deadliest in the world and horses are particularly sensitive to it; as one 2010 article dryly noted, 'it takes more botulism to kill a mouse than a horse.'

The toxin interrupts muscular nerve impulses by binding to nerve cell endings with debilitating results: horses become progressively weaker and less mobile and, in severe cases, paralysed. Horrifically, sensory nerves are unaffected, meaning that as a poisoned horse physically deteriorates, it continues to experience hunger, thirst, pain and anxiety. Without prompt treatment, botulism is almost always fatal. Prompt treatment consists of botulism antitoxin used in conjunction with antibiotics and supporting care. In the 1950s not only did no such remedy exist, but the general understanding of the disease was seriously inadequate.

Accordingly, when Reg became aware of a unique, recurrent illness in Oakey during his first year of practice in 1952, he began a long battle against botulism without fully comprehending what it was he was battling. Until around 1968, instances were sporadic and mostly confined to stock horses and children's ponies, but then the illnesses began to appear in stud farms too. By 1969, Reg remarked that he had 'narrowed the suspected cause of the deaths down to either botulism or brown snakebite', the symptoms of which 'are almost identical, with the only significant difference being that horses sweat more from the snakebite.'

By the following year, Reg 'had become determined to treat all foals for snakebite, but we managed to save only about one in ten. We then considered the dose to be inadequate, but further testing proved the dosage was more than sufficient. We therefore had to eliminate snakebite.' Despite a better understanding of the situation, the death toll remained high; the 16 per cent success rate was mostly due to good nursing and care by the foal's owner rather than clear treatment methodology. The situation must have been terrifying for stud owners on the Darling Downs: approximately 200 horses had died by 1988 and Reg estimated '95 per cent of all cases have been confined to a ridge of country in a line from Toowoomba through Wellcamp and Biddeston to Mt Tyson – making it the most intensive area for the disease in Australia.' Widely regarded as the 'nursery of the stud industry ... in Queensland', the Darling Downs' numerous pre-eminent thoroughbred and standardbred horse breeders faced devastating losses. Reg believed one thoroughbred stud alone had lost as many as 100 horses, ninety-five of whom were foals.

By 1980, he felt that he'd run out of options. 'It had to be botulism.' But with that established, what could he do? Type C and D botulism vaccines had long been available for treating cattle, because 'almost all cases of botulism in cattle ... in the southern hemisphere in general are due to botulinum types C and D.' But while some vaccines are effective across species, cattle vaccines didn't work on horses and botulism continued to cut a swathe through the local studs.

Part of the problem was that there was little interest among government laboratories in investigating the origins of the disease. Reg had been trying since the mid-1970s to interest an organisation in developing a vaccine, but the specific requirements and high costs meant many were reluctant to invest. With the illness isolated to the Downs, 'the Commonwealth Serum Laboratories said the idea was too uneconomic for such a small area.' Doggedly, Reg continued to, 'mumble in people's ears and grizzle about it' in an effort to garner support.

In 1985, he had the breakthrough he'd been waiting for. The Department of Primary Industries' Animal Research Institute in Brisbane approached him via a researcher called Dr Rod Thomas. Thomas was already conducting research into botulism on cattle and 'became deeply involved with the development of the vaccine.' Reg sent him samples from afflicted and dying foals and he was able to isolate type B botulism as the organism most commonly found in the horses suffering on the Darling Downs.

This was a remarkable discovery. For context, over thirty years later, the Western Australian government's agriculture advice about botulism in cattle is that 'Type B toxin is more often observed in Europe and northern America.' A 2010 report on a twelve-horse outbreak in Victoria noted that 'cases due to type B have been reported *mainly in Queensland*' [italics added]. More than twenty-five years after Rod Thomas identified the type B strain among the samples Reg had sent him, these remarks demonstrate the unique circumstances in which Reg operated and the rarity of type B botulism. Thomas's discovery also explained why Reg's attempts to treat affected horses with the common cattle botulism vaccine had failed: each type of botulism must be treated by its own, antigen-specific vaccine.

'Once [the strain] was isolated,' Reg said, 'the problem had been virtually solved.' All that remained was to develop a vaccine (to immunise horses against botulism) and an antitoxin (to treat those animals diagnosed with the disease). The antitoxin proved its worth in December 1987. Two months earlier, a single dose had failed to save the life of a Toowoomba foal, and Reg resolved to act more aggressively. When another colt presented with symptoms of botulism just before Christmas and didn't improve markedly after one dose of antitoxin, Reg administered another twelve hours later. The colt, who had been 'given just a 5 per cent chance of survival', began to noticeably improve within a few hours. Six days later, the colt was well enough to go home and seven weeks after the ordeal, the colt was joyfully racing the cars that sped past his paddock. It was a landmark moment, but despite the proven efficacy of the antitoxin, limited doses were available.

Vaccine manufacture was similarly limited; the DPI produced only 2000 doses total. But although Reg 'advocated a wide-spread vaccination program throughout the affected area of the Darling Downs', believing that annual vaccination of mares could prevent a recurrence of botulism in their foals, this did not occur. The localised nature of the problem made commercial production of the vaccine economically inviable. Reg seems to have accepted this with his usual equanimity: the hard work, after all, was done. 'I do believe the DPI will continue to provide doses,' he told the *Chronicle*'s reporter, Mark Bousen. 'At least they have all the information and knowledge available to do so – we have the answers now.'

Bousen remarked, 'Dr Pascoe tries to play down his role in the development of the vaccine and anti-toxin. However, there is no doubt his continued pressure, research and involvement were the major factors that led to their development.' Reg simply preferred 'to describe his victory after a thirty-five-year battle as "a satisfying win against disease",' but thirty years later, he remarked that his diagnosis of botulism in horses was one of his most difficult but rewarding successes. Over the decades, and while maintaining a busy clinic, he chipped away at such issues until he found an answer. In doing so, his investigations across the spectrum of equine medicine shaped Queensland and Australian veterinary science.

7
Growing Professional Veterinary Bodies

Reg entered the veterinary profession at a time when veterinary science in Australia was still in its infancy – both technically and organisationally. There was need for the growth that would transform a fledgling, semi-professional occupation into a well-structured, well-regulated and well-respected profession. Central to this growth was the establishment of professional bodies which facilitated ongoing education for veterinarians of all backgrounds, regardless of their intended trajectory; regulated standards of treatment and client interaction; and advocated on behalf of the profession with external agencies such as state and federal governments.

In all these activities, Reg was a vital player. Indeed, across the various associations with which he was involved – and there were many – he was invariably the dominant influence. He played an indispensable role in founding and cultivating professional organisations at both the state and national level. And, while equine associations predominated, Reg supported several crucial generalist vet groups too: doing so was characteristic of his unwavering commitment to elevating the calibre of the entire profession.

Like his capacity for academic work, his contributions to the development of the profession while maintaining a successful practice would not have been possible on his own. The support provided by his OVH partners, David Laws and Paul Green, was essential. As Reg became increasingly involved with both established and emerging organisations, his partners kept OVH on an even keel.

Reg devoted countless billable hours and years of his life to industry associations, but he doubtless would have dismissed his contributions as unremarkable. Certainly, he believed it was everyone's duty to strive for the continual betterment of their profession. Writing in 1975 for *Apsyrtus*, the journal of the UQ Veterinary Students' Association, he pointed to the need for all members of the profession to invest in those organisations that fortified their work: 'any professional body can only be as good as the effort put into it, not by the dedicated few alone, but by the whole graduate body.'

It was only by virtue of cooperating, Reg believed, that they could achieve the best possible outcomes – and that required *everyone* to donate something of themselves, without the need for recompense. As always, he led by example, doing so for over forty years across several of Australia's most important and enduring veterinary organisations.

The Australian Veterinary Association

In 1960, Reg was elected president of the Private Practitioners Branch of the Australian Veterinary Association, Queensland Division. This was notable for a few reasons, not least because of the existence of the Private Practitioners Branch at all. At its inception, the Australian Veterinary Association (AVA) 'was initially a province of veterinary schools and government veterinary surgeons' from the Department of Primary Industries (DPI) and Department of Agriculture. Members of the privately practising profession were a rarity (though Reg joined in 1948, before he even qualified for that title).

This skewed proportion of representation in the AVA had changed rapidly throughout the 1950s as 'more and more new graduates entered purely private practice.' In the same period, a group called the Association of Official Racing Veterinarians (AORV) was formed, whose membership almost solely comprised veterinarians employed by racing clubs on race days. In time, these two organisations came together, and Reg would be pivotal in their development.

AVA membership offered Reg the chance to expand his professional network and begin sharing ideas and building his profile. As he would later recount, once during the early years of his membership, he attended a Queensland division meeting as the invited speaker. A senior, esteemed clinician was also there, a man widely perceived as the founder of equine medicine in Queensland. He was somewhat frail and when his car pulled up out the front of the building, Reg strode over to help him up the stairs.

'Thank you, young man,' the older vet said. 'Tell me, do you know who the speaker is today?'

'Yes,' Reg answered without blinking. 'It's Reg Pascoe, from Oakey.'

There was a pause, then the older man nodded. 'Can you just help me back down the stairs?' Without any further thought, he got into a cab and went home again. Reg stood there for a moment watching the car disappear, then turned back to the business at hand. *Oh well*, he thought, *I'll go and give my talk now*. It was a timely reminder that even 'when you think you're doing a good job, you're not going to please everyone.'

Reg was a member of the AVA from 1948 until 2008. After serving as president of the Queensland Private Practitioners Branch in 1960, he was elected president of the Queensland Division in 1975–1976. The division presented Reg with the Distinguished Service Award – Queensland Division in 2001 in recognition of more than forty years' service.

Reg was made a fellow of the Australian Veterinary Association in 1982, an honour which recognises members 'who have rendered outstanding service to the association.' The fellowship is the most senior award for service to the AVA and its criteria state it should only be given 'for truly outstanding service' to, among other areas, 'an AVA Division or Special Interest Group.' Reg had more than fulfilled this by 1982; in addition to his work with the AVA, he had played a pivotal role in the 1971 raising of the Equine Special Interest Group within the association (covered in more detail later in this chapter).

Four years later, in 1986, he was awarded the AVA's Gilruth Prize. Conferred for 'outstanding service to Veterinary Science in Australia', the Gilruth is Australia's highest veterinary honour. Reg was surprised to be a recipient. He noted in a newspaper interview that 'most of the winners have been people employed in laboratories or government positions', a historical precedent that was far removed from his own path. It was not possible to find a historical description of the requirements for receiving the Gilruth between its inception in 1953 and 1986, but the selection criteria outlined by the AVA's nomination guidelines (current in 2020) include eminence, quality of service, duration of contribution and impact on the Australian veterinary profession – but most vitally, that 'the awardee's work has brought great credit to the profession or made a major contribution to veterinary science in Australia over many years.'

The Post-Graduate Foundation

In 1970, Reg began producing what was to become a copious number of equine lectures. Some of the most influential and important were those made to the Post-Graduate Foundation in Veterinary Science (PGF), a Sydney-based organisation that had been established by the authority of the University of Sydney Senate under director Dr Tom Hungerford. The PGF was created to promote and accommodate ongoing veterinary education for professionals beyond their BVSc. It was a cause Reg ardently supported.

That year, he presented his first lecture on 'Surgical Diseases and the Problems of the Newborn Foal.' His approach was methodical, concentrating on evidence-based practice and diagnosis. Even as recently as 1970, equine medicine was still in its infancy; as Scone veterinarian Bill Howey recalled, 'we didn't really know all that much'! This was evidenced by the numerous ways in which equine medicine often drew on human medical practices, particularly for surgical techniques. Along with key figures such as the Scone Equine Hospital's Murray Bain, Reg advocated for and actively advanced the use of more rigorous, science-based exploration. His continued dedication to developing resources for other veterinarians and his ever-inquiring mind placed him 'at the forefront of postgraduate education in Australia.'

Reg's contributions to the growing body of scientific veterinary knowledge were a direct and almost natural sequelae to his own innate personality traits, most notably, his curiosity. (The 'almost natural' is a vital caveat; inevitably there are brilliant and curious minds who *aren't* particularly invested in sharing this knowledge for the greater good.) Reg's curiosity drove his quest for answers, and pursuing greater knowledge led him to become an expert equine surgeon and achieve similar mastery of other disciplines. He specialised in surgery, skin diseases, and reproductive techniques, most notably but he saw no part of his vocation as beyond his remit or undeserving of his interest. As Bill Howey observed, 'He was almost the complete package and there weren't very many, if any, who were.'

The confluence of these characteristics led Reg to chronicle the many interesting cases that came through the doors of OVH. The extent of work required to achieve these clinical research outcomes was, and remains, a source of awe among the profession; it 'defies belief', friend Trevor Heath said. Not content to relinquish to anyone else the responsibility for capturing the visual evidence of his research, Reg took most of the photographs for his papers. In the numerous small equine handbooks he produced for the PGF, including one on equine skin diseases and disorder called *Skin Conditions of Horses*, the vast majority were Reg's. He was never without his 35 millimetre slide camera and took any opportunity to document points of interest. His collection of thousands of images enormously helped his efforts to share what he had learnt.

Reg's initial contributions to the PGF also included a handbook on equine restraint techniques. Here, for the edification of the newer members of the profession, he encapsulated the grounding that Robbie Burns had given his students in the late 1940s and which remained so relevant to the equine vet's work: ubiquitous use of chloroform as an anaesthetic meant a thorough education on restraint techniques was essential to protect both animal and vet. Chloroform was an unpredictable sedative. It was poured onto a sponge, which was then placed in a leather nosebag and affixed over the horse's face. The horse then inhaled it until the drug took effect. It was hardly an exact science. Correctly and thoroughly restraining the hind legs, especially during castrations, was essential to ensure that if the horse unexpectedly regained consciousness, he'd be unable to kick the vet, who would be in a vulnerable position. The PGF handbook made readily accessible to all veterinarians the crucial knowledge that Reg used almost every day and carefully instilled in his own veterinarians.

One vet who worked at OVH in the early 1970s remembered Reg mentoring him in correct equine restraint techniques very early in his tenure and the lesson stuck. 'It's stood me in good stead right the way through.'[14]

The Australian College of Veterinary Scientists

In 1971, Reg joined the newly formed Australian College of Veterinary Scientists, an educational and regulatory institution modelled on its British counterpart, the Royal College of Veterinary Surgeons. Today, the organisation is known as the Australian and New Zealand College of Veterinary Scientists (ANZCVS) in acknowledgement of the New Zealand veterinarians involved since the body's inception. The idea for an Australian college originated in 1958 as a subcommittee of the NSW division of the AVA, but didn't come to fruition until the 1967 AVA Annual General Meeting passed a resolution to form the ACVS.

Establishment of the ACVS enabled Australia to transition veterinarian registration from a state- and territory-based framework to a national system, which many hoped would ensure better standardisation. It was another keen interest of Reg's, but more likely his main motivation for participation was linked to the organisation's concurrent educational goals. The ACVS's aims were to 'advance the study of veterinary science and to bring together members of the veterinary profession for their common benefit, and to hold, conduct or arrange examinations of professional proficiency for the purpose of determining qualification for Membership and Fellowship of the College.' This statement, however, ignores one of the key facets of the ACVS that would have appealed to Reg.

Jakob Malmo, an illustrious dairy vet who similarly became involved with the ACVS at an early stage, explained, 'The College was initially developed to allow veterinarians *in practice* the opportunities to further their education and qualifications.' Though there were opportunities for vets to attend university for further study, prior to the establishment of the college there were no clear developmental paths for those who wanted to pursue further education while continuing clinical practice. Reg was a clinician, with no intentions (at that point) of becoming an academic; supporting a body designed to educate veterinarians of his ilk was common sense. It also offered him opportunities for his own professional growth.

Initially, the college achieved its stated goals by having applicants undertake both a written and an oral exam. Later, a fellowship was instituted as a higher level of qualification, requiring vets to have completed several years of training and undertake further written and oral exams. Eventually, this fellowship became a method by which practising vets could become registered specialists, neatly dovetailing with Reg's pursuit of the ongoing professionalisation in Australia.

Professor Doug Blood from the University of Melbourne – one of the first elected council members and its initial chief examiner – offered Reg the opportunity to become an inaugural fellow of the college in 1971. The chief examiner considered Reg's career to that point – not only his academic publications, lectures and presentations, but also the time invested in running what was, in essence if not in name, a specialist practice – as sufficient evidence to support his right to be an inaugural fellow. Uncomfortable with the thought of being given an exemption, Reg refused, telling Professor Blood he would prefer to do the entrance exams like anyone else.

Though he joined the ACVS as a member in 1971, he wasn't awarded a fellowship until 1975, when he received the sixth-ever issued Veterinary Specialist Registration in Equine Surgery. Ultimately, consensus suggests Reg became an ACVS fellow without being examined. That he had, only two years earlier, become a fellow of the Royal College of Veterinarians in London for his research on equine fungal disease, doubtless supported the ACVS's amenability to doing so.

Reg was an active member of the ACVS for over forty years and his passion for the new organisation was unassailable. As Jakob Malmo said, 'Reg always worked under the assumption that we can do things better, [so] let us do things better.' In the organisation's earliest stages, Reg, like other members, travelled to Brisbane five or six times a year to attend meetings. He worked to develop the college's annual science week, aimed at providing further educational opportunities both within and without the ACVS, and later served as president from 1977 to 1978. Both in this role and throughout his engagement with the college, Reg played a major part in developing the registration of veterinary specialists.

In the beginning, however, there wasn't much to work with. To help create the foundations upon which to build the ACVS, Reg set about generating support and enlisting other specialists. He was a useful person to do so; refusing a determined Reg Pascoe was a rare occurrence! One of his targets was a UQ Veterinary School staff member, a pathologist called Roger Kelly who had moved to Brisbane from South Australia in early 1971 to complete his PhD. Reg's unique, liminal position within the UQ Veterinary School – not an official staff member, but deeply involved with and influential in developing the course's equine medicine aspect – meant the two men had had some passing interactions. When Reg needed a pathologist, Roger was in his sights.

The ACVS required a minimum number of founding members to examine candidates and so Reg began assessing the UQ staff. Roger was an AVA member attending a trade display when he found himself cornered by Reg and another colleague; almost fifty years later, his memory of Reg's determined recruitment strategy remained sharp. 'Now listen here,' Reg said to the younger man. 'You're a pathologist and you've got experience in examining and assessing people's abilities in pathology: we need you to be a member of this college.'

Taken aback, Roger began executing his best evasive manoeuvres. 'I understood it's for practitioners,' he said, 'and I'm not a practitioner. I don't particularly want to – see, I'm busy doing a PhD and I'd have to go and do more examinations to be any use to you.' Reg told Roger in no uncertain terms where he thought Roger's duties lay. 'He didn't *actually* stand on my foot,' Roger remembered, but it was pretty close to it. Yet despite Reg's best efforts, Roger somehow managed to wriggle his way out of the situation without committing himself to the ACVS – a remarkable effort by any measure.

Reg's activities within the ACVS demonstrate his immersion in this forum alongside his other professional commitments: he established both the Equine Disease and Surgery chapters in 1979, serving as the chair for both in their inaugural year. His long-term involvement also included stints as the examiner for both medicine and surgery – even though, strictly speaking, equine medicine wasn't his speciality. Although his breadth and depth of expertise more realistically precluded such typecasting, many veterinarians believed Reg was 'a surgeon with expertise in skin disease and reproduction.' His ability to serve as the equine medical examiner, then, is yet another testament to his diverse range of experience.

Peter Huntington, who joined the ACVS in the mid-1980s, recalled Reg invigilating his oral examiner for equine medicine. He was nervous. Yet despite Reg's intimidating reputation, Peter found that Reg's approach recognised that the examiner had to facilitate, rather than impede, the candidate. Reg was well-acquainted with the challenges students faced in performing under exam conditions, and Peter remembered that Reg 'gave you the right clues to demonstrate what you knew, rather than what you didn't know because you were nervous.'

His work with the ACVS was in keeping with one of his key passions throughout his career: the standardisation and professionalisation of veterinary science. Growing up in a rural area, Reg had spent his childhood surrounded by animals, especially as Vyvyan's passion for dairy farming consumed the family more and more. It is logical to assume he was exposed to the ramifications of shoddy vet work and the consequences of a lack of vet support, but also those general social qualms about the legitimacy of, and need for, vets on country properties. A historical lack of standardisation had damaged the profession's reputation and Reg saw the cost of this first-hand, particularly once he graduated and began practising in Oakey.

His answer to improving perceptions of veterinary science was to demonstrate and exact the highest possible standards of science-based care, clinical excellence and professionalism. More broadly, he strove for the continued advancement of the industry by tirelessly pursuing more stringently regulated standards – his work across various organisations, including the ACVS, was driven by this fundamental goal.

It was through the ACVS that a young veterinarian called Barry Smyth renewed his acquaintance with Reg in the late 1970s when he served as secretary of the Equine Chapter of the Australian College during Reg's tenure as chair. A 1972 University of Melbourne alumnus, Barry first met Reg not long after graduating, when he attended an equine reproduction course in Queensland run by Reg and Dr John Hughes from the University of California, Davis, whom Reg had met on his international travels in 1968. 'Of course, I had heard of Reg before,' Barry said, but 'that would have been the first time I had any personal dealings with him.' Participants attended lectures in Brisbane then travelled out to Oakey to see OVH and visit a nearby stud where Reg performed hands-on demonstrations of the course's key techniques. He also showed the course the innovative crush he had devised and had built by Lloyd Iland – the same local engineer who built Reg's revolutionary hydraulic operating table. Like the table, the crush remains in use, and its ingenious design and ease of use sparked Barry's interest. 'You just flicked a lever and the whole crush came apart ... [so] you could release a horse and people didn't get hurt.'

Barry's initial impressions of Reg were coloured by a sense of awe: he was an 'intense person' and tended to overwhelm people, especially junior vets. When Barry graduated from vet school in 1972, Reg had a 'formidable reputation as a top-shelf operator' and more than lived up to it; anyone seeing him in action quickly realised 'he was a man who walked the talk.' But despite his renown, Reg remained approachable. He was 'always keen to have a talk with anybody ... [and] learn as much as he could from anywhere he thought he could get new information.'

When Reg flew to Melbourne for a meeting in the late 1970s, Barry arranged to collect Reg from the airport and drive him to his hotel. On the way, they discussed key issues of interest, but even with this focus, they arrived at the hotel parking lot with several items outstanding. Barry parked and suggested that they head inside to continue their conversation. Reg's response surprised him. 'Oh no,' he said. 'We'll just chat in the car here.'

Fair enough, Barry thought. The men held their meeting – which lasted for some time – in the car; Barry was grateful that they'd arrived after metered parking hours had finished for the day. The experience stuck with him. He had always known that Reg was pragmatic, a man without any 'airs and graces about him [who was] always very professional'; but that interaction taught Barry something new. 'Reg was prepared to get the job done with the available resources and do the best job.' Even if that meant sitting in a car.

Between 1980 and 1994, while Reg served on the assessing panel, Barry completed both his ACVS membership and fellowship examinations in equine surgery. Like Peter Huntington, he found Reg to be a fair examiner. 'He was prepared to accept an answer so long as you could provide evidence and references to back [it] up even though it might not have been the exact one he was looking for.' Reg's approach was that of someone who understood that the fundamental purpose of examinations: to demonstrate true comprehension, as opposed to the simple rote learning that might tick an assessment box but was liable to founder under the pressures of clinical practice.

Reg's commitment to the Australian College of Veterinary Scientists proved essential to its growth and its entrenchment as a key aspect of the profession in Australia. The college has helped to develop veterinary science and as Jakob Malmo noted, the ACVS 'has provided a path for veterinarians to become registered as veterinary specialists', which has become 'a very important part of the veterinary professional landscape.' Much as Reg had dreamt, the college continues to provide an opportunity for the profession to lift its standards, and his work developing it ranks as one of his most enduring legacies.

The Australian Equine Veterinary Association

In 1971, the same year that the ACVS was formed and just over a decade after the establishment of the AVA, Reg helped form the Australian Equine Veterinary Association (AEVA). What is today more simply called the Equine Veterinary Association (EVA), was born of the increasing desire among AVA members for an equine branch, a move supported by the Association of Official Racing Veterinarians, which in many ways served as the forerunner of the AEVA.

The US and Britain had formed their own equine veterinary associations, the American Association of Equine Practitioners (AAEP) and the British Equine Veterinary Association (BEVA), in 1954 and 1961 respectively, and Reg recognised their value: he joined both organisations in the early days of his move towards equine specialisation (joining the AAEP in 1966 and the BEVA in 1968). It's likely that other prominent Australian equine vets did the same and, together, these two bodies provided a blueprint for what an Australian organisation might look like and what services it might deliver for its members.

As these influences permeated throughout the profession, a group of visionary veterinarians – including Reg – met in Canberra in 1971 for the AVA conference and conceived the AEVA. Among their number were luminaries such as Dr Virginia Osborne, one of New South Wales's first female registered veterinary surgeons and herself a revolutionary equine reproduction specialist; and Dr John Bourke, a seminal figure in Australian (particularly Victorian) thoroughbred racing who became a leading international authority on the use and effects of drugs on horses and was central to the introduction of drug testing for racehorses.

With a plan formulated, the group dispersed. The following year, they reconvened in Brisbane at the 1972 AVA AGM, where the AEVA was officially born as a 'Special Interest Group' under the banner of the AVA, with a concomitant constitution, rules and bylaws. Under command of inaugural president John Bourke, the formal establishment of the AEVA witnessed the beginning of a professional body exclusively concerned with all aspects of equine veterinary practice.

Seeking to address what they identified as fundamental issues within the industry (be they vet-specific or more generic), the AEVA created a variety of subcommittees in which Reg invariably participated. Each centred on a particular area of concern; thus, one subcommittee examined the challenges associated with achieving and ensuring fair and legal horse insurance, including the obligations of veterinarians, insurance companies and owners; another focused on producing the *AEVA Blue Book: A guide to the examination of the horse* (now in its fifth edition) and innumerable hours were spent creating, discussing and editing content to the highest possible standard. Reg was respected by his fellow members of the AEVA executive both for his impressive national and international network, and his decades of experience.

The incipient AEVA strove to build on these promising beginnings and Reg was proactive in captaining the organisation through difficult waters. On one occasion, he travelled overnight from Toowoomba to Scone in regional New South Wales, spending twelve hours on a bus to present at one of the early AEVA fundraising meetings. Bill Howey collected him from the Scone transport depot at 4 a.m.

Reg later served a twelve-month term as president from 1973, a period in which the association struggled to survive. Bill Howey recorded, 'With no money and no assets and few financial members the EAVA [sic] struggled to stay afloat for a number of years. The Association relied entirely on the goodwill and self-support of the elected delegates. Predictably, early Executive Meetings were not well attended with usually only 4/5 from the Eastern States [re]presented.' The cause of this sometimes poor turnout is self-evident; for many years, attendance at the typically Sydney-based meetings was self-funded and participation voluntary, a combination which necessitated a major commitment from those involved.

Despite the challenges, the nascent body endured. Dubbed 'the father figure of the AEVA',[15] Reg was a constant in the organisation's life; regardless of the travel required, he was present at every meeting, providing a steady guiding hand. His passion for the AEVA and its work extended far beyond his twelve-month presidency – a devotion recognised a decade later in 1983 when the AEVA named him a life member.

If its founding members' intentions were to bring together the Australian equine veterinary community in a meaningful and educational way, then the AEVA far surpassed their expectations. Its effectiveness as a networking and developmental force is evidenced by the fact that it soon became one of, if not the, key bodies through which Reg met many of the younger Australian vets who credit him with directly exerting a positive influence on their careers.

One of Reg's many addresses to the Equine Veterinary Association.

David Johnson met Reg at an AEVA conference in 1982 but their friendship really began six years later when David joined the AEVA committee. Having graduated from Sydney University in 1980, he was still young and fairly junior and when charged with convening the 1989 Coffs Harbour AEVA conference, he took his seat in the committee meeting only to find himself subject to a conversation that ran a 'bit like the Spanish inquisition.' Reg grilled David about everything from his alma mater to whether he had children and David hung on for the ride. '[Reg] was a fairly scary character for us young guys; everyone respected him, and he was admired and looked up to, but you didn't cross him.'

The Coffs Harbour conference was a success. In the course of its planning and execution, David and Reg became good friends, and Reg made himself available to assist however he could. 'He really helped me,' David remembered, and their work 'fundamentally changed how the EVA did conferences.' David's hard work in this process was enough to warrant Reg's respect – because while Reg was never free with compliments, he did have subtle ways of demonstrating his approval and those around him soon learnt to take these signs for the praise they disguised. After the conference ended, Reg said to the younger man, 'Well, I might have been to a better conference, but I can't remember it.'

David interpreted this to mean the event had gone well; Reg likely thought it had gone excellently. It was a credit to David's name and had perhaps unforeseen implications, because as he pointed out, 'Reg was fairly old-school; you had to earn your stripes.' Having done so, David became part of a circle of people who, ever after, were the tacit beneficiaries of Reg's mentorship; once someone proved their worthiness, he became deeply invested in their career and often also an important figure in their personal life.

David went on to work with Reg on the committee in various positions and found that Reg was always supportive of him regardless of the role he was in. Reg was, however, generally 'an advisor to everybody. If you were unsure, you asked Reg what to do.' Such mentorship was not confined to AEVA committees or the yearly conferences: Reg seemed to pop up all over the place. Working at the Coffs Harbour Cup one year, David heard a familiar voice and turned around to see Reg standing on the other side of the running rail ready for a quick catch-up.

More often, if David wanted advice on a case or a client, he knew that Reg would be able to help. Reg's interest in developing both the Australian horse industry and young veterinarians, and what David fondly recalled as his 'heart of gold', meant he was always available. And Reg's vast store of knowledge – 'more than most of the textbooks or people that were speaking' – made his assistance particularly valuable, especially when any veterinary matter was being debated. If you found yourself in a robust discussion, Reg was a good ally to have; 'he never lost any of those arguments, so he was a great person to have on your side.'

Reg was also, as it so happened, a great person to have a social outing with prior to a meeting. Like David Johnson, Adelaide-based equine vets Sandy and Bill Harbison first met Reg through the AEVA, and something just clicked – despite a twenty-five year age difference, the couple became close friends with both Reg and Joy. Sometime later, as the South Australian AEVA rep, Sandy invited Reg to Adelaide to speak at a local conference. Together with Bill, they headed to Springton in the Barossa Valley to have lunch at a little café beforehand, only to find themselves enjoying one those lunches that went on all afternoon. It was so engrossing they barely made it back in time. Needless to say, both Reg and Bill looked somewhat worse for wear.

'The honourable speaker,' Sandy recalled, had 'enjoyed the Barossa wines particularly well.' Or to be more accurate, 'Reg was half-pissed,' Bill chortled. Well-lubricated and operating at full volume, no one else seems to have caught on. Under his direction, Bill was deployed to work the slide projector, where the effects of the afternoon kept dragging his eyes shut. As Reg roared through his presentation, he decided upon a solution to Bill's heavy eyes: every time Reg wanted the slide changed, he'd grandly cuff his friend around the back of the head.

James Gilkerson, a University of Sydney graduate now based in Melbourne, had never heard of Reg Pascoe before he met him at a conference in 1995. The following year, he gave a talk at the same conference where Reg was the timekeeper. Reg introduced the speakers, but not without issuing a warning. James remembered him saying, 'You've got ten minutes. At eight minutes, I'll ring the bell once; at nine minutes I'll ring the bell twice. If you're still talking at ten minutes, I'll hit you with the bloody bell, okay?' When James laughed, Reg levelled the younger vet with the renowned Pascoe stare and added, 'If you think I'm joking, son, you just keep talking.'

Smile gone, James toed the line and managed to avoid being hit with the bell, which he gratefully tallied up under his 'wins' column. The experience wasn't traumatising enough to put him off presenting another talk the following year. It seemed to go well and Reg asked several questions at the end, but when James went to sit down, Reg stood, tapped James's PhD supervisor on the shoulder and motioned him to the back of the room. James's stomach plummeted. *Oh my god, what have I said?* he thought. A number of speakers remained and good manners warred with curiosity as James agonised over what the men might be discussing. Curiosity won out.

He found the two men in the bar. Reg turned as James walked in, wide-eyed and anxious, and gave him a friendly nod. 'That was a really good talk,' Reg said. 'You've changed the way I think about this disease. Can I buy you a beer?' James nearly fainted. He joined the two men and accepted the drink. Reg followed up the beer with some hard-hitting questions he'd refrained from asking in public and they had a vigorous discussion about the paper and its implications.

The conference dinner was that night, and James sat with his wife and an assortment of other vets when they began announcing the prizes. 'Are you in the running?' James's wife asked, and James shook his head. The only one he thought he might have put his hand up for was the Reg Pascoe Clinical Prize. Inaugurated by the AEVA in 1995, in 2020 it's called the Equine Veterinarians Australia Reginald R Pascoe Prize and comprises 'a grand perpetual trophy, an individual engraved glass memento, and $1000 for EVA members and $500 for non-members.' Candidates hold, or are two years into, a specialist qualification or advanced research degree and the prize stipulates that they must 'present the best clinical or research paper at the combined ANZCVS / EVA abstract session ... The topic may include any clinical or research project exclusively involved with horses.' In 1997, at least two other pre-eminent veterinarians had given talks at the conference. Both were registered specialists in their field who were presenting excellent research to their assembled colleagues. James was only a PhD student. He was chatting to his next-door neighbour when his wife tapped his shoulder. 'That was *you*,' she said. James stood up, flabbergasted, to receive the Reg Pascoe Clinical Prize. The path to the stage took him past Reg's table, and Reg stopped him on the way to shake his hand. 'Told you it was a good talk,' he said.

Though he wasn't one of the judges, apparently Reg had spoken to the people who were, letting them know in no uncertain terms who he thought deserved the prize that year. James noted that in the Australian veterinary community, the prize is seen as 'recognising scientific rigour and novel, clinical application of knowledge and pursuit of excellence.' It's an apt prize to bear Reg's name, because, as James said, 'they're the things that I associate with Reg.'

James felt he had established a relationship with Reg that night. Their main interactions occurred through EVA conferences (particularly the annual, multi-day Bain Fallon lecture series), but like David Johnson, James found Reg approachable and supportive when he occasionally had questions. Reg had a mind like a steel trap, not just for science, but for people too. The first time James rang OVH, he introduced himself, adding, 'you won't remember me' but Reg surprised him. 'James,' he said, with the ease of long acquaintance despite the younger man's uncertainty. 'How're you going?'

If James rang and Reg wasn't available, he never failed to return the call. 'What can I do for you?' he'd ask when he rang back. It was a question that underpinned his dealings with so many members of the profession: what *could* Reg Pascoe do for them? One year, he asked James to travel to Queensland and talk to the Horse Industry Council; it was some time before James realised that the council hadn't requested that Reg find them a speaker. Rather, as a member of the board of directors, Reg had promoted James to his fellow executives as an interesting and worthwhile presenter.

This is a single example but there are myriad others. Reg's passion for community created a web of relationships that James dubbed 'the Pascoe network': an extensive, diverse and collaborative system of friends and colleagues working informally together to enrich their careers. Arising from Reg's commitment to cultivating dedicated and impassioned young vets, its existence was proof in action of his deepest beliefs; the quiet, unassuming work done under its aegis reinforced an ethos of collaboration, service and the pursuit of excellence.

The influence of the Pascoe network was greater than Reg might have imagined. If, at any point in his career, he'd felt a niggling doubt that his efforts were akin to shouting into a void, then the Pascoe network was the (perhaps unrealised) validation of his endeavour: his echoes reverberated over and over, extending far beyond their immediate and most obvious beneficiaries. Reg moulded the Australian veterinary community in the most subtle, vital and indelible of ways – the type of influence which proliferates, predominantly unseen, from the innermost circle outwards and across generations of veterinarians who never even met him.

The most valuable thing Reg taught James Gilkerson was not to fear investigating ideas: to accept that not understanding a concept did not consign you to never understanding it but was instead an invitation to continue learning. The Pascoe network was fundamental to this: discovering a problem was an opportunity to make a connection.

It was also about pulling together to work out a solution and the people who operated within that system were deeply invested in doing so. They took their responsibilities seriously; when James put a problem out into the network, the answers – or the titbits pivotal to piecing the answers together – would begin trickling in with little further prompting. Dedication and collegiality predicated the network's success, and becoming a member was an unspoken mark of Reg's esteem. As James said, 'I knew I must be doing something right when I got a phone call from someone who said, "I asked Reg Pascoe a question and he suggested I call you." ... I thought, *Ooh, I'm in the Pascoe network.*' Inclusion was an honour, but there was an accompanying responsibility to live up to the distinction.

During his forty-year association with the AEVA, Reg received several prestigious awards. Following the conferral of his life membership in 1983, he was awarded the AEVA VMS Award for Excellence in Veterinary Medicine over consecutive years in 1987 and 1988, then again over a decade later in 2001 – an achievement described in a 2004 AEVA article in the *Australian Veterinary Journal* as 'the AEVA's highest annual award.' He was subsequently made a life fellow in 2003. This landmark decision, the letter of recognition noted, instituted Reg as the 'first and only' life fellow, an honour unanimously acclaimed by the more than sixty AEVA members.

Perhaps his most enduring commemoration by the AEVA, however, is the Pascoe Oration. Inaugurated in 2004, the oration is presented by an Australian veterinarian of some renown. Barry Smyth, who was present at the Darwin EVA conference for the first Pascoe Oration, recalled how the prospect of this newly created award in his honour left Reg unsettled. Barry had spent the week prior to the conference travelling happily with Reg and Joy and some other vet friends around the Northern Territory. But as the presentation date drew closer, Barry noticed a change in Reg's demeanour. Few, if any, would have ever before seen Reg anxious at the prospect of getting up in front of an audience – having spoken at conferences and presented papers across Australia and around the world, he was a confident and erudite presenter. On this occasion, however, Reg was 'genuinely was nervous about having to give this presentation in his own name and the inaugural one too ... He was most relieved when it was over.'

Five years later in 2008, Reg's decades-long contribution to the AEVA (by then renamed Equine Veterinarians Australia or EVA) was recognised with one final award. Running into Reg at a conference in Yeppoon, James Gilkerson asked whether he would be attending the conference later in the year. When he received a negative response, James said, 'We've got a prize we'd like to give you.'

Reg was unmoved. 'I've got all the prizes you guys at the EVA have.'

'Well, we've got a new one,' James said, undeterred. The EVA Award for Services to the Horse Industry had been established in 2007 to recognise members who had 'made a major contribution to the Australian horse industry through leadership, enterprise and service to the betterment of horses, their owners, and the community.'

'Oh,' Reg said, thinking about it. 'Is this the first time you've given it?'

James shook his head. 'No, we gave it to Trish [Ellis] last year.'

'Well, that's a good person to follow on from. I'll come.'

Four years later in 2012, after a more than forty-year association, Reg officially retired and relinquished his membership of the EVA.

National and State Research Bodies

Reg's enthusiasm for clinical research meant he was well acquainted with the unique challenges of investigating equine conditions in Australia, and his personal experiences kindled a desire to help make conducting research more accessible and realistic for other vets. This stance explains his involvement in an early-1970s movement that sought to create a strong, resilient framework for supporting Australian research. The result was the inauguration in 1972 of the Australian Equine Research Foundation (AERF) in Victoria and, twelve months later, the establishment of the Queensland Equine Research Foundation (QERF).

The AERF was formed to address a historical lack of funding, support and interest in Australian equine research, a situation which hampered practitioners' ability to investigate equine disorders with breadth and rigour. Vets could draw on international research papers for pathologies that were common around the world, but found themselves constrained when it came to understanding and treating conditions unique to Australian horses. Leading practitioners at the time knew local research would fix the problem, but also that any would-be researchers were hindered by inadequate funding.

This is not to say there was no money in racing, which has historically been one of the biggest sources of revenue and will likely continue being so for the foreseeable future. Each state's various racing (or jockey) clubs had their own funding and, whether it was widely acknowledged at the time or not, these organisations had a vested interest in the ongoing development of equine science. However, a unified body was needed to coordinate the research, and so the AERF was conceived.

Several renowned equine vets were central to the formation, including leading practitioners such as Murray Bain, Les McMenamy, Len Fulton and Ken Cox, who at the time was chair of the Victoria Racing Club. Rex Butterfield, who had been the founding president of the Australian College of Veterinary Scientists, was also central to the new endeavour. The inaugural chair, he later handed over the reins to Reg's friend, Keith Hughes. Records chronicling the inception of the AERF are scant, but Keith attested that 'Reg would certainly have played a part in [its] formation.' While Reg may not have been the frontrunner, other contemporaries have stated that 'of all Australian veterinarians, [Reg] would have been the most influential in the establishment of research foundations for horses in Australia.'[16]

The AERF met biannually and received and processed research grant applications. Reg assisted in adjudicating these matters in his capacity as a member of the advisory committee which he'd joined in 1975 and served on for twenty years. Most of the applications came from academics who were required by their universities to conduct a certain amount of research under the university's auspices. They typically had access to laboratory support and enough time to conduct the research. Practising veterinarians also participated – while Reg was an exceptional example of someone who pursued clinical investigation, he was certainly not alone – but they usually worked in partnership with an academic, whose theoretical understanding and laboratory facilities were an ideal complement to the practitioner's practical expertise.

Although the AERF and its subsidiaries were the main recipients of equine research funding in Australia at the time, the AERF operated primarily on the basis of voluntary levies – a 1999 report noted it was 'supported by industry contributions and grants, donations and appeals.' Whether this was augmented by lump-sum grants from the federal government (as with the QERF, examined in more detail below) is not clear, though it seems likely that this must have occurred intermittently to allow the organisation to survive. A resilient operation, however, it was not.

It's likely that several state-level research bodies were derived from the AERF. Certainly, those individuals involved in establishing the AERF were also active in pursuing state-level bodies to coordinate equine research (for example, Rex Butterfield provided essential impetus in the creation of New South Wales Racing Research Fund, which existed under the auspices of the University of Sydney for many years).

In 1973, the QERF was established through the provision of a three-year, $100,000 state government grant which sought to promote research into diseases and the improvement of bloodstock lines. Managed by the chair of the Queensland Racing Club, the foundation was supported through a series of annual funding allocations. Inevitably, the origins of this money changed over time; a 1987 Queensland cabinet minute submitted by Russ Hinze proposed that the funding which had previously come from the Local Government Department now be provided by the Racing Development Fund. He noted that 'financial assistance for research projects which benefit the racing industry in Queensland should be funded by the racing industry when and where possible', and his submission was approved.

Reg's passion for Queensland vets was legendary, so it was natural that he was more involved with the QERF than its national counterpart. He began serving as a councillor on the board in its inaugural year in 1973 and remained there for the next two decades.

The AERF, with its strong ties to the Victoria Racing Club, was dominated by people from the racing, breeding and sectors of the industry; vets were less common. Reg was therefore among the organisation's foremost veterinarians for decades and formed strong friendships with the other veterinarians involved in the two foundations. Trevor Heath, who was dean of the UQ Veterinary School during the 1970s, was also on both the QERF and AERF boards, and in these capacities, the two men found themselves meeting every few months.

Trevor quickly developed respect for Reg, recalling, 'I always genuinely enjoyed [our] interactions.' Although they worked in different areas of the profession, their views often aligned, and Reg's direct and practical approach to problems resonated with Trevor. Although some friends and acquaintances recall Reg as being intermittently (or perpetually!) gruff or intimidating, Trevor didn't witness that. Perhaps that speaks to the two men having a narrower context to their friendship than others in Reg's life; or perhaps their similarities saw them united in their views and rarely on opposing sides.

'People literally referred to him as "God",' Trevor said. 'They weren't being cynical; I think it was a genuine reflection of their respect for him. Because he really was *the* leading light in equine work in a public sense.' Trevor believed that Reg's fulfilment of that role, and his ability to shape the Australian veterinary community from a small, remote country town in rural Queensland were among his most noteworthy accomplishments.

But as Reg would learn countless times throughout his career, the dynamism and commitment of one person – and even a group of similarly passionate people – cannot create success in a stagnant pond. By 1984, the AERF and its subsidiaries were dying. The foundation's dependence on various voluntary horse industry levies was promising: after all, research funded by these levies was to the benefit of the industry at large. Yet a lack of interest from some factions and outright opposition from others meant that resource avenues failed one after another. Keith Hughes recalled that an inescapable amount of 'politicking went on trying to get the money.' As with many such organisations before it (and as would happen again with organisations to which Reg had devoted himself), a lack of money combined with internal disputes gradually spelled the AERF's doom.

The 1980s witnessed growing government interest in supporting research across primary industries – but unlike other major moneymakers in the rural animal sector, horses didn't provide a readily apparent income source. The cattle industry levied milk; the pig industry, pork products. Money from these ventures could be funnelled back into industry-specific research. Attempts to introduce levies in the horse industry struggled, then foundered, and with no money coming in, there was little appeal for the federal government's investment. The *Primary Industries and Energy Research and Development Act 1989*, however, established the Rural Industries Research and Development Corporation (RIRDC), a statutory authority which was to play a key role in the future of the AERF.

The RIRDC managed research and development (R&D) projects with the aim of improving rural industry productivity. Industry funds, such as those raised by product levies, were matched dollar-for-dollar by the Australian government to support ongoing development. Within a year of its creation, the RIRDC was engaging with the AERF, holding workshops in 1990 and 1991 to discuss the organisation's future. By 1995, the declining AERF was subsumed into the RIRDC. The newly created RIRDC equine R&D program began in February 1995 with much of the funds provided by the Conference of Principal Racing Clubs (the national governing body for racing clubs at the time) from racehorse registration fees. Several other industry groups, including the AEVA, indicated they would likely provide ongoing financial support.

The RIRDC equine program ended in 2015. In 2018, the newly established body, AgriFutures Australia, instituted the AgriFutures Australia Thoroughbred Horses R&D Program which draws its funding from a statutory thoroughbred breeding levy which is matched by commonwealth funding.

The AERF and its subsidiaries did not survive, but does that negate the time, energy, effort and belief invested in them? Certainly, they provided a service to the Australian horse industry that is hard to quantify: the research outcomes directly resulting from the AERF's facilitation were likely invaluable to regional equine science. For Reg, who had already played a role in launching some of Australia's most important professional bodies and thrown himself headlong into participating in others, such an outcome was likely its own quiet reward. His involvement was inevitable, a continuation of his developmental efforts within the Australian community.

Whether he was disappointed by the AERF's eventual dissolution is hard to know, but it's more likely that he was, as usual, pragmatic – as long as there was continuing support for Australian equine research through the RIRDC, he was probably satisfied with the outcome. While the research made possible by the AERF was readily apparent, his contribution also had more far-reaching effects. Keith Hughes believed Reg's efforts were crucial in creating the conditions for future successes. 'Reg's involvement with the AERF went on to really make RIRDC an effective body ... [the AERF] was an embryo of the idea of having a research fund that could look at all facets of horse research.' The energetic participation of key individuals like Reg, Rex Butterfield and Keith among others created the foundations for the robust and well-resourced Australian equine research framework they had imagined.

The Veterinary Surgeons Board

In 1974, Reg resumed his post on Queensland's Veterinary Surgeons Board (VSB) after a five-year hiatus. Having first joined in 1958, the reasons for his absence are not recorded anywhere but the period coincided with the Oakey Vet Hospital's transition from clinical focus to equine work. 'Late in 1968, the equine hospital became a reality.' Reg referred specifically to the facilities he had designed and built to allow the clinic to properly tend ill and injured horses. Guiding OVH through this phase must have entailed countless hours of work both as a vet and a business owner. He was highly active in a number of other organisations during this period – he was awarded his fellowship by the Royal College of Veterinarians in England; began producing a number of papers; was actively recording interesting clinical cases that came through the doors of OVH and, as we have seen above, was fundamental in the establishment of the AEVA, ACVS, AERF and QERF. The only notable thing about the five-year hiatus from the Veterinary Surgeons Board, then, is that it wasn't longer – or that it ended at all. From his return in 1975, he would serve on the Queensland board until his retirement in 2001, a total of forty-two years.

The Veterinary Surgeons Board of Queensland is the state's

statutory authority for regulating veterinary science. The board ensures proper registration of providers and is responsible for administering disciplinary action in instances of misconduct. Of its six-member legislative committee, two are elected by the profession on a triennial basis. These two positions are prestigious because they reflect the profession's high opinion and faith in the members' ability to justly arbitrate veterinary standards and professional compliance. Queensland vets trust that their two elected peers will deal fairly with them if they are accused of professional misconduct. Equine vets have, historically, been quite rare but Reg was an automatic choice every year. As Dave Lovell, another Queensland vet who later served on the board, recalled, 'There was never any question about who was going to win the election. [Reg] was put there by the profession and there was no challenge to his right to be there.'

Reg's interest in education and its powers to enhance veterinary science were at the forefront in his work with the VSB. The sanctions available to the board weren't strong; the focus was on encouraging continuing education to pre-empt circumstances that might bring a veterinarian and their practice into question. It was this continuing education, Lovell noted, 'that was always part of Reg's reason for being.'

In 1974, Reg had his first meeting with a young, Kiwi-born veterinarian by the name of Vic Menrath. A UQ graduate who was building a practice in Brisbane, Vic strongly objected to the board's stipulation that he include a central drain in the operating theatre of his new hospital. It was, Vic thought, a big and costly undertaking with little rationale behind it, and he told the board members as much. Vic found himself in a robust discussion with Reg but, as was frequently the case, Reg's argument won out. The facility requirements remained extant.

It was not Vic's first encounter, however, with the Pascoe name. Dubbed 'the grandfather of feline medicine in Australia,' Vic served as an external examiner for UQ in the early 1970s, assessing students' small animal knowledge. One particular year might have rocked his faith in the university process; it was, he remembered with a shake of his head, 'really, really bad.' One student after another entered the room; and one student after another had no idea how to answer Vic's questions. Then a young man came in. He stretched himself out in the chair and put his hands behind his head.

'You're John Pascoe?' Vic asked.

'Yes,' said John, utterly unconcerned about the looming examination. They exchanged small talk before Vic asked, 'What are you going to do post-graduation?'

There was no shadow of a doubt in John's reply. 'Horse practice.'

'Well,' Vic said, 'I'm afraid if you want to get a veterinary degree, you have to know something about small animal medicine.' They commenced the examination, and to every question Vic posed, John's answer was the same, 'I wouldn't have a bloody clue.'

Vic wrote a zero on the paper and, afterwards, headed to the examiners' meeting to discuss the situation.

'Has anybody got any problems?' the dean asked.

'Yes,' Vic said. 'I've got a problem. John Pascoe, I'm afraid, is going to have to re-sit.' There was a moment of silence, then a wave of dismayed murmurs arose around the table.

'Vic,' the dean said, voice laden with meaning, 'that's *Reg Pascoe's* son.'

Vic was bemused. 'What?'

'He did so well in everything else,' the dean said, apologetic. The remainder of the board began muttering again. Before Vic knew quite what had happened, John had been passed. 'I was bloody furious,' Vic remembered. 'I think John never knew.'

Sitting on the VSB gave Reg a unique insight into the state of the profession in Queensland, information that served him well across many of his endeavours, but could also be a cause for concern. He had noted some years prior in the UQ *Veterinary Journal*, 'Another area of grave disquiet is the increasing evidence of discourtesy, rudeness and poor client relations by some practitioners ... leading to investigation by the Veterinary Surgeons Board. In many instances, this has been due to lack of professional bedside manner, poor contact with the client concerning costs and prognosis, together with a generally disturbing attitude of treating the public as being an uneducated illiterate mass, when in fact today, your clients are on the whole, better informed and more interested than ever before – even to the stage of seeking legal advice for redress on their grievances.' Mistakes were part of life; condescending to clients was not. To Reg, if the situation deteriorated to the point where clients felt legal action was their only recourse, the profession was failing miserably to inculcate the necessary values in its community.

Queensland Veterinary Bodies – AVA Queensland Division and the Darling Downs Equine Group

In 1975, Reg undertook a two-year post as president of the AVA's Queensland division. Among the vast number of boards, committees, foundations and associations he served on and championed, it's tempting to question their true purpose. At some point, they seem – as least to an outsider – to blur into one. First and foremost in importance is their capacity to bring together inquiring minds that question the status quo. People who pursue their own education tend to congregate with those similar in temperament and devote themselves to passing on what they've learnt to those who'll listen.

Reg built an extensive network of friends and acquaintances within Australia and around the world, and it was this network that facilitated many of his most noteworthy achievements. The countless people whom Reg mentored or helped was, in and of itself, one of his greatest achievements. Tom Hungerford's Post-Graduate Foundation in Veterinary Science; the AEVA; the Australian College of Veterinary Scientists: these bodies, like the many other professional organisations both nationally and internationally, played a vital role in the growth of his professional influence, and in the development of equine veterinary science.

Reg's service as president of the AVA Queensland division is important because, like the VSB and the PGF, the AVA and its divisions are not equine-specific: they support and provide service to *all* Australian vets. Reg's involvement testifies to his commitment to his profession, but also how he perceived both veterinary science as a vocation and himself as a practitioner. An equine specialist Reg undoubtedly was, but first and foremost, he was a *veterinarian*, and recollections from numerous colleagues about his cross-species surgical and diagnostic skills demonstrates how fundamental this ideal was to his professional identity.

Reg's attitude was similarly evident in his work with local veterinary organisations, such as the Darling Downs Equine Group. Rather than viewing such a small, grassroots body as inconsequential, he recognised how local groups were key adjuncts to larger professional bodies, vital in sharing educational, growth and relationship-building opportunities which might otherwise be less accessible to rural practitioners.

Group president in the mid-1990s, Chris Reardon recalled that the region was blessed with several experienced senior vets in locations from Goondiwindi to Chinchilla. The annual meeting was an affable affair, marked by strong bonds of collegiality. Reg was always interested in hearing about how the association was progressing whenever he caught up with Chris. He thought it important the profession perpetuate and support groups dedicated to cooperation and development. His support, as son David Pascoe recorded in 1988, was evident in the way that he was 'involved in the Darling Downs branch meetings, serving as a leader and presenter of lectures on a myriad of veterinary research and treatment topics.' If there was one thing Reg could do, it was to bring both his knowledge and the wisdom of other accomplished veterinarians to the broadest possible swathe of the profession: the help and guidance that he felt had not been readily available to him as an isolated, rural veterinarian, he would give to others.

Equine Veterinary Education and the Inception of the Bain Fallon Memorial Lectures

In June 1978, the inaugural Bain Fallon Memorial Lecture series was held over three days at the Wentworth Hotel in Sydney. The conference was the result of collaboration between two successive AEVA presidents, Geoff Hazard (1977) and Bill Howey (1978), who imagined a conference that would 'advance the professional development of equine veterinarians in Australia and ... establish through [A]EVA an international network of experts and an annual forum through which knowledge and research could be shared.' They named the conference for Murray Bain and Peter Fallon, two pre-eminent veterinarians who both died prematurely in 1974. Since its inception, the 'Bain Fallon' has become internationally renowned; the flagship of the AEVA.

The conference's prestige owes much to Reg. As AEVA education coordinator throughout the 1990s and early 2000s, the annual lecture series was his primary responsibility and he brought every shred of his expertise to bear and capitalised on his network to mould the event into the success he knew it could be. Many see it as his greatest legacy to Australian veterinary science.

Technological advances over the last two decades have made it easier to pursue ongoing professional education. For the majority of Reg's career, however, there was no internet. Where online education now bridges vast geographic distances, veterinarians in the 1990s and earlier were dependent on lectures and conferences. For many Australian equine vets, the Bain Fallon conference was *the* annual event, and Reg worked hard to make it valuable for them.

Reg spent more than fifteen years as a consultant for the Australian Blood Horse Breeders Association (ABBA) to the International Disease Reporting Committee, which fostered his international connections. He served as a consultant to the University of Florida in 1977; the Philippines in the early 1980s; and to a prominent stud farm in India throughout the 1990s. This is hardly an exhaustive list and it fails to reflect how his dedication to his own ongoing education prompted much of his own overseas travel and brought him into contact with many expert equine vets, expanding his network of potential Bain Fallon lecturers.

What is certain is that Reg actively harnessed these connections to the benefit of Australian vets. Though active on several of the AEVA's subcommittees, he was most heavily involved with the education subcommittee, often alongside several other academic vets, and his twelve years' tenure as chair from 1989 to 2001 provides some indication of his investment in this aspect of the AEVA's work. He was ideally suited to the role. His contacts were invaluable when searching for experts to present on different topics and this, in conjunction with his decades-long relationship with the University of Queensland, made him well placed to be a key advisor on lecture programs, possible future speakers, and how to proactively shape the trajectory of professional education through the AEVA.

Years of active participation on the international veterinary stage and attending countless overseas conferences allowed Reg to readily identify ideal speakers. And, whether by dint of cajoling or more domineering methods, he managed to get those speakers to present at the Bain Fallon each year. He also cultivated the conference's program to reflect the most pertinent topics. Dave Lovell recalled, 'it was remarkable how he was able to cover virtually any topic that you needed to know to be up-to-date in the practice.' Lovell would know: he had a front-row seat to the process for years. He sat on numerous executive committee meetings focused on selecting speakers and noted that while Reg didn't originate the Bain Fallon lecture series, 'as time evolved, I believe that he was singlehandedly responsible for its emergence [as] ... a premier world educational event.'

Reg's commitment the Bain Fallon is testament to his belief in the ongoing development of Australian equine vet science. It also recognises that his own pursuit of professional growth might not be so accessible to others in the profession. Lovell acknowledged Reg's numerous contributions to Australian and international vet science but was unwavering in his belief that Reg's stewardship of the Bain Fallon formed his greatest legacy. Brian Sheahan, a Brisbane vet who met Reg at the first Bain Fallon conference, agreed, remembering 'I called him God', the nickname both a measure of his admiration and respect, and a sly quip that Reg always appreciated. 'Glad you know your place, son!' Reg used to reply.

'Reg's legacy was education,' Sheahan said. 'He believed in quality research and education and enabled so many in the profession to benefit from his teachings.'

Fighting to Build a National Body – The Australian Horse Council

In 1977, an event occurred overseas that indirectly set in motion one of the most challenging endeavours of Reg's career: contagious equine metritis (CEM), a bacterial infection of the genital tract of mares, broke out in England and Ireland. The scare prompted the

Australian Federal Department of Health to send Reg and a bacteriologist called Bruce Clarke to the UK as Department of Health consultants. They spent two weeks in August visiting England, Ireland and the US to learn first-hand of CEM's ramifications. Reg recalled, 'We were fortunate that in the two weeks we were visiting ... the causative organism was isolated at the Cambridge General Hospital Pathology Department.'

Reg and Bruce returned home to present their reports to the Department of Health and share their findings with the Thoroughbred Breeders of Australia at a specially convened meeting in Sydney. The timing couldn't have been worse. While Reg was overseas, the Hunter Valley in New South Wales had seen an outbreak of spontaneous abortions due to the equine herpes virus 1 (EHV1). Overwhelmed with containing and responding to EHV1, Australian thoroughbred owners and breeders were in no place to appreciate the serious risk posed by the outbreak of CEM overseas. Dealing with the infection's potential consequences was put on the backburner, to disastrous effect. Later that same year, in the early spring of 1977, the first case of CEM was diagnosed at a stud on the outskirts of Scone.

The venereal disease had almost certainly been introduced in 1976, and perhaps even earlier. Regardless, failing to give CEM its due amid the chaos of the EHV1 outbreak had been a serious miscalculation on the industry's part – it would take three years of concerted effort to eradicate CEM in Australia and end up costing the country $12 million ($53 million in 2020). For Reg, the disastrous sequence of events illuminated the shortfalls of the Australian horse industry: it was a community ill-equipped to proactively address serious issues such as EHV1 and CEM and lacked the flexibility and interconnections necessary to react rapidly and effectively in the face of such calamities. It was a deficit Reg was determined to rectify.

As time passed, the impact of his trip to the UK – compounded by the Australian outbreak of CEM and the EHV1 scare – stayed with him. As he considered what had occurred and the shortfalls that led to the disaster, he came up with a plan. He determined that the solution 'was the establishment of better communication between government, horse organisations and racing authorities', and envisaged a network of interconnected bodies working towards a common goal. Ideally, this would take the form of a national council, comprising a series of state councils overseen by a single super council.

In 1980, Reg was commissioned by the Bureau of Animal Health and given a federal grant to conduct a survey of the Australian horse industry. Foremost among the bureau's concerns was a lack of basic information about the industry and how this deficiency shaped our ability (or lack thereof) to respond to novel diseases. The investigation's terms of reference requested Reg review the existing processes for liaison between the federal government and the industry and then recommend a system that would facilitate something more robust and reliable (be it routine or ad hoc). Pivotal to this was the idea of establishing an Australian equine database in which national horse populations, breed distribution figures and up-to-date information about diseases and other risk factors would be recorded. Coupled with more robust communication across the various facets of the industry and different levels of government through the creation of the horse council as a single point of contact, the system would hopefully ensure an agile and adaptive response to emergencies. The bureau's task provided Reg with the ideal opportunity to advance his ideas for change.

'With assistance from the Thoroughbred Breeders Association (TBA),' he noted, 'the Australian Equine Veterinary Association, the Victoria Racing Club and the Australian Equine Research Foundation, together with a federal grant, I visited all mainland states to sell the concept of horse councils.' The travel allowed him to meet with a 'good representation of the horsemen' and he held wide-ranging consultations with representatives of state departments of agriculture, as many equine breeding groups as could be coordinated, the Australia Bureau of Animal Health, the Australian Equine Research Foundation, and university veterinary schools (particularly on matters involving the specialist field of equine virology). His interactions impressed upon him the need for a council – first implemented on a state level, then federally – and this was reflected in his report published in 1982.

At the time, Australia had no way of accurately determining the national population and distribution of horses. This information, Reg noted, was crucial for providing a baseline against which to compare survey data, create procedures to investigate unusual diseases, and support the manufacturing, marketing and servicing aspects of the industry with information necessary to their enterprise planning and functions. This included coordinating the management of horse imports and exports, which carried a risk for disease transmission. A single coordinating body could standardise the recording and transmission of information across a vast range of fields, as well as support key equine research. Most crucially, however, a comprehensive national organisation was the only realistic path to the establishment of the resilient, enduring and uniform system required to reduce risk in the event of dangerous disease outbreaks. With one eye on the consequences of the poorly handled CEM outbreak, Reg was also aware of the broader need to enhance general management of Australian horses, including a national identification system and the implementation of modified quarantine and exotic disease control policy to safeguard against future outbreaks.

The first draft Reg wrote was modelled on the American Horse Council: a logical choice because the American organisation offered the ideal template. Based in Washington DC, the American Horse Council was created in the late 1960s. By 1970 it had formed a 'Coalition of State Horse Councils' to manage issues across the industry – a body which in 2019 covered forty-three of fifty US states. Quentin Wallace, who served on the Australian Horse Council, noted that the American counterpart 'lobbies before Congress and federal agencies for the interests of the horse industry, and serves as a unified voice for the horse industry'; moreover, it 'gets consulted by the [US] government whenever there's any [equine] matter that's of a national or federal importance.' This national unity and fruitful, reciprocal relationship with government were the primary aspects the Australian Horse Council sought to emulate.

Such 'national unity' however was the obstacle over which the AHC was to find itself stumbling again and again. Divisions are old and run deep. In an industry already biased towards state-based organisation, the AHC first had to overcome entrenched factionalism. It was only by bridging the divide between the different groups that the foundations of an effective national council could be built. As Reg pointed out in his report, even the term 'industry' itself was misleading, suggesting a functional coherence that simply did not exist. 'The horse "industry" is at best a nebulous description of a largely disassociated group of people with a common interest.'

There was a disconnect between racing (specifically thoroughbred racing) and other equestrian pursuits, both in terms of funding and perceived importance or prestige. Horse racing is high profile, easily accessible and recognisable to the general public and, most notably, a serious moneymaker: a 2018 economic impact study indicated the racing industry complete (including thoroughbred breeding and training sectors) was worth a cool $9 billion per annum and employed more than 70,000 people full-time. However, the racing industry saw little reason to support of a national coordinating body; their path into government was well-established and any national horse council seemed to promise little of value. This historical clout that racing has had with government – far more than most other facets of the horse industry – combined with the state-based nature of racing at the time, meant the sector was at times a reluctant participant in the concept of a national horse council … and always less than fully committed to the venture.

Yet, as University of Melbourne graduate Peter Huntington recalls, the racing sector played a strangely paradoxical role in the Australian Horse Council's eventual creation. There has always existed a state-based hierarchy, predicated on the successes of each state's racing and breeding industries. Victoria – home to Flemington Racecourse and the Melbourne Cup and historically considered 'the home of racing in Australia' – has long ruled supreme. This was particularly true during the 1980s. Victoria was the undisputed premier state, New South Wales came in second and Queensland trailed behind in third.

Racing's predominance in Victoria meant there was a concentration of wealthy and influential individuals who were invested in addressing racing-related issues; this was central to the formation of the Victorian Horse Council (VHC) in 1980. The VHC was the first state-level horse council in Australia. Ironically, the broader racing industry wasn't all that interested in supporting a national body. Peter Huntington served on the VHC in the 1980s and remembered that part of the challenge was that the people who were driving those working state-based bodies 'didn't necessarily have the time or the energy to put into the national one as well.' Their focus on the state-level organisation simply didn't allow them to participate in a national body.

But despite its money and power, horse racing actually makes up only a small proportion of the total industry numbers. In 2007, the New South Wales government estimated that 'thoroughbred racing comprises only 20 per cent of the horses but is the largest economic sector of the industry.'

Patricia Ellis, an acclaimed Victorian equine vet who was both a foundational member of the AEVA and served within the Australian Horse Council for many years, well understands the challenges. Communicating with non-racing groups was like herding cats, she noted dryly, but the locus of the issue was the narrowness of people's general scope of concern. 'The average horse owner's problem is the last thing that happened to him or her,' Patricia said. 'They're only interested in generic issues if it directly affects them, and they can't see that there's a need for preparedness, there's a need for education.'

Reg knew the sacrifice that was needed to ensure the national council's success. He'd spent decades involved in the creation of equine veterinary organisations in Australia, and almost every one had begun their life with little to no funding. It had been years before the original EVA brethren had been able to attend interstate meetings without paying for their own travel and accommodation, but an acceptance of the situation and commitment to the organisation they were building had seen the EVA flourish.

Others were less convinced. Those who couldn't see the value (for them) in a national council were reluctant to contribute money for permanent administrative staff. At its core, Peter Huntington noted, the issue of 'who would pay for it and how you would enforce it was too big a bridge to get the horse industry over the line.' When there *was* money, everyone wanted their fair share without much recognition of priority. 'The pony clubs wanted money and the racehorse people wanted money.'[17]

For many, particularly the smaller breed associations, it was a challenge to see the bigger picture. Focused as they were on the management of their breed rather than the industry as a whole, they struggled with the idea of a need for a voice to government and the importance of international imports and exports. It's likely that many wondered what purpose a state or national council could serve for them – let alone one for which they were expected to raise funds, possibly by levying their membership. It was a rocky foundation on which to try and build; though Reg strongly believed a council would benefit *all* horse owners in Australia, many found his vision unpersuasive. Personal agendas ruled. Finding a consensus, or even just common interest across the groups, continued to be the deciding factor for the venture's success – or lack thereof.

The 'abortive attempt for a horseshoe levy' exemplifies that struggle. Seeking to raise funds to make the national council self-sufficient enough to be effective, the horseshoe levy proposed that a percentage of the monies from all horseshoes sold would be used to finance the council's management. There were both advocates and decriers for the scheme, but even when – somehow – a majority solution was reached (with the exception of only one faction), the levy was rejected by the federal government due to the industry's failure to achieve a unanimous agreement.

Depending on who you ask, the finger of blame lands anywhere along the spectrum of horse industry sectors. Bill Howey pointed to the lack of support from the major (state-based) racing organisations. Racing's lack of interest undermined the national body's efficacy, he argued, so that the AHC could never manifest the desired influence within federal government. Peter Huntington similarly believed varying levels of engagement across major organisations was to blame – the thoroughbred breeders, under the driving hand of Colin McAlpine were enthused, but many others, such as state-based racing groups, were not.

Inadvertently, the community itself became the impetus for achieving a national body. At every level it was veterinarians who were most invested in the idea of a high-functioning, cross-disciplinary and national council. Veterinarians inevitably work across all sectors and to some extent were removed from the politics, no more invested in the quarter horse lovers' interests than the stock horse breeders, the thoroughbred racing groups, or the pony club enthusiasts. The inevitable chasms between these different divisions were a factor in the AHC's struggles for coherence. 'A lot of horse owners are passionate about their own particular passion, own particular area of the industry and to some degree look down on the other sectors,' Peter Huntington pointed out. 'That was why it was very hard to get a national body together and functioning.'

A dressage rider need not have anything to do with thoroughbred racing, or a stock horse breeder with a small town pony club … but inevitably, at some point, *every* horse will need a vet. Working at the coalface of equine disease, vets had a greater grasp of the ramifications of outbreaks and the challenges around how diseases spread. Such knowledge made the idea of a national council – including, most notably, the greatly desired creation of national horse and breed registers – appealing. Further, the consequences of Australia's mishandling of the CEM outbreak in the late 1970s must have been uppermost in many vets' minds, and probably also explains a similar passion among thoroughbred breeders – another serious disease outbreak, without a coordinated response that was only achievable through a coherent national organisation, could have even more dire ramifications. But while these veterinarians were the ones who saw the most value in the success of the National Horse Council, they were not influential enough to create the momentum needed to make it work.

Unlike many others, Reg had industry clout and he brought every scrap of it to bear in his fight to establish the Australian Horse Council. He was rigorous in considering how best Australia might better manage and coordinate its industry and firmly believed the approach he conceived to be the best. The sluggish, fragmentary response he encountered in the early 1980s must have felt like salt in the wound when he compared it to the success of the American version. It says much about the environment in which he was operating that, despite his best efforts, it wasn't until 1984 that concrete steps were made. By that point, 'only the Victorian industry had managed to set up a state council and any moves to establish a national body had foundered on disagreement, self-interest and apathy.'

In February 1984, the state division presidents of the Bloodhorse Breeders' Association of Australia (subsequently the Australian Bloodhorse Breeders Association [ABBA] in 1987 and the Thoroughbred Breeders Association [TBA] from 1994) convened in Adelaide. Under the direction of the association's federal president – Reg's long-time friend and colleague Colin McAlpine – they discussed forming a national council framework. Reg took the opportunity to advance several suggestions. At the meeting's conclusion, the association decided it was time that key players within the industry be brought together to discuss the idea of a national council and they asked that Reg, supported by EVA and Australian Equine Research Foundation executives, to issue invitations to attend a meeting in Canberra in March.

As Colin opened the meeting on 30 March 1984, he drew attention to the central role Reg had played in bringing the various factions together. Since they had met in February, he noted, Reg 'has worked at [an] almost dynamic level to get this meeting today under way.' What Colin didn't say – but what everyone else doubtless knew – was that the fact that the meeting was occurring at all was a triumph. Reg's work to 'bring all the big players into the [one] room' was a monumental feat.[18] But it would have been impossible without the investment of others, most notably Colin.

Even so, the path ahead remained rocky.

Colin reinforced the need the Bloodhorse Breeders' Association saw for the National Horse Council of Australia and noted what he and the association felt were key areas of concern to take up with the government, including the import and export of horses; drought relief; and tax relief.

Following Colin's introduction, Reg stood up. He provided a brief overview of the sequence of events that had led them to that room on that day, 'because it demonstrated that the prodding of emergency is what gets most things done.' He recounted the CEM disaster that had shocked the industry in 1977 and ignited his passion for reimagining communication throughout Australia's various equine organisations. There were seven listed reasons for the formation of a council: interface with government agencies; association with the National Farmers' Federation; research; welfare issues; communication and dissemination of information; identification of horses; and production of suitable vaccines and medicaments.

However, these were not Reg's primary focus. Instead, he spoke of the philosophy underpinning the formation of a national council. The diverse collection of people and interests that made up the industry fragmented it and many despaired of it ever becoming a cohesive body. The only way forward was consensus and unification. 'We must realise that one horseman's problem is *everyone's* problem,' Reg said. 'Strength can only be obtained through unity. We all have goals and objectives that can best be produced if we work on a united basis ... This concerns all horse owners alike. If there is a problem that concerns the country as a whole, we must know who we can talk to and who we can deal with.'

The CEM outbreak had highlighted the country's communications deficiencies. The government had encountered a disease that Reg understood – but, he pointedly told his listeners, 'I did not know who to tell what it was all about.' The ramifications of that failure continued to resonate; as Reg reminded the gathering, Australia in 1984 was still banned from exporting horses to South Africa due to the CEM outbreak. There were also risks in not having well-educated and well-informed people involved in legislating and managing equine issues. Reg left no one in doubt as to his views on this. 'When you have people involved who have no horse sense, you can get bad legislation developing and common sense is not sufficient to overcome bad legislation once it becomes law of the land. We must be in a position to prepare well-documented cases to defend those procedures which are deemed necessary for the proper husbandry, use and care of horses. It is only by united effort that this can be achieved and when it is seen to be the unanimous decision from a national body representing all horses.'

He emphasised that the 'importance of a cohesive national body must be further reinforced by ... education, research and communication.' Education had always been one of Reg's foremost concerns, and whether it was provided in riding schools, agricultural colleges, or the veterinary schools of universities, he argued it should be of paramount significance to all involved. But adroit management was crucial. 'We want the best available education for all aspects,

[but] we do not want to waste resources ... We do not want overproduction and we certainly do not want the production of an article for which there is no demand.' And in the establishment of a national council, education offered an additional benefit: it would only be by inculcating a belief in the value of a council at grassroots level across organisations around the country, that the cooperation necessary to the council's longevity could be assured.

Meanwhile, the research which was central to developing equine understanding and advancing the industry was underfunded and under-supported. The AERF and its smattering of state research foundations must be managed to avoid duplication of effort to 'conserve whatever little funds have been currently available.' A national council could also fight for the (then non-existent) federal grants required to support essential research.

Reg finished his address and sat down. A man called Barry Cassell, a member of the Australasian Andalusian Association, stood and put forward a motion to establish the National Horse Council of Australia. The Australian Endurance Riders' Association's Elizabeth McCallum seconded, and the motion was carried unanimously.

At 3 p.m. on 30 March 1984, the Australian Horse Council was born.

When the time came to depart, Colin McAlpine couldn't let the meeting finish without a final word. 'It would be very remiss of me if I didn't make a special mention of Dr R. R. Pascoe, who put everything together for us today ... Others helped but he was the man who did all the work to make the meeting today possible and to work on all the items put forward.' When he asked the meeting to show its appreciation for Reg, his words were met with thunderous applause.

But as the group discussed the new organisation's terms of reference, Reg had a reminder for them all. 'We are dealing with a national organisation and there is no room for pettiness, internecine fighting or for anything other than business of a national level. If everybody keeps the point before them all these problems would be solved in a few minutes because basically there are no grounds for a fight.' It was a sensible, practical attitude – quintessentially Reg – and in seeking to pre-empt such issues, he had accurately foreseen the challenges to come.

Despite the relevance of the issues being discussed, most state governments issued apologies and didn't attend the meeting. With the exception of Queensland, the state bodies were 'holding watching briefs' saying 'they wished to see the National Horse Council of Australia formed but ... could not see at this stage any point in having direct intervention.' Such passivity was indicative of the attitude towards the venture and though state horse councils were subsequently established in Queensland, South Australia, Western Australia and New South Wales, the realisation of Reg's original vision was turbulent and the outcome short-lived.

What is now called the Australian Horse Industry Council (AHIC) found the first few years of its existence challenging – and, though it survives today, the organisation is far less than what Reg had imagined it might be. What successes it has had are due to the dogged persistence of a few forceful, hard-working and dedicated people: people committed to the industry's wellbeing – irrespective of personal agendas.

After the initial meeting in Canberra, there 'followed a very difficult period in the establishing of this framework ... factional infighting weakened its authority, lack of funding could have dug its grave and funds ran out. The attempted efforts to use various funding avenues – such as levies on foals, racing horses, and the abortive attempt for a horseshoe levy – all took their toll.' Elected as one of twelve trustees in late 1985 and then secretary the following year, Reg had a front-row seat to these struggles. He played a leading role in the 1986 formation of the Queensland Horse Council and served as its trustee and honorary treasurer for thirteen years, for which he was awarded a QHC life membership in October 1999.

The state councils however were riven by squabbling. Faced with recurring dissolution due to the very 'pettiness [and] internecine fighting' he had so presciently warned of, Reg often took matters into his own hands – but even his redoubtable efforts weren't enough. Patricia Ellis recalled one instance in the late 1980s-early 1990s when the NSW Horse Council seemed, yet again, on the verge of collapse. Reg gathered a selection of his fellow AEVA members to attend the council's meeting and try to provide a voice of reason. Walking into the room, the AEVA group were confronted with various members of the NSW Horse Council arguing. 'All of a sudden, Reg hit the desk in front of him with a great thump and said, "Right, you people! Time to pull together."' It was a summons impossible to ignore. The councillors sat up and took notice of his words ... but in his absence, the council inevitably struggled once more. If Reg could have held them together – state and national councils all – with his own blood and bone, he would have. As Patricia Ellis recalled, 'Reg single-handedly was the secretariat for quite a long time in the early days; at one stage, he was pretty much a one-man band, horse-council wise.'

In 1992, the Australian National Horse Council became the Australian Horse Industry Council. It was a move that sought to better recognise and incorporate peripheral components of the industry – not just the breeders and the vets, but also the farriers, the float-makers and the feed companies. A month later, in April 1992, Reg resigned as secretary of the AHIC and, in recognition of his 'outstanding wisdom and determination in carrying out various positions' within the organisation, was made the AHIC's first honorary life member. The reasons why he resigned are not entirely clear, but it's possible he felt he had driven the idea as far as it could go; perhaps he hoped that the shift to the AHIC would better align with all he had envisaged and that with the change, it was safe to let go. Or perhaps after more than a decade of devoting himself to the endeavour when so many others refused to meaningfully contribute, he was just tired.

The dream into which Reg poured so much time and determination has never truly materialised. Those industry rifts that hindered it have only deepened over time: today, Racing Australia and Australian thoroughbred breeders hold no seats on the AHIC. Most state councils have vanished or have splintered into specialist group councils that still fail to provide the central point of coordination required to make a national body truly effective. Of those states that continue to maintain 'horse councils', these too are limited to certain industry sectors. Though truest to Reg's ideal, the Queensland Horse Council (following several reconfigurations) describes its organisational focus as the 'Performance and Pleasure

Horse Industry, which comprises of all equine interests other than racing' – though it maintains 'an excellent working relationship with the Racing and Thoroughbred breeding sectors.'

The consequence is that when a crisis has arisen, the national response has been suboptimal, even though such incidences have simultaneously reignited national awareness of the need for a central coordinating body. The AHIC, member Quentin Wallace noted, 'was given a boost when the flu epidemic hit, because government wanted to deal with a single body', but the fragmentary response born of previous neglect doubtless left a sour taste in many mouths. In 2010, following the 2007/2008 equine influenza crisis, the Queensland Horse Council submitted a proposal to support formalising the horse industry's inclusion in Australia's Emergency Animal Disease Response Agreement (EADRA), noting, 'No organisation, government or industry, performed with great distinction during the 2007/2008 Equine Influenza crisis. It was an incredibly hard lesson.' The EADRA is a response plan under the management of Animal Health Australia – clearly, the QHC had identified just how desperately the Australian horse industry needed better coordination to avoid recurrent poor handling of disease outbreaks ... much as Reg had realised with the 1977 contagious equine metritis outbreak. Not much, it seemed, had changed.

Reg's good friend, UK vet Derek Knottenbelt, recalled Reg's 'understanding of other people's inadequacies', but this failed Reg when he conceived that bright vision of the AHIC. Achieving it required vast numbers of people to set aside their personal priorities and take a broader view of the needs of the industry: to consider the implications not only for their specific area of interest, but for *all* horse people in Australia – and to invest both time and money in safeguarding that population and preparing for the possibility of a crisis. This idea of a thorough and effective national body seemed logical to Reg – investment in the community was, after all, a guiding philosophy in his life – but more than that, he recognised how intertwined are the fates of all members of the industry. CEM had taught him that lesson, and he had learnt it well. But in his assumption that this would be true of everyone else, his faith in others stretched too far.

That's not to say that he was alone. Far from it. Beyond the initial passion of Colin McAlpine, there have been countless others who have continued to fight for that dream. But there is only so much individuals can overcome when faced with what Reg's colleague at the ACVS referred to as 'trying to do the job of a multibillion-dollar industry with no resources and no personnel.' Even Reg Pascoe, it seemed, had to let some dreams go.

8
Publications and Symposia: the Sharing of Knowledge

Reg was dedicated to sharing his knowledge with others. He was an active participant in countless symposia and produced countless professional publications for a practising clinician. Whether it was his research into little-understood equine pathologies or his devotion to fostering professional organisations, Reg's endeavours were the tangible manifestations of his belief in sharing the benefits of his hard-won experience – and his valuable clinical findings – for both the individual's edification and for the broader ongoing evolution of veterinary science as a discipline. In Chapter 6, Derek Knottenbelt noted the risk in assessing Reg's influence purely on the basis of his publications. Derek recognised the importance of interpersonal interactions which are never captured in print. Regardless, examining Reg's participation in international conferences and some of his most notable publications goes some way towards capturing both his own belief in education through sharing his knowledge, and the lasting reverberations of his work.

Reg saw participating in conferences and writing for publications as simply good professional practice. 'Clinically interesting material is often overlooked in busy practices, but is rewarding both personally, and for the practising profession as a whole for such material to be published.' The activities also formed part of his personal ethos: sharing what you knew so that everyone could benefit.

US veterinary reproductive specialist, Dr Cheryl Lopate, who worked at OVH in the mid-1990s, recalled Reg's attitude toward education. 'He tried to impart his knowledge to as many people as he could in an easy-to-understand format; he never wrote things to be confusing or to sound professional. He wrote things that were very explanatory. He has [written] so many books on clinical conditions and how to manage clinical cases rather than the minutiae of academic research.'

Reg worked hard over many years to build his expertise, but he shared it as readily as if he had chanced upon it, rather than by dint of his own endeavours. The challenges of his early years never left him, prickling like bindis caught in his clothing. Perhaps the effects of those early experiences only grew stronger and more acute as he grew older and recognised just how much good one person could do.

Of course, his academic pursuits had to coexist with his clinical work. One of his vets from the early 1980s, Andrew Dart, pointed out how well Reg could not only balance academia and a busy practice, but to do so without the support networks that many other successful academics enjoyed. Reg had 'always seen so much – from that little town in the Darling Downs – that he was right up on the world stage' alongside some of the finest international professors and academics. But where many had financial backing and staff support to achieve their breakthroughs, 'Reg was just doing it quietly on the side.' And what he was doing on the side was extraordinary.

The late Professor Dave Hutchins (or 'Prof' as he was known) was one of Reg's most renowned contemporaries, an internationally lauded clinician and pioneer in both equine surgery and medicine in Australia. They were colleagues through the AEVA and the PGF in a relationship Prof described as characterised by 'mutual professional respect.' There were similarities between the two men: beyond their stellar careers, both were innovators, passionate about education. In a 2019 conversation between Prof and his protégée, equine internal medicine specialist Dr Leanne Begg, the two agreed Reg was 'observant and meticulous at recording his clinical observations ... His ability to do good clinical research stands him out among his peers.' Just as crucially, Reg's publications enabled him to share that research in meaningful ways. 'He published impressively and was without doubt one of the leaders in veterinary science in Australia of his time.'

The Inaugural International Symposium on Equine Reproduction (ISER)

The year 1974 saw the inaugural International Symposium on Equine Reproduction (ISER) held in Cambridge, England. The conference was an initiative of a keen young British veterinarian called 'Twink' Allen, who was supported by a cadre of well-known British and international vets including founding members Doug Mitchell, Bill Pickett, Peter Rossdale and John Hughes (whom Reg had met during his 1968 study trip to the University of California, Davis).

Twink imagined a forum for 'biologists and veterinarians interested in equine reproduction to exchange and argue their views, to review the present state of knowledge of the subject, to produce guidelines for future research, and to foster international friendship and collaboration.' Given that description, the event naturally piqued Reg's interest. He was one of about twenty-five in what Twink remembered as a 'very jolly, noisy, badly-behaved bunch of Australians and New Zealanders' who attended. Bill Howey, the Scone veterinarian who worked with Reg at the AEVA, attended as well and retained fond memories. And while Reg was certainly quieter than the rest, he didn't hold himself apart, particularly when the group got going and there was fun to be had: 'he was very much part of the gang.' There was a clear line in the sand, however. When, after a dinner at King's College one night, Twink and some colleagues had to fish a number of the visitors out of the Cam River into which they'd ducked for a 3 a.m. swim, Reg was noticeably absent.

Impromptu river swims notwithstanding, the inaugural ISER was a success. The symposium proceedings were edited and collated, titled 'Equine Reproduction' and published as a supplement to *Cambridge's Journal of Reproduction and Fertility*.

Reg and Twink stayed friends after the symposium and met many times, both at conferences and outside of them. Twink visited Reg and Joy in Oakey almost a decade after the inaugural ISER, enjoying their hospitality for several days (including a scintillating dinner with all four sons present) and visiting the hospital.

Beyond Reg's impressive conference presence, the strongest impression he left upon Twink was of his incredible mind. Reg was a good practitioner who had built an excellent practice, but fundamentally he possessed the 'inquiring mind of an academic and a researcher'; he was a man, Twink believed, who would 'have succeeded admirably in an academic career.' Perhaps so, but such a life – in an office, behind a desk, away from the outdoor life in which he thrived – might have underwhelmed Reg. Reg, Twink remembered, 'did enjoy the outdoor life and veterinary razzmatazz and going round to the stud farms and getting all the mares pregnant.' For all Reg's love of research, it was being a vet in the field or in the clinic that truly drove his work.

Professional Ethics Publication

Reg's professional successes, his interest in developing Australian veterinary science, his involvement with key veterinary organisations, and his enthusiasm for cultivating junior vets inevitably positioned him as a leader in the profession. But he was never one for the limelight. His leadership was less about standing on podia and calling the masses to arms and more about exemplifying what a vet – and more fundamentally, a person – should be. It resonated deeply with those who witnessed it. 'Everything he did was for our profession and the good of our profession rather than for himself,' veterinarian Jane Axon said.

There were certain lines in life that Reg believed should never be crossed. Ensuring these boundaries remained sacrosanct and openly condemning what he saw as unethical behaviour ineluctably positioned him as a role model for 'great professional ethics.' When another veterinarian sold and distributed drugs over the internet without in-person consultation, Reg (who couldn't countenance treating an animal without even *seeing* it) was very clear in his condemnation of such. And he was never backwards about sharing his concerns. Addressing the profession in a 1975 journal article, he noted, 'This increase in veterinary population will lead to more active competition between practices which, if allowed to drift into unethical procedures in the quest for the dollar, can only bring harm to our good professional standing of today.'

ISER III and IV – Sydney, 1982; Calgary, 1986

In 1982, as a member of the small, six-person symposium committee, Reg played a crucial role in coordinating the third ISER in Sydney. Alongside industry stalwarts such as Bill Howey and Rex Butterfield (the founding president of the ACVS), they were joined by forceful South Australian vet Peter Irwin as chair and the quiet, unassuming New South Welshman Phil Knight as treasurer. Audrey Best completed the team as secretary, a role for which she was well suited. She had long been a central figure in the AEVA in her role as secretary: past AEVA president Ian Nielsen recalled that she ran the show. She was 'a bit of an authority figure and terrifying to most committee members' he added but he concurred with Bill Howey's observation that Audrey possessed superlative administrative skills. These were to be essential to the successful conduct of ISER III.

Most of the ISER III organising committee had attended the inaugural symposium in Cambridge eight years earlier and the second in Davis in 1978. These experiences were positive, and everyone seems to have felt that they would be hard acts to follow. But once their hats were in the ring and Sydney was set as the location for the next ISER, there was nothing else for it but to fully commit to the venture – and so they did.

Between 1978 and 1982, the organising committee managed their meetings as a kind of sub-committee of the AEVA, aided by the fact that Howey, Irwin and Reg were all past AEVA presidents. Bill recalled that in their meetings Reg was pragmatic, yet he doubtless would have viewed the whole concept as another great challenge and quietly thrilled to the prospect.

There can also be little question that the six members of the committee dug deep during this time – Bill Howey noted that their meetings were self-funded, which provides some idea of the tight budget they were operating under. Professor Rex Butterfield leant on his connections at the University of Sydney to secure a week at the university's multi-purpose performing arts Seymour Centre for free, rather than the typical $20,000 it should have cost the symposium.

Their efforts were worth it. The committee gathered the necessary disparate pieces to present an excellent conference – not only a scientific success, but also yielding a healthy financial return. Attendees came from thirteen different countries, including Saudi Arabia, Japan and West Germany ... though the ongoing Cold War precluded the participation of several scientists from those countries (such as Poland) living behind the USSR's Iron Curtain. In the obligatory conference photograph, the front row of the third ISER was replete with what Bill described as 'the very cream of the academic upper echelon involved in equine veterinary research up to that time.' 'It's my view that ISER III in Sydney is/was by far the biggest achievement by the equine veterinary profession in Australia in its entire history – fifty years since 1971.' And of course, here too, as always, was Reg: sitting quietly at the heart of yet another triumph.

Four years later, Reg was joined by his second eldest son, David, at the fourth symposium in Calgary, Canada in 1986. Though John was not present in Calgary, there were many other occasions when, Twink recalled, 'the mafia were together.' The Pascoes sat, sons on either side of the father, all three asking the kinds of pointed questions with which Reg had been challenging speakers for decades. 'If anyone disagreed with what they suggested or had another view,' Twink recalled, 'then the rest of the family would unite and come down on whoever was questioning them very severely and determinedly and some jolly good arguments would go on.' Twink had by that stage known Reg for some time, and felt all three Pascoes enjoyed the robust discussions. Reg's inquisitive nature – and his legendary stubbornness – was alive and well in his two eldest sons.

Clostridium perfringens Type A

Among the countless academic papers that Reg published throughout his career, some were particularly groundbreaking. Following his role in isolating botulism in horses in the mid-1980s, he began exploring another lethal organism that was killing foals across the Darling Downs. In 1988, along with OVH veterinarian Andrew Dart and researchers at the Toowoomba laboratory, he published a paper on the group's discovery.

The responsible organism, *Clostridium perfringens* Type A, is member of the Clostridia genus – anaerobic bacteria that include many pathogenic species such as those causing tetanus, gas gangrene, botulism and other forms of food poisoning. These bacteria multiply rapidly, releasing toxins that are lethal and can kill an animal within days. While mature horses and foals are equally susceptible, foals, like most newborn animals, are dependent on their mothers for initial immune protection (which passes via the colostrum). Their smaller size means that they become more quickly dehydrated when suffering diarrhoea and are more vulnerable to disease.

Reg and Dart saw this first-hand during the 1988 season. Suffering from bloody diarrhoea, foals were dying rapidly – a 2009 article recorded the death of a foal within sixty hours (less than three days). But in 1988 there was no record of *Clostridium perfringens* Type A: for Reg and Dart, it would have been bewildering and horrifying to witness.

The two men did the only thing they could: put their overalls on, got down into the muck and began searching for an answer. Gathering samples from every case they saw, Reg and Dart enlisted the help of the Toowoomba laboratory. 'We isolated [this] organism – *Clostridium perfringens* Type A – which had never been seen anywhere else in the world,' Dart remembered. But despite this watershed moment, the discovery passed mostly unremarked upon: they published a paper in the *Australian Veterinary Journal* in October 1988 but 'no one really said a whole lot about it.'

Some years later, Dart was working at the University of California, Davis when a similar outbreak occurred among newborn foals. He suggested testing for *Clostridium perfringens* Type A but no one seemed to pay him much heed. Later on, a New Zealand pathologist told Dart they had discovered the lethal organism in the foals. The pathologist was astonished by the finding. 'We should write this up,' he said. 'It's never been reported anywhere else in the world.' Dart said nothing. The pathologist returned the following day, shaking his head. 'You bastard,' he said to Dart. 'You and Reg published about this two years ago.'

Dart's response could have been learnt at Reg's knee. 'Well, I have been trying to tell everyone that,' he said with a shrug.

Post-Graduate Foundation's 'Equine Dermatoses'

Reg's interest in skin conditions continued 'widening considerably due to lack of published information in Australia and reported skin conditions on horses in other countries.' As he stepped into that waiting void, his growing expertise meant he began receiving lecture, article and other publication requests throughout the 1970s and 1980s. He spoke many, many times for the University of Sydney's Post-Graduate Foundation (PGF; today the Centre for Veterinary Education [CVE]) on everything from ultrasound to the evolution of the horse, specific equine eyelid conditions through to lameness.

In the late 1980s, he wrote a small paperback handbook for the PGF called *Equine Dermatoses*. Veterinarian Hugh White, who in 2021 had been the CVE's director for thirteen years, recalled *Equine Dermatoses* as a convenient little publication that filled a crucial gap in general understanding. It was 'the sort of thing people could throw in their car, keep in their glovebox and pull out when they saw something where they weren't quite sure what it was.' With its collection of photos for identifying skin conditions, most of which were likely taken by Reg, the book rapidly became the 'go-to handbook for people in mixed practice or people in horse practice' and the PGF sold countless copies throughout the 1990s.

Colour Atlas of Diseases and Disorders of the Horse

Galvanised by his early successes in equine dermatology, Reg's irrepressible curiosity and the general dearth of data led to his 'investigation into various conditions which were likely to be of importance to horses in Australia', as he recorded in his 1982 doctoral submission. The result, noted his assessor, was that, '[Reg] was instrumental in making several significant scientific advances notably in dermatology and virology ... without his initiative many studies could not have been carried out.' The report commended Reg's prolific experimentations and his dedication to the profession. 'He is recognised today as one of Australia's leading equine practitioners, and as one who has made a significant contribution to our knowledge of the horse in health and disease. His published work has led to his being recognised for his distinguished contributions not only in this country, but on the world scene. Mr Pascoe's originality is that of a veterinary practitioner, a highly skilled clinician, who observes an abnormality and recognises it as a unique syndrome. He then thinks about the condition, identifies the problem, and seeks to answer it by logical investigation.'

In particular, the assessor drew attention to Reg's exploration of rain scald and its implications (see Chapter 6). His efforts to determine the cause and optimal treatment for the condition exemplified his analytical bias in his clinical work – it was both a skill and a marker of his breadth of veterinary knowledge that he was able to identify that what he was seeing had never been described in literature before or, if it had, was yet lacking a tested scientific explanation or identification of a causal organism.

It was important to note, the assessor added, that despite Reg's reliance on external laboratory support, he was the primary instigator of, and pivotal to, the completion of such research work. 'The original stimulus, the diligent clinical investigation and a good deal of the experimental work was carried out by Mr Pascoe. Without his original observations and hard work, the causal agents of a number of these conditions [such as coital exanthema and equine herpesvirus 4 in virology, and fungal conditions in dermatology] would probably still be unidentified ... in the thirty years he has been in practice Mr Pascoe's contributions to knowledge have been quite extraordinary and should be seen as an example to all clinicians.'

These excerpts from the assessor's report provide insight into Reg's standing; moreover, they offer context for the work that he did with British equine internal medicine specialist, Professor Derek Knottenbelt, in the 1990s. While Reg's publications and work for the PGF demonstrated his passion for sharing knowledge, his friendship and collaboration with Derek perhaps best illustrated Reg's dedication to sharing his expertise across the profession.

Reg's address to the Graduands upon the occasion of being awarded his Doctor of Veterinary Science.

Derek and Reg first met at a British Equine Veterinarians Association (BEVA) conference in 1991. There, as it had for others many times before, Reg's breadth of experience inadvertently swiped the floor out from under Derek. Presenting a new condition for which he had four exemplar cases, Derek was expounding on his treatment method when a voice from the back of the room piped up. 'Do they look like *this*?' Reg asked, meticulously describing the condition on which Derek was presenting before following up with a detailed account of how he thought the horses were probably reacting to Derek's treatment so far.

'Exactly!' Derek said.

'Well,' said Reg, popping Derek's bubble, 'they're about to go to shit now.' To Derek's four cases, Reg had seen a dozen: the first six had died under his care; the latter six, with whom he had changed his approach, had lived. After the day's presenters had finished, the two men made a beeline for one another. Reg freely shared his experiences, discussing what had so far worked and what had failed. This first encounter left a deep impression on Derek, and it initiated a long and fruitful collaboration.

When a publisher approached Derek in the early 1990s and asked him if he'd be interested in writing an equine textbook with Reg, he was flattered. 'I thought, frankly, I'd died and gone to heaven ... Anybody who knew anything about horses anywhere in the world from a veterinary perspective, knew of [Reg] and had experience of things that he had done and said and written.'

The two men were kindred spirits, sharing a passion for photographing everything they saw in clinical practice. Armed with their vast collection of images, Derek and Reg set about writing the *Colour Atlas of Diseases and Disorders of the Horse*. They corresponded via email for a time before Reg bit the bullet: putting their textbook together would be far easier and more efficient if they were in the same place. 'I'm coming to England,' he told Derek, who happily concurred.

Reg and Joy travelled to Liverpool to stay with Derek and his wife, Morna. Joy and Morna quickly got acquainted and, as they explored the local sights together, Reg and Derek knuckled down at the desk. From the first, their decision to collaborate in person was validated; they spent the first week hunched over an X-ray viewer turned on its side into which they fed thousands of slides, poring over the images to find which might best fit the book. This process, and the deep, lasting friendship they built throughout, was beneficial to them both. Reg greatly enjoyed Derek's company – they found plenty of time for laughter amid their work – so much so that he and Joy returned several times over the years.

'The more I spoke to him,' Derek recalled, 'the more I realised that although we knew that he was a fantastic clinician and a great guy, that was nothing ... a lot of what I learned beyond my normal practice life was as a consequence [of time spent with Reg] ... It was absolutely clear to me that this guy was, frankly, a veterinary god.'

Together, their effect was electric. *Colour Atlas of Diseases and Disorders of the Horse* became a bestseller for the genre, reprinting multiple times. Translated into at least four different languages, Derek noted, 'It was clear that we had something going for us.'

Equine Stud Farm Medicine and Surgery and a Final Contribution

Almost a decade after *Colour Atlas of Diseases and Disorders of the Horse* was published, Reg and Derek were given the chance to work on another book in the early 2000s. Joined by the skilled minds of two American reproductive specialists, Dr Cheryl Lopate and Dr Michelle Leblanc, the four wrote *Equine Stud Farm Medicine and Surgery* for Dutch scientific publishers, Elsevier.

By the early 2000s, Reg had been working in equine reproduction for over six decades and according to Derek Knottenbelt, 'his experience of stud farm medicine and reproductive surgery and so on was just amazing.' Cheryl Lopate knew that it must have been Reg who had suggested her inclusion. She was aware of the faith he was showing in her to 'choose me over all [his] other friends and specialists [in the US] ... I was very honoured.' With Derek as the editor, each contributor was assigned a separate section; once their work was complete, they sent their portion to Derek, who compiled them.

Like Reg and Derek's earlier *Colour Atlas*, the new textbook was a practical, hands-on guide designed to be accessible to vets of all experience levels. Reg and Derek again enjoyed themselves immensely in the process. Derek remembered fondly that, 'We met at so many places across the world and every time we met, it was just like we'd seen each other yesterday.'

Reg was to make one final contribution to the world of equine veterinary textbooks. When he decided to retire – yielding to the passage of time and the promise of pursuing other passions – Derek approached him with a new idea. Knowing of Reg's interest and exploration in the field, he suggested an equine dermatology book. It was tempting, but after considering it, Reg said no. 'I'm a bit tired of all that,' he added. 'But good luck with it. I'll help you out where I can.'

'He did,' Derek recalled. 'An awful lot.' Reg's help was so vital to Derek's work (for he ended up writing the textbook predominantly on his own) that he titled the book *Pascoe's Principles and Practice of*

Equine Dermatology. At the front, he wrote how he had met Reg and Joy, and thanked Reg for all his help in bringing the book into being. It sold out, with a second edition released in 2014.

Even if Reg was no longer working in the clinic, his passion for veterinary science and the scores of close connections he'd made throughout his career remained constant. He continued to send Derek pictures and other information for a subsequent neonatology book Derek wrote. In this, Derek believed Reg was especially unique. 'There aren't many people like him in the world. There are a lot of greedy people, a lot of people who attacked him about everything that they know, but he was never like that. He was just always so open and so willing to share things.' Yet Reg's expectation of reciprocation was minimal. His desire to share his knowledge was centred on improving the profession and it was important to him that he lend a hand wherever he could – 'he was one step ahead of us all really and he wanted to help, he wanted to contribute.'

It is this trait, perhaps more than any other, that characterises Reg's publications history: he recognised and believed in the value of collaboration as a method for developing veterinary science and bettering the community as a whole.

Part IV —
Contributions to the Australian Veterinary Industry

9
A Vet and a Businessman: Provet

Reg was always considering the bigger picture. He dedicated his life to fostering a strong, agile and responsive Australian veterinary community and this dedication extended well beyond just veterinary bodies. He believed cooperation between veterinarians was essential to the profession's growth and, just as crucially, to the ongoing education of horse owners about both the range of treatment options available and the quality of care they should expect. Reg began working at a time when Australian vets had limited options for procuring supplies and were generally viewed, at least in his region, with scepticism. Overcoming these obstacles left an indelible mark, most evident in his belief in regulating the industry and for a tight-knit, professional and perpetually evolving equine vet community.

In the 1980s, Australian veterinarians were experiencing a unique and rather thorny issue: how to easily and at reasonable cost buy the supplies they needed to do their job. It wasn't that there weren't any available. There was a thriving overseas market, upon which Australian vets were almost solely reliant. The problem with being dependent on imported products was ensuring they were supplied on time when competing with global demand, and the risk of sudden and unexpected price surges if a product was in high demand elsewhere.

The range of imported products was also narrow, due to the relatively small Australian market. Importing goods is only profitable if there are enough customers and the issue was compounded by vets' loyalty to their chosen supplier. Vets inadvertently dispersing their product requests across multiple suppliers meant that distributors couldn't justify bringing in products for such a small client base. Ironically, this same loyalty reduced competition between companies: there was no real impetus for distributors to provide a wider range.

The biggest worry of all was getting the medicines required. There were virtually no pharmaceutical products manufactured in Australia and the imported options were limited. The human medicines that veterinarians occasionally used to treat animals were only available through medical suppliers. Most vets thought pet products were too commercial to stock in their practices, so veterinary wholesalers didn't carry them – but there were very few pet stores available for the public to buy from anyway, and vets who wanted to fill the gap struggled to find suppliers. (In 2021, large warehouse-style pet stores are ubiquitous, but this is a new phenomenon.) Emerging diagnostic equipment such as X-ray (made purely for human hospitals and astronomically expensive), and machine options for laboratory work such as blood tests (still done in labs, by hand, using test tubes and reagents), were inaccessible to most.

The result was a disorganised and fractured system of different suppliers selling different products, mostly from overseas. Procuring clinical supplies was a difficult, unwieldly and time-intensive process for Australian vets. To add insult to injury, the market was not a particularly honest one either. Of the three major national wholesalers who served as the local distributors of the international companies, all provided a mediocre and apathetic service that cared little for helping clients get what they needed ... yet did so at a generous profit margin. Several drug distributors were receiving discounts of up to 15 per cent from manufacturers with the understanding that these savings were being passed onto the Australian veterinary profession, who of course rarely saw the rebate.

Into this frustrating gap stepped Queensland veterinarians – and brothers – Vic and Bob Menrath. The situation 'really got up my nose', according to Vic, and so he began his own small wholesaling operation on the side of his busy clinical practice, buying directly from the manufacturers. At the time, Vic was running the Kessels Road Veterinary Hospital (KRVH) in MacGregor, in Brisbane's south – the practice regularly had a large pharmaceutical bill. Vic's idea was to circumvent those companies that were taking advantage of vets by overcharging them, go direct to the manufacturers and capitalise on their discounts. It worked and, before long, Bob and Vic were buying supplies on behalf of other colleagues too. But their efforts drove home the complexities of trying to bypass the system and coordinating with various manufacturers soon turned their endeavour into a logistical nightmare.

If the brothers had gallantly bowed out at this point, no one would have blamed them. Nevertheless, the underlying problem persisted. What if, Bob and Vic wondered, their side venture could become a stand-alone enterprise? This new Australian veterinary wholesale distributor, which they dubbed 'Provet', might be the panacea for an industry struggling to adequately fulfil veterinarians' clinical supply requirements.

After developing a business plan, Bob spent several months quietly discussing the idea with various friends and colleagues. He recalled, however, that 'it soon became obvious that there would likely be some considerable limitations to [the company's] growth, given its ownership by a colleague and potential competitor.' Sole proprietorship would place the owner in a unique power dynamic with colleagues with whom they were potentially competing for clients. This was germane because Bob and Vic's successful, five-clinic Kessels Road Veterinary Hospital structure had brought difficulties with several other Brisbane vets who saw their operation as a threat.

Allowing Provet to be seen as a KRVH enterprise could undermine its legitimacy. But sole proprietorship was also risky as the venture would be dependent on the business nous of a single party, the Menrath brothers. A collective business venture, on the other hand, not only brought with it greater commercial impartiality, but also dispersed the management of the company's teething problems, which were likely to be substantial in the early years.

Bob and Vic were aware of the challenges; other vets had seen the opportunity and two 'would-be, supply-all distributors [had recently gone] belly-up within a couple of years in Brisbane alone.' The causes are not entirely clear, though one apparently became insolvent due to misuse of funds. The other was a cooperative (a member-owned business in which all members have equal voting rights, regardless of their level of investment), which fell prey to some members' sense of entitlement to benefits that the company couldn't reasonably absorb. Provet, Bob was determined, would not suffer a similar fate: his business plan was comprehensive and supported by expert consultation.

In 1981, Bob began actively mobilising support. Making Provet attractive enough that colleagues financially backed it would spread the risk. The more vets fiscally and ideologically invested in the concept, the more they were likely to use its services. The brothers considered other potential directors to join them on the Provet board, which would both shift the burden of financial risk away from their practice and defuse the sole proprietorship issue. Reg's name came up as an option. He was influential in Queensland and 'everybody admired him', Vic recalled. The brothers decided Reg was the large animal and equine veterinarian representative whose support – and preferably active involvement – they wanted.

Vic and Reg had met in 1974 through the Queensland Veterinary Surgeons Board (VSB), on which Reg had sat since 1958. Since that time, Vic had also become a member of the VSB and joined the ACVS Board of Examiners, which Reg first joined in 1980. Their roles meant they spent a lot of time together. On the VSB, their responsibilities included reviewing cases regarding the conduct of practising veterinarians in Queensland before formulating a reply to the writer about how they as a board would respond. It was a rigorous and demanding process, one that Vic remembered as difficult at times. But more often than not, Reg 'would just rattle off [the solution]' leaving his fellow board members gobsmacked – and Vic awed.

On the ACVS Board of Examiners, Reg and Vic regularly met in Sydney to run the membership and fellowship exams and, while doing so, weren't always on their best behaviour. On one occasion, Vic recalled arriving at the hotel next door to the university and heading to the reception desk to check in. Reg entered the lobby and clapped a hand down on Vic's shoulder. 'Let's have a couple of beers,' he said. But when he went to check into his own room, there was a problem. 'Oh, I'm sorry, Dr Pascoe, you haven't got a room,' the receptionist said awkwardly. Reg was infuriated, but no matter what he did, there was no room to be had.

'Reg, why don't you come and stay in my room?' Vic offered. With two beds, it wouldn't be a problem, and the two men headed out 'on the turps.' Vic wasn't sure whether Reg had ever been out on a night of heavy drinking, but they had a great time. It was only later, as they called it a night, that Vic remembered: he was chief examiner for an eight o'clock examination the following morning with a co-examiner who hated his guts. As the two men, pleasantly inebriated, stumbled back to the hotel, Vic told Reg, 'I'd better bloody ring up reception and make sure that I get woken up in time. I'd hate to be late.'

'Don't worry,' Reg said. 'I'll wake up. I have an internal clock. Five o'clock, I'm up, end of story.'

Vic woke the next morning at 7.45 a.m. to Reg snoring like a jet engine. He scrambled to dress and run to the examination. 'I never forgave him,' he remembered, laughing.

Reg made a habit of jumpstarting Vic's heart. On another trip, this time to Newcastle for a board meeting, they decided to head to the beach for a swim. Reg was fit and strong and had swum capably in the ocean without fear his whole life. Vic wasn't a great swimmer and he recalled paddling in the shallows while Reg was much further away, somewhere 'out there in the bloody surf.' And then Vic couldn't see him anywhere. Panicked, he ran up and called the lifeguard, raising the alarm ... only to find out that Reg had swum down the coast and 'just got out on the beach and was walking back again. I could've killed him for that.' Theirs was a strong, resilient friendship, and when Vic imagined undertaking a mammoth new professional venture, he knew he wanted Reg in his court.

Bob Menrath had met Reg at conferences and had heard he was well-known throughout the industry and ran a successful equine practice in Oakey. But Bob also knew that Reg had been involved as an external director in a privately owned veterinary distributor that hadn't made the grade. If Provet were to succeed, it was vital to know *why* this forerunner had failed.

The brothers approached Reg. Their recollections of how they did so, however, differ somewhat. According to Vic, 'Reg didn't hesitate when I rang him ... He just knew, straight away, that it was going to work.' Bob's account seems truer to the man than Vic's. '[The meeting] was set up by Vic, and I visited Reg at his practice in Oakey. He gave me his full attention and listened carefully to my plan and asked many questions. What its background was, how far we had developed it, and the business plan I had written. And I remember the words well: "Why would you want to do this? I have been involved in a vet wholesaler and it was a disaster. It's not going to work. Vets don't work well together."'

Reg had spent most of his career promoting collaboration and friendship within the veterinary community. It has to be assumed that his concern was not vets working well together – as they clearly could and did in a clinical capacity – but rather the challenges of business management and potential conflicts of interest. Vets inevitably compete with other vets for clients. A venture like Provet would demand these concerns be put aside. This was different to other cooperative ventures that Reg had facilitated or participated in: the numerous successful professional bodies of which he was a member were all about uniting practitioners on shared industry issues, or in pursuit of common ideals. But they weren't businesses per se. And, aside from basic administrative expenses, they didn't involve money.

Bob was taken aback. 'It was an unexpected and disappointing response. Fortunately, I had not raised the question of a directorship, but his intimate experience and knowledge of a failed venture made me all the more interested in having him on our potential board.'

The men spoke about the failed wholesaling company of which Reg had been a director. More than forty years later, the details are hard to pin down: Joy doesn't remember Reg acting as a director for another company, though they and many other vets owned shares in a popular distributor that later collapsed, costing many people a lot of money. But Bob believed Reg was a director because he explicitly recalled Reg saying that, if he got involved with Provet, he wanted to be legally protected as he previously had not been.

Regardless, the men spoke in great detail about this other venture, examining why Reg thought it had failed and discussing how it had been organised and developed. They noted poor, ad-hoc decisions made by an unrepresentative and unstructured board as part of the company's downfall, as well as the deficiencies of a club-based organisation. For the Menrath brothers, this was the clincher. They needed to create a structure which would simultaneously provide directors with control while allowing clients an opportunity to share in the ownership and the profits.

With Reg's input and in consultation with their lawyer, it was decided Provet would be established as a unit trust. A unit trust is an unincorporated mutual fund – a pool of money collected from numerous investors – that allows an organisation to hold assets and distribute company profits to individual unit owners rather than reinvesting those profits back into the fund. The idea was that the company's available units would be divided into A, B and C class units: A-class units would form the majority and be reserved for registered veterinarians, with some B-class units for staff and C-class for others, such as the general public. The vets who helped finance Provet would thus have vested financial interest in promoting and ensuring its success. The legal discussions led the men to impose stipulations in the trustee company articles that protected company directorships for some years before rotational elections would occur. This would ensure Provet's stability in its formative period.

Throughout the latter part of 1981, Bob and Reg had numerous meetings to better understand the task ahead and work out how this new venture would differ from the failed cooperative. It was sometime during this period that Reg, persuaded by the preparation and care taken in drafting the proposal for Provet, agreed to become a director. Bob noted the fact that Reg waited 'was indicative of his professional personality. He was thoughtful, considered and analytical in his evaluations, needing to be fully informed. He made his decisions with care.' And though their memories of how Provet came about might differ, on one recollection the brothers were in perfect agreement: they were elated to have Reg on the board.

Vic and Bob Menrath were already named in the company's documentation and they invited three further directors to join them: Reg, Tony Nicholls and Tony Thelander. Since the project was still in its development stage, the three other men agreed to be appointed the following year, when Provet officially began. In the meantime, Bob began scoping expressions of interest throughout the veterinary profession. Throughout the first half of 1982, he visited veterinary colleagues as well as product manufacturers and various banks to secure support for what he described as 'a veterinary distributor which was a company rather than a cooperative.'

In his favour was the project's unique management structure, designed following conversations with Reg: a pre-selected board comprising five well-known and respected vets who 'would be appointed if the profession supported the concept and was prepared to contribute by taking up units in the trust.' Veterinary clinics could buy products at a competitive price while, if they wanted, have a share in the ownership and the profits. The slogan? 'Make a profit while you buy and when you sell.'

In early 1982, they held an interest meeting attended by over one hundred vets. The five prospective directors roused their colleagues' enthusiasm for the concept and after a four-hour meeting, sixty-five vets were convinced, contributing almost $200,000 and promising their patronage. Bob recalled, 'The following weeks were a blur of frenzied activity. We appointed an already well-informed and ready-to-move general manager, Stan Johnston, who was a respected veterinary pharmaceutical representative with endless enthusiasm and energy.'

The Menrath brothers had put up much of the business's initial expenses – absorbing the costs of accountancy and legal advice, as well as other general costs. They identified an operating location, too, on Elford Street in Brisbane's Fortitude Valley: ironically, in the same building as a space vacated by a recently broke veterinary wholesaler. Fitting out the new office space, Bob and Vic put together a small staff and 'started a business based on a service delivered the way we knew veterinarians would want to be treated.'

The brothers and other investors took units in the unit trust as return for the cash investment. Heavily committed, financially as well as philosophically, the board agreed to forgo payment for their work. The directors, Bob noted, agreed on the premise that they 'were not paid for the first couple of years, until we were sure that we were going to be successful.'

One of Provet's aims was to become the supplier who 'provided a one-shop stop for all of a veterinary practice's requirements.' The company fulfilled its objective well beyond what the Menrath brothers imagined and it was an offer few practices could resist. Provet rapidly gained traction – first in Queensland, then interstate, until practices who remained committed to their original wholesaler comprised a minority. The first few years were frenetic. Provet 'guaranteed to supply anything in the veterinary and medical field and sourced the most exotic equipment and product for any client veterinarian', Bob pointed out. And, to make the deal even sweeter, they delivered products so quickly they left other suppliers scrambling. As long as the order was in before noon, Provet prided themselves on being able to supply most routine products on the same day. Before long, Provet was supplying clinics Australia-wide.

New opportunities came knocking. The company invested in a warehouse in Newstead, Queensland in 1984 and then bought a second warehouse in Brisbane's Fortitude Valley two years later. Construction began in Townsville in 1985, the same year in which the company pushed south of the border to invest in a New South Wales warehouse. The expansion into Townsville was important; the subsidiary, which was dubbed 'Provet Nth Qld', provided an alternate distributor in the state's far north, an area which was supplied solely by Provet's main competitor at the time.

In 1986, Provet's expansion saw the company eyeing the acquisition of a another distributor called Veterinary and Medical Suppliers (VMS). Based in Newcastle, New South Wales, VMS was roughly the same size as Provet and, Bob pointed out, 'gave a great service. It had an additional attraction in that it had a very successful track record over twenty years and supplied Australia-wide from a fledgling instrument and equipment division that sourced and repaired stuff.' With the owner, John Wotherspoon, looking to retire, it seemed a straightforward process. Reg, who knew John well, formed part of the negotiating team, but discussions quickly hit a snag. Despite wanting to retire, John saw the process as a gradual one in which he would ease out of his business, rather than a rapid, total handover. It was an unattractive proposition for Provet; they wanted to secure the purchase as quickly and cleanly as possible without any dangling loose ends. The two businesses found themselves at an impasse without any clear way forward. It was at this point that a man named Ian Bryant entered the picture in what appeared to be a moment of great serendipity.

Bryant was a successful veterinary manufacturer who produced some pharmaceutical product lines and had recently resurrected a struggling wholesaler in Melbourne. The success prompted his interest in breaking into the Sydney market but, wary of the risks of expanding too quickly on his own, he foresaw another option. He contacted John and Bob and proposed a joint venture: in conjunction with Provet, Bryant would jointly acquire the majority of VMS while John retained a share in the business. Provet was therefore also acquiring a reasonable proportion of the risk without the full benefit of owning the company outright, but Bryant had a good business reputation and if it allowed Provet to acquire VMS, his proposition seemed mutually beneficial.

Bryant wanted to achieve wholesale distribution Australia-wide – which was Provet's aim – and he brought to the negotiations his considerable experience and success in the industry, from which Provet believed they could learn a great deal. The resultant tripartite agreement saw Bryant holding the lion's share (50 per cent) of the new Sydney-based company, with VMS and Provet owning 25 per cent each. Provet was only four years old at this point, but its success had already been meteoric; Bryant was granted permission by the board to capitalise on the power of that success and call the new company Provet.

Bryant went to work and soon the Sydney-based Provet business had a sizeable share of the market – but the progress came at a cost. Bob remembered Bryant as 'an excellent operator but a brittle person and in business matters easily offended', a man who believed things had to be done his way. It was an unprecedented and unpleasant surprise when Bryant called Bob one day to tell the board that he 'had prior claim to the name Provet and was going to ensure we paid him for its continued use.' Bryant seemed to genuinely believe he had a legitimate claim, but Provet was a globally unregistered name the board had borrowed from a US company; they were in the process of trademarking it as a business name in a number of other countries but trademarking at the time was slow and complex process. Fortunately, the Queensland-based Provet having already used the name for four years weighed the argument heavily in their favour and the board decided to fight Bryant for it.

Eventually, they won a favourable settlement. Finalised around the same time that Bryant unexpectedly died from a heart attack, the settlement stipulated that Bryant surrender the Sydney-based company to Provet. After a considerable amount of time, money and emotional energy spent fighting the suit, the directors emerged with Provet in New South Wales.

Subsequently, Provet acquired another small veterinary distributor in New South Wales. The Wagga Wagga business was a subsidiary of a larger stock and station agency that, fortuitously for Provet, was keen to exit the veterinary supplies distribution industry. After the heartache around the partial procurement of VMS and the debacle with Bryant, it must have been a relief that this purchase was successful and seamless.

Soon after, Provet finalised the acquisition of VMS. During the process, the Provet board recognised that their current, all-Queenslander line-up limited their reach into other key areas of the national market. In 1986, a New Zealander called John MacLachlan and two new South Welshman joined the board, bringing their numbers up to eight. Garth McGilvray had been president of the AVA, while Nigel Nicholls was an equine practitioner who had known Reg since the early 1970s – and both were former directors of VMS.

In 1990, Bob Menrath left full-time practice and was appointed CEO of Provet. The company's growth had been rapid in the early years and the trust now held a net worth of roughly $20 million. Continued success demanded someone be on the ground on a day-to-day basis to manage the business and that someone was Bob. Under his leadership, Provet set up in New Zealand in the early 1990s, acquiring an existing supplier and developing three further sites in Christchurch, Palmerston North and Auckland. Western Australia was next and Provet purchased 20 per cent of a company in Perth before acquiring the other 80 per cent a few years later. To add Victoria to the fold, Provet bought a company in Melbourne, then established one in Tasmania, another in South Australia, and later, one in Darwin to serve the Northern Territory.

Provet's widespread distribution of (predominantly leased) warehouses was, Bob noted, 'certainly more costly than a more centralised warehousing', but it was a successful model. It enabled a local experience from a giant national distributor, a feeling Provet encapsulated in their slogan: 'a national company with a local focus.'

Expansion meant the company was able to address the fundamental problem facing distribution in Australia: the tyranny of distance. Distance affects the costs, but dispersed warehousing and local Provet businesses could mitigate this. Moreover, the structure acknowledged the varying clinical requirements among the broad array of Australian veterinary practices: local businesses became intimately acquainted with what their clients needed and could react accordingly, which built trust and meant vets could rely on Provet. This was essential because clients' needs are often urgent. Bob wryly noted that vets are typically 'not well organised as stock controllers – so same-day deliveries are universally expected.' To meet this need, Provet fielded a fleet of its own local delivery vans augmented by contractors, which by 2010 numbered roughly eighty vehicles.

In the early 1990s Provet expanded internationally. With the Australian market secured and the company continuing to grow, they decided to push into Southeast Asia and the Middle East. The demand for Provet products in these regions, particularly throughout Asia, had been increasing and the board recognised that continuing to use Brisbane as Provet's export centre was simply too expensive. A regional facility was the logical choice, but there were risks to international expansion: many practices had long been supplied out of England and would have to be enticed to commit to using Provet.

Provet contacted an Australian expat vet in Hong Kong who found someone interested in running a distribution centre. Using local contacts and fostering local business relationships was important, and it took Provet roughly three years to achieve a full branch operating out of Hong Kong. It became quite successful, and since the new branch was capable of delivering across China, the expansion allowed Provet ready distribution to that market at lesser cost than managing exports from Australia. But Bob noted that Reg's warning about international expansion was a sage one. 'We seemed to have endless local problems in Southeast Asia,' he recalled. 'The culture was different, and margins were low,' which was likely tied to the struggle to establish concrete operating parameters. Unlike Western businesses, where contracts define the conduct of business, Chinese business culture is tied to the art of negotiation; many Chinese businesses prefer to engage in an ongoing, dynamic process, which proved challenging for Provet to navigate.

Not long after opening in Hong Kong, Provet opened a warehouse in Singapore. The Singapore branch, however, never really took off and faced with Malaysia's dominance of the market, Provet withdrew. British suppliers also took steps to establish a foothold in Hong Kong, the competition driving down margins for Provet so that continuing to operate the branch became untenable. Eventually, they sold out to the local manager.

The company's advances into the Middle East unfolded in a similar vein. Provet's business in the region had started mainly through the provision of equine products for countries such as Bahrain and the United Arab Emirates which had extensive racing stables. Reg, in particular, Bob remembered, 'knew a few of the many Australian veterinarians employed there to look after the numerous equine operations owned by local sheiks.' The high volume of these sales had generated pressure to open an office or a warehouse, but the board hesitated, unsure of the viability of pushing into the Middle East.

English wholesalers had traditionally supplied the region and while there appeared to be enough demand to warrant Provet's expansion, everyone was aware of the risks. It seemed too good an opportunity to pass up, so they didn't – but after about two years, they pulled the plug. They had tried hard to make the venture financially viable, but Bob recalled that the 'graft and corruption and the lack of ethics' that the new branch faced made it difficult to run the business as intended. His observations, similar to those surrounding Provet's experiences in Southeast Asia, speak to the challenges of extending operations into an international market – ultimately, the business culture in the Middle East was incompatible with how the Provet board wanted to operate.

There were, however, numerous opportunities for expansion closer to home. The model which the board had always been interested in was something they all desired as practitioners: that of 'an across-the-board supplier that supplies all the needs of a vet practice.'[19] The late 1980s and early 1990s saw the emergence of technology, particularly the potential for digitising stock control and client management. None of the board members understood much about IT at that stage. Those who were younger and more interested knew a little, but on the whole technology was a vast and murky world, one that was seemingly almost unnavigable. Still, they were open to the possibilities and the local manager at VMS arranged a meeting for Bob with a young, intelligent IT graduate called Andrew Foote from the University of Sydney, then working in a government facility. 'It was like talking to a person from another planet,' Bob recalled.

Andrew was not only brilliant, but persuasive too. He convinced Bob that he could design a system which would integrate all of Provet's many various operations into a single, readily understandable user interface that gave a comprehensive picture of the business's health across the full range of performance metrics. Viewed from the highly networked, ultra-technologised world of the twenty-first century, such interoperability in business IT is not only norm, it is so run of the mill as to be of little interest – but to Bob and the Provet board in the early 1990s, what the young IT engineer suggested sounded too good to be true and it revolutionised the company's future operations.

This ingenious young man, dubbed 'Nasa', was the first member of a unit that grew to some thirty people over the next six years. Under Nasa's management, the IT team created a computer program that incorporated into a single system stock control, accounting, client management and internal business development – in short, everything required to successfully and efficiently run a veterinary clinic. Later, the IT group grew into a stand-alone subsidiary when Provet bought an IT company in New Zealand which was already in the process of developing its own business management system. Under Provet, this system was reworked into a program for veterinary clients, leading to the supply of in-house software, including training programs and updates. These systems were all linked to the Provet mainframe – which conveniently made it harder for practitioners to move away from working with Provet as their supplier.

By the beginning of the new millennium, Provet had achieved the aim of providing a 'one-stop shop' for veterinary professionals. They sold over-the-counter products and supplied all a vet's required diagnostic equipment including X-rays, ultrasounds and CT scanners, as well as pet toys, feeds and other animal supplies. They provided surgical and clinical instruments, no matter how exotic, and all the necessary disposables. Eventually, the company could even supply specialised architectural information to design veterinary clinics that could meet a practice's every modern diagnostic need, including operating theatres furnished with all the requisite equipment: everything, Bob noted, 'to satisfy the most demanding surgeon.'

Pharmaceuticals, including those human medicines previously only available through medical supply companies, were available through Provet. For a period of time, the company even supplied a number of pharmacies around Queensland, though this didn't last; being required to furnish products on incredibly short notice (as little as two hours) proved an insurmountable obstacle. Rounding out the gamut of services offered, Provet acquired a marketing company that provided government-approved (and partly funded) veterinary nurse training programs, OHS training, HR control, and other amenities that were sometimes overlooked but contributed to a smooth-running vet clinic.

Provet really could, it seemed, do everything.

What Provet couldn't do, however, was hold back the advance of time. The early 2000s threw up a challenge that might have curtailed Reg's involvement in the company's meteoric rise: his seventy-second birthday. Australian legislation at the time stipulated company directors had to retire at age seventy-two – an event Reg was by no means ready for. As the inauspicious milestone approached, Bob and Reg spoke on at least one occasion about the impending restrictions. 'We've got to try and find a way around it,' Bob mused. 'Perhaps you could serve as an "advisor" to the board without actually being a company director.'

Fate intervened. Reg was two months past his seventy-second birthday when, in August 2001, the *Abolition of Compulsory Age Retirement (Statutory Officeholders) Bill* 2001 was passed. It stated that if a person were appointed by special resolution at the company's

Annual General Meeting, they were able to act as a director past the age of seventy-two: serendipity, it seemed, had played her hand. Reg remained on the Provet board.

Three years later in 2004, two events of note occurred. The first was that Provet listed on the Australian Stock Exchange. The company was continuing to grow at a rapid rate and by 2010 was opening a new warehouse annually. At the start of a ten-year building lease, Provet would aim for 50 per cent floor occupancy over time – but in some buildings, growth was exponential, and the company exceeded its initial targets. Such rapid expansion meant the unit trust structure that had served Provet well for over twenty years and provided the stability of a consistent board of directors, was no longer the best option.

There was no public market to arbitrate the company's unit value and with increased frequency of unit trading, the board had sought to provide an indicative price, meeting at least twice a year to evaluate the business. The board was open about their method – advising that they used the publicly available estimated value of the company from its most recent audit and the most recent unit sale price to indicate likely market value – but it was hard to be timely and accurate. This method, Bob pointed out, also 'placed the board in a delicate and dangerous position of potentially being accused of influencing [the] unit price.'

With the ATO already taxing Provet as a public trading trust at company rates, the decision was made to list on the Australian Stock Exchange. It was a process Bob Menrath recalled as 'complicated, tortuous, expensive and [as taking] a great deal of time.' Over a year, Provet spent around $2.5 million, with all eight directors contributing to the process under the directions of a company of specialist accountants and lawyers. As they ploughed hours into reviewing the management processes, it became increasingly clear that continuing to combine the positions of chair and CEO into a single role was no longer appropriate. Bob Menrath had spent twenty-three years wearing both hats: it was time for change.

From this decision was born the second event of note in 2004 – Bob approached Reg in private to ask if he would be interested in chairing the Provet board. To Bob's surprise, Reg turned him down.

'I need more spare time, not to increase my workload,' Reg said. He was seventy-five by this stage and Bob later wondered whether their challenging conversations about compulsory retirement a few years earlier, before the new bill was passed, had continued to weigh on Reg's mind. He and Joy had recently bought a motorhome and Reg wanted to travel more; chairing the Provet board didn't feature in those plans.

He did stay on as a director but as time passed and he grew older, his capacity for managing the meetings diminished. He had always been a masterful storyteller, fellow Provet director Garth McGilvray recalled, but now when he spoke to Reg on the phone, the stories had grown 'longer and longer ... he'd run them around and round all over the place.' Reg was acutely self-aware and recognised what was happening. He confessed to Garth in 2009, 'I feel like I've got hold of a bit of string but it's getting longer and longer, and I can't really catch up.'

It must have been excruciatingly difficult for Reg to confront the effects of ageing and admit that he was starting to feel like he wasn't pulling his weight. For more than fifty years, his mental acuity had characterised his life, had driven everything he did – and now it was starting to dull, in a subtle and inexorable way that he could not prevent.

Hearing what had been unsaid in the conversation with Reg, Garth spoke to the board. Some had been present on a night not long before when Reg had taken a couple of wrong turns on the way out to dinner after a board meeting. Around the same time, Bob recalled that Reg suggested he was finding it increasingly difficult to make time available for Provet; what Reg didn't say, but Bob walked away thinking, was that his heart wasn't in it anymore. Listening to Garth, the board agreed that he should go and further chat to Reg about his future with Provet. It was an unpleasant task with which to be saddled, but Garth didn't flinch. He hired a car and headed out to Oakey where he was served a cup of tea while Reg put some toast on and forgot about it, so that it burnt.

They sat down together, these two men who had worked closely together for more than two decades, and Reg levelled a stern gaze. 'Okay, Garth, let's not beat around the bush,' he said. 'What do you want me to do?'

Reg had given him the opening, but Garth couldn't help dancing around the point. 'The board is concerned that it's becoming a struggle for you to attend the meetings.'

'So, you want me to resign.' It wasn't clear if it was a question or a statement, but it was there now, laid out on the table before them. Being forthright and unflinching in the face of an unpleasant issue was the only way that Reg knew how to deal with a problem, and he saw no reason to deviate from it now. Provet had been a big part of his life and the beneficiary of his wisdom, energy and countless hours for over a quarter of a century. 'It was such a part of him,' Garth recalled, 'and he was a part of us.' Leaving must have felt like a kind of death, one Reg didn't want to face. But he still did not shy away from the truth. Perhaps he realised how devastating it was, too, to be sitting across the table in Garth's seat; Reg was always aware of the people around him. In approaching it as he had, by being self-aware and then direct with the knowledge at hand, he had made it as easy as he could for his friend.

'Yes,' Garth said, finally. He lingered a while, then got in the car and drove away. What had it cost him to serve the Provet board this way? He recalled pulling over by the side of the road and dry retching at the enormity of what he had just done, and at the knowledge that Reg Pascoe's role on the Provet board was now over.

Not long after Reg's resignation, Provet received an offer to sell out to an American company, Henry Schein. The company agreed, and Provet – employing close to 400 employees and boasting a national turnover of over $300 million a year by this stage – was officially announced as sold in October 2010.

What made Provet successful was also what made it different: the attitude of the board and its ethos permeated throughout the company in myriad small but important ways. Predominant among these was the emphasis on serving the vets they counted as their clients. The recollections of Glenda Sinclair, a Provet employee for decades, illustrate this philosophy. Glenda was a young woman when she began working in Brisbane for the customer service team in 1991. She remained there for eighteen months before heading to Townsville to work in the North Queensland branch. Then, in 1998, she returned to Brisbane to assume Stan Johnston's mantle as general manager. In this capacity, she gained considerable insight into both the Provet board and the company as a whole.

The directors came from different backgrounds and pursued varying professional fields of veterinary medicine, but they were unanimous in their understanding of Provet's purpose. As it grew larger and busier, the company retained the fundamental philosophies that had driven its establishment in the first place: a desire to provide a reliable, high-quality service to veterinarians. It was a core lesson that resonated with every Provet staff member. Glenda remembered, 'The one thing that [Reg] always reminded me about was to look after the client ... As long as you look after the client, as long as you do the right thing by them, they'll do the right thing by you.'

The board's attitude engendered a strong and resilient sense of community within Provet, and the directors as a group underwrote these ideals by purchasing from Provet as clients. They believed in what they were doing, not just as businessmen but as vets, and they reinforced this every time they bought supplies through the company. But Reg's approach was particularly unique. Of all the board members, he was the only one who still personally submitted the order for OVH's clinical needs. 'From his point of view,' Glenda said, 'the inventory was a huge investment. It was extremely important, and he didn't delegate that to anyone.' As he placed the order with Provet's customer service team, Reg would take the opportunity to chat with them about their work, sometimes asking to be patched through to Glenda if he wanted to check in or purchase something outside of the usual order. As a consequence, he was both highly visible and interactive with the company. It reinforced to the staff that he believed in the value they were providing, that he was deeply invested in Provet beyond his work as a director, and that he esteemed and appreciated the staff's toil.

Ever curious, Reg enjoyed satisfying his interest about what was going on at different levels within the company: he wanted to ensure the clients were happy, the staff were happy and, Glenda recalled fondly, that she was happy as the general manager. He knew that different facets of the business worked in symbiosis and a disruption in one inevitably undermined the others, but both his and the board's approach illustrates that their concern extended beyond simply commercial wins.

Provet's success was determined by how the directors handled the 'business end' of things, and in this, they had established advantageous conditions from the start. Reg's previous experience with veterinary distributors had been plagued by a single central problem: that the structure of the company had permitted some of the directors to withdraw money from the venture and leave it floundering. His conversations with Bob about the issue had informed the subsequent construction of Provet's operating framework and rendered the issue moot – both through Provet's decision on the company's structure, and the careful planning and forethought of the board in the early days and during periods of expansion.

Doubtless there were hiccoughs throughout Reg's long association – the name claim debacle with Bryant being the most notable – but the company's successive victories might make it look in hindsight as if Provet's success were the easiest thing in the world. Of course, that wasn't the case. Provet's success was the result of stringent administration and good business practice. The board were rigorous in their management. Monthly audits ensured they knew their cash position to the dollar – in the early years, stocktakes were frequent and the annual, end-of-year inventories were attended by the full board to ensure everyone had an intimate understanding. These monthly, two-day gatherings often included specialist seminars designed to continue developing the directors' business acumen and understanding of both the market and operating within it. Throughout the meetings, Reg was always the considered voice of caution, requesting the board examine and re-examine any proposal to avoid repeating the mistakes he had seen before. He thought carefully before he spoke and everyone listened.

Bob recalled the early decision to institute a committee system for Provet's board of directors. The committees included risk management, human resources, audit and finance, and planning, among others, and the structure dictated that each director serve as chair for one committee and member of two others, rotating their assignments every few years. As Bob recalled, doing so 'ensured the development of an involved and well-informed board' and he had fought to fill that board with the strongest businessmen that Australia's veterinary community had to offer.

Regardless of their abilities, however, the business world still posed distinct challenges from those associated with running a veterinary practice. Aware of this disparity, the directors actively pursued professional growth, and undertook a diploma in business – a notable commitment, considering the demands on their time with their respective practices, families, and serving on the Provet board itself. After completing the diploma, the board members were required to sit an examination and fulfil the stipulations set forth by the University of Sydney Graduate School of Business. Having done so, the school recommended each director be recognised as a fellow of the Australian Institute of Directors. Bob noted, 'I always felt it was a tribute to the seriousness in which each and every one of our directors regarded their position on the Provet board.' The process was invaluable and gave each member a deeper understanding of the business world that would stand them in excellent stead in the future. As a group, they joined a range of professional bodies, continuing to learn from various sources that allowed them to better integrate into the business world.

Nigel Nicholls joined the board in 1986 and was CEO of Provet at the time of writing in 2021. He first met Reg in the 1970s at an equine vet conference when he was only a recent graduate, recalling, 'quite frankly he terrified me, and I think that's a common experience with most people.' As their association grew through the AEVA, Nigel realised that Reg was less scary than he might appear, and the two men became good friends. By the time Nigel joined the Provet board, they knew one another very well. '[Reg was] probably the most important mentor I've had in my life,' Nigel said. When Nigel succeeded as Provet CEO in 2005, Reg played a valuable ongoing role in the boardroom until his retirement in 2009.

As CEO, Nigel experienced the extreme scrutiny that accompanies such positions. With the 2004 decision to take Provet public, he was accountable to Provet's shareholders but, just as crucially, he was also accountable to his fellow directors. They were savvy, well-educated and occasionally hard-hitting. During their meetings, as he fielded questions about how he was implementing the board's strategies and the state of Provet's everyday operations, Nigel could sometimes see Reg mulling over a particular thought or an idea. The sight always caught Nigel's attention. *What's he going to hit me with now?* Nigel would wonder, keeping a weather eye on the older man. He knew Reg never spoke without first carefully considering what he would say and that whatever he said would be significant; it wouldn't be malicious, but Reg could and often did pose questions that would make others stop and reassess. There was no doubt of Reg's technical and scientific abilities, but particularly in his work with Provet, it was his integrity that distinguished every move he made.

Nigel found this valuable. Reg expected that Nigel would respond to his questions in the spirit in which they were posed, with a thorough and honest answer; he did so with the belief that it was better to have a problem or a concern out in the open and deal with it honestly than dance around the issue while it mouldered out of sight. The Provet boardroom was characterised by frank and open discourse which was vital when dealing with gnarly business issues.

At Provet's Annual General Meeting each year, the board members would sit up the front and answer questions from the floor. Their responses were carefully considered and they did their best to be thorough. As chair, Bob Menrath was responsible for the AGM's overall conduct, but the various directors each managed a specific aspect of the meeting, which usually aligned with the committee of which they were the chair. On one occasion, a veterinary colleague whom Bob described as 'one of our lesser client shareholders and a recurrent pest', asked a question relating to an issue that Reg had spent considerable time earlier in the meeting addressing. It was a risky business, not paying attention to what was going on. Reg turned to the shareholder, his gaze sharp behind the glint of his glasses, his voice gruff. 'If you had listened, you would have known that we've already covered this *ad nauseum*.' Then he turned away again. The AGM moved on.

Reg could be tough, but he was also fair and his work with Provet was characterised by a pervasive and touching concern for, and connection with, his colleagues and employees. Glenda Sinclair recalled being invited to the OVH Christmas dinner along with some other Provet staff on a number of occasions. The dinners, which in the 1990s would have been huge and no doubt boisterous affairs, were held at the now-defunct Weis restaurant in Toowoomba. Surrounded on all sides by the OVH staff, Glenda recalled that Reg would get quite emotional when he stood to address them.

When he poured his energy into something – be it OVH, a professional body or Provet – these efforts were his all, and they came from the deepest, kindest part of him, even if that part did occasionally have a rough edge. That philosophy of service and community underpinned Reg's entire career. He believed that life shouldn't centre on your opportunity to benefit from a situation but on what you might bring. 'The rest,' he said more than once, 'will look after itself.'

His longstanding battle with Stan Johnston over Provet's 'blue tubs' goes some way to illustrating this point. Provet delivered orders to its customers in large blue plastic tubs, which the client was expected to unpack and return when the next delivery van came in. But Glenda noted that the tubs 'are quite rodent-proof', and Oakey had been suffering a mice plague for what seemed like aeons. By the time Glenda took over the general manager's role from Stan Johnston in 1998, Reg and Stan had been arguing for ages about Reg's refusal to surrender the tubs his orders came in.

'Stan,' Reg said on more than one occasion, 'I'm your client and I have a need. These tubs suit my need and I'm going to be keeping them.'

'No, you're not, Reg,' Stan shot back. 'Because those tubs are Provet property and we don't have enough of them. It's not my fault you have a rodent problem – I want my blue tubs back.'

'This went on and on and on. It was sort of still simmering when I came on,' Glenda recalled. Of course, once she was in the seat, one of Reg's first orders of business was to determine what her approach would be regarding the issue. 'Now, what're you going to do about this?' Reg said.

Unconcerned, Glenda answered, 'Reg, you can have as many blue tubs as you want, I'll just buy some more.'

'Good. Good answer,' Reg said. Glenda thought she scored a brownie point that day, but the infamous blue tub battle was about far more than Oakey's rodent plague. Reg's point, Glenda said, was that, as a client, he had a need that Provet could meet. 'Even though it was outside of [the usual services], it was something we could do for a client. And if we *could* do it, then we *should* do it.' That was the simple philosophy that served as the company's foundation: if there was a possibility they could provide it, Provet never said no.

Even as a director of an internationally successful company, Reg was first and foremost a vet. His principles may have cost business opportunities; when he and Glenda were discussing treating horses' leg wounds one day, Reg snorted at the idea of using a specific wound-cleaning treatment. 'All this bloody guff that people go on with,' he said. 'Just get a garden hose and put it on there as hard as the horse can stand and hose it out every day and it'll get better.' As Glenda noted, there were always people looking for Reg to endorse their products, particularly those for horses. Had he done so, there doubtless would have been a significant market solely on the basis of his recommendations, but he was both honest and practical and wouldn't change his ways.

Honesty, practicality and the determined, skilful work of first the five, then later eight, Provet directors allowed Bob and Vic Menrath's great idea to become a roaring success. Over the seventeen years that Reg sat as a director on the board, the unit trust grew from a small concern into a large, multimillion-dollar company, the first port of call for most practising Australian vets.

10
A National Veterinary Exam

In 1983, Reg was a founding member of the Board of Examiners for the Expert Panel on Veterinary Science, a specialist branch of the National Office for Overseas Skills Recognition (NOOSR). NOOSR was a federal organisation designed to assess foreign professionals who wished to work in Australia if their tertiary degree wasn't recognised in the country. (In 2020, this function falls under the Qualifications Recognition Policy Unit in the Department of Education.) Professor Doug Blood's efforts in creating the Australian College of Veterinary Surgeons for veterinarians to gain non-university postgraduate qualifications had raised awareness of the risks associated with admitting unregulated overseas veterinarians. Any veterinary practitioner who received their qualification from certain universities within the British Commonwealth system was accepted as possessing a degree equivalent to those granted by Australian universities ... but with an increasing number of veterinarians from outside the British system moving to Australia to practise, an independent regulatory process was needed.

The Australian veterinary community was invested because an internationally qualified vet whose skills were not up to scratch had had the potential to undermine the profession's reputation as a whole. Standards had to be high enough that overseas-qualified vets would not bring the profession into disrepute. Just as important, overseas vets represented competition and so a rigorous examination designed to objectively adjudicate their skills and proficiencies would ensure Australian vets weren't unfairly disadvantaged. Those involved had to get it right.

In 1983, UQ Professor Mike Rex instituted the National Veterinary Exam (NVE). Reg was an enthusiastic advocate for registration as a way of maintaining high standards. 'It was an unusual thing for a practitioner – a really busy practitioner – to get involved with,' according to Leo Jeffcott. But then, it was nothing out of the ordinary for Reg. And though some noted that the challenge of such organisations was the realisation that once you were in the thick of it you had to actively propel them forward, that too was familiar to Reg.

The examination committee was made up of expert vets with varying specialities, ranging from equine to small animal specialists, pathology to production animals. Then as now, the NVE comprised three components: an English test, a multiple-choice exam (three 100-question quizzes), and a clinical exam. Each component had to be passed before proceeding to the next.

A mix of vets on the board was crucial to ensure that the process could assess whether the candidate's professional knowledge was sufficient to practise in Australia. Though their areas of interest differed, the examination committee were all vets, and many of them had worked in academia. Fellow board member Virginia Studdert noted that Reg 'bridged the gap between academia and private practice, which was good – he was the perfect person for that job.'

Virginia remembered Reg very clearly. 'He had a way to him. He was very good at running meetings, but with humour; he was disarmingly humorous. And relaxed. He was always relaxed. You never got to see that he was feeling there was any pressure on him, even though he managed to keep things running and he got outcomes that I think were satisfying to him. He had an idea of what the outcome should be and somehow everyone came around to agree with him; I don't remember any discord at all.'

Board meetings were typically held in Canberra or Melbourne over a period of several days. These trips featured at least one group dinner and while Reg was always charming and effective during business dealings, it was in these relaxed social forums that he was at his most entertaining. He was a natural raconteur: personable and engaging, his dry wit, seemingly endless catalogue of tales, and keen eye for the humour in any given situation making his stories enormously enjoyable. He spoke of rural Australian life that in a Melbourne restaurant must have seemed light years away. In a favourite of Virginia's that she asked him to retell more than once,

Reg parked in a paddock to tend a wounded horse. Did he leave the car door or the boot open? In all likelihood, yes. OVH vehicles carried all necessary supplies and Reg would have wanted easy access without having to open a door or fumble around with dirty hands. When the job was done, he returned to the car to discover a huge snake had slithered in and made itself right at home. Even if it wasn't poisonous, it easily could have been – Reg was well aware of the dangers awaiting the unwary in rural Queensland paddocks. The shock probably made his heart stutter. And the crowd laugh.

The early years of the NVE required considerable time and effort on the part of the board members, who were working to implement the exam framework with little pre-existing foundation to draw upon. Certain assessment sections had to be created from scratch. Some board members were able to capitalise on their own professional expertise – Reg undoubtedly wrote some of the multiple-choice questions, particularly equine ones – but to generate a broad question bank for the MCQ papers they also invited other vets to send in questions. The result, remembered board member Roger Kelly, was 'a real mixed bag.' Some of the questions were hopeless. Others had flaws but, with some reworking, could be used. Contemporary academia uses a series of sophisticated statistics and assessment metrics to differentiate 'good' multiple choice questions from 'bad', but in the absence of these methods, the board was reliant on their own instincts. Fortunately, Reg's instincts were sharp.

In 1991, after eight years on the board, Reg became acting chair for the NOOSR's Board of Examiners. The following year, he was confirmed as chair and chief examiner, where he remained for almost two decades. Around the same time, pathologist Roger Kelly joined the board. Twenty years earlier, Reg had tried to persuade Roger to join the fledgling ACVS and failed. Now, the incumbent NOOSR pathologist decided to resign and sent Roger a letter to ask whether he'd be interested in the position. As he mulled it over, Reg got in touch to pose the same question. Faced once more with a determined Reg Pascoe, Roger recalled, 'I felt sufficient residual guilt … to think, this time I must help, instead of ducking and weaving and getting out of it as I did last time.'

It was fortunate for all that he did so: Roger's academic experience proved invaluable. Possessing a thorough understanding of the theory of assessment – particularly the methodology behind multiple-choice question design – he identified fundamental defects undermining the NVE. It was clear that the 'cobbled together' multiple-choice exam, particularly the pathology section, was flawed. 'There's a lot of work to be done here to get some of these exams up to scratch,' Roger told Reg. 'Some of these questions are really awful.'

Reg accepted the criticism with his usual equanimity. 'Right,' he said. 'Well, welcome aboard.' The rest was implied: *let's get to work.*

Leo Jeffcott, who presided over the NVE from 2010 to 2020, noted that it took 'an awful lot of work to keep [the NVE] fine-tuned.' Reg did so for decades. The MCQ aspect in particular was continually refined but doing the same with the various multiple-choice questions was never truly complete and remained one of the board's key responsibilities. The worst examples were culled or rewritten early in the process, but, inevitably, there remained questions that were flawed or needed revision and so Reg and Roger spent long periods pulling questions apart. Every so often, the light of inspiration would hit, and Reg or Roger would write a new question, which circulated among the committee members so they could assess it and ensure its validity.

In these robust discussions, Reg was superlative. He possessed an acute memory for veterinary knowledge: one OVH vet remembered Reg mentioning 'trivia' he'd learnt from a paper in vet school more than thirty years earlier.[20] He paired this formidable recall with untiring efforts to stay abreast of current veterinary knowledge, though he was by now in his early sixties. Roger recalled that Reg 'was still sharp right up until the last when it came to his knowledge of equine diseases', and this mastery made his emails 'good intellectual exercises.' He enjoyed their exchanges, where his own keen eye for academic rigour and Reg's penetrating mind grappled to resolve an issue.

Reg respected Roger's opinion and he was always receptive to discussing concerns; it didn't take much convincing to show Reg that an exam question needed to go. He wasn't emotional or possessive about the content even if the dog in the fight was his own. 'If it worked better, then he accepted it,' Roger said. 'He was quite gracious in that sense.' And Reg expected the same of others. If it became clear that a question was flawed, he didn't attempt to defend it – even if the specialist in that area was disgruntled at the prospect of revising it. Flexible and 'intellectually supple' as Roger described him, Reg willingly adapted his ideas and methods where it was clear to him that it was beneficial to do so.

Once the candidate passed the multiple-choice exam, they were eligible to progress to the clinical exam. Here too the board faced challenges perfecting the assessment process. In its earliest forms, the clinical exam had between ten and twelve components ranging across veterinary specialities. The variety of experts on the NVE board were necessary to ensure that 'their' section of the assessment could adequately test a candidate's proficiency. Reg assembled the various sections of the exam and the two equine components – equine medicine and equine clinical skills. Malcolm McLennan, a dairy cattle veterinarian who started as a clinical examiner when the exams began in 1983 and later joined the NVE board, summarised Reg's influence by noting, 'he really had carriage of that whole exam and took it from nothing to where it is today.'

The clinical exam consisted of both theory and practical knowledge elements across the full spectrum of clinical work. In its early days, the NVE used animals from local RSPCAs to assess candidates' surgical competency. Dogs scheduled for euthanasia were used so that examinees could show their ability to successfully anaesthetise the animal, then perform a desexing operation including suturing before the dog was put to sleep. If the vet was able to perform the surgery under the critical eye of one of the university's surgeons, he or she was deemed competent and given a pass. Today's clinical examination has not changed much, though the section assessing small animal surgical ability emphasises the ongoing welfare of the animal and operations are conducted with no intention to euthanise. The December 2020 Australasian Veterinary Examination candidate information handbook notes: 'The Examiner's judgement on the safety of the patient may modify the course of the procedure. A lack of knowledge or competence will require the procedure to be terminated in the interests of the animal's welfare.'

Aside from this, in 2021 the clinical exam comprises twelve assessment sections administered over four to five days. Each section lasts between one and two hours and is overseen by two examiners. It is a precise and taxing marathon undertaken for the right to practise in Australia. Assembling the NVE in the 1980s, foremost in the Board of Examiners' minds was the need to remain above scrutiny. Inconsistency among examiners, particularly, and failures to apply the criteria with due rigour, would undermine the process and comprise the NVE's purpose. To ensure its legitimacy, the clinical exam was therefore developed with a keen awareness of the risks: the ability to practise in Australia was lucrative, so the risks of corruption or mishandling were judged to be commensurately high.

Assigning two examiners to oversee each assessment capitalised upon what is termed 'the Hawthorne Effect', which recognises that we behave better when we're being observed or even when we simply *think* we're being observed. Having examiners work in pairs provided each assessor with their own independent arbiter. Colleagues were there to keep one another honest and ensure the exam was conducted *well*: that the right questions were asked, that candidates were neither threatened nor disadvantaged by their examiners and, by the same token, that candidates weren't attempting to bribe examiners. The board also decided to intermittently send some board members to, as Roger phrased it, 'mooch about during the examination process.' This was how Malcolm McLennan first got to know Reg. As Malcolm and other examiners assessed aspiring practitioners, Reg and another board member would appear quietly in the background and 'prowl around the various examination stations' before vanishing. If the intent was to ensure examiners always felt they were being watched (and maintained higher standards because of it), it seems to have worked.

The board's oversight of the process added another layer of legitimacy. It was a stressful situation for candidates and examiners alike and the range of nationalities and backgrounds added further complexity, as assessors needed to be aware of different cultural practices that might affect performance. Requiring an orthodox Muslim to handle a pig during the clinical examination, for example, would not only be deeply offensive but would make completing the exam impossible. Such issues had to be carefully considered in order to make the process as fair as possible.

It was also vital examiners didn't influence the results and Roger recalled the challenges associated with ensuring the process was unassailable. 'Sometimes you'd have snappish examiners who were clearly threatening: their body language wasn't appropriate or when they hadn't had much experience in the process of oral examinations, they could be asking the wrong questions or asking them in the wrong fashion.'

Reg was not immune to such foibles. As Roger pointed out, Reg had to carefully walk the line 'between being approachable and not too threatening and frightening, and also making sure all the procedures were being followed.' Yet he could be a forbidding character if he wanted to be, sometimes even without trying, and his tolerance for cultural differences and their potential effect on performance was low, especially in the early days. He expected candidates to rise to the occasion, regardless of their background. 'They just have to survive the process,' he would say, in the gruff, no-nonsense voice that made it hard to argue with him. *Stop being too soft on them*, the words implied.

Reg (second from right) and third year BVSc classmates at UQ in 1949: a generation of vets who 'had it pretty tough.

'Reg didn't believe in mollycoddling people,' Roger noted. '[He] was from another generation that had things pretty tough.'

This extended to the establishment of Reg's practice. Isolated from other veterinarians, he had no professional support, and in the early days had worked long hours alone with the only help provided by Joy. It was a professional path which, in some ways, made him less sympathetic to certain factors at play for NVE candidates.

Yet as time moved on, so too did Reg's attitudes. He empathised with candidates, realising that, though different to his own, the challenges they faced were equally onerous. As the NVE chair, he became increasingly sensitive to the ways in which cultural differences could be distracting or might undermine a candidate's confidence. Reg's friend Garth McGilvray, with whom he worked at Provet, remembered, 'He was very firm about the standards, and he wasn't going to allow [them] to be lowered, but he thought the support for [candidates] genuinely trying to pass the exam should be given by the profession. And that showed the very soft side that he had for people – if he chose to support somebody, he really stuck up for them.'

Malcolm McLennan recalled witnessing Reg's gradual change in attitude after he joined the NVE board in 2008. Reg, Malcolm pointed out, had a 'reputation as being a fearsome person to deal with.' He was a hard taskmaster and Malcolm recalled wryly that he could be more than a little 'whatever Reg says, goes.' But there was also 'quite a softer side to him as chair of the NVE.' When the board gathered to discuss candidates who had failed in parts but might still be eligible to undertake supplementary exams, Reg's compassion was evident.

The clinical exam requirements were stringent, and success required passing all twelve stations. If, however, candidates passed at least eight, they were eligible to undertake supplementary exams: a second chance without having to wait twelve months to try again. There were always candidates whose performance had been borderline and enabling them to take supplementary exams was life-changing for many.

Reg was determined to maintain the profession's standards, but he also recognised that intransigent pedantry wasn't the right way to go about it. He was down to earth when it came to rules. He wasn't a renegade, but recognised that no framework is universal and that mindlessly applying rules without considering an individual's nuances and circumstances was, in fact, the easier and thus weaker approach. It was harder to analyse and adjudicate complex situations than to simply tick a box and declare the matter finished. If he thought there was a better or fairer way to get the job done, he wouldn't hesitate. And, as Virginia Studdert noted, he 'got away with it', no doubt because when pressed, 'he could defend his interpretation' and do so compellingly.

With his appreciation of the challenges candidates faced continuing to evolve, Reg pursued opportunities for those borderline cases to take a supplementary exam. 'There was a side to Reg that really went out of his way to help people,' Malcolm McLennan recalled; 'he wanted to give candidates a go' to get across the line. It wasn't a simple path – other board members opposed him at times and Reg didn't always win every battle – but he saw it as the *right* path, and that was more important. In pursuing this balance, his work with the NVE encapsulates his efforts to balance his drive to maintain practitioners' high standards across the profession with his deep love for education and his passion for helping others achieve their potential.

The NVE and the expert vets who ran it was merely one branch of the diverse NOOSR portfolio, itself a subdivision of a Commonwealth department today called the Department of Education, Skills and Employment. As the turn of the century approached, the department realised it would be easier, cheaper and more sensible to outsource from NOOSR this specific and complex veterinary skills recognition exam, for which they had very little skills or experience. The Commonwealth's attention turned to the state and territory veterinary boards. Here, it seemed clear, were the organisations through which the NVE should be run. Surely ownership of this crucial regulatory process by states and territories was the ideal solution? Few in the profession agreed: state-level management would bring coordination and standardisation challenges that threatened the fundamental purpose of the NVE. For Reg, recalling his extended battle to corral various aspects of the horse industry into a cohesive national council, it must have seemed like another logistical nightmare.

This time, however, a group of motivated vets set to work finding a solution. Galvanised by the impending devolution of the NVE from the federal government, the Australasian Veterinary Boards Council (AVBC) was incorporated in Victoria in December 1999. Its vision was to provide a legal entity to speak and act on behalf of all veterinary registering authorities. To do so, its members comprised the state and territory Veterinary Boards of Australia, the Veterinary Council of New Zealand, the Australian Veterinary Association Ltd (AVA) and the New Zealand Veterinary Association Ltd (NZVA).

With the approval of the AVBC's charter, the NVE was transferred from NOOSR to the AVBC. It was a sensible move, Roger believed. As the overarching regulatory body for the vet boards who would be responsible for 'registering veterinarians and making sure their qualifications are up to snuff', the AVBC was the logical choice.

Current President Julie Strous was instrumental in establishing the AVBC. And, through the organisation's relationship with the Queensland Veterinary Surgeons Board, and the AVBC's assumption of responsibility for the NVE, she renewed an old acquaintance. She first met Reg in 1976 as a first-year vet student at UQ when Reg was guest lecturing. Vet students, she recalled with a laugh, 'are well practised in bluffing. You can't survive that course unless you can bluff, because you cannot physically hold in your head all the information that is required of you. And most lecturers are fairly sanguine about that. They say, "Oh right, you obviously haven't done your reading," but they'll let it go. Nup. Not with Reg. He would not let that go. And he would always call you out if you hadn't done your proper preparation, for sure.' A first-generation university student, Julie already felt completely out of her depth. She also had no experience with horses and so was doubly nervous about equine lectures and pracs – the very places where she encountered Reg.

Later, when she had graduated and was practising in northern New South Wales, she encountered a horse with a case of 'Queensland itch.' Caused by hypersensitivity to insect bites, particularly those of midges (a common Queensland nuisance), Queensland itch is a recurrent seasonal dermatitis – the very kind of condition Reg was renowned for understanding and managing.

While Julie was still intimidated at the idea of it, her boss was relaxed at the prospect of asking Reg for help.

'I'll just give [him] a call and find out what to do,' he said easily. Picking up the phone, he called OVH and, shortly after, Reg despatched his chosen solution. Julie was stunned. It seemed incredible to her that, amid a busy practice, Reg had fielded the call and leapt in to help solve someone else's problem.

Yet despite knowing of his generosity, walking in to find Reg at the head of the NVE Board of Examiners still caused that exact same adrenaline spike Julie had experienced at university almost thirty years earlier. 'It was kind of like a reflex reaction,' she laughed. In time, she got to know the man behind the legend, learning of his hobbies; hearing him speak of his grandchildren; and uncovering the strength of those personal and professional values that underpinned his career. 'I really got to like him,' she said, 'and was just amazed at how intimidated I had been all those years ... But having said that, he always made you sit up a bit straighter.' It was a trait that helped made him such a strong leader. As in his other pursuits outside of OVH, his stewardship of the NVE was exemplary.

11
The OVH Equine Teaching Unit

From the day Reg entered the University of Queensland's transient post-Second World War halls as a student in the 1940s, he was loyal to his alma mater. In 1955, three years after graduating, he returned to the UQ Veterinary School as a guest lecturer and external examiner in medicine and surgery. He fulfilled these roles for the next decade. As OVH grew, demanding all his energies, he took an extended hiatus from teaching, but he always came back: as a guest lecturer over several two- to three-year periods between 1970 and 2000; intermittently as an external examiner over the same time span; and from 1998, as an adjunct professor.

Keith Hughes, a UQ alumnus who graduated in 1957 and later became dean of the school, recalled Reg's presence as an external examiner during his fifth year. Though already a skilful practitioner, Reg's examination methods were unorthodox – likely a symptom of developing teaching methodologies, for Queensland's veterinary science discipline was still in its infancy. As was to become an ongoing theme in Reg's career, the students were scared of him, but whether he was aware of this or not, he refused to compromise on his approach.

Arriving for his duties, Reg would bring a bag full of old instruments. When the examinee entered the room, Reg would withdraw an instrument at random. 'Now, what's that?' he'd ask, nodding towards the item in his hand. Most of the students 'didn't have a bloody clue', Keith remembered. And for those few who did, there was inevitably a follow-up question. 'Well then, how was it used?'

'Of course,' Keith said wryly, 'we didn't have a clue to that question either.'

Given Reg's stern demeanour, the experience was likely a

daunting and unnerving one, but it was perhaps not much different to what students expected. Such methods, and their at times brusque delivery, were typical of veterinary science at the time. And, of course, a student's ability to answer tricky 'surprise' questions factored little in Reg's appraisal.

Reg was in the process of developing his own ideas about Australian veterinary science and how it was being managed and taught at UQ. He cared about maintaining standards across the profession, and he saw guaranteeing the quality of graduating vets as vital to doing so. But his relationship with UQ was complex. Loyalty played a role, but it centred on his commitment to ensuring the best education of Queensland vets. Working with UQ gave him access to one of the things he wanted most: to play a role in educating the next generation.

His reasons for doing this were manifold. Reg had been a member of the first Bachelor of Veterinary Science class to complete all five years of study in Queensland and he had an intimate knowledge of the course's strengths – and weaknesses. Those limitations would have remained with him, knowledge that irked and itched. A 1975 letter, published in UQ's *Apsyrtus* newspaper, adjured the profession to 'be watchful of the development of our Veterinary School that our graduates are not reverting to "theoretical" vets with insufficient clinical grounding.' They must all, he added, 'ensure our graduates will meet the demands of their day with the training they have received.' Supporting UQ allowed Reg to work toward achieving this goal and rectifying the shortcomings of his own experience. External support diversified students' professional exposure, facilitating their best possible education. He was also paying homage to the university lecturers who had shaped him and his own career.

Finally, he had a vision of OVH as a 'holistic' equine practice. The hospital's isolation demanded greater clinical diversity than other practices, and in conjunction with his belief about what constituted a competent clinician, this goes some way to explaining the gamut of capabilities that Reg believed OVH should offer. His vision comprised five distinct branches: equine reproduction; equine surgery; equine dermatology; bovine practice and small animal treatment ... and teaching.

Equine reproduction, he had pioneered. Through his work with Queensland thoroughbred studs in the 1960s and 1970s and particularly with the integration of the ultrasound in the 1980s, Reg had become a leading specialist. To equine surgery he had similarly dedicated himself for many years: he was among the first to perform colic surgery, developing techniques and establishing them before sharing his knowledge with the rest of the profession. His work in dermatology had begun with his innovative investigation into rain scald in the mid-1960s. His findings – in conjunction with his publications of the University of Sydney's Post-Graduate Foundation (today the Centre of Veterinary Education) *Blue Book on Equine Dermatoses* and collaborations with Derek Knottenbelt on multiple textbooks – established him as a pre-eminent international equine dermatology expert.

Though he had begun focusing on horses in the 1960s, he had a foundation in bovine science from his early work on the DPI's tuberculosis testing contract, and OVH continued to provide cattle care predominantly through Paul Green's work. And, despite OVH's renown as an equine specialist, it was also registered for small animals.

The only thing he still needed to do to fulfil his vision was teaching. He felt established practitioners should contribute to the education of the next generation. He went on to do so enthusiastically for decades.

OVH had facilitated these ends. Since its inception, the UQ Veterinary school had required students to undertake clinical placements in the final few years of study, an assessed program known as 'seeing practice.' Earlier versions of the program were skewed towards observation. Keith Hughes recalled, 'You went out with a practitioner and you watched what they did. They let you do a few things that were non-invasive – like pregnancy diagnosis of cattle ... you didn't really do any practical surgery, but you observed it.' This was not to say that students missed out on practical skills, since the various units included surgery, but the concept of 'seeing practice' was about just that: *seeing*, not *doing*. During one university Christmas break, Reg spent time on a stud Jersey dairy farm at Devon Park near Oakey as part of this process.

Leanne Begg, who did seeing practice stints at OVH in 1986 and 1987, remembered that Reg 'didn't speak to the students in the whole week that I was there ... we posed all our questions to Andrew Dart who was working as an associate.' It was only during the Christmas party that Reg had a few drinks and came over for a chat. The students were flattered, Leanne recalled, the experience 'a bit like speaking to God!'

The 1990s were a challenging time for higher education in Australia. Increased participation had seen government funding abolished in 1989 by the Hawke federal government and the re-introduction of fees – a system that nowadays includes the Higher Education Contribution Scheme (HECS). As government money dwindled, belts tightened – and tightened again. Then Treasurer Paul Keating travelled around the country selling the new budget to academics, some of whom remembered that his presentation 'was devastating ... It was about how [universities] were going to have to learn to work with fewer dollars.'

Head of the UQ Veterinary School from 1990 to 2000, Keith Hughes had unique insight into the political machinations and financial considerations that underpinned the university's struggles. To this day, vet schools remain one of the more uncommon faculties in contemporary tertiary institutions: in 2020, only seven of Australia's forty-three universities offer a Bachelor of Veterinary Science. From the initial trio of Sydney, Melbourne and Queensland, Perth's Murdoch University had added a school in 1973 and Townsville's James Cook University did the same in 2006 (though JCU's initial offerings were confined to postgraduate courses). 'Veterinary science was the most expensive faculty' for these universities, Keith remembered; whereas medical students practise in state-supported hospitals, veterinary students must practice in university-provided clinics and the associated expenses are substantial. Confronted by federal financial pressures, the faculties – and in particular the vet schools – had to find ways of reducing teaching costs.

The ramifications were invidious and far-reaching. Predominant among these for UQ's Veterinary School was the risk of losing recognition by the Royal College of Veterinary Scientists (RCVS) in London. RCVS accreditation ensures Australian graduates are eligible to register as practitioners both in the UK and in several other countries, such as New Zealand, Fiji, Hong Kong and Singapore. To retain this privilege, Australian vet schools are intermittently assessed by RCVS inspection teams. If UQ failed such an inspection and lost this recognition, their graduates access' to international opportunities would be curtailed. The university's appeal would almost certainly decline. Dwindling numbers could put the existence of the Veterinary School itself under threat.

In the middle of Keith Hughes' tenure as dean, and confronted with these issues, the school reduced staff numbers. These reductions were keenly felt in the equine aspects of the course. Horses are expensive animals to buy, maintain and treat. Though Keith noted that 'the University of Queensland did a very good job with what resources it had', doubts swirled in the community as to the school's ability to teach equine medicine and surgery as it had in the past and to maintain standards.

While hosting London's Dean of Veterinary Science, who'd come to Australia intending to recommend that the Royal College cease recognising degrees conferred by UQ's Veterinary School, Keith took the inspection team to the research facility and farm at Pinjarra Hills. Perhaps the dean had never seen the facility before, or perhaps he saw Keith's determination and tireless efforts to maintain the school and was looking for something to get them over the line. Whatever it was, Keith remembered that when they visited Pinjarra, the team 'changed their minds, because they didn't have anything like that in the UK.'

But the bigger issue remained. Keith wasn't keen to try the school's luck a second time and they couldn't rely on goodwill or the hope of impressing visiting RCVS teams enough to get over the finish line.

The school had several long-term problems, such as the fact that the campus's location on the outskirts of Brisbane made it hard to reach with a horse truck. More immediately, budget constraints continued to impair the school's operations. This meant that the already tired and inadequate St Lucia equine hospital was unable to be properly refurbished. The university was forced to close it in 1999. Now UQ didn't have an equine hospital or a surgical facility and even if they had, staffing shortages meant they couldn't provide a surgery department to teach those skills.

Of course, students still had to conduct 'seeing practice' and the concept continued to evolve alongside students' changing expectations. In 2021, it remains a cornerstone of the degree with UQ BVSc students completing Extramural Studies (EMS) in their fifth year: thirteen weeks of clinical placements of two weeks each at small animal clinics, large animal clinics, mixed practices and the RSPCA, and a week at an abattoir. In the remaining four weeks, they consult with the EMS team to choose their final placement location.

In the late 1990s, seeing practice increasingly aimed to provide better, more meaningful instruction by offering a variety and opportunity of experience not possible within the confines of a university. Students needed a baseline: they couldn't reasonably go to a large animal practice without ever having learnt how to handle a horse. And if the vet school couldn't teach an equine component, they weren't really fulfilling the requirements for producing a graduate.

The community grew worried that UQ had become incapable of adequately teaching equine medicine and surgery and some even began murmuring that perhaps the Veterinary School would need to be closed entirely. For the state's oldest and most prestigious university – and one of Australia's elite 'Group of Eight' – this was a dire threat.

Keith got in touch with Reg. He knew Reg was, and had always been, hugely supportive of UQ; he likewise knew that Reg would be aware of the problems the school was facing. Reg believed Queensland had to continue offering a Bachelor of Veterinary Science so aspiring local vets weren't required to travel interstate. 'He was totally committed to that,' Keith said. And if ensuring that outcome meant Reg personally stepped up and made it happen, then he would do so.

Together, the pair conceived what was to become the University of Queensland Equine Teaching Unit (ETU) at OVH. The UQ lecturer in equine medicine at the time, Chris Pollitt, recalled, 'There were quite a lot of options apart from inviting the Oakey Veterinary Hospital to undertake management of the fifth-year veterinary students' equine rotation, but the Oakey Veterinary Hospital was really the only viable [one].' OVH was the only place that had the qualified and experienced equine staff able to immediately produce lectures and handle students.

Reg with the RVCS accreditation team, who ensured that the Equine Teaching Unit at OVH was sufficient to ensure UQ veterinary students received an accredited degree.

Chris invited Reg to deliver the course's equine dermatology lectures and, in conjunction with some other lecturers, handle the surgery component. He likely failed to anticipate the additional administrative burden this presented; despite Reg's keen interest in innovation and incorporating the newest technology at OVH, he remained wedded to some old-fashioned methods. Like many of his era, he possessed vast slide collections – records from various conditions and cases seen throughout his extensive career. Such slides had been Reg's way of chronicling his life – personal as well as professional – for decades, yet they were quickly being superseded as the Microsoft Office suite dovetailed with other teaching technologies. Reg however kept using the increasingly obsolete

WordPerfect, which had been a dominant player in the word processor market in the 1980s and early 1990s, and other Corel software. This posed challenges for lecturing at UQ.

He confronted the need to use data projectors to present lectures with his customary equanimity and refused to convert to PowerPoint. He had used the Corel software for years and found it excellent – even though the UQ data projectors were incompatible. So he completed his lectures in Corel, transferred them onto to floppy disk, and gave them to Chris Pollitt. Chris recalled, 'I had to transfer all of his lectures from WordPerfect to Word and publish his lectures, print his lectures out so that the students had them and then convert his slide presentation.' It was time-consuming work.

Reg might have been reticent to change software programs, but he was determined to take responsibility for the ETU and make it a world-class experience. Some thought this was madness given the continuing pace of work at OVH. He turned seventy the year the ETU was established but seemed inexhaustible and didn't appear worried about the additional workload. In fact, he relished the opportunity. OVH vet Jayne McGhie recalled, 'He loved to teach the students ... He loved to tell them stories ... He liked to inspire them.' The creation of the ETU provided the final aspect of the comprehensive practice life Reg had always envisaged. He plunged ahead.

Negotiating with UQ on how the ETU would be created and managed must have been complex, even with Keith's enthusiastic cooperation. And while it should have been daunting, there's little indication that Reg hesitated. As Jon Hill, dean of the Veterinary School from 2008 to 2012, noted, 'Someone with Reg's character just took it upon himself and said, "This has to happen."' The decision made, Reg was immovable. If he participated, it would be on a twelve-month trial and the contract would have a clause to allow either party to back out, with a period of notice. 'I still own a clinical practice and I have a responsibility to that practice,' he told them. And after years of gratis service to his alma mater, he stipulated that he would have to be remunerated. Done properly, as he intended to do it, it would take a lot of time and energy, and Reg knew his worth.

Chris Pollitt remembered that Reg said 'he couldn't [run the ETU] as a donation. It had to be on a commercial basis: he had to charge for the time that the veterinarians used to deliver those lectures, his own time, and the time that they [spent managing the students]. He reckoned that it was a full-time salary for an entire year of a junior staff member at Oakey. So, he charged that, and it was paid.'

Coordinating the creation of the ETU would have been complicated, but Reg made it happen by the force of his character alone – a process aided by his ability to successfully communicate with different groups of people. As easily as he could chat across the rail in a paddock, he would adapt, speaking a different language to communicate with large, bureaucratic institutions. Throughout, Jon Hill noted, 'He used the same consistent approach, which is that [he] just kept pushing hard – and direct.' It worked. Keith relayed their discussions to the university's deputy vice-chancellor who was interested. The main obstacle to remedying the school's deficiencies was time, and that, UQ didn't have; the threat to the university's reputation if forced to close the Veterinary School was looming large. This meant securing a quick solution was paramount, the priority justifying the cost. They pushed ahead.

UQ fronted construction costs for the new facility and spent some $80,000 to $100,000 for a demountable building. The teaching facility included a lecture room with desks and some computers, as well as a kitchenette, shower and toilet: all the resources necessary to teach the students. Reg outlined what he felt was necessary to achieve success, and in consultation with UQ lecturers and OVH veterinary staff, devised a teaching plan.

The UQ equine rotation was three weeks long and, in accordance with Reg's plan, Chris Pollitt would take the students in hand for the first week. It was essential that they were equipped with and had practised several procedures that Reg felt necessary – such as stomach-tubing – before they arrived for their two-week rotation in Oakey. Reg's insistence on this pre-training may have been prompted by some previous student encounters; Joy recalled students who arrived in Oakey having never passed a stomach tube in a horse, believing it unnecessary since they intended to focus on cats and dogs after they graduated. Most concerning, some had never had any exposure to large animals and feared horses in principle, let alone when required to treat them. Reg had little tolerance for this. 'If you want to pass and get a veterinary degree,' he told them, 'you have to do *all* species.'

At Oakey, Reg's word was law.

For the latter fortnight of their equine rotation, approximately twelve students came to Oakey and lived in the caravan park across the road, allowing them to return outside of work hours to revise or prepare for exams.

It was all carefully planned, but the scheme's reception was less than positive. Andrew Van Eps was a fifth-year student in 1999 and intended to pursue equine practice after he graduated. For Andrew and the few other students of his cohort interested in horses, the closure of the UQ equine hospital was a blow, and news of the creation of a teaching unit at OVH didn't alleviate the concern. 'Everyone was sceptical that there would be any sort of clinical rotation set up in time for it to be reasonable, because it takes a lot of time and planning to put in place a decent experience for students.' Everyone was aware of the limitations. 'We'd heard, not unexpectedly, that we wouldn't be allowed to work too much on client-owned animals.' This wasn't uncommon. It would be a rare equine practice that allowed students to treat the animals of paying clients.

Keith recalled the student reaction as being rather more dramatic. As they were putting the ETU concept together, the students said, 'This is terrible! We're not going to be registered because we're not then going to be taught [enough].' Their apprehension was understandable. Though renowned bovine veterinarian Jakob Malmo had instituted a similar model for cattle in Melbourne, there were no external equine teaching units operating in Australia at the time. The ETU was unusual, Jon Hill pointed out, as was the collaboration between Reg and UQ (though it has since been replicated). It was a 'real one-off to have a private practice teaching, educating the veterinary students on the equine rotations' – hardly an auspicious situation for students nervously considering their future careers. And, as always, there was the issue of money.

Frank Low, who went through the ETU as a fifth year in 2000, was vice-president and later president of his year of the student union. His positions gave him insight into the behind-the-scenes struggles which preceded the establishment of the ETU. The union had a small pool of money and Frank recalled occasional issues with university funding that brought Reg to the union's doors. 'He would ask us to find some supplies or some dental gear [or anything else] that he needed to help teach ... that the university had trouble getting for him.'

Despite the funding issues and student worries, Reg created a program which satisfied all the requirements of the fifth-year rotation within the space of a few months. It was comprehensive enough to ensure graduates were as skilled with horses as any from Melbourne or Sydney. Keith argued in fact that the ETU provided better training than most, if not all, other universities, and that included anything UQ had taught to date as well. How? Reg was a perfectionist, but Keith attributed the venture's success to something different. In universities, lecturers would typically be academics whose knowledge was broad but not necessarily deep or specialised, and who were physically removed from practice. In contrast, vets instructing in the ETU at OVH were seeing clinical cases every day. They were also all specialists. An Australian expert on equine reproduction, David Pascoe provided both lectures and practical demonstrations. The students quickly recognised this expertise, and it garnered their respect, further improving the learning environment.

The challenge was balancing OVH's core purpose as a functioning veterinary hospital with its new role as a teaching clinic. Chris Riggs, who worked at OVH in the 1990s, was invaluable in helping resolve this issue. As he considered the prospect of incorporating the ETU into OVH, he approached Reg to discuss boundaries. His experience at a university and his clinical work in Oakey made clear to him the risks of inadvertently conflating the two arenas. 'I think this is going to work,' he told Reg. 'And it's going to be of value to these guys. But if you're teaching, you've got to be off the clinic.' The risk otherwise was that the high standards of service Reg esteemed would suffer, whether in one group or the other.

When a client came in with their horse, they deserved all the treating vet's attention – no one would argue with that – but, Chris noted, if OVH didn't clearly separate clinical work and teaching, then the steady stream of clients would mean the students would 'play second fiddle [to the clients] and it wouldn't be fun. They'd feel like you weren't giving them the attention and you weren't doing a proper job.'

Reg was convinced – short-changing the students would have been repugnant to him. He separated the clinic from the ETU. Teaching OVH vets were off the clinic, which meant they weren't responding to incoming cases; they might be peripherally involved but their focus for that day was solely on teaching. 'It made it much more civilised,' Chris said. 'And much better because you could really focus on the students.'

That didn't mean there was no crossover. Recognising that the value of running classes in a clinical practice was that it enabled student exposure to interesting cases, Oakey vets ensured they grabbed that chance wherever possible. Students started each day by conducting hospital rounds with the teaching staff, but if something interesting cropped up later, the vets on clinic let the lecturing vets know, and the students were turned over to have a look before resuming their normal routine.

The vets who worked at OVH recalled the experience with enthusiasm. 'It was a great thing,' Chris Riggs said. 'It was really impressive how – almost overnight – we put in those demountable buildings and turned them into seminar rooms and other facilities.' Andrew Van Eps agreed. 'We went from obviously being really concerned about our clinical year education to being very thankful that we'd had that opportunity.'

The students' experience was thorough and dynamic, delivered by veterinarians eager to maximise the opportunity. They started at 7 a.m. and kept students busy with both lectures and practical lessons until 6 p.m. Running the ETU in a clinical practice limited students' access to live clinical cases, but Reg overcame this by creating detailed, challenging and realistic scenarios using cadaver limbs and simulated wounds. This resulted in problem-based learning tutorials and practical hands-on experiences that left a deep impression. Presenting a scenario, Reg and his vets asked students 'to formulate a plan' based on their observations. The method provided fertile ground for reinforcing Reg's favourite lesson: the value of knowing and applying the principles of veterinary science to a problem.

In his early years of practice, Reg had encountered something unfamiliar on almost a daily basis. He knew that instructing students in rote responses was ineffective and possibly dangerous both to the animal and to the students' careers. Instead, as he had been taught, he taught students how to react when presented with a conundrum, reinforcing the value of adhering to the basic principles of investigation and appraisal. Dr Cheryl Lopate, the US equine reproductive specialist who spent time at OVH, recalled that Reg 'was very good at teaching veterinarians [how to be] veterinarians. He would tell the students to analyse the issue thoroughly, drawing on the combination of their existing knowledge and their thorough examination of the animal to come to a sound decision.'

This investigative paradigm was the cornerstone of Reg's clinical skills. His vets only thrived at OVH by demonstrating these analytical capabilities, and they strove to inculcate the same approach through the ETU. One occasion seared itself into Andrew Van Eps' mind. The rotation was completing a scenario when a classmate glanced at a wound on a cadaver leg and dismissed it. 'This has just a small tear in the skin, we'll just suture it up,' the student said. Without speaking, the supervising OVH vet took the leg and bent it at the joint; the flexion revealed a ruptured tendon. The truth was there, hiding from sight, and it was their task to delve deep and uncover it.

For Andrew, that seemingly small moment exemplified not only the value of remembering the basics and applying them in a logical way, but also the possibilities in the structure and delivery of teaching. Several such episodes at OVH stuck with him, particularly how learning resonated when the experiences were relevant and interesting.

Reg could be gruff and some students were scared of him, but Cheryl remembered 'a kind and empathetic teacher.' It was unavoidable that, throughout a degree, there would be some lecturers whom students were terrified of. Andrew pointed out that there were those who would upbraid students simply as a matter of course, perhaps to remind them of their place in the hierarchy, but he was quick to note that that wasn't why students were nervous around Reg. They were aware of the respect in which Reg was held by the profession and, just as importantly, his tendency to be sharp-tongued. Students were anxious about slipping up and getting on the wrong side of him. But Reg didn't rebuke them without just cause and that even-handed treatment balanced his bluntness. Knowing he was a hard taskmaster was acceptable when coupled with an underlying fairness, 'but people were definitely on their toes around him, always', Andrew added dryly.

Reg was well aware of the effect that he had. Decades of dealing with people and mentoring junior vets meant he understood human nature and knew how to keep people vigilant – but also how to put them at ease. He often cracked jokes to break the ice, which was effective: laughter seemed to unknot most stomachs. But that only lasted until he asked another question, and once again nerves descended like a swarm of flies in Oakey's summers. Reg liked having fun and Frank Low's class joked around, pulling pranks during their time in the ETU. Reg loved the class's penchant for shenanigans. 'Everybody would say he was very serious, but he had a bit of a comic side to him,' Frank said.

Reg also loved to challenge people, and made a point of pushing the students every day, forcing them to confront the limits of their own knowledge and broaden their horizons. Not everyone was responsive to his methods, Frank remembered. Some 'gave up and clammed up.' Reg felt that such reactions indicated a student's inability to survive the challenges they'd face in the profession and, where he thought it necessary, he told them that he thought they couldn't handle it.

That bluntness was quintessentially Reg, as anyone who made a foolish comment in the ETU quickly discovered. Andrew's rotation was receiving a class on wound management when one of his peers suggested they treat a wound by urinating on it. Reg was silent for a long time before he looked the young man in the eye. 'You're a raw prawn,' he said and turned away to continue the lecture. The phrase resurfaced more than once over Andrew's equine rotation. But the students formed a deep affection for Reg, his vets and the practice, as demonstrated by this poem composed by a 2002 UQ fifth-year rotations in honour of their time at the ETU:

There was a vet called Pascoe
Who could solve any fiasco
From any problems with skin
To fixing a wound on the shin
He could cauterise sarcoids
Or chew off any haemorrhoids

He could solve any problem with legs
With hessian bags, phenol and pegs

Then there was a vet named Joan
Who could tackle anything on her own
Her speciality was dealing with foals
So sick their hearts full with holes
No better rectal ever has been done
From the top of a 44 gallon drum

Then there was Steve
In his wrangler jeans
With his tight butt spreading the seams
What a glorious sight at a trot of a hike
He thought we were dumb
But we were too busy looking at his bum

Along came Christene
Who was new on the scene
An angel in disguise
Who saved us from demise

Paula the Brit
Patient and full of wit
We nearly made her cry
By spraying methylene blue in her eye
She showed us how much fun
You could have with lube
And a nasogastric tube

There wasn't a day without an X-ray
We sat down with Tim
In a cosy room with lights dim
Our solution to the cases were
A bullet in the head
They were better off dead
unlike Tim who was realistic
We might have been a little pessimistic

We were visited by Glen
Who took time out from the races
To help us with thoroughbreds and pacers

Then there were the repro boys
With their ejaculation and stimulating toys
David, Dave and John
And their horse with a hard on
With helmet in hand
We expressed the horse's glands
He then blew his whole wad
All over the collecting student's bod

We all had fun at Oakey
Even though we suffered frost bite
Thank you again
We now view horses in a different light.

Reg retired from teaching in 2003. Many of those educated through the ETU during its first four years counted themselves lucky – whether they went onto become equine vets or not. Chris Pollitt remarked that Reg had no 'formal training' as an educator, which is true, but his ability to teach in a way that was engaging and meaningful was beyond reproach. According to veterinarian and friend Julie Strous, 'He did love to educate, and he did love people – he wanted to bring the best out in them too and encourage them along that same path. He did have a real joy in learning and seeing other people, seeing the light go on.'

Of the students at OVH during Reg's management of the ETU prior to his retirement, only a small number wanted to pursue equine medicine. That was the norm, but it was difficult for Reg when he came up against classes where *none* of the students wanted to do equine work. He was so enthused about his profession, so happy to sit and talk to the students in the evenings and so invested in conveying his own passion that he could be left dejected by discovering that some just weren't interested.

Nevertheless, he left an indelible imprint on them all. Andrew Van Eps believed a good educator can teach a student something fundamental that stays with them, and is able to be taken away and applied elsewhere, even if the subject at hand isn't their primary calling. Reg 'was somebody who undoubtedly did that.' Yet when course evaluation forms were distributed for the students to provide feedback on the ETU's effectiveness, Reg had a problem. Confronted with recurrent sixes and sevens, he was nonplussed. *What aren't I doing right?* he wondered.

Seven out of ten was hardly an acceptable result for the effort he and the OVH staff had put into the scheme. While he was mulling over what was going wrong, one of UQ's small animal lecturers heard about the evaluations and asked Reg if she could discuss the results. Reg agreed. It was only when the professor arrived to congratulate him on such stellar student ratings (and to ask how she might replicate his work), that Reg realised: he'd been assuming a scale of one–ten, where universities use one–seven! For all his concern about the effectiveness of the ETU, the program he had designed, implemented and directed was consistently ranked by students as one of, if not the, best course at UQ.

At the end of 1999, the deputy director of studies for veterinary science at UQ, John Thornton, reflected on the integration of the Equine Teaching Unit at OVH in his annual address to the graduating class. 'The joint venture with Oakey Veterinary Hospital this year is clearly and significantly different to previous years. As you are all aware there was a combination of circumstances that led to the initiation of this venture to provide clinical teaching in equine medicine and surgery. As with many situations in life, a short-term resolution of a difficulty may well prove better run some ways than the original situation. This is also true for the present arrangements with OVH. The enthusiasm of Dr Pascoe, the scope of his practice and the willingness of his colleagues together with the efforts of Dr Chris Pollitt resulted in an "equine rotation" that was comprehensive, instructive and well received by all groups during the year.' It was hard-won wisdom and Reg put it to good use. A decade later in 2010, he gladly shared it to help his friend and colleague Bruce Pott establish student placements in his clinic for James Cook University's new equine component. It was, clearly, a model that worked.

Yet despite the proven success and value of the ETU, when Keith Hughes retired in 2000, his replacement begrudged the expense Reg's services. There was, Keith recalled, 'some resentment there that Reg was ripping the school off.' Was he? Reg rarely, if ever, strayed from a strict moral code that governed everything he did. His career was marked by altruism: few professionals give as freely of their time and expertise. It's unlikely that he deviated from this trait in managing the ETU.

Jon Hill, who did practical work with Reg in the 1980s and became head of the Veterinary School in 2008, marvelled at Reg's generosity when he realised the extent to which the ETU had acted as UQ's saviour a decade earlier. That the university had paid for OVH's management of the ETU was a just recognition of the commitment of time and expertise, but the money wouldn't have fully compensated the practice. It was, Jon pointed out, 'a commitment to education broadly and particularly to UQ.'

Part of the issue was that in the absence of a cost-benefits analysis, there was no data available to use as a point of comparison for what Reg *should* be charging. Historically, there had been ongoing incongruence between the funds allocated for the completion of a veterinary science degree, and the actual costs of achieving the outcome; Chris Pollitt noted that the Veterinary School 'was always in debt to the university in those years.' Reg's carefully determined fee had come as a rude shock.

The ETU remained in place for a decade, but it was unavoidable that money worries, an awareness that in-house training would be cheaper than outsourcing to a private practitioner, and the university's desire for greater control over the BVSc, factored into the push for the establishment of an equine hospital at the UQ Gatton campus. In a move that merged the state's two oldest higher education institutions, UQ had absorbed the Queensland Agricultural College at Gatton in 1990. The two had long cooperated in teaching and research ventures and in 2010, UQ's Veterinary School relocated to purpose-built facilities on the UQ Gatton campus.

Reg was nearing eighty. He had relinquished directorship of OVH in 2001 and stopped teaching in 2003, and yet for the final time, he rallied to the support of his alma mater when they needed his help. When a capital campaign was instituted in 2007 to raise money for the relocation of the Veterinary School, Reg was invited to join the committee and said yes without a moment's pause. On one hand, he experienced a sense of loss associated with the end of the ETU: he had worked hard and had enjoyed teaching the students. On the other hand, however, he knew that reintegrating the equine component of the BVSc into the university curriculum was vital to the long-term health of veterinary education in Queensland.

Jon Hill was also on the committee, and believed Reg brought great value to their endeavour. Reg was both well-known and a natural leader; had made many notable contributions to the UQ Veterinary School, particularly in the provision of the ETU; and had of lot of experience with fundraising because of his volunteer work in the local Oakey community. There was an array of different personality types on the committee, and Jon recalled that Reg's presence was interesting precisely because he was 'very direct and action-oriented' but was now working with people who were, in Jon's words, 'not necessarily outcome-orientated.'

Given Reg's drive and energy, the situation would have been frustrating. There was a problem that needed smart decision-making, planning and execution – all traits by which Reg had organised his own professional life for sixty years. Yet achieving that now seemed impossible, or at least hampered by bureaucratic nonsense.

'When [Reg] was asked for his opinion, it was always how to timeline and what could be achieved and let's get it done now,' Jon said. Where others dithered and plotted out circuitous strategies, Reg remained grounded in the immediate: what could they do *today* to move forward in the coming month? Who was going to take responsibility for the next step? In doing so, the pragmatism and direction he offered the committee was invaluable ... no matter how frustrating he may have found it.

Reg's influence was interwoven into the fabric of many aspects of the new Gatton campus Veterinary School. In a turn of events that he describes as 'serendipitous', Andrew Van Eps returned to UQ in 2009, a decade after he graduated, to create the new UQ equine hospital. He had spent much of the previous ten years in the US, studying for his PhD at the renowned University of Pennsylvania. His esteem for Reg's management of the ETU remained undiminished and he often thought of OVH during his postgraduate studies. Other training just wasn't as good. The ETU and the dedicated OVH vets working there had left an indelible mark on him; in comparison, other education felt like a water skimmer darting over the surface of a pond.

In his first year back at the University of Queensland, before the equine hospital was opened, Andrew was responsible for the final year clinical rotation and designed many facets of the course based on how Reg had taught his class. When the equine hospital eventually opened, he continued to include these lessons from Reg, many of which remain an important part of the equine rotation.

Reg's legacy to UQ was long and fruitful. Yet when the Gatton campus was opened, there was little recognition for all his hard work. Prior to the vet school's reopening, Andrew Dart gave Reg a call. He had been Reg's friend for twenty-five years and had witnessed Reg's ongoing investment in UQ. They had spoken many times of Reg's efforts for the vet school, which Dart (and perhaps Reg, too) thought were underappreciated. Dart couldn't resist a wry joke at Reg's expense. 'Reg, they're going to name a building after you!' he said with a laugh.

Reg just laughed in return. 'No, they won't,' he said, and he was right. Dart later stated that he felt UQ 'used Reg time and time again.' He remembered, 'They offered to name a carpark after him and he sort of had a laugh at that, thinking they maybe could have done more than just a carpark. But that was the sort of thing that always happened to Reg – he'd put in all of this effort to help the university and they always give him a bit of a chastising.'

Chris Pollitt agreed. 'The name Pascoe has never been fully acknowledged by the veterinary school. There's no building, lecture theatre, room, named in Reg's honour – I always thought there should be.' Chris believed this could be attributed to lingering resentment that 'Reg made the school pay' for the ETU, but the truth is more complicated. University buildings are often named after financial donors to incentivise fundraising; while Reg's omission might have been due to ill-feeling, it may also have simply been seen as expediency. Whatever its origins, this final rebuff wounded Reg. In 2016, when the University of Melbourne came knocking at the door of Jim Vasey's practice, Reg advocated caution.

2002. Reg in the main OVH office with a group of Japanese veterinarians undertaking a UQ seminar run through OVH.

It was not the first time Reg's relationship with UQ had hit rocky ground. When the position of professor of veterinary surgery became available in 1974, Reg's ears pricked up. Recognising the colossal change that moving into academia would have on the life he and Joy had built, Reg mulled over whether or not to apply. When they talked it over before the interview, he told Joy, 'You know that if I get this, we'll have to leave here. What do you think about living out Kenmore way?' South-west of the Brisbane CBD, Kenmore is close to the Pinjarra Hills UQ Research Facility, roughly a twenty-minute trip to the St Lucia campus. While today the area is significantly more developed, it was 'a bit rural back then', and seemed to offer an ideal compromise. Joy agreed.

Reg loved surgery and the position seemed to him to offer a chance to pass that love onto others and so he put his name forward. OVH veterinarian Max Wilson remembered being flabbergasted. 'We'd just assumed that he would never walk away from that place until he was well and truly ready to retire – or in a box.' OVH was a thriving vet hospital – but Reg was prepared to leave it in others' capable hands or let it go entirely, to take the position at UQ.

Arriving in Brisbane for the interview, Reg found himself in the waiting room alongside another applicant. Professor Mike Rex, the associate professor of surgery at the University of Melbourne's Veterinary School, was an anaesthetist with an impressive résumé. On paper Reg should have been an equally ideal candidate and he likely expected the atmosphere to reflect as much even though his history with UQ was characterised by pull and push. There were many times over the years, Dart recalled, 'where Reg was rebuffed and chastised by the university for his opinions or the way he did things. But whenever they needed something done, [UQ] used to come to Reg and Reg used to always say yes.'

When he appeared before the interview panel, Reg discovered that his reception was considerably less welcoming than he might have imagined. 'Why would you be interested in this position?' the panel asked. 'Is it to earn more money?' Nothing could have been more insulting for a man who had always put financial gain low on his list of priorities ... particularly when delivered by an institution which had for decades benefited from his magnanimity. He may have misinterpreted the thrust of the inquiry; the intent may have been different, the delivery more clumsy than antagonistic. But the result was the same.

Reg stood and coolly met each panel member's gaze in turn. 'I would earn less money here than I would in practice,' he said brusquely, and walked out.

Mike Rex sat outside, awaiting his turn with the panel.

'The job's yours,' Reg said. He returned to Oakey.

Reg and Mike went on to work in close concert on various committees during Mike's tenure – most notably in managing the National Veterinary Exam – and Reg's loyalty to UQ continued, but not without damage. In the preceding eighteen years, he had spent twelve as a UQ guest lecturer. Following the professorship interview, he didn't return to those responsibilities for another thirteen years. The change could also be attributed to the additional workload Reg undertook beyond OVH in that period, but it begs the question of whether the interview stung enough to cause him to take a step back from the university.

The situation was galling, but it was an unwitting boon to Reg. Joy believed it was the best thing that could have happened. Reg was a formidable surgeon, but had he become a professor, his talents would have been constrained within the university system and that would have frustrated him. A man who prized his autonomy and refused to dilute his opinions might have felt frustrated in an academic setting, for while he 'offered a lot of himself to the university, he did not tolerate fools or political games.'[21] His steadfast refusal to compromise his own moral code meant he could be abrupt, even abrasive, when saying things people didn't want to hear. He believed neither in the posturing inherent in campus politicking, nor in prevaricating when faced with a tough situation. And, as Andrew Dart summarised, 'fundamentally, [UQ] wanted the experience and expertise he had to offer from so many years of self-discipline and commitment, but did not want the straight talk.'

Rather than having to concentrate more stringently on research and pursue a PhD, Reg was free, a liberty he exploited to pursue the advancement of veterinary science in Australia. More importantly, at least from the university's perspective, his continued clinical practice at OVH enabled the creation of the ETU – that singular innovative solution – when UQ needed it the most more than twenty years later.

Reg's relationship with the University of Queensland was an intricate tapestry, woven over many decades. In creating and running the ETU in 1999, he added another thread, perhaps the most resonant and beautiful of them all. Throughout his career he repeatedly demonstrated the ability to adapt to new information and situations, a flexibility that underpinned his success across numerous fields. He couldn't stand stagnation. Yet in other ways, he was immovable: there was an unspoken but immutable moral code etched deep into his bones and he lived every day by its tenets, chief among which were integrity, loyalty and service. It was a seeming contradiction: the curious explorer and intellectual pioneer on one hand, the steadfast pillar of constancy on the other.

But therein lay the nexus of his character.

It was this character that underpinned his long relationship with UQ, that precipitated the ETU, that made it into a success – and that influenced those who studied at OVH. 'It was really impressive,' said Andrew Van Eps and, 'to the credit of Reg, in particular, it was a really fantastic experience.' He saw Reg as the godfather of horse medicine and was grateful to have been given the chance to learn from him. Frank Low agreed. Reg created an incomparable experience at OVH for UQ students. 'There's no one like him now and I don't think there ever will be.'

Part V —
Going to Work for God

12
Reg and the OVH in the 1970s

Reg's life was eventful. Numerous people and organisations vied for his attention as he sought to balance a busy professional life with his family and Joy wryly noted more than once that she sometimes wondered if she had married twins. With so many competing concerns, a lesser person might have felt like they were being torn to shreds. Reg thrived on it. At the centre of it all was the Oakey Veterinary Hospital. Whatever might be occurring beyond the clinic, OVH was the heart of Reg's professional world, and his devotion was unwavering.

As 1970 dawned, Australia entered an economic downturn. Inflation began to increase, heralding a decade of poor economic performance tied to a drop in international demand for Australian exports. Coupled with a rise in interest rates, a slump in the agricultural industry meant expansion of OVH slowed. But while the physical expansion of might have paused, neither the surgery nor its clinicians sat around idle. Far from it.

OVH received its accreditation as both a small and large animal veterinary hospital early in this period. Clinics had to meet rigorous standards and it was unusual for a vet hospital to be accredited for creatures *both* large and small. Reg, writing for his Doctor of Veterinary Science (DVSc) submission in 1984, pointed out that OVH was the 'only combined large and small animal hospital in Australia.' Lou Winkel, who worked as a vet nurse at OVH at the time, recalled Reg's management of the accreditation process. He made a point to involve his staff, introducing them to the accreditors, and afterwards inviting some, including Lou, to join them for lunch up at the house.

The house was only a brief stroll away, sitting up on the small hill from where it gazed out over the hospital like a benevolent guardian.

The proximity did little to separate Reg's professional and personal lives and his passion for his work regularly crossed the divide. In 1971, their eldest son John enrolled in a BVSc at the University of Queensland and two years later, his younger brother David followed suit, commencing a Bachelor of Vet Science.

The college life Reg had missed out on was possible for his two sons and for the next nineteen years, there would be a Pascoe at King's College. 'Reg and Joy would've paid college fees for a longer time than anybody else,' according to family friend Trevor Heath. The boys' emulation of their father seemed preordained: they'd been steeped in the intricacies of veterinary science their whole lives. David later recalled that as a young boy, 'We always had vet students staying and Reg would get out his slides. We kids could answer the questions because we'd seen all the skin conditions before, but the poor vet students hadn't a clue what they were looking at.'

A steady stream of students or junior and visiting vets undertook their fifth year BVSc 'seeing practice' at OVH. David Laws was one of the first in 1954 but Reg actively encouraged many others – both from UQ and further afield – to come and work with him in Oakey. Those who worked with Reg closely over many years knew 'the Boss' well, better than most. The sheer amount of time the OVH vets, nurses and administrative staff spent with Reg meant they were privy to a veterinary giant at his best – and his worst. Every relationship was slightly different; each person took away their own unique image. Their collected stories offer a humorous and insightful picture of Reg in his most natural environment, doing the work he loved best.

David Skerman, OVH vet 1969–1974

In 1969, in the final year of his BVSc, a young man called David Skerman from a rural Queensland dairy farm spent a month at OVH in two fortnight blocks. At the end of his 'seeing practice', he asked Reg about his job prospects.

'The only possible option for you here,' Reg told him, 'would be if Les decides not to go on.' Les McMicking had graduated from UQ a year ahead of David and joined OVH at the start of the year. 'But,' Reg added, 'if Les decides to leave, I'd be happy enough to take you on.'

As it turned out, Les decided he wanted to see the world and so David started at OVH two days after graduating from UQ. The practice was still small, comprising only Reg, David Laws, Paul Green and Hazel Ward, a vet nurse who managed much of the small animal and lab work. As the youngest and the newest member of the team, David Skerman remembered, 'I got to do whatever nobody else wanted to do. But I didn't mind.' OVH saw such a variety of clinical cases – from the eighteen thoroughbred studs on the surgery's books, to the trackwork being done in Toowoomba – that it was an ideal place for him to consolidate his studies. And it didn't hurt that he thought the OVH surgery facility better than UQ's, nor that, as a country boy from a dairy farming background, he was already at ease around large animals.

Reg had an innate ability to size up the professionals he welcomed into his practice, detecting potential in those he would mentor. 'Sometimes I look back and wonder the basis of Reg's assessment of other people – he had no résumé from me, I had no experience,' David said. The relationship necessitated trust on Reg's part, a trust that was fundamental to the practice's success. The nature of large animal work and the requirement for vets to attend on-property calls meant it was impractical for Reg – or David Laws or Paul – to hover over a junior vet at every moment, and from the start they often conducted lone calls. Returning from on-property work, David remembers being quizzed by the partner trio, exchanges that encouraged him to think more broadly about his available treatment options and consider the best ways of doing things.

He was never cast adrift without support, though: if time permitted, Reg always offered to oversee and assist with surgical work. Stud work was managed on-property by the attending vet, with only incidents requiring surgical intervention brought to the hospital, but other complex and interesting cases regularly arose. In the clinic, everybody saw it. Horses floated in from both the local area and further afield exhibited a wide range of conditions, and anything that was even slightly unusual was discussed in detail. OVH operated on the premise that exchanging ideas was fundamental and discussion was central to daily practice life. Even at the operating table. Reg ran surgeries like a conductor before an orchestra; as he wielded the scalpel, another vet or nurse would be managing the anaesthetic, while someone else applied a tourniquet to a horse's leg to prepare for surgery. All the while, David remembered, 'You'd be exchanging views and stories of the day's proceedings or particular cases.'

Outside of OVH, the ante-mortem cattle jobs that had been Paul Green's responsibility fell to David. This mainly involved inspections at the Oakey abattoir, which had been established in 1956. It was owned by a short-tempered man called Fred Keong, who was seen as one of the district's toughest businessmen, infamous in the stock and station industry for his unpredictability and his tendency to swoop in and purchase large herds of cattle in a single go. David typically started work around six in the morning and as he checked the cattle to ensure they were fit for slaughter, it provided him the chance to see tuberculosis and a wide range of other conditions first-hand.

The ease with which the local community, including Fred Keong, accepted David – 'the new, fresh-faced boy on the block' – was testament to the esteem in which Reg and the OVH practice were held. It was a far cry from the suspicious attitudes Reg had first encountered upon graduation almost two decades earlier.

David Lovell, EVA Colleague

David Lovell graduated from UQ in 1970. Joining a Dalby practice in 1972, he became Reg's opposition; yet despite this rivalry and Reg's fierce possessiveness, Lovell found Reg to be a great source of help and advice during the early years of his career. Reg fostered a collegiate environment that extended far beyond OVH. 'There was no one in Australia, in my opinion, that came anywhere near him in the fingerprint that he ... put on all of us.'

What was notable in this, and played a big role in his influence, was Reg's accessibility. He was always available to discuss horse issues: with clients, with horse owners, with other veterinarians. If someone had a problem, Reg was there to help. In part, this was smart business. As Reg said more than once, he knew that of those he spoke to, sooner or later, someone would send him a horse for treatment. But even Reg's own words covered a deeper truth: he truly cared about serving his profession and his clients. Decades later, a colleague noted Reg's opinion that equine vets existed to help improve the health and welfare of horses was inspirational, providing a much-needed contrast to the view that every time a vet looked at a horse or discussed it with an owner, they merely saw dollar signs.

Reg believed in the sharing of knowledge, knowledge that he had worked hard to acquire, but dispersed freely. His attitude was a reaction to the striking *lack* of support that had been available in his early years: remembering the difficulties he'd faced, it would have been odious to Reg to neglect the community. His work was not simply a job to him, but a calling, a vocation that enthused and energised him.

Shirl Adamson, OVH staff, 1974–1989

In January 1974, a fifteen-year-old girl called Shirl Adamson began working at OVH. She was a Queensland kid from Maryborough whose family had recently moved to Oakey when her parents bought the local hotel. Having completed Grade 10 in Maryborough (and not enjoyed the process), her father's ultimatum that she either finish school in Oakey or get a job sent Shirl out looking for work. Scouring the newspaper, she stumbled upon an OVH ad that stated the practice was seeking a 'girl Friday.' Derived from Daniel Defoe's novel *Robinson Crusoe* in which the protagonist rescues a young native man on a Friday and so creatively dubs him 'man Friday', the old-fashioned term referred to any resourceful assistant.

That sounded okay, Shirl thought, and she applied. A few weeks later, the phone rang. The voice on the other end was the OVH office manager, informing her that she hadn't been the hospital's first choice, but their initial hire hadn't lasted the distance. Shirl was next in line. The role involved everything from manning the reception desk when clients brought in their animals, to cleaning out the kennels, and even assisting in the operating theatre during surgeries. She fell to it with a vengeance.

Shirl enjoyed the work and quickly built a strong relationship with Reg. Though he could be a hard man to work for, he was consistent and kind; after she lost her father in August 1974, Reg became Shirl's role model. She respected him and Reg provided a steadying hand

and safe port of call, always available with advice as she navigated the challenges of her teenage years. Reg's advice was sometimes delivered bluntly, but Shirl learnt to wait and to listen, and then follow through as best she could. He was her friend and mentor, and Shirl cherished their relationship; for fifteen years, she was a dedicated and enthusiastic OVH employee, playing an important role in the practice's growth.

The hospital changed greatly during her time there. It 'just got bigger and bigger and busier and busier as the years went on', she recalled. You never knew what was going to happen on any given day – every one was different – and that made it interesting. Though it must have been daunting at first, especially as a teenager thrown into this complex and dynamic environment, she quickly carved a niche for herself. This acclimation would have been helped by one of the fundamental philosophies of OVH: individuals were empowered in their area of expertise and acknowledged by other staff as the master of that domain.

Shirl saw this idea play out across all levels of the practice. Countless vets worked there during her time, but she remembered that they were always respectful of what she was doing and seemed to similarly respect one another. One of the greatest lessons Reg taught her was the importance of always listening to people and appreciating them for what they did. It was a principle that he and his partners strove to exemplify for all OVH staff, and one demonstrated in Reg's management of Shirl's professional development.

Shirl was young and inexperienced when she started at OVH, but Reg didn't care about that. She was bright, hardworking and determined to grapple with anything that came her way, traits Reg prized above most others. He spent time developing her skills and confidence in handling the surgery's administration. When an administrative issue arose, Reg headed to Shirl to discuss the matter – but in the end, 'he would always leave the final decision up to me.' Reg respected Shirl's opinions and if she came to him with a suggestion for an improvement, he always sat and listened. He never condescended to her, and she never forgot it. 'He didn't speak down to me as if I was a layman at any stage, ever.'

Shirl worked hard to make life easier for Reg. If he had morning surgeries, she headed into work early to ensure the associated administration was complete and the process ran smoothly. She never doubted Reg's gratitude. 'I always knew that he appreciated anything that I did.' Throughout her time at OVH, this appreciation ensured Shirl received a nice bonus each Christmas. 'He was a very generous man.'

Glenda Sinclair, who worked with Reg at Provet, recalled the company's annual Christmas promotion: any client who bought a certain amount of product received a free Christmas ham. Every year – to the point that she began planning for it well in advance – Reg would ring Glenda. 'I need thirty-six hams this Christmas,' he'd say, to ensure every OVH employee received one. 'How much do I need to order to get those?'

Reg was a loyal Provet client as well as a director and together, he and Glenda would tailor OVH's order so that he could secure the requisite number of hams. Afterwards, of course, Glenda faced a 'great big logistical nightmare' in ensuring all the hams arrived in Oakey at the right time, but the kindness of it touched her heart. 'Nobody,' she said pointedly, 'ordered thirty-six hams. Nobody except Reg – because he wanted to make sure everyone at the clinic got their ham from the clinic at Christmas.'

But then, OVH had always been a family business. Both Reg and Joy cared deeply for the staff and Joy was always available on the other end of the phone if someone needed something. Lou Winkel remembered that 'she was always there for a chat and if we were working really late, she'd bring us down food.' Joy recognised there were challenges to working in a male-dominated environment; perhaps she also realised such challenges could be more marked for young women who typically had less experience and education than their male colleagues in those days.

Reg was often abrupt when dealing with people, and in his practice, his expertise and his authority reigned supreme. For teenage girls – with only high school-level education, lacking a strong male figure in their lives, and professionally inexperienced as well – entering such an environment meant they were likely to be highly susceptible to influence. Lou believed Reg recognised the power imbalance and he ensured the girls were treated with respect, working with Joy to protect and guide them.

On several occasions during her time at OVH, Shirl was working at her desk only to look up and find Reg standing beside her. 'What're you doing next week?' he asked.

'Working, I suppose,' Shirl replied slowly, perplexed by the question.

'No, you're not,' Reg said, his tone brooking no dissent. 'Mrs Pascoe's just booked you a holiday on Great Keppel Island.'

There was a reassuring stability in working for Reg Pascoe and Shirl was never in any doubt about where she stood. 'He certainly let me know if I did anything that I shouldn't have,' she recalled. His rebukes could be sharp, but if she knew she'd done the wrong thing, she just 'copped that on the chin' and apologised, taking responsibility in a way Reg respected. They had a great connection and Shirl was not only Reg's right hand, but developed an excellent read on his character. She understood what he was likely to want in each situation and if someone suggested something new, she knew when it was time to run it past Reg to avoid anyone overstepping the line.

By the time she was in her twenties, Shirl had developed the resilience and self-possession ideally suited to working closely with Reg. She typically sat doing the accounts in Reg's office, a situation which drew incredulity from others. 'How do you stand sitting in there with him all day?' they would marvel. But Shirl's response was as laconic as her boss's might have been. 'He's all right,' she'd say. Years of working together taught her how to weather the storms. Like Reg, Shirl was practical, and she recognised that everyone had bad days now and again. It was obvious when Reg was having a bad day and if he came in for the morning and Shirl realised that he 'wasn't going to be the friendliest person that day', she gave him a wide berth. Where that wasn't possible, she was adept at recognising when the issue wasn't about her. Her method was simple and effective: she'd stroll down the corridor as he yelled at her, and she continued walking when he demanded that she 'get back here.' Once he'd cooled down, he would eventually stop by her desk and apologise for yelling.

While she loved working at OVH, there was one aspect of the job she didn't like: the annual yearling sales on the Gold Coast, where hundreds of foals had to be inspected and certified. Reg was in high demand among buyers who wanted his keen eye to assure them that a horse was sound for sale or could be insured. 'Pulled from pillar to post' in Shirl's words, he'd return to OVH every time with hundreds of certificates to process. With no computer systems, the responsibility of typing them up fell to Shirl and the other administrative staff. It was painfully repetitive and a marathon job.

But Shirl knew it had to be done because Reg always wanted to help people. It's that trait, more than others – including his generosity, like when he and Joy gave her beautiful crystal champagne glasses for her twenty-first birthday – which Shirl remembered most. He always strove to be as 'helpful as he could.'

In 1977, OVH digitised their processes. 'To handle the increase in practice accounts and animal history files,' Reg recorded, 'a thirty-megabyte computer was added in 1978. [It was] programmed under my direction and proved valuable in both the accounting and the easy retrieval of animal histories.'

Along with a local software programmer called David Mallen, Reg and Shirl sat down to work out what needed to be done. They imagined a structure that would allow the clinic to maintain digital client records and manage the accounts. Together with Mallen, they wrote the program then Shirl and Joy put it into action.

In the early days, OVH's 'computer room' stored a machine that was bigger than a filing cabinet. Opening the front door of the computer revealed massive data reels, similar to cinema film reels, that had to be regularly rotated – new ones inserted, old ones changed out for back up. With the massive amount of clinical information stored in the computer, it might chew through up to five reels a night. Shirl sometimes set her alarm for the middle of the night to drive to the hospital and change the reel over.

Reg's innovations at OVH soon spread across the country. The software programme he, Shirl and Mallen designed and implemented later became the basis for similar systems at the University of Sydney's Veterinary School Farm at Camden as well as a large Sydney-based equine practice.

Max Wilson, OVH vet 1973–1989

Having graduated from the University of Queensland, Max Wilson headed south of the border to the job he had secured in a New South Wales practice. Not long after he got there, however, he was shown the door: with the transition of the TB and brucellosis testing that had once been Reg's bread and butter from private practitioners to DPI veterinarians, much of the clinic's workload dried up and there wasn't enough to keep Max on. 'Surplus to requirements,' as he dryly recalled.

He returned to Queensland on the hunt for a job and approached a Toowoomba practice, only for the vet to suggest Max head out to Oakey and see Reg. 'It never would have occurred to me in a million years to go to God for a job,' he recalled. Reg's reputation was well-established, and like other UQ graduates, Max had met him through the vet school. Excluding a clinic in Brisbane (whose capabilities and facilities failed to compare), Oakey Veterinary Hospital was the only proper equine facility in Queensland – and one of the few in the country.

Now that it had been planted, the idea took root. Max headed to Oakey dressed in what he felt was appropriate interview attire – coat and tie, long trousers and well-shone boots – but arrived to find Reg, Paul and David dressed in anything but office wear. Unbeknown to Max, Reg had already done his due diligence on the new applicant, so what followed seemed to Max to be a casual kind of chat. At the end, Reg simply said, 'Yeah, you've got the job. Start next week.'

Start he did. In fact, Max worked the next three weeks without a break. He finally screwed up the courage to approach DJ Laws and ask whether anyone at OVH ever got any time off.

'They should,' said David, squinting at the new vet quizzically. Hectic clinic life seems to have driven more mundane considerations from the busy vets' minds and it's impossible to know whether each partner thought one of the others was handling the new guy. But, the question asked, David fixed the problem. 'You can have next weekend off,' he said. Max must have been relieved; everyone at OVH worked hard. Reg, David and Paul were no exception, toiling long days down in the trenches with their team. 'They didn't ask us to do anything they didn't do or wouldn't do themselves,' he recalled.

Thus began Max's sixteen-year stint at Oakey Veterinary Hospital, making him – outside of David and Paul – one of the practice's longest-ever employees. They were golden years and the skills that

Max learnt underpinned his successful career post-OVH as an equine reproductive practitioner. But the relationship meant more to him than that: Reg was good to him, and Max inadvertently found himself slipping up and calling Reg 'Dad' on a few occasions.

OVH was more professional than anything Max had seen previously, and Reg expected higher standards of his staff than anyone Max had come across. As David Skerman had found, Reg was a stickler for junior vets being able to justify their decisions and their views. 'As a new graduate,' Max remembered, Reg 'wouldn't let you say, "that's black" without proving that it wasn't white first.' It was challenging, but greatly rewarding too, forcing people to think deeply about what they were saying and why. It saved them, Max thought, from starting to 'believe their own bullshit', as others might. Reg had no tolerance for that. He knew that most clients wouldn't know if a vet was telling the truth or not, instead trusting and relying on them to do the right thing. Reg hated the thought of his vets, or indeed *any* vet, bluffing that way; everyone at OVH was to invest the time and thought into making sure not only those things were done correctly but that everyone, at every level, knew what they were doing.

Reg didn't bring people into the practice who had stellar references, advanced degrees or international qualifications. 'He was more interested in poor suckers ... whom he could teach his way, right from scratch,' Max said. More than twenty years later, a journalist described the OVH employment philosophy, noting, 'Most new veterinarians are recruited by word of mouth and personal recommendation. [Reg] has no aversion to the employment of new graduates, feeling it is the motivation of the individual rather than their experience that is important, and tends to employ the brightest available – with the proviso that they are not totally clumsy. He says that practice expertise can be taught, providing the basics are in place prior to graduation.'

Few vets were established professionals, especially in the early years. Reg's reasoning was sound: he could inculcate his methods and his professional philosophy in those open-minded and as-yet-unformed veterinarians who were eager to learn. The pay-off was manifold. By imbuing others with his own passions – for the highest possible quality veterinary care; for curiosity and the pursuit of improvement; and for innovation in the face of challenge – he foresaw one of his most lasting legacies as the people he left behind continued developing the profession. These vets came from UQ, from around Australia, and later, from around the world. Typically, they spent a few years with Reg before moving on to establish their own practices, pursue further study overseas, and enrich others through the lessons they'd learnt.

The number of vets who worked at OVH is testament to Reg's passion and the effectiveness of his approach. But throughout, these colleagues tended to have one thing in common: they were quick-witted, adaptive to Reg's manner and responsive to his teaching. If they failed any one of these criteria, they would never work at OVH. Of course, some were intimidated by and even afraid of Reg's fame, or affronted by his at times brusque and confronting manner.

'Reg was – well, he was God,' Max recalled. 'There weren't too many people around who could provide any decent service as far as horses were concerned ... [so] Reg didn't really feel he had to be nice to people, they were going to come to him anyway.' Reg's phone manner appalled Max. Characteristically terse, Reg would eschew pleasantries, answer in monosyllables, and then hang up. It wasn't until later, when he was managing his own busy practice, that Max finally understood Reg's methods. Unnecessary conversation extended the call when what you needed was to get people off the line quickly because there were another ten callers waiting.

Reg's blunt manner wasn't limited to phone calls. Anyone who met him would likely have concluded that 'he didn't suffer fools.' Reg formed firm ideas about people and once his mind was made up, these rarely changed – even in his later years, when some believe he 'mellowed out', his appraisals were rapid, incisive and nigh on immovable. It was a trait that could make for some awkward situations, as Max witnessed first-hand.

During his time at OVH, an investor bought a small stud on the Darling Downs. This particular gentleman was one of the Gold Coast's 'white shoe brigade' – a group of wealthy and politically conservative Queensland property developers whom many regarded as aggressive and gaudy. The investor was friends with an existing

OVH client called David, who had also bought a stud south-west of Toowoomba and asked Reg to handle the mare work for him. David wasn't really the sort of bloke Reg would normally warm to, Max thought. They had different lifestyles and work ethics: when Reg agreed to help, he told David he'd arrive at 5 a.m., unimaginably early for most people. But David wanted Reg for the job and so was there ready and waiting. Whatever Reg's personal opinions, the two men ended up working well together.

That said, there were limits to Reg's forbearance and the fancy Gold Coast newcomer inadvertently found those limits. Hoping to secure Reg's services for the new stud, David brought his 'white shoe' friend to OVH. He asked the receptionist to bring Reg out and, when Reg appeared, David made the introductions. 'He's bought a little stud over at Southbrook,' David said. 'He'd like you to do his work. I thought you might like to show him around the surgery.'

There was silence as Reg scanned the developer from head to toe. 'No, I don't think so,' he said, turned on his heel and walked out. Max was in the room with the receptionist and their jaws dropped. 'We didn't know what to say to the poor bugger,' he recalled.

Reg's high expectations weren't restricted to OVH's staff or clients: Pascoes, Max noted, 'set a very high standard for themselves.' Everything at OVH was state of the art and the clinic's capabilities were excellent, elevating the practice above most others in the country. In 2021, New South Wales's Scone Equine Group is the largest and among the best equine veterinary care providers in Australia, but when Max arrived at OVH in the 1970s he thought Scone was 'almost subservient to Reg.'

The quality of the facilities, staff and processes at OVH was driven by Reg's desire for excellence and his pursuit of innovation and progress. Inevitably, financial considerations played a role: certainly, the quality of care provided by the vets at OVH made the hospital profitable, 'but that wasn't his motivation', Max said.

Reg never forgot where he came from and understood the financial challenges that the vagaries of the seasons and other similarly uncontrollable factors visited upon rural communities. David Laws' son (and later OVH partner) Glen Laws recalled Reg would be flexible about fees when necessary – there was more than one occasion where Reg performed 'surgeries on the cheap just to get them done.' Beneath his gruff exterior, Reg had a soft side. Certainly, he wanted to support breeders and the Australian breeding industry.

Reg in the OVH holding yards with one of the many thousands of horses he treated over the decades.

Particularly in the early days of a stud, people who were developing bloodlines (a breeder's efforts to incorporate a new characteristic into their chosen family of horses so subsequent generations demonstrate that trait) weren't necessarily making much money. Charging them a large fee was impractical and, as another OVH vet noted, 'I don't think Reg really wanted to.'[22] There were also instances where Reg saw something as being in an animal's best interests and would reduce his fee accordingly. The same vet noted simply, 'Money wasn't a big deal for Reg.'

Suggesting Reg was the sole driver OVH's excellence would be reductive; Paul Green and David Laws were just as committed to the practice's quality of work. As partners, the trio strove to ensure everything they did was of the highest possible standard: they attended conferences to remain abreast of industry developments and emphasised that such continuing education shouldn't be limited to new graduates. Speaking to a journalist in 1986, Reg noted, 'In order to maintain the high standards we have set, everyone who works here attends conferences, makes overseas trips to make themselves totally aware of the latest developments and surgical procedures.'

Though he was the principal director and maintained oversight of everything going on, Reg eschewed the micromanagement that might have stifled others' development. If any of the vets needed help, everyone else pitched in and lent a hand – but what he considered appropriate standards among the OVH staff also meant, according to Max, that the vets didn't come close to 'finding our feet.' This, Max thought, even extended to David and Paul, noting that Reg would always check David's accounts before they were sent out. Neither Paul nor David seemed to resent this; Max believed that 'they all looked up to [Reg] as a superior veterinary surgeon, especially when it came to horses. They didn't question that very much.'

There's likely some context missing here. As Max noted more than once, Reg was God – but such comparisons often obscure the truth. OVH's success was the result of the strong partnership trio. Paul said that Reg didn't interfere, and each handled their own work, under their own steam. He also pointed out that 'whenever one of us needed some help with something, all the others were always there willing to step in and give their assistance.' Like all successful partnerships, it was a case of give and take.

Still, staff knew there was little point arguing with Reg – he was usually right. But he was also even-handed and got his way because he was rarely too harsh or unfair.

Although a public figure for much of his career, Reg was private about his personal life and his emotions. However, many who worked closely with him received slivers of insight into the man behind the professional demeanour.

On one occasion, Max, against practice policy, visited a client outside of working hours. He knew Reg's thoughts on the matter: you worked hard during the week, but the weekends you had off. Of course, this didn't apply to Reg, but he expected it of his staff. This particular weekend, Max wasn't rostered on when he received a phone call from client out at Goombungee, north-west of Oakey, begging Max to come out and have a look at his horse. It was hard to refuse when someone *begged* you; besides, it was less than thirty minutes from the hospital. So Max agreed. When he finished, the client handed him a hundred dollars in cash and Max nodded his thanks, but he couldn't leave without a final word. 'Don't you tell Reg I've been to see you.' He drove back to OVH, dropped the payment off in the work till without alerting his boss and went home.

The following day, the client's concern hadn't abated and he took his horse into OVH to see Reg. As Reg examined the foal, the client said, 'Oh, I wasn't happy with it yesterday. I got that young Wilson fellow out and I gave him a bit of cash and he had a bit of a look at it.'

The result, Max remembered, was less than pretty. 'Reg came after me – woah, he was not happy.' But Max hadn't really done anything wrong; a minor transgression of a rule Reg himself didn't adhere to. Max had put the money in the till, and that knowledge steeled his spine in the face of Reg's anger. He let Reg rant for a while, then drew himself up and looked his boss square in the eye. 'Reg, you should know me better than that,' he said, his voice quiet and firm.

Max's words stopped Reg in his tracks, and to the younger man's astonishment, he practically broke down. 'I don't even know what my sons are doing sometimes,' Reg said. Then he walked away.

Caught in an unguarded moment prompted by the challenges of ongoing family friction, it was one of the rare occasions in which Reg unintentionally revealed his personal distress in a professional setting. It's not hard to believe that the emotions Reg felt about this sequence of events – the relief of discovering his mistake and at the same time, the shame of having misjudged and accused of wrongdoing someone he trusted and cared for – caused the walls to crack, ever so slightly.

In 1983, after working at OVH for a decade, the partners sent Max Wilson on paid long service leave to the US. Perhaps a little cynically, Max thought it a clever strategic move. Once he came back he couldn't very well leave the OVH. But it was by no means a bad deal. With some assistance from Reg's eldest son John it was arranged that Max would take up a role as a visiting professor at the University of California's Davis campus for three months on OVH's payroll. It would be a great experience and a chance for professional growth.

Before Max left, Reg gave him some advice. 'If you're smart, you've learnt a little bit while you're here. When you get to the States, if you're smart, you know nothing. Absolutely nothing ... If you tell them you know nothing, they'll teach you everything they can. If you try and make out you know stuff already, they won't teach you a bloody thing.' It was sound advice and Max learnt a lot.

Two years later, the OVH partners put a proposal to Max and two other young veterinarians, Peter Lyons and Lindsay McNaught. The three younger men were offered the opportunity of buying into the hospital as junior partners, with the intent that they take over from Reg, David and Paul when they were ready to retire. Lindsay took one look at the offer and shook his head. 'That's not good enough,' he said.

Although they were appreciative, the three younger men felt the deal wasn't financially viable. Perhaps the required buy-in was too high for not enough return, but it seems that there was no further negotiation and the idea was shelved. Thirty years later, Max still thought it a shame they hadn't been able to come to an agreement. But Reg could be intractable and perhaps some of the younger vets were too.

Max stayed at the OVH for another four years. Then, in 1989, the same year that Peter Lyons left the practice, Max did the unthinkable: he set up his own practice in direct competition with Reg. It was, he remembered, almost an absurd notion. OVH 'was the biggest and best practice in Queensland in the time, if not Australia' and Reg's influence was unparalleled. But Max felt he had no choice. Though unintentional, Reg's mastery of OVH's clinical work prevented Max from growing into the practice as he wanted, and after fifteen years of service, he expected to be made a partner and felt, colleague Chris Pollitt noted, that he deserved it. Reg, David and Paul evidently believed Max *did* deserve it: had they not, the offer they made in 1985 would never have been forthcoming. But that offer, made in perhaps the only way Reg had seen he could, had been rejected and whether the younger men felt they'd done so for good reason or not, Reg never forgot their decision. It seems the OVH partners didn't offer again and Reg's blunt clarification that a partnership would not be happening in the way Max had envisioned must have been hard to swallow.

Max and Reg were close. Max's decision to not only leave OVH but to establish a competing practice, particularly after declining Reg's earlier offer, wounded Reg. Everyone recognised that the decision caused a rift between the two men and Reg treated Max coldly afterwards. But Max retained fond memories of his years in Oakey, which shaped him as a vet.

Jim Vasey, OVH vet 1976–1977

Jim Vasey was in his final year at UQ when he rang OVH in April 1976 asking whether he could come out west for a week of prac work. Reg was absent on Jim's first day, but he returned on the second and took the young student with him on that morning's calls. John Pascoe was a year ahead of Jim, David Pascoe a year behind, and while Jim might have known little of Reg, he was left in no doubt that Reg knew more than a bit about him.

As they sat down to lunch together, the inhospitable conditions awaiting Jim after graduation were at the forefront of the young man's mind. Having done some work experience down south, he knew that Australia's agriculture industry in the mid-1970s was in trouble. In Victoria, he recalled, 'the government was giving dairy farmers ten dollars a cow to shoot them and put them in pits.' Jim had witnessed the traumatic practice first-hand.

'How am I going to get a job?' he wondered aloud as he and Reg discussed the industry hardships.

Reg levelled him with a stern glance. 'You'd better ask me at the end of the week.' Then, his sons' tales of this young man uppermost in his mind, wryly added, 'That'll make you behave yourself.' At the end of the week, Reg delivered. 'I don't know what I'm going to pay you,' he told Jim, 'but I'll give you a job.' That was how Reg used to employ people, Jim remembered. 'He wouldn't advertise, he'd just take pot luck. Some would work, some wouldn't.'

'Okay,' Jim said, 'that'll do me.' For the rest of his final year at university, Jim took every possible opportunity to visit OVH, driving up on weekends and on his days off. 'I'd have to leave Brisbane at about two in the morning to get there at four,' he remembered, arriving in Oakey to jump in the car with Reg 'and drive around the countryside looking at horses.' Jim was still green and there was a big age difference between the two men ... but he felt that they 'became colleagues from the word go', establishing a strong and lasting camaraderie.

Reg often returned to the clinic after his stud rounds tired and grumpy from an early start. Other staff might have done their best to avoid setting him off, but Jim had a deft touch and there's little doubt that Reg had a soft spot for him. When the boss started to grumble, Jim would intervene. 'Come on, Reg, don't be grumpy,' he'd say. Jim 'was only fresh out' of university, but this light admonishment would summon a wry smile to Reg's face 'and he'd settle down.' Jim had a rare quality which Reg respected. Along with Reg's eldest son John, Max Wilson recalled that they were 'the only people I'd ever seen who could actually put Reg on his guard a little bit, because they knew a hell of a lot.'

Jim found in Max 'a good person to help guide me': the older vet simplifying life for the newcomer by drawing up a series of maps that showed all the farms in the area with their names and best access routes. Other wisdom, however, could only be gained by experience – your own or someone else's. John Pascoe had graduated from UQ as dux of his year at the end of 1975 and returned home for roughly twelve months of hands-on experience; during Jim's stint at OVH, John was out one night handling calls when he got a flat tyre. No big deal. He put the spare tyre on and saddled up again ... only to score *another* flat not long after. Stranded, he called his dad.

Reg was 'pretty mad that John didn't have two spare tyres and he had to go and get him', Jim recalled, but realised that the shoe must once have been on the other foot – Reg's habit of carrying two spares had come about through his own hard lesson. 'Whatever's happened to you guys, it's already happened to me,' Reg told the two young men dryly.

Apart from spare tyres, a few pieces of advice stayed with Jim. Always cautious when handling large animals, Reg reminded him on more than one occasion to ensure his mind was on the job. 'The day you get kicked by a horse will be the day you come back from holidays,' Reg said. He'd just returned from a brief absence one day when, standing with Jim in the crush, he bent to begin bandaging a horse's injured leg. The horse kicked out, striking Reg in the face, splitting his lower lip. Confronted by blood gushing from his boss's face, Jim bundled Reg up and took him to a local doctor. He sat nearby while Reg, pumped full of morphine, was 'off with the fairies saying stupid things while this guy stitched up his lip.' The lesson stuck.

Having demonstrated the risks of complacency, Reg warned Jim that making assumptions when examining an animal could imperil the patient ... and the vet's reputation. 'You want to be careful that you don't make a hasty decision, because it could come back to bite you. With every case, be careful – look carefully, think carefully, make sure you've considered all the possibilities.'

Jim Vasey spent eight months working in Oakey – 'a beautiful part of the world to live in' – before receiving an offer to buy into a clinic down south. Reg was bluntly honest about his prospects. 'You'd better take that,' he said. 'I can't offer you anything like that.' Appreciating his boss's candour, Jim accepted, but he and Reg stayed firm friends, sharing a room from time to time while attending international conferences and often calling one another to discuss cases.

13
Reg and the OVH in the 1980s

In 1979, the Oakey Veterinary Hospital underwent a growth spurt in what Reg termed the 'stage three development.' Stage one had been the 1964 completion of the first hospital building, a cavity concrete block facility measuring 6 by 12 metres. Then, following Reg's tour of prestigious practices in the UK and US, the second stage in late 1968 greatly expanded the facilities. Stage three saw the addition of a large examination area containing two examination crushes – one without posts at one end to permit unhindered limb radiography; the other designed for standing surgeries and reproductive examinations. More staff facilities were constructed, while the clinic's X-ray capabilities were expanded with an automatic X-ray processor and an additional portable X-ray machine to cope with the growing stable and track practice commitments.

The hospital now employed seven full-time vets, and the expansion included a large new vets' office, a nurses' office, and interview and consulting rooms. A laboratory was added for bacteriology, blood chemistry and microscopy as well as, on a lower level, an autopsy room and general storage room. Four reinforced cavity-block stables were constructed, together with further holding yards and two loading bays for the increased number of horses being treated and stabled at the practice. The practice's state-of-the-art facilities played a role in the ongoing international interest in OVH. But there was also another factor.

Reg and Joy's two eldest sons had both completed their veterinary studies at UQ before moving overseas. After finishing his PhD at the University of California, Davis in 1986, John Pascoe stayed there as an associate professor of veterinary surgery. David Pascoe was also in California, doing a PhD in equine reproduction. He returned to

Australia in 1986 and in 1988 received a Membership and Fellowship in Animal Reproduction specialising in Equine Reproduction in 1988, before becoming both a Registered Specialist in Equine Reproduction and an OVH partner the following year.

*Reg and Joy with their four sons. John and David became vets, while Roess and Andrew became medical specialists.
From left: Roess, Andrew, David, John.*

Mike Huber, OVH vet 1980–1984

In July 1980, a young American vet by the name of Mike Huber graduated from the University of California, Davis with a job secured at a practice in Morgan Hill in northern California. During the last twelve months of his studies, however, Mike had become friends with John and David Pascoe, and the Australians slowly began sounding him out on OVH's behalf. When the Pascoe brothers asked what his plans were after graduation, Mike said unenthusiastically that he had a job opportunity waiting for him in Morgan Hill.

'Maybe you should go work for the old man?' John said casually.

It was, Mike remembered, 'a seed that he planted, and that over time began to germinate.' Curiosity aroused, he needed details. 'John, I want to go to a good practice,' he said. 'Tell me about it.'

'Well, there are three partners,' John said. 'It's a mixed practice and it's really big – and it's in a beautiful part of Australia. You'll love it.'

'John would talk it up, then David would talk it up,' Mike remembered with a chuckle. 'The more I thought about it, the more it appealed. I was afraid about going to another country, but if I could pick a country that I could practise then [Australia] would be one of them.'

John and David's description of OVH promised experiences 'as good as any practice I could find in the US or even better.' Keen to ensure his first year of real-world education provided him with such opportunities – and driven by the thought of seeing another country – Mike decided he would go to Australia and spend six months working for the hospital during the breeding season before returning to California and the job he'd secured. His parents thought he was crazy.

Mike applied for a working visa, but during his interview at the consulate in San Francisco, his interviewer pulled a map down off the wall. Jabbing his finger at the paper, he said, 'You're going down the east coast of Australia. Beautiful beaches, beautiful people. You'll love it. You ought to apply for a permanent migrant visa.' When Mike looked uncertain, the man pointed out that there were limitations to the standard working visa. 'If you want to stay one day later, you won't be able to.' Mike intended to work for six months, then travel for another six. He applied for a permanent migrant visa instead.

Landing in Sydney, he then took a small prop plane flight to Oakey. Reg came out to meet him at the airport and Mike was amazed. 'He had a massive practice and he was the one to meet me.' Reg loaded him up and drove them both home. As they hurtled along, he asked Mike what his biggest worries were.

'Poisonous snakes and spiders,' Mike said. He knew Australia was home to some of the most dangerous creatures in the world. Reg just laughed. He recognised the challenges Mike was facing. 'I felt like a fish out of water,' Mike confessed. 'Not only did I speak differently, but I was a brand-new graduate. Never practised. I was in a new country … I was trying to be good at what I was supposed to be good at.'

Mike must have felt like he was being asked to scale a mountain, but Reg didn't seem to care too much about his lack of experience. He and Joy welcomed him into their home as he got to grips with the minutiae of daily Australian life. When he gawked at the geckos walking up the walls, Reg and Joy chuckled. 'I was so captivated by some of these things that were so unusual for me,' Mike recalled.

Reg enjoyed challenging his protégés, but he knew the difference between a challenge that allowed growth, and one which hindered it. He made sure Mike was comfortable and accepted by the community by taking him on his daily calls for the first month or so. Seeing them together reminded OVH clients that it was Reg who had hired Mike – they could rely on the soundness of his judgement – and that, like all OVH vets, he had Reg's trust and support. 'He couldn't have done a better job of helping me out,' Mike recalled. Whenever Mike went out on calls, regardless of whether he was treating large animals or small, people knew who he was. 'I had already been around with the Boss, and I was accepted. They gave me a hard time about talking the way I did and thinking the way I did and all that, but they were very accepting, and it made a huge difference.'

Reg and Mike had agreed prior to Mike's arrival that he would have the opportunity to handle some of the hospital's breeding work on his own. With a few new studs coming onto OVH's books, Mike was assigned to one as the lead vet. It was a big responsibility but he fell to it with gusto. Reg was made sure he was all right, talking him through the stud work each week, checking up on how he felt, asking whether he'd run into any problems. And, once he was assured the younger man was feeling comfortable, he challenged him with bigger jobs like managing the worming requirements for nearby horse farms.

Nowadays, equine worming is a fairly straightforward procedure. All it requires is for a veterinarian to put paste in the horse's mouth. It's not the most pleasant job, but it's relatively simple compared to methods in the 1980s. Back then, Mike had to 'tube worm' the horses, a labour-intensive job that required the vet to pass a tube down the oesophagus into the horse's stomach. Reg sent Mike out to Gainsborough Lodge just outside of Toowoomba, where the young vet wormed 170 horses in a single day. 'I was absolutely exhausted!'

But there were rewards – not just the tangible experience Mike was gaining, though that was valuable – but the feeling of being a member of a team, working for and with someone he respected. 'Reg made me feel really special when he said, "You did a good job." It was special to be assigned things that he used to do himself and know that he thought enough of me to give me those assignments.'

Reg's clinical prowess with animals of all sizes left a deep impression upon the younger man. 'He wasn't fearful that he'd forgotten. He wasn't aloof as if he just did equine only and he wasn't going to work on small animals.' More striking, however, was Reg's ethos, which reverberated throughout every corner of OVH. Mike's memories encapsulate one of the most enduring and fascinating contradictions that characterised Reg Pascoe's life: his combination of self-assurance and expertise with the humility of service. He was a skilled equine surgeon, supremely confident in his abilities and his experience, but he retained a lifelong respect for clients and for the animals that he cared for.

His accessibility was another trait etched into Mike's mind. Though the Pascoe family home was right behind the practice, there was no gate or sign to keep people from coming up. 'People would walk through the door with a dog in their hands.' Reg would then accompany them down to the hospital until the on-call veterinarian arrived to tend the animal.

Compassion was a cornerstone of Reg's professional philosophy and he demanded OVH staff similarly value it. During Mike's time in Oakey, another young vet, a country kid who'd joined at the same time Mike, lost a pet cat under anaesthetic while performing a routine procedure. The young vet had to tell the owner, so he headed to the group office, stuffed to the gills with every veterinarian then on-staff, and picked up the phone. 'It's the vet from Oakey,' he said when the owner answered. 'I've got to tell you; we had some bad luck. We lost your cat today. It was an anaesthetic death and I regret it happened.' There was a pause while the woman on the other end responded to this heartbreaking news. 'Well, you can always get another cat,' the vet added. 'It's just a cat.' He didn't look around, but if he had, he would have seen every other vet in the office exchanging loaded glances; the silence was as heavy as a closed fist squeezing the air from the room. Mike laughed, remembering the young man's obliviousness. 'He didn't think anything was wrong.'

Reg waited until the vet hung up, then asked for everyone to leave the room. Calm and controlled, he didn't raise his voice, but he made it abundantly clear the younger vet had 'to leave his country mentality somewhere else and start being a little bit ... considerate of people's emotions.' Reg didn't want to ever see or hear him treat a client that way again.

Mike Huber had intended to travel for six months when his stint at Oakey ended then return to the US but it didn't quite happen that way and he ended up staying for another three years. One winter, the Darling Downs suffered tremendous rains; widespread flooding submerged roads and properties. Driving on calls for the practice, Mike's little ute got stuck.

'No problem,' Reg said easily. 'Put yours somewhere and you can use the hospital's ute.' It was much bigger than Mike's ... but it, too, couldn't handle the flooded Darling Downs. Driving through three feet of water, Mike finally drew the line. 'I can't get around on calls,' he told Reg. 'The ute's just not tall enough. I'm going through too much water.'

'Why don't you take the Merc, then?' Reg said. Mike baulked. The Mercedes SUV was an expensive, recent acquisition and Reg had been 'bragging about this thing for the previous two weeks.' The *last* thing he wanted was responsibility for the boss's new pride and joy. But Reg was unperturbed. 'No, it'll be right,' he told Mike. 'You'll be fine.'

'I think he was relieved that I was at least out doing the calls,' Mike remembered. And the luxurious SUV seemed to handle the water okay, which was a relief.

At the time, Mike was living in a granny flat on the nearby Donaldson property and Reg insisted Mike take the Mercedes home of an evening. Arriving home one night, Mike parked the SUV outside the granny flat – directly over the pipeline that ran out to the unit.

That night they got a lot more rain.

The following morning, Mike received an early call. He jumped in the Mercedes and switched it on. 'It started up fine and smooth as can be.' But that was where things started to go pear-shaped. 'I put it in in reverse and started to back up and then the wheels started spinning,' he remembered ruefully. He shifted it into four-wheel drive and tried again. One of the wheels spun on him, but still he wasn't worried. He was a country kid and knew a thing or two about driving on boggy ground and freeing up stuck vehicles. He tried the usual trick, driving back and forth a few times to get it out ... but all that happened was the car got stuck deeper and deeper in the mud. Mike's heart sunk.

'Warranted to *never* get stuck,' Reg had bragged just the other day, and here Mike had gone and done just that. He called the Boss and Reg showed up, not concerned in the slightest. 'I'll get it out,' he said, jumping behind the wheel. But the SUV wouldn't budge. The tow truck was next to try. But by that point, Mike and Reg had high centred the car, its chassis sitting on ground. With the ground so boggy, the tow truck couldn't risk coming off the road, so they put a line on the bumper. The SUV still wouldn't shift. Finally, unwilling to risk tearing the bumper off, Reg and Mike sent the tow truck away.

'We're going to have to jack it up,' they decided. But the ground was far too sodden. They had to wait a whole, agonising week for the rain to stop and the waterlogged ground to dry out. Coming home to the sight of the stranded Mercedes every night, Mike felt like crying. Finally, some drier weather and a stack of sandbags under the wheels allowed them to free the vehicle. 'It was a victory to get it off, but neither one of us were cheering,' Mike recalled with a laugh.

When Reg was about business, he was about business, but he could be thoroughly charming when he chose to be and believed in balancing out the hard work with relaxation. OVH had several parties in the clinic during Mike Huber's time there and he recalled that though Reg was always there at the beginning – acknowledging the team's effort and toasting their hard work – he would only have one drink or so before he and Joy left the staff to enjoy themselves. 'Reg, why don't you stay?' Mike asked once. 'Why don't you drink it up and have fun?'

Reg smiled. 'No, Mike. I love the people I work with. I respect what they do for me, and I want to acknowledge them by having a party, but I don't want to get in the thick of it as far as drinking and carrying on and getting out of control.' And the parties did get out of control at times. With the benefit of hindsight and experience, Reg's reasoning is clear to Mike. His absence meant the staff could have fun without fear of looking foolish in front of the Boss. They had certain expectations, and Reg's decision meant everyone could preserve the balance of respect and camaraderie that allowed OVH's staff to be a professional family, while he maintained a professional distance.

Mike left OVH in 1984 and took up a position in a busy US practice. Up until that point he had really thought he would end up staying in Australia. 'I'd like to stay,' Mike told Reg. 'Is there any opportunity for me to do that?'

Mike was a good fit at OVH and had become part of the practice family, but Reg answered regretfully, 'Max [Wilson] has been here twelve years now. We're going to give him first opportunity to buy in.'

'So I left,' Mike remembered, and it was a tough thing to do. But about six months into his new job, he phoned Reg. 'Do you have any openings?' More than twenty years later, he laughed at the memory. 'I heard that if you ever left Reg, you'd never get hired back, so I kind of knew what the answer was.' There were no openings. Years later, Reg rang to ask if Mike would like to return to OVH as the hospital's specialist surgeon. 'I was still in the middle of my residency,' Mike said, 'so I couldn't, but it made me feel good that he thought enough of me to consider asking me.'

'[Reg] taught me things that I'll never forget and certainly pass onto residents that I work with – that's a legacy.' A veterinarian and a surgeon, Reg was also 'an artist' in Mike's opinion. His surgical abilities were incredible: he was efficient and quick without sacrificing skill. One such example was his deftness at left laryngeal prosthesis surgery, a treatment for 'roarers', horses suffering a respiratory defect of the larynx causing a 'roaring' noise during exertion. A procedure that would take others up to ninety minutes, Reg could do in half the time, with 'great results.' Mike similarly recalled Reg's skill at repairing third-degree rectovaginal tears in mares. Though not life-threatening, the condition prevents mares getting in foal and is complicated to remedy; with roughly a 30 per cent success rate, the surgery is 'wrought with failure.' Most surgeons require multiple attempts for success, but Mike said, 'when I do it with [Reg's] methodology, it always works.'

The acquisition of skills is vital, and there's no doubt that Reg rigorously instilled them in his veterinarians, but that's not all you remember about someone. On any given day, Mike recalled fondly, Reg could 'pull you aside and be relatively stern but make it a learning opportunity. And at the same time have you in stitches laughing about a joke.'

Jane Axon, EVA colleague

Jane Axon graduated from UQ in 1985. Throughout her time at university, she'd heard that Reg Pascoe ran a world-renowned equine practice at Oakey, but knew little more. It wasn't until years later, working in a rural South Australian practice, that her interest in equine work blossomed and she became involved with the Equine Veterinary Association (EVA). Like many Australian vets, it was through this organisation that Jane first met Reg at the annual Bain Fallon conference series, which served as an equine vets' community event. Her increasing exposure to equine science, she remembered, also meant a growing understanding of Reg's accomplishments and who he was.

Reg's presence at veterinary conferences was unforgettable. As Max Wilson recalled, 'He did so much work and looked at so many horses and had an opinion on everything.' Following presentations, it was customary for the floor to be opened to the audience for questions. Reg was renowned for taking a seat at the back of the room and listening carefully. Once the speaker finished, Reg would 'almost always be the first one to ask a question.'[23] Some recalled that he raised his hand – one vet remembered he could see 'the lecturer melting as he's trying to see what Reg would ask.'[24] Others, like Andrew Van Eps, remembered simply that 'a voice would just come from the back of the room, and everyone would be silent. It was sort of like God speaking.'

'Well, I don't really agree with you,' Reg would typically open with, followed by what Andrew Dart recalled was his favourite question: 'How many of those cases have you seen?' No matter the presenter's response – and, in hindsight, Dart wondered whether the figures were accurate, or inflated in the hopes it might spare them

Reg's questioning – Reg would 'always be able to trump them with a larger number.' There were multiple occasions, Dart said, where the lecturer had seen perhaps two or three instances of a disease. Reg would shake his head. 'I've seen *thirty-six* of these and I've found the opposite.' His depth of experience 'blew these speakers away.' Max agreed, remembering that Reg 'was renowned for doing that at conferences'; the effect so pointed that some visiting international lecturers apparently began warning their peers to check he wasn't going to be there before giving a presentation.

'Reg was a real policeman of equine veterinary standards,' said Andrew Van Eps, and this concern for integrity wasn't constrained to the speakers behind the lectern. Mike Huber recalled being at one Sydney lecture about reproductive surgery when, at the conclusion, an audience member stood and said forcefully, 'I don't know why we don't do caesarean sections in mares. I've done a caesarean section in a standing mare and –'

Reg got up without raising his hand. 'Sir, either you are a liar and you've never done one or you are not in your right mind, because if you knew what was involved with doing a C-section on a horse, you wouldn't even think of the idea or consider the idea of doing it with the horse awake and standing up.' His voice remained level, but no one in that room was in any doubt as to how he felt about the issue. They quickly moved onto the next speaker. 'That's the way Reg Pascoe was,' Mike remembered, 'he could silence an audience with his statement.'

Jane Axon wasn't immune to this effect, which cowed more experienced and senior vets. She had seen Reg 'absolutely grill' presenters and when she discovered he was one of the adjudicators at the Bain Fallon, her upcoming lecture began to take on the dimensions of a Herculean ordeal. As Reg reached over to pin the microphone to her shirt, Jane's apprehension got the better of her. 'Shit, I'm nervous,' she said.

Reg gave her a wink. 'Oh, you'll be right.' He returned to his seat. It was a defining moment for Jane: it broke down his daunting reputation, what Jane called the 'ice that was around him and I realised he was approachable and a ... *normal* person behind the name of Reg Pascoe. And he was fun-loving and obviously had a sense of humour.'

Her recollections of Reg's conference participation are less confrontational than those remembered by others. Rather than challenging the speaker, she described a more unassuming method, where his questions were intended to prompt discussion. 'He did have humility,' she said. 'He did not boast, he was not blowing his own trumpet – at all. If he did have something to say about himself, he would do it in a very passive way ... his facts were correct, but he'd never put his hand up and directly dispute the lecturer's competence or knowledge.'

Reg understood the role of perception and ensured, since his earliest days in practice, that he was always neat and well-dressed. 'He always presented himself well – professionally, not in a pair of shorts or a T-shirt,' Jane said. This was in no small part thanks to Joy. Chatting with Jane at a conference one day, Joy checked her watch and excused herself. 'I've got to go now and iron Reg's clothes,' she said with a smile.

Reg's commitment to this public image was about respect, both for his clients and as a representative of the veterinary profession. It subtly broadcast what he thought was appropriate behaviour for an Australian veterinarian, a lesson that couldn't help but be observed and assimilated by others. The different facets of Reg's persona – his moral code, his professional ethics, his clean-cut image – could not be separated from his successes. To achieve the latter, junior vets would be wise to echo the former. In perpetuating these standards for himself, Reg's ascendancy and the respect in which the profession held him inspired others to emulate his example. 'Because he presented himself so well and always acted professionally, I wanted to aspire to do that as well,' said Jane.

Not long after delivering her first conference paper, Jane worked for several years with Jim Vasey who, after his short time at OVH in 1977, had stayed close friends with Reg. Today, Jane is an expert in equine neonatology, a subspecialty focusing on the care of newborn foals, but back in the 1990s, she remembered ringing Reg for help when she encountered difficult cases, ever grateful for his support. As she increased her knowledge and experience, Reg's long history of research spurred her own. 'Here's this man, Reg Pascoe, who's been doing [research] for the last fifty years!' They became, as Jane fondly recalled, 'bloody good mates', linked by a common belief about how veterinary science should be done, and what was important in the profession. Their friendship was typical of Reg; he would readily form 'a bond with a person of any age who was driven and passionate about the profession.'

In 2018, Jane took to the microphone for her turn at the Reg Pascoe Peroration. It was the first Bain Fallon since his death, and her topic was inspiration. Standing before the assembled veterinarians, she mused on the influence that Reg had had on her career. 'Reg was someone I called with a difficult case, and I knew if anyone had seen or knew what was going on with the case, Dr Pascoe would. He was always available and would help you in such a way as to not make you feel completely stupid. He was a true teacher and mentor. And as I grew into the veterinarian I am today, I found his professionalism, his desire to understand the diseases he encountered, his clinical research and his clinical skills such an inspiration. He inspired me to improve all those skills during my career. And as Christine Johnston ([EVA] president 2001) said, "If we all took one leaf out of Reg's book, I think we would be better vets and probably even better people." I couldn't agree more.'

Jon Hill, 1984 seeing practice at OVH

Jon Hill completed his seeing practice at OVH in 1984, coming 'face to face with the Legend.' Reg was renowned, particularly among the UQ student body, for being 'a very stern, uncompromising man with very high standards and very limited patience.' Jon remembered that seeing practice at OVH was 'widely known to be a potentially terrifying experience if things went wrong and an uplifting one if you avoided trouble.' It was an ominous portent, but Jon quickly found that if he was willing to learn, Reg was willing to teach him.

His introductory experience was quintessentially Reg: simultaneously terrifying and exhilarating. At their first meeting, Reg told Jon to jump in the shiny Mercedes SUV of which Reg was rather proud. 'We're going to go and see some horses,' Reg said. That sounded promising, but Jon didn't yet know that Reg's driving was a legend all its own. UK vet 'Twink' Allen, who worked with Reg on the International Symposium on Equine Reproduction and visited Oakey in the 1970s, remembered that Reg 'would roar along with about one finger on the wheel, sitting sideways in the saddle at about 80 miles an hour, chatting away in the car ... he was a very good driver.'

Jon also couldn't know that Reg was to use that car ride the same way he used every car ride – as an opportunity to further develop his passenger. 'It sounds trivial, but it was important to him,' a friend remembered, that when people were in the car with Reg, they were 'not allowed to talk about anything else except veterinary science.'[25] Reg was conscious of the numerous competing demands on his time and wanted to make the most of every opportunity: these students 'were there to learn and he was there to teach them.'

While Reg drove at whatever speed 'flat-out' foot-pressed-to-the-floor was, Jon negotiated an extensive question and answer – for every answer Jon provided, Reg followed up with another question. Jon likened 'the exhilaration of going at high speed with the need to reply precisely and accurately to these questions being fired at me' to playing a grand final match: an activity where you were 'absolutely hyped for an hour and you get out' and almost collapse with relief in the aftermath of adrenaline. But his first impression was that Reg 'led by example and was so consistent in his approaches [and] behaviours' – and that impression endured.

In 1986, two years after his practical experience in Oakey, Jon began working at an established vet practice in Warwick. The experience gave him the opportunity to see Reg in a new light. Jon's new workplace saw OVH as a direct competitor and Reg as a professional rival; Reg saw a chance to continue developing another young Queensland vet. When faced with a challenging case, Jon recalled, he would pick up the phone and ring Reg. 'I didn't ring any of my bosses, I rang [Reg] and he was just incredible.' But it was the fundamental professional ethos from which this readily offered assistance sprang that most deeply resonated. Reg's 'behaviour and leadership was rock solid ... he was committed to the animals, to the clients, to the profession and so he was willing to help at any time.'

Of course, as the owner and director of a veterinary practice that relied on referrals, Reg's approachability and availability was also simply good business: strong relationships with other vets would inevitability lead to more referrals. Similarly, building rapport with the local community was vital. Reg was fond of reminding junior vets, 'If you are invited in for a cup of tea, coffee or cold water, be very careful about saying "no", for this is a great time for networking.' But while Reg understood the importance of networking for the success of his business, his focus was always the elevation of veterinary science and serving the profession.

Although Jon called occasionally for advice on tricky cases, Reg wouldn't have batted an eyelid had he *not* done so – there was no expectation of reciprocity. Reg was just happy to help a new graduate, giving the kind of guidance he wished he had received in his own formative years. Now, he gave it freely. Reg's time was precious and he never wanted to waste it, but even after Jon moved interstate, Reg was always available for a chat. And as always, he appreciated robust dialogue. 'If you were connecting with something – a topic that was relevant, interesting,' he would gladly delve into such conversations ... but 'if you started waffling, then: conversation over.' And while Reg may have warmed more to those he esteemed, fundamentally, in Jon's opinion, 'The way that he treated people just didn't seem to vary.'

Andrew Dart, OVH vet 1986–1988

Like Jon Hill, many of the young vets who came to work at OVH were UQ graduates. Reg was passionate about developing Queensland and Australian equine vet science and kept an eye on potential talent – and it was this keen eye that led him to a young graduate called Andrew Dart.

Born and bred in Brisbane, an equine placement in his final year of university in 1984 led Dart to switch from a career working with small animals to working with horses. Towards the end of that year, he headed to Sydney with a few mates to attend a postgraduate course on equine medicine and surgery. He was also more than a little motivated by a sense of adventure and the promise of Sydney's nightlife. But the course was well-regarded, popular with overseas speakers, and it was here that Dart first encountered Reg.

Although well-known in the industry, during courses and conferences Reg was often apart from the group, happy being alone with a cup of tea and a biscuit or a sandwich. As the others in the room at this particular course mingled, no one ventured too near – whether it was Reg's silence, or perhaps his reputation, or the 'intimidating sort of way' he watched the rest of the room – it was enough to scare young students (and others, not so young, or inexperienced) into keeping their distance.

Frivolous conversation never interested Reg and he was often reticent among crowds of strangers. Some saw this as standoffish, even arrogant. That was inevitable, given his clinical reputation and his habit of dressing down speakers, students and fellow vets alike. It wasn't until later that Andrew Dart realised Reg's tendency to sit apart was his way of dealing with awkward situations. Along with the widespread student belief that Reg was a hard taskmaster, this is what Dart took away from the course that day.

The following year, Dart secured a one-year internship at the University of Sydney, still seen as the premier Australian institution for veterinary science. Unsure where he wanted to go next, and a little lost career-wise, the internship went poorly. As 1985 ended, Dart's outlook was grim. His bid for a university residency had been unsuccessful, and the job applications he'd subsequently submitted had ended the same way. He was sitting in the tearoom and feeling rather sorry for himself one day when Reg walked in. Dart didn't recognise him. Reg fetched a cup of tea, sat down and after a few moments' silence, asked Dart where he'd studied.

'Queensland,' he said and, at Reg's further prompting, he filled in the gaps.

'Sounds like you need a real job,' Reg said. He thought a 'real' job wasn't necessarily a university position, but something in the industry proper, dealing with clients and their animals. And that's precisely what Reg offered him. 'You've got a job next year if you'd like one. Turn up at my place on the first of January.' With that, he left the room.

Years later, John Pascoe laughed at Dart's account of the exchange. 'That's not the story Dad told me. He said he came down to Sydney and took [Dart] out for a very expensive lunch before he offered [him] a job!' Regardless of how it came about, Dart didn't see

Reg again on that Sydney trip, and didn't dare ring him to confirm the details.

When his internship finished, he packed his bags and headed to Queensland. He arrived at Oakey Veterinary Hospital on 1 January 1986 at 8 a.m. to find the place deserted. He set off up the hill towards the Pascoes' house, but caught sight of movement in the old blue shed that had once been the clinic and now served as Reg's workshop. He looked through the door to find Reg hunched over one of his beloved woodworking projects.

'What're you doing here?' Reg asked.

Dart was thrown. 'Do you remember me? I met you in Sydney and you offered me a job ...?'

Reg harrumphed and eyed the young man fiercely. 'Yeah, but I'm wondering what I'm hiring. You can't be all that bright.'

Dart was unnerved; this was not going at all how he'd hoped. 'What do you mean?'

'No one works on the first of January. Come back tomorrow.'

Dart was elated: he had the job. But rather than leaving, Reg set him to work in the shed, helping with some carving and sweeping the floor before he took his new vet up to the house for lunch. There, Reg and Joy organised some temporary accommodation at the local pub until Dart could find something more permanent.

The adjustment from university life to clinical work was challenging. Though Reg wasn't judgemental about his new recruit's difficulties, Dart confessed that he struggled at the start. OVH was a very different environment to what he'd previously encountered and Reg could be authoritarian. 'He was straight down the line: it was [his] way or the highway.' Reg provided the opportunity but it was the recipient's responsibility to take that opportunity and make it into something. And while meeting the Boss's expectations might not have been easy, it *was* simple: you just had to get on with the job and do the work to a high standard, and in the manner that was expected. 'If you wanted to argue or play games,' Dart recalled, 'well, that was just bad luck.'

Reg had little time for people who didn't want to work hard and though he accepted that everyone made mistakes, according to Dart, he 'never gave you a pat on the back or ... words of encouragement.'

Despite this, he maintained keen oversight of his staff and if a situation got sticky and you needed help, you could be certain Reg would be there to provide it.

Safety net or not, gaining the practical experience that Reg esteemed was never going to be easy. He firmly believed in the value of learning by doing – the more experience, the better the vet – and he never hesitated to remind his junior vets how more experience translated to more expertise. 'When you've seen twenty cases,' he would say, 'remember that I'll have seen fifty, and I'll still know more than you do.'

How best to ensure vets got the broad knowledge base and practical exposure they needed? Dart discovered that the partners at OVH, despite being on call overnight, never seemed to answer after-hours calls: most of them ended up in his lap instead and he typically responded to cases on his own, forcing him to find his feet and fast. He handled both equine and small animal cases and filled in for Paul Green doing dairy work. As time passed, he was allowed to perform more and more equine-exclusive work.

'For someone who was lost, with no real direction or understanding of the industry or what I needed to do to get where I wanted to go, [Reg] quietly pushed me in the right direction.' At OVH, Dart's clinical exposure was broad and his years there were a formative period in his life. The guidance he was given both personally and professionally was pivotal to this growth. Reg and his partners handled the latter – Dart, over time, became more akin to Reg's personal resident – while Joy provided a warm, caring and practical ear during several difficult periods. 'It felt almost like a family.'

The staff at OVH worked hard to save those horses that they could, but, inevitably, they were not always successful. Euthanising animals is a distressing concept for most people, but it's an essential part of a veterinarian's job. As noted in Chapter 6, Reg had a six-shooter that Dart remembered as 'a Wyatt Earp-type thing.' In the 1980s, once euthanised, disposal meant taking the animal's body to the local tip, which is where complexity arose. The average adult horse weighs anywhere from 400 kilograms to a tonne, and with no sling or crane systems, the arrangement prior to euthanasia was crucial. After parking the surgery ute below the lip of the loading ramp out the back of OVH, Dart would bring the horse up and position it right next to the edge of the ramp, so Reg could shoot it.

The idea was that the horse dropped on the spot or fell into the ute, because there was no other way of getting the body into the tray otherwise. Dart's job was to stand and hold the animal still while Reg handled the pistol, but 'I used to hate guns, and still don't like them' and he couldn't stop himself reflexively closing his eyes when Reg fired. That was the first and most difficult part of the process ... but as Dart discovered, even the simpler aspects could become complicated.

The most direct route to the tip passed the primary school so for decorum's sake, the hospital placed a tarpaulin over the ute's tray, covering the animal. One day, Dart remembered, 'The kids were all out – whether it was after school or whether it was during the lunch break – and there were [horse] legs and bits and the tail sort of hanging out from under this tarp.' It was hardly wholesome lunchtime fun for a group of children – though, being country kids, most of them probably viewed the strange midday experience rather prosaically, or maybe as an interesting diversion. The school thought otherwise. Not long after, Reg received a call from the headmaster; OVH, he was informed briskly, was going to need to find a different route by which to take euthanised animals to the tip. 'Of course,' Dart remembered, 'I got into trouble for that!'

It wasn't to be the last time. For the most part, Andrew Dart and Reg had a respectful, amicable relationship. But Reg's dominant personality and innate stubbornness resulted in conflict when it collided with similar traits in others. 'The first time we ever had a fight was probably two years into my time there,' Dart recalled. 'I used to have to anaesthetise horses for him. Back in those days we had the tilt table and ... I used to give [the horses] this heavy sedative and then tie the horse to the table and then we'd give them the main anaesthetic.' He typically performed this step alone. But on one occasion, Reg came storming in as Dart was still getting the sedated horse secured. Reg could often be impatient, particularly when it seemed like someone wasn't getting the job done, or executing it to the standard he required, and today was one of those days.

'Why isn't that horse on the table yet?' Reg demanded.

'I'm getting there, Dr Pascoe,' Dart replied. He motioned towards the sedative bottle and added, 'I've run out, I need to make some up.'

Glancing at the bottle, in which some dregs of the drug remained, Reg harrumphed. 'That'll be enough. Just get it anaesthetised.' Dart didn't argue. He gave the horse the sedative and, with Reg by his side, tilted the table so that the horse was lying on its side.

'Of course,' he remembered, 'it *wasn't* enough. The animal wasn't quite anaesthetised: it was paddling with its legs and moving.' Reg and Dart tried to hold the animal still in what would have been an awkward, unnerving situation, one that carried risk both for the horse and the two vets.

'Get some more drug!' Reg said.

Dart was impassive. 'There's none made up, Dr Pascoe.'

'Well, why the hell's nothing made up?'

'Because you were bloody impatient and couldn't wait!'

Reg grunted an acknowledgement and the horse was tilted back to standing while they made more of the anaesthetic. Later, Dart recalled that Reg 'came up to me and apologised and said it was his fault. It was the only time that I ever heard him say it was his fault. That was the other thing about him; he was always right but he didn't mind admitting when he was wrong.'

As time passed, Andrew Dart found the learning curve at OVH began to level off. He was eager to pursue his passion and train as a surgeon, but Reg was already a passionate and enthused surgeon ... and he didn't let go very easily: as a journal article from 1986 records, 'All surgery on racehorses is performed by Dr Pascoe.' Planning for his retirement and grooming a successor – particularly in surgery, his own area of expertise – seems to have been far from Reg's mind. It was time, Dart realised, for him to move on. He was keen to work in the US, but as he began looking further afield, he was stymied. Reg had strong ideas about Dart's future and felt there was only one place for Dart to work next and he was going to make it happen. So, to potential employers who called seeking a reference for Dart, Reg was blunt. 'He doesn't want to go to your university,' Dart overheard Reg say on more than one occasion. 'He wants to go to Davis. If it's good enough for my sons, it's good enough for him.'

This isn't going to turn out well, Dart thought. His blood must have been running cold at the prospect of Reg chasing away his career prospects, but he didn't realise that John Pascoe was the head of surgery at Davis at the time. He was also unaware of Reg's international reputation; having OVH and the Pascoe name on his CV, and having co-authored a number of papers with Reg, made for a compelling endorsement of his skills. Much as Mike Huber's career had been shaped by the 'Pascoe Mafia's' careful cultivation, Dart unknowingly received similar treatment.

He was working with Reg one day conducting an endoscopy when a call came through the two-way intercom. 'It's John Pascoe on the phone to speak to you,' Shirl said.

'Tell him to ring back later,' Reg said. 'I'm busy.'

'He doesn't want to talk to *you*,' Shirl said, unfazed. 'He wants to talk to Andrew.'

Dart's ears pricked up, but Reg was unsympathetic. 'If John wants to pay his salary, he can pay it – or else he can ring after hours,' he said, and turned back to the task at hand, leaving Dart to wait all day for John to ring back. It was worth the wait. John offered Dart the very job he had wanted and 'it suddenly dawned on me that Reg had done this for me.' It was a gratifying realisation.

Soon after, Dart set about finding something to give Reg as a thank-you and parting gift. Joy had mentioned that Reg had owned several Labradors over the years, adding on more than one occasion how much he loved dogs – but also needed them to keep him company and distract him from overwork. *I need to get Reg a dog*, Dart realised. Luckily, he knew just where to find one. Earlier that year, he had treated a black Labrador bitch with a broken leg. The dog arrived from Roma on a Friday afternoon and Dart set the limb with bone plates before kennelling her for recovery. When he came in on Saturday morning he found the cage door open and the dog gone. He was petrified. 'You don't lose animals on Reg's watch.' Panicked, he spent hours searching – driving into town, visiting the police and service stations, asking anyone and everyone if they'd seen a black Lab wandering around with a bandaged leg. Every inquiry yielded disappointment and finally, he conceded defeat. Returning to OVH, he began trudging up the hill, dread in every step, to tell Reg that he'd lost the dog.

But to his surprise, when he rounded the back of the house, he found Reg sitting on the verandah, throwing one of his gardening gloves for an excited dog to retrieve. The very same black Labrador with the bandaged leg. Relief flooded through him, closely followed by consternation: the dog needed confinement and rest – not to be running around. But he took the soft approach. 'Thank god you've got the dog,' he said, walking over to Reg. 'I've been really worried.' Reg didn't respond. 'It's got a broken leg,' Dart added, trying to make his concern more evident.

'I know that. I've kept an eye on it.'

Dart tried one more sally. 'This dog needs to be rested,' he said, but Reg was unperturbed. He fixed Dart in his sights and said, 'If you've done a good job, it won't be a problem.' And sure enough, despite its impromptu jaunt, the black Labrador recovered very well.

When Dart came up with the idea of getting Reg a puppy, he called the owners and put his name down. 'I arranged for my parents to go up to Roma to pick up the dog and bring it back via Oakey,' Dart remembered. In May 1988, a few months before he was due to leave for the US, and a weekend when he was on call, his parents walked in at midday, ready for lunch. The Saturday morning surgery was finished, and Dart approached Reg.

'Dr Pascoe, my parents are visiting,' Dart said. 'Do you mind if I go up to Toowoomba and have a bite of lunch with them?'

There was a pause. 'Who's on call?' Reg asked.

'Well,' Dart said slowly, 'I am, but I'll only be a phone call away.'

'No,' Reg said. 'You don't do that while you're on call.' His tone brooked no argument, but Dart wouldn't have challenged that proclamation anyway: Reg was the Boss, and that was that. He headed outside to tell his parents. The puppy – 'a huge, big, fat thing' was sitting on the front seat with his mum. Dart scooped it up, took it inside and handed it to Reg. 'Thank you very much for all your help,' he said. He nodded at the puppy now squirming in Reg's arms. 'That's the only surviving pup from the litter, the rest died.'

Reg was staggered, but he covered it well. 'Right, well, I suppose you can go for lunch. But don't be a minute more than an hour.' And with that, he turned and headed up to the house, where Dart later heard that the great man had had 'a little bit of a cry.'

Reg named the pup Midnight – quickly shortened to Middy – and the dog soon became a key fixture of OVH. For more than a decade, they were rarely seen apart. 'You knew Reg was coming when he walked in,' Cheryl Lopate recalled, and then Reg would leave; Midnight 'would linger around for a while and then he would head back out.'

Reg taught Middy tricks and to fetch the paper but, Dart remembered wryly, Reg 'would never get him castrated' ... probably because '[he] likely thought it would be good if [Middy] would sire a few progeny.' The dog had an unconquerable urge to wander, but when Dart pointed out to Reg that getting Middy castrated might help with the problem, Reg waved it off. 'It was almost like he was proud that [Middy] would go off and wander around Oakey: everyone knew the dog.' It was the greatest gift anyone could have given Reg.

Reg and his beloved Midnight ('Middy'), the dog gifted to him by friend Andrew Dart.

Reg and Andrew Dart stayed good friends after the younger man left for the US and often spoke on the phone. One day during his stint in Davis, distraught, Dart called Reg. Performing rectal examinations, the young vet had inadvertently torn some horses' rectums, a fatal mistake. 'It's a pretty devastating thing to do,' he said decades later. 'It's a fairly small accident that can lead to very significant ramifications. It's one of those things that most veterinarians hope never happen to them.'

'If you haven't torn a rectum, you haven't done enough rectals,' Reg said laconically, a response that, on face value, was unsympathetic in the face of a friend's distress. But Reg knew that mistakes were a part of life and the attitude at OVH was that everyone made them, but you just got on with it. It was all part of the learning experience. 'You don't sit round crying or kicking the can, you pull yourself up and dust yourself off and learn from your mistakes and get on with it,' Dart summarised. Years of experience taught Reg that there was no such thing as a 'perfect method' – every strategy could be improved on.

Practical experience was the great teacher, Reg was fond of reminding junior vets. And no one was above it. One visiting American vet recalled that Reg was always ready with his favourite, good-natured rebuttal if the staff ever acted 'all high and mighty.' 'Tell me when you've palpated a *hundred thousand* horses,' he would say.[26] It was clear that the process never truly ended; Reg would simply try something different, applying new ideas to find a solution. As Dart noted, 'Reg's point [was] you can never stop learning, you can never stop developing and the more you see, the better you're going to become ... He put those sorts of things into perspective really well.'

Reg often used humour to defuse tense situations or to find fun in the long days. He was a dedicated practical joker and a great lover of laughter ... never more so than when in good company and with a fine red wine in hand. The king of the snappy one-liner, he had a humour so dry it fairly crackled underfoot and, at times, could feel biting rather than amusing. His quips could be devastating, but for the most part, those who knew him remembered often laughing (rather than crying) at remarks delivered with his trademark mischievous glint in his eye.

His larrikinism is immortalised in the EVA's annual Wolf Blass Award, a prize given to the EVA member who has provided the most amusing or outrageous act or deed performed at the Bain Fallon week of lectures. One year, surrounded by friends and colleagues – and a few drinks in and feeling up to some devilment – Reg noticed his friend, Mike Sier, dancing with the wife of famed Barossa winemaker, Wolf Blass. The next morning, Reg made a phone call. This was nothing new: a friend recalled that Reg loved 'trying to trick people, trying to set them up', and prank calls were a favourite way to do so.[27] In his strongest German accent, Reg convinced his friend that he was Wolf Blass, seeking revenge for Mike's dance with his wife the previous night. Mike fell for it, hook, line and sinker: he panicked, worrying that he'd offended an honoured guest. More than thirty years later, the Wolf Blass Award remains one of the EVA's most appreciated accolades. Despite Reg's insistence on professionalism in the practice, he encouraged his staff to have fun in the everyday – as long as it didn't interfere with the provision of quality care to clients.

His wit could be cutting and to some, it may at times have seemed cruel. After Andrew Dart left OVH, Reg took on a young female vet who became the unwitting butt of his wisecracks. One day, while Dart was back for a visit, his young replacement had taken some X-rays for Reg's review. When she brought them over, each film was underexposed – the result of not enough power to the machine. 'I'm sorry, Dr Pascoe,' she said. 'They're all underexposed.'

Reg considered this. 'Well, what machine did you take them with?' When she told him, he nodded. 'All right. Did you use an extension cord?'

'Oh yes. I had to use a couple to get the power from the shed to the horse.'

'Well, you should know better than that,' Reg said, like it was obvious.

'Why?' she asked, unnerved by the prospect of one of Reg's renowned tongue-lashings coming her way.

As solemn as the grave, Reg reminded her, 'The more cords you use, the further the electricity has to travel from the wall to the machine. That's why the X-rays are underexposed.' A seemingly helpful titbit which, Dart recalled with laughter, was 'obviously a load of codswallop.' Still, the new vet looked at Reg and whether she had any qualms about this information or not, decided that there was no way Reg was having her on ... Or maybe that challenging the Boss wasn't worth the risk. 'Is that right, Dr Pascoe? I'll have to remember that next time.' After she left the room, Reg looked over his half-moon glasses at Dart. 'It's very hard to find good help,' he said.

Dart's friendship with Reg gave him ample opportunity to relish the Boss's sense of humour. Visiting Oakey for lunch one day a few years later, Dart found himself the unwitting cause of strife. Reg had been teaching Middy tricks since he was a pup, with mixed results. Before Dart left for the US, one trick was a game of 'hide and seek.' It involved Reg making Dart take his socks off to give the dog the scent before he sent Dart off to hide in one of the clinic's cupboards. Middy, Dart remembered laughing, was hopeless. Bored of silly games, the dog often got distracted and ran off to some more enjoyable pastime. Meanwhile, trapped in a cupboard, Dart had to wait it out, and any attempts to attract Middy by cracking open the cupboard door were met with a quick scolding from Reg. But by the time Dart returned a few years later, Reg felt he'd cemented some even better tricks worth showing off – except he made it clear he'd not be doing them while Joy was around.

The Pascoe house had a small eating nook adjoining the kitchen. An inbuilt bench ran along the two far walls, with a laminated table and a few chairs sitting closest to the kitchen countertop. It was here that Dart sat for lunch with Reg and Joy this particular day. As soon as Joy left the room, Reg turned to Dart with a conspiratorial whisper. 'Hey, watch this.'

At a gesture from Reg, Middy leapt from floor to the bench seats; from bench to table; from table to kitchen countertop. He was standing there, looking back at his two-man audience with undisguised canine pride, when Joy came back into the room and 'all hell broke loose.' Furious, she said, 'Get that dog off the counter! If you ever do that again, the dog will be outside – and so will you!'

'When Joy got angry, Reg was like a little schoolboy,' Dart remembered with a chortle. Duly chastened, Reg quickly summoned Middy back to the floor.

Reg Pascoe: the reserved, humble man; the driven professional; the great practical joker and larrikin. 'He did have definitely a bit of a wild streak,' Reg's friend from Provet, Garth McGilvray, recalled. He thought Reg was better behaved around his wife; there were clear 'differences from time to time when we were away because he did keep a very austere, formal sort of façade with Joy around, but without Joy he often relaxed and became the life of the party.' But it wasn't always the case.

Andrew Dart recalled a family dinner with Reg and Joy on the Gold Coast during a conference where Reg, for some reason, 'felt very much at home' at the BYO Korean barbecue restaurant. He 'got himself quite pickled' as the night wore on. 'With a few drinks under his belt ... Reg [got] funnier and funnier and sillier and said silly things – and of course the sillier he was, the angrier Joy got with him.' It was a funny, memorable evening – made even more so 'when Reg got up to go, he found that his legs were a little bit loose, and we had to carry him home.'

While Mike Huber recalled Reg keeping a professional distance at staff parties, in the right company, the gloves came off. Sue Hollindale, who joined the OVH administrative staff in the late 1980s, remembered that Reg 'was a bit of a rabble rouser with Colin McAlpine.' The equine vet and stud owner were in their seventies when they got themselves and the rest of OVH banned from the local RSL – the result of a water pistol fight. 'It wasn't like he was one of the young men running rampant ... he was the Boss; he was encouraging everyone to be light and relaxed.'

As Reg grew older, his sense of fun seemed to intensify, rather than diminish. He exemplified the adage 'work hard, play hard' for no one worked harder than he did. But few played as many pranks, caused as much mischief, or enjoyed themselves as thoroughly, either.

14
Reg and the OVH in the 1990s

The 1990s were Reg's final decade in practice. At age sixty, he showed no sign of slowing and this period saw some of the greatest changes and growth in the hospital's history. But the decade dawned inauspiciously, to say the least. 'A serious world financial depression for the horse industry occurred in 1988–89,' Reg recorded, 'greatly affecting many of our clients and leading to an increase in unpaid fees. This, coupled with a period of high bank interest rates and almost ten years' continuous drought caused a marked slowdown in yearly case intake.'

Though he ensured the clinic's amenities remained of the highest quality, where additional equipment was needed (such as a Frigtronics cryosurgical unit), it was leased instead of bought outright 'to preserve financial liquidity.' In an account he wrote in 2000, Reg defined the staggered development of OVH in terms of stages of expansion. Following the third stage in 1979, stages four, five and six occurred between 1992 and 1997, with the addition of the ETU in 1999 considered stage seven.

In 2000, the equine hospital alone saw an average of over 1500 annual admissions for a variety of treatments, from major surgeries (approximately 350–450 horses), to minor surgeries (200), and reproduction cases (80). The remaining cases were mostly lameness and other medical issues. Ensuring the work was performed to the highest standards was the dedicated team of personnel. Reg continued to pursue partnerships with passionate, like-minded vets – and there were many, both at home and abroad – and the team boasted eleven full-time vets and one part-time vet, as well as four vet nurses, a part-time farrier, and several administrative staff.

The mention of a 'part-time vet' deserves further examination.

Though even-handed in his dealings and generally lacking prejudice, Reg certainly felt there was a 'right way' to be a vet, and this belief sometimes failed to recognise the complexities others faced. In 2021, his views may seem archaic, even elitist, but they're representative of common attitudes in the profession and more broadly of a generational shift.

As recently as 2019, a British veterinary blog wrote of the need for vet practices to recognise and adapt to millennials' workforce expectations, including work-life balance and part-time work. Meanwhile, a 2008 paper released by the Australian federal government described the deliberate limitations to part-time work imposed by Australian industrial and institutional arrangements throughout the 1970s and 1980s due to fears that it would threaten full-time employment. Apprehension about flexible working arrangements was common. The 1990s saw fewer impediments and a gradual acceptance of part-time employment.

A colleague noted that when it came to part-time work, '[Reg] was no different to other male principles of veterinary practices at this time.'[28] But for someone so frequently so ahead of his time, his stance was undeniably conservative. 'I never thought he was sexist – I think he was very careful,' veterinarian and friend Julie Strous recalled, 'even for someone of his generation; a lot of the problems that that generation had, he didn't have.' Yet towards those women who wanted to work part-time while raising children, Reg's sentiments weren't favourable, an attitude that, over the years, some found galling.

While easy to dismiss as the simple condescension of a male professional who had benefitted all his adult life from the efforts of a supportive, resilient and adaptable spouse, Reg's concern with the feasibility of part-time work was more complex. In a 1999 newspaper article, 'When questioned about the reasons for [the Oakey Veterinary Hospital's] success, Dr Pascoe stated it was because of the continuous diligent attention to client relations, prompt answering of calls twenty-four hours a day, and provision of expert veterinary services at all times.'

Reg was devoted to veterinary science and his work was a higher calling. He understood 'that to be a professional was to work in the best interests of society', Julie said, and certainly he 'sacrificed a lot of his personal life' to do so. This included doing large amounts of voluntary work. 'The sheer scale of what he gave back in the profession ... [would not] be easy to find, perhaps not even in his generation. That was quite remarkable.' Jon Hill agreed, observing that Reg 'felt an obligation and a commitment to further the profession', and he pursued it steadfastly. This, for Reg, was the definition of a 'professional': someone who put society first and who worked long and hard in service of it ... Someone, in other words, who worked full-time, or even *beyond* full-time.

The lessons he learnt as a child during the Great Depression and the hard years following never left him. He grew up in a time when people didn't have much, but what they had, they shared: the only way to survive was to pull together. Those early years also instilled in him that legendary industriousness that awed colleagues, clients and friends. His disdain for part-time work was a product of both his personal dedication to his calling and his belief that if you chose veterinary science, then it should be the predominant preoccupation of one's life: both for the edification of the vet, and for the provision of care to the client. As his friend Chris Johnson said, this attitude was made possible due to Reg's personal circumstances. 'He could be like that because he had such a support network at home.' But Reg was also adaptable. There are numerous instances in which he revised an entrenched belief after considering new information or a changing situation. Perhaps, with the evolution of the profession towards greater workplace flexibility, he may once more have changed his mind.

Chris Riggs, OVH vet 1998–2001

Unlike many others who joined OVH, Chris Riggs had been qualified as a vet for over a decade when he met Reg in the early 1990s at the annual British Equine Veterinary Association's conference. A lecturer at the University of Liverpool's School of Veterinary Science, Chris sat next to Joy at the conference dinner and found Reg an interesting puzzle: he was impressive, obviously experienced, and very opinionated ... but beyond that, he wasn't sure how to read him.

Around this time, Reg and Professor Derek Knottenbelt began working together on the *Colour Atlas of Diseases and Disorders of the Horse*. Reg's repeat visits to Liverpool brought a secondary burgeoning friendship with the young lecturer. During one of these visits Reg saw Chris perform an equine surgery. He watched with interest as Chris worked and liked what he saw. 'You'll have to come and work for me one day,' he said casually. It was, Chris thought, a throwaway line – he had yet to learn that Reg wasn't really a man for throwaway lines.

Soon after, Chris made plans to travel to New Zealand as part of a research venture with Massey University. He'd always yearned to live there. *If I go there, I'll stay*, he thought to himself as he prepared to leave. But his visit was plagued by terrible weather, leaving a sour taste in his mouth. He changed his mind. Sometime later, he spent a week in Oakey with Reg and Joy. They were welcoming and hospitable, and Chris was 'absolutely taken by Queensland.' The vast open blue skies of summer, the beauty of the bush around Oakey; it was the opposite to how he'd felt during his trip to New Zealand. The visit also allowed him to deepen his relationship with Reg.

In 1998, perturbed about the trajectory of his academic career, Chris shared his fears with Reg. 'I was going down too narrow an avenue too early and I really wanted a lot more experience,' he remembered. Reg, who had employed Andrew Dart a decade earlier with the promise of 'being right at the coalface', knew he could help. 'Why don't you come out and work for me?' he suggested. It was the ideal offer, but the situation wasn't straightforward – Chris remembered it as 'a bit of a jump off a cliff' for his family. His son was only nine weeks old when they left the UK, and his father was dying from cancer. Enthusiastic about Chris's prospects, he was nevertheless concerned that there was no contract securing his future. But on that front, Chris wasn't worried. 'I had complete confidence in Reg. He was one of those blokes that you could really trust.'

When Chris and his family arrived at Oakey in September 1998, they found the second home they hadn't known was waiting for them. They bought a house on the hill behind the practice, so that Chris's daily commute meant jumping over the fence near Reg and Joy's veggie garden and strolling down to the practice. Often, he recalled, he would head to the barn early and there was Reg 'on his own, just standing there looking. Taking it in.' The scene remained etched in Chris's mind; many people, he thought, had lost the ability to truly observe and absorb what was before them, to ponder and analyse rather than simply skim the surface. But in those quiet, reflective moments alone in the barn, Reg was drinking in the world that he had built and that he loved so deeply. More often, Chris would find Reg already hard at work at the hospital and the pair would have 'a good old chin wag' to start the day. 'He had such a good way of summing things up,' Chris remembered.

Chris found this period of his life idyllic. For three and a half years, the Riggs were at home in Oakey, drawn into the OVH community and made welcome by Reg and Joy, whose personal support they treasured. With an infant son, Reg and Joy's kindness meant 'there was always that feeling [of having] someone senior and wiser and with the ... mental resources to get you out of a pickle if you got in a pickle.' And Chris loved OVH. 'It was an amazing experience. My knowledge ... expanded massively. Not just in dealing with technical, clinical things and good ways of dealing with them' but also practical, useful surgical procedures. 'Reg was superb at all that stuff, and he was good at teaching. He'd pick one or two things and say, "All right. I'm going to teach you and Steve." And he'd take us through a case each.' Reg was methodical, Chris said, 'very precise and very particular about the things we'd done and [became] very grumpy if the recipe hadn't been followed.'

Chris's surgical experiences, however, occurred among a myriad of other facets of life in Oakey. Reg's passion for self-education and investigation imbued everything he did; Chris 'learnt how to deal with people a lot more, how to deal with situations and how the practice contributed in some small way to the gradual ongoing expansion of OVH. The history of Oakey Veterinary Hospital is mapped out on all the different bits of concrete.' Whenever there wasn't much going on in the clinic, Reg would call a friend of his with ready access to concrete, which 'would suddenly appear', Chris remembered, 'and we'd lay a new path somewhere. I learnt how to lay concrete as well ... it was good fun.'

Another day, another slab of concrete poured in a free moment around the clinic. (Photo courtesy of Dr Chris Riggs)

Of course, life at OVH also had its hiccoughs. Reg had brought Chris in as a specialist surgeon, someone who would take some of the load from his shoulders, but that was challenging for other surgeons who had already been at OVH for some time. 'Aussies aren't quite as laid-back as everyone says they are,' Chris said wryly. There were several 'fairly tricky moments' in the early days as other vets chafed under the new staffing arrangements and struggled to redefine their niche.

Trickier still, however, was the inadvertent challenge Chris posed to the Boss's sovereignty. As he took the lead on certain surgical cases, people would bypass Reg and pose their questions directly to Chris. Though he was managing cases that Reg had never even seen, it was still difficult. Reg had maintained complete oversight of OVH, and particularly of equine surgeries, for forty years and the unintentional effect of a newcomer's ascension, was one of 'implied criticism – although that's exactly what you got the person in to do.'

Like most successful and rarely countermanded individuals, Reg was not good at receiving criticism ... not, of course, that many people within the practice openly criticised him. In spite of his humility, he also was very proud: in his practice, in his experience, and in what he had learnt and achieved throughout his career.

Speaking to Chris's mother one day, Reg said, 'Australians are really thick-skinned – apart from the bits where they're thin-skinned.' This was true for Reg too; there were aspects of his life and his work about which he could be as sensitive as anyone else. His path to success, Derek Knottenbelt pointed out, had seen Reg encounter 'significant failures that he found hard to accept', but in response, he had become 'more determined and more forthright' rather than cede victory. Isolated and without a mentor to guide his steps, Reg 'had to think on his feet and develop reasons for failure of surgical techniques and procedures and then set out to find solutions. He did not do what mere mortals do and accept the dogma.'

To persist in the face of failure, to harness that failure and move forward requires fortitude and resilience, characteristics common to all successful individuals who forge new paths. It's also necessary to let go of one's pride. A delicate balance must be struck between knowing there is much to learn, and not being overwhelmed by the mountains yet to be climbed. That Reg was able to do so as a young man was a feat, and the process must have, at times, shaken his faith. Criticism could feel like a dismissal of his experience and knowledge for which he'd fought so hard and so long.

When the Equine Teaching Unit (ETU) began at OVH, Chris was talking one day to students about a type of bandage traditionally used at OVH. 'Of course, there are alternatives,' he added. Reg 'went absolutely ballistic.' 'Do you think I wasted fifteen years of my life using that bandage?' he barked.

Reg was open to discussion, Chris remembered, but there was a right time and place: if you chose 'the wrong time, then just be careful.' But Reg was also always open to new ideas and to failing on the path to success.

Reg with a foal undergoing the hessian-binding treatment described by Dr Chris Riggs. (Photo courtesy of Dr Chris Riggs)

Chris remembered his 'amazing ... youth-like willingness to try new things', even when they were 'really bizarre things that no one else would try', like their experiments using hessian sacks to correct rotational deformities of foals' legs. This openness to innovation and commitment to ongoing learning left a deep impression on Chris. 'Every day I'd learn something new.' It was an attitude encapsulated in a slew of sayings and quotes. Chris's favourite is an excellent summary of Reg's approach to his work: *persistence wins the day*.

From 2003 to 2019, Chris filled the highly prestigious Head of Veterinary Clinical Services at the Hong Kong Jockey Club before moving to the role of Head of Mainland Veterinary Operations. Although Reg's clinical expertise helped hone Chris in ways that have since served his international career, one of the strongest impressions of Reg once he'd left was his connection to his calling and to OVH. 'He really loved it; loved the animals, loved the horses and really cared about them.'

Sue Hollindale, OVH admin staff 1992–2002

Sue Hollindale joined OVH in 1992, arriving not only with no previous experience with animals, but no knowledge of Reg Pascoe at all. 'We travelled past the hospital every time we left town,' Sue said, 'but I never [knew] what that was, or who ran it ... [Reg] was a world-renowned veterinarian and even when I started there, it still took me a little while to know how important he was to the industry.'

'That's not a problem,' Reg said during Sue's interview when she mentioned she had no experience. Under the desk, Middy lay asleep on Reg's feet. 'You don't need any kind of special knowledge about animals: I have vets and vet nurses with that expertise, and you'll be working in reception.' This, Sue recalled, was fortunate; Reg 'was never able to teach me anything very much about animals.'

Sue was a diligent and valuable member of OVH's front office. Her polling booth experience with 'stroppy people coming to the front desk to place their votes' during elections was invaluable when dealing with OVH clients, but it was just useful when dealing with staff arguments. Reg might have been in what some referred to as 'his mellow years', but his ability to get under people's skin was undiminished: when his ire was aroused, his tongue could be sharp, his censure devastating. Chris Riggs noted some found Reg's dominance overbearing and combined with his at times brusque and satirical manner, disharmony occasionally ensued. He was capable 'of upsetting people enough that [they] talked about leaving', Sue remembered, though this appears to have been mostly limited to one particular vet with whom Reg regularly clashed. Chris Pollitt, who worked with Reg in the ETU and remembered that Reg never had much time for him, noted 'I don't think [Reg] held back humiliating people much', and some certainly experienced this more than others.

Strong personalities polarise, and Reg was blunt with everyone regardless of who they were. Another OVH vet, Jayne McGhie, remembered, 'He didn't mince words. For some people who can't hear the truth very well, maybe that just didn't work for them.' There were undoubtedly those who found Reg hard to deal with. 'It was always Reg's way or the highway.' 'He was proud of what he'd achieved,' Reg's friend Julie Strous mused. 'He loved the thought that he didn't suffer fools – and sometimes he wouldn't be as kind as he should be. He'd call people out and embarrass them in front of others.' Doing so could leave people rankled. The well-timed, perfectly aimed and cutting remarks at which he was so skilled were designed to take people down a peg and would have smarted on bruised egos at times. He wouldn't sugar-coat the truth when uncomfortable things had to be said. Jayne knew the attacks weren't personal – though it's impossible to know whether others also realised this. 'I wouldn't have expected him to have a personal attack on anybody,' she said. It was more that 'if you'd done a poor job, he'd tell you.'

Strained relationships seemed to have been the exception at OVH. Reg is predominantly remembered as a man who treated people impartially. The refrain that he mellowed over time is a recurrent one, and tales from the last decade or so of his clinical practice evince a gentler Reg than the earlier years. Many previous OVH staff speak with respect about Reg's egalitarian treatment of people, from stable hands to administrative staff and vets alike. Reg's vet nurse Lou Winkel said, 'It didn't matter who you were or what your position was or how much money you had or what part you were going to play in the practice ... he was always fair to people.' Sue, too, remembered Reg 'as a common man', dealing with staff, friends and clients as his equals and as deserving of respect as any expert professional. Despite occasional confrontations, he was a consummate communicator when it mattered. 'One of his major strengths was his ability to communicate and pass on to all the rest of us how important that was,' recalled Brisbane vet Dave Lovell.

Sue Hollindale thrived under Reg's leadership. For all that he eschewed verbal praise, his appreciation for and faith in people was self-evident in the way he managed his staff. As he had with a teenage Shirl Adamson more than fifteen years earlier, Reg handed over control of the front office to those who knew it best. Active in implementing new ideas and technology within the clinic, Sue's role expanded as digitisation became increasingly important. This meant she assumed responsibility for all of OVH's word processing, and digitally inputting vets' field work reports. She also created and managed an OVH newsletter.

Reg, Sue remembered, 'allowed me to do what I needed to do without really interfering in my role.' He gave her the autonomy 'to develop and find my way and then bring in new things.' And in his desire to implement new ideas, he continually pushed the boundaries of Sue's knowledge. 'He wanted me to create a merge document so he could send out all these letters to his horse council people. So, I had a week to learn how to create a merge document and be able to merge addresses with putting fields into a letter.' Handing out new problems for Sue to solve was how he showed his faith in her.

From the small group of three women working in the office when Sue first arrived, the practice soon grew in infrastructure and personnel. She joined OVH around the fourth stage of expansion, which included the completion of a full arthroscopic surgical suite in 1992 with a video camera and monitor, plus abdominal telescope. The operating theatre table that Reg had designed twenty years earlier needed to meet increasing demands for colic and joint surgery positioning: it was fitted with hydraulics, and the previous mild steel construction (originally chosen to defray the cost of producing the table) was galvanised. The exposed surfaces were replaced or sheeted in heavy gauge stainless steel. This aside, Reg felt the practice's stage four expansion was moderate compared to earlier stages. 'A totally enclosed shed with [capacity for] 1500 hay bales and 500 bags of lucerne chaff was added' and the growth of small animal practice necessitated the 'expansion and re-vamping of two small animal consulting rooms, new small animal surgery and new laundry/sterilising room with a 150-litre steam autoclave and 60-litre ethylene oxide gas steriliser added, allowing our capacity to handle increasing surgery more efficiently.'

Sue was at OVH during the stage five expansion, which centred on the addition of new holding paddocks for what Reg referred to as 'problem mares, chilled and frozen AI mares' – referring to the increasing use of artificial insemination in equine reproduction under David Pascoe's expertise. Swathes of new equipment were bought, including a CO_2 laser, endoscope and monitor, thermography camera and improved ultrasound. And, as Sue recalled, 'large animal nurses went from one to three ... quite quickly in the first five years' she was at OVH. Several international vets – from America, the Netherlands and elsewhere – came for short stays, while several Aussies joined for longer periods.

Reg's commitment to the continual evolution of OVH wasn't just focused on veterinary science. He was a consummate businessman and Sue had recently arrived when he decided OVH staff needed uniforms to ensure a high standard of dress and the maintenance of a clean-cut, professional image. While this is the norm in 2021, it was rare in most workplaces at the time. Reg allowed the office staff to choose their uniforms themselves, but retained oversight of the choices and veto on the final decision.

Reg cared deeply for those who worked for him, and was often involved in managing his staff through the vicissitudes of life, both professional and personal. He protected the security and comfort of his staff in the clinic and ensured, regardless of position or experience, that everyone was treated with respect. Sue recalled one instance where this was particularly important for her.

'One of your vets just criticised me in front of the clients,' Sue told him one day, frustrated and embarrassed. 'It was very unprofessional.' Reg listened carefully and then Sue returned to her desk. She had faith that he would fix it. And he did. 'Dr Pascoe had my back and he took it from there never to happen again.'

Sue experienced some confronting and challenging personal circumstances during her time at OVH, and Reg was always understanding and supportive. And generous. Once, when he and Joy went travelling, Reg came home with a Western Australian wildflower paperweight for Sue and a porcelain mug with Kangaroo Dreaming art. And when they went to Spain, he brought her a small decorative plate as thanks for looking after his personal mail; they were small things, but Sue still remembered them over twenty years later.

Jayne McGhie, OVH vet 1995–2003

When Jayne McGhie first met Reg, he 'scared the living daylights out of me.' She was doing work experience in Oakey during her BVSc and had always wanted to be an equine vet and spent her first few days too scared to talk to him, simply 'following everybody around like a puppy.' When Reg finally asked Jayne for her opinion on a radiograph, it seemed a make-or-break moment. Though briefly stymied, she gathered herself and plunged ahead with an answer, recalling, 'It was like a trial ... If you [hadn't] known or if you messed up, you might never have gotten the time of day.'

But despite all she'd heard, Jayne didn't experience his reported gruffness. 'He was always calm and understanding. I had a great time.' When she graduated from UQ in December 1994, the positive memories were enough to convince her to take a punt. Though she had already secured a job for the following year, she couldn't help dropping a résumé in at OVH.

'Well,' Reg said, 'do you want to start?'

'Really?' Jayne asked, taken aback. Reg shook her hand and that was that.

Her eight and a half years at OVH provided an amazing foundation for her career. 'As a new graduate, I couldn't have gone into a better practice.' During that time, Reg was in many ways a father figure. 'I tell people that I ate more meals at Reg and Joy's when I was employed with them than I had in my home sometimes.'

Reg's friendship and guidance were pivotal to Jayne's professional success and the ethos he espoused resonated deeply. People always had to prove their worth, but once they had, Reg's willingness to guide and mentor them was boundless. He made a particularly big impact on the younger women who worked at the practice, treating them with kindness and respect, and encouraging their further education.

Reg was role model, mentor and father figure, perhaps even without any real intention of being so. His affection for, and protectiveness of, his OVH family came naturally to him. As he had with Andrew Dart, more than twenty years earlier, Reg guided Jayne into working at the University of California, Davis with his son John Pascoe in the mid 2000s. That role helped with her subsequent residency as a small animal surgeon and, 'that all stems back to Reg. He made things happen with people's careers.'

He also safeguarded those careers, particularly in the early years. If one of his vets erred, the ultimate responsibility for what happened remained with Reg. Perhaps it was for this reason that he told Jayne, 'I never tell people that they do a good job, because they always turn around the next week and do something silly.' But as he impressed upon Andrew Dart, he knew that learning involved making mistakes. In vet science, errors can prove fatal, but they are also an essential step in the journey to competence and expertise, and Reg always ensured his protégées were given room to err.

'I'd only been working for him for a couple of days,' Jayne remembered, when 'I made one of the biggest mistakes that I've made in my career ... it was a terrible day.' Faced with a horse that needed to be euthanised, Jayne bungled it and the result was gory and stomach-turning. It was also painful for the horse, the thought of which horrified Jayne. Shaken, she returned to the practice, where Reg met her in the car park. It was a moment that might well have ended her career, but within half an hour, she was sitting at a table in the clinic with the partners and the client whose horse had been euthanised, listening to the stories of their own professional disasters. They sat with her over cake and coffee and let her know she wasn't alone, and that it would be okay.

That didn't mean mistakes went unnoticed, or that the lessons weren't reinforced. 'I remember Reg yelling at me several times – in fact, more than several – for doing stupid things.' On one occasion,

Jayne had a mare in the crush down at the reproduction hut (which staff had fondly dubbed 'the love shack') for a procedure. She was using local anaesthetic and decided to forgo a 'twitch', the small rope noose attached to a stick and placed around the upper lip or ear to apply pressure and subdue the horse. As she began to work, she discovered she'd 'missed a spot' with the local anaesthetic, recalling that the mare 'exploded in the stocks. There [were] hooves and Christ knows what everywhere.' Reg came down from the office to help wrest the animal under control. Afterwards, he unleashed on Jayne, letting her know how stupid she'd been. The use of appropriate restraint techniques, crucial in large animal work, had been drummed relentlessly into Reg at university and remained a cornerstone. Jayne's slip-up contravened both his own convictions and the methods he'd taught her. Jayne was gutted and awed by Reg's fury. Later, they sat down together to discuss the incident in more depth. Jayne was nervous about what he'd say, but Reg surprised her.

'What would I have done if that mare had hurt you?' he asked. 'Don't ever worry me again like that. Don't do anything stupid where you might hurt yourself.' His anger, Jayne realised with a shock, came about because he was worried that something bad might have happened to her. As he told vets, time and again, working with animals could be dangerous, and the aim was to finish every day unhurt.

Reg had a policy that whenever things went wrong, admonishing and managing his staff was a strictly in-house matter. 'He would be right there to back you up if you did something right,' but even if 'you did something wrong, he would take your side.' He made sure that OVH fixed the problem, but 'he would defend you first and then sort it out later.' Reg was canny about understanding personalities and relationships, especially when it came to recalcitrant clients. Jayne was on call one Christmas holidays when a call came in. Reg dropped it into her lap. '[The client] absolutely hates the other vet on call,' he told her. 'I can't send him – you've got to go.' Attending this client, whom Jayne remembered as 'a big German, grumpy man' who intermittently unleashed on the vets, was a painful prospect. 'You know it's going to be terrible,' Reg told her, '[he's] going to tear you to shreds.'

It was an accurate prognosis. The client 'had been grumpy as all hell.' Reg was always on the other end of the two-way radio, but Jayne left the property emotionally bruised and battered, just as Reg had predicted. Upon her return to OVH, he met her at the clinic and invited her up to the house for a meal.

OVH was Reg's life: a passion and a calling not restricted to work schedules or other arbitrary boundaries. The practice's proximity to his house meant Reg was never really 'off work' – even on weekends, he'd often wander down to the surgery to see what was going on and supervise what his vets were up to, a pair of coveralls thrown on over his pyjamas.

The workload at OVH could be gruelling and the work ethic expected of the vets was tough. 'We just worked and worked and worked.' During Jayne's time there vets spent at least a few years working twelve days on, two days off. Andrew Dart recalled that Reg 'appreciated people who were happy to work and to enjoy their work … that's what he saw as being successful.' He wasn't particularly interested in set hours or strict schedules. He believed in working until the job was done. And if, Dart said with a laugh, that happened to be 10 o'clock at night, well that was when it was.

There was always something new to learn. Jayne sometimes felt as if she was being paid, not to do a job, but for the privilege of learning at Reg's side. His belief in education and self-development extended to his tolerance for both his staff's use of clinic resources and management of vet–client relationships. 'If you're learning something new,' he said, 'just charge the client what you think best. If you want to do that call for a hundred bucks because you're going to learn, do that.' Jayne took the message to heart: her enthusiasm for treating injured wildlife extended on at least one occasion, she remembered, to 'dragging the X-ray machines out to a farm that had a kangaroo that had a broken leg – a dislocated hock – and [putting] a cast on.' These intermittent excursions with the portable X-ray machine were always funded by OVH; it was the practice's money that she was spending, and Reg reminded her of it from time to time … but he never stopped her.

He was so pragmatic in so many other ways that the idea of OVH rescuing and caring for orphaned joeys seems uncharacteristic, anathema to a man that one might assume would view such incidents as a natural by-product of life. But Reg's close friend Tony Nicholls recalled that Reg 'spent considerable time, energy and money on efforts to treat and recuperate koalas.' An endeavour outside the scope of his practice, no matter how hard Reg tried, it was 'always a bit of a lottery on whether or not his efforts would be successful, despite using multiple blood tests, dietary changes [and] varying husbandry techniques.' This, however, was also relatively common in the industry at the time; 'many of us in the veterinary industry used to do a whole lot of [pro bono] work with ... native animals,' Tony remembered. 'People just came to expect us to do it all.' An industry survey around that time revealed that the hours spent treating native wildlife across Australia's veterinary profession amounted to millions of dollars of free work.

During Jayne's years at OVH, rescued joeys were so common that they became a standout memory for almost everyone who visited. She had raised joeys and other orphaned or wounded wildlife since childhood, so the temptation was irresistible. *I'm just going to keep one or two*, she told herself. Rescued joeys lived near her desk, where she could feed and care for them around her work. A bag hanging on the back of the vets' office door provided a simple replica of the pouch in which the babies would normally have grown up and small bells around their necks would tinkle merrily as they hopped back to the pouch after a brief excursion into the wide world. As they grew, bigger bags were necessary, and anyone walking past would see two big ears and pointed face hanging out of the pouch – and maybe a paw or two. When US vet Cheryl Lopate arrived in 1997, a joey ended up in her care. 'We had a joey each,' Jayne recalled with amusement. 'We had them in our cars, we had them around the hospital ... and Reg would pretend to be grumpy, but I knew he wasn't.'

'Those bloody joeys,' he'd say as he walked past. He tutted at the new arrivals and grumbled about their antics, but he never forbade Jayne from fostering them. And whatever else might be going on at the time to irritate him, the kangaroos were never to blame. It was a singular indulgence that was tied in part to Reg's fondness for Jayne, but he also simply liked having the joeys in the practice. If he thought no one was watching, he'd reach into the bags to play with them, though of course, Jayne noted, 'he would never let anybody know that.' But there were limits to his patience.

'Get your bloody joey off my desk!' Reg bellowed along the corridor one day. Hurtling down to Reg's office, Jayne discovered that one of the joeys had jumped up and peed all over his letters. On another day when Reg was roaring around the corridor about the joeys, Jayne came out to discover one had escaped its pouch and was standing, quite unconcerned, in the stocks under a horse's belly. 'Get your bloody joey,' Reg growled at Jayne, and she scooped up the little adventurer into its bag. 'I knew that stuff would hop around the hospital,' he said darkly.

Jayne could also sometimes be found climbing onto the hospital roof to gather branches for rescued koalas. She always seemed to have one animal or another down her shirt, which she would frequently pull out to show others. 'Look what I've got,' she'd say, holding her shirt open to show Reg a baby koala. His response was characteristically dry but he never dressed Jayne down; he saw her passion as a gift. He was also open to learning from her experience with native animals. When she quietly proposed 'the tree test' to him one day, he was bemused, forced to admit he had no idea what she was talking about. 'You place the treated koala at the base of a tree and if it climbs up, it'll probably live,' Jayne said. If not, the odds were slim at best.

'It's the best test of likely survival I've ever found,' Reg admitted later. It was a story he greatly enjoyed recounting to others and a friend noted how it spoke to Reg's character that he was willing to do so. 'He was not afraid to tell a story where he was the butt of the joke.'

Fittingly, it was Jayne who gave Reg his much-loved last Labrador, a golden puppy named Sassy. Reg and Joy were on holidays in 2000 when Middy the black Lab died. It was a terrible time and everyone could see that Reg felt the loss keenly. 'He got so grumpy after Middy died and he didn't have a dog,' Jayne remembered. It couldn't continue and she told Joy she was going to get Reg another dog. Joy wasn't sure – she told Jayne no, in fact. But Jayne's mind was made up.

She waited until the time was right, then bought the puppy. It was around Christmas in 2000 and so she placed little reindeer antlers on its head and took up to the house. Two of Reg's grandchildren were there and were thrilled at the unexpected appearance of the fat, wriggly little yellow puppy. Reg was less impressed. 'He didn't even want to speak to me,' Jayne said, unfazed. But as Middy had before her, Sassy went about winning Reg over as only a dog can. 'She was running around trying to be friends with him and he was acting grumpy ... and then he wanted to be friends with the dog and the dog would ignore him. And he'd get rather cranky,' before insouciantly 'dragging [a string] behind him so she'd follow him along.'

Reg and his final golden Labrador, Sassy, a gift from Dr Jayne McGhie.

Whenever Sassy did anything wrong, Jayne knew about it. 'Your dog's hiding from me,' Reg would say when Sassy lay down and blended into the laundry's yellow tiles, but though he often sounded irritated, he bonded with the puppy. When she tragically died of tick paralysis only a few years later, he grieved the loss of his friend. He never got another dog.

'I can't verbalise the impact that [Reg] had on my life,' Jayne said, except that he was 'incredibly kind.' Remembering her years at OVH brought back so much joy. 'I look back and I don't think of any bad memories.'

Dorraine Waldow, 1996–1997 breeding season

Dorraine Waldow had recently completed a residency in theriogenology (a branch of veterinary science specialising in reproduction) at the University of Florida when she first met David Pascoe, who was at the university as a visiting clinician. The effect of the Pascoe Mafia was in force again, and Dorraine soon headed to Australia, where she spent a breeding season at OVH from August 1996 to February 1997.

Her visit coincided with the implementation of Reg's next phase of evolution for OVH. 'Stage six in 1997 saw a major reorganisation of the hospital yards. The original outside stables and yards were showing signs of wear, so they were demolished and replaced with a new set of fourteen steel box stables, also containing feed and treatment rooms. The eight demountable stables installed during this process have been retained for outside use. A covered farrier's shed/forge has been added. A self-contained intern flat was added close to the main hospital. A reproduction bar (9 x 14 metres) containing a laboratory, storage area for frozen semen, an examination crush (stocks) built adjacent to the outside paddocks with subdivision of some of the existing paddocks as holding yards for these mares, allowed expansion of AI and ET [Artificial Insemination and Embryo Transfer] in the practice, increased convenience, comfort, better [and] more efficient handling of repro cases.' It was ideal timing for the American vets, all reproductive specialists, who came to work at OVH over the next few years.

Reg, Dorraine remembered, was 'one of the best people I ever worked for.' He fostered a 'we're all in it together kind of attitude' that made OVH an intimate work environment in spite of its size. It felt like family, she recalled, a warmth which was particularly welcome because she missed her own. Dorraine shared a house in Toowoomba with another visiting US vet called Karen. There were 'tonnes of times everyone as a group went out to dinner', and her memories of Christmas in 1996 demonstrate the lengths to which Reg and Joy went to nurture their people. She accompanied Reg and Joy to a Christmas performance at a little community hall in Oakey; a small, local event, but Dorraine thought it beautiful. When 'everyone stood up and sang "Waltzing Matilda"' together to piano accompaniment, it brought tears to her eyes.

The vets formed close friendships while working at OVH and these bonds endure. Dorraine, Jayne McGhie and Cheryl Lopate (who arrived the season after Dorraine) are still close friends and credit their time in Oakey for bringing them together. 'A lot of big instances in my life all originate from my time with Reg,' Jayne said. This sense of community among the OVH staff was cultivated both in and out of work hours.

Every day, the hospital stopped work and had morning tea, a comforting and sacred ritual. Everyone would gather in the covered area Reg had built and sit on the 'talking chairs' to discuss whatever was on their minds.

Reg, captured in the middle of a discussion.

Cradling his customary cuppa, Reg 'would park himself right there, usually in his pyjamas with his coveralls over [the top]', Dorraine recalled. 'He'd sit down and just settle the world's problems.' The simple intimacy of those short breaks stayed with her, not least of which was Reg's habit of chaffing her about her love of iced tea; in retaliation, she always kept a jug of the American concoction in the fridge. The morning tea tradition wasn't confined to OVH. It was the same when Reg went out to the big horse studs. 'Before he even palpated your eighty-five horses, he would sit down and have tea with the owners.'

But Dorraine was there to learn and there were always opportunities for that. 'If there was an emergency – a colic or something – in the middle of the night, he always called [Karen and I].' 'We're about to cut a colic!' Reg would say, referring to the need to treat a horse's abdominal pain, often related to gastrointestinal conditions. 'Do you want to come down and not miss out on the fun?'

The contrast between vet science in the US and Australia was a recurrent source of fascination. 'We're not in your country now,' Reg would say, laughing at Dorraine's surprise over one difference or another, such as sterilisation techniques for equipment. Mainly concerned with the in-house breeding work, Dorraine managed approximately one hundred mares who had to be artificially inseminated, then cared for until pregnancy was confirmed. When others were away or unavailable, however, she also covered for vets on clinical calls out to client properties. The first time she did so, she ran into a strange problem.

'Gosh,' she said to the rest of the staff when she got back to the clinic, 'I really didn't have enough needles and syringes.' There was a bemused pause. 'What do you mean?' someone asked. 'You had plenty.' To her evident confusion, the other staff explained where she'd gone wrong: every time she gave a horse an injection, she was supposed to rinse the needle and syringe with the bag of saline and reuse it. OVH reused surgical face masks in the same manner, something which Dorraine had never encountered before.

'[Australians] didn't have a lot of the same infectious diseases that [America] had,' she explained, and what would have caused an uproar in the US was, at the time, safe enough not to cause a blip on Reg's radar. Reg believed in being practical and thrifty in matters both large and small. For example, the clinic typed up their own labels for medications on a typewriter; it was so fundamentally simple and sensible, it felt like a breath of fresh air. Though loyal Provet customers, OVH also made up many of their own medications including a progesterone implant, which involved 'boiling the oils and adding the progesterone powder ... suspending it and putting it into bottles [to] inject into mares that weren't producing enough of their own.'

Repeatedly reinforcing attitudes turns them into habits, even when tensions are high and situations at their most dire. Veterinarians are often confronted with difficult and at times gory predicaments, and OVH was no different – in fact, Dorraine recalled, 'everything was so much more dramatic because horses would come in off the farm or whatever back 200 acres, having not been seen for months.' They would arrive with huge sticks protruding from their flesh, or sometimes with years-old foreign bodies that were working free.

Reg's stoicism and his refusal to succumb to stress in high-pressure circumstances were vital when dealing with such challenges: composure begets composure. It was reassuring for junior staff when even the most serious and graphic cases were met with Reg's customary impassivity. Dorraine had that lesson reinforced numerous times. The most striking example was that of an unfortunate horse who arrived with extensive superficial damage to its torso. Trying to clear a fence, the animal had caught its chest on a post, peeling the skin away from between its front legs and along its belly in a bloody sheet a metre long. Unperturbed, OVH staff swiftly secured the horse in the stocks before grabbing a couple of chairs and starting to drain the wound. Reg, clad in coveralls over his pyjamas, took a seat and set to stitching the skin back together. It might have been a rent tablecloth for all the agitation he showed. The moral was clear: panic only exacerbated a bad situation; serene confidence redeemed it.

'There'd be people who'd come once a year with one horse,' Dorraine recalled with amazement. 'They would come the night before and camp out and they would have a little pick-up truck or a little ute with [rails] on the side to keep the horse in. Or an old trailer and they would just unload the horse and have the horse tied out by the trailer.

They would literally camp out so that, in the morning, when Reg got there, they would be the first one to have whatever done.'

Cheryl Lopate, 1997–1998 breeding season

Twelve months after Dorraine arrived at OVH, US vet Cheryl Lopate received an email from Reg. Like Dorraine, Cheryl had just finished her residency in comparative theriogenology at Purdue University in Indiana. Would she be interested, Reg wondered, in going on sabbatical and working for a breeding season in Oakey?

The offer was tantalising so she accepted, spending six months at OVH. While her caseload was predominantly in equine reproduction, Cheryl also got to work with food production animals (a term which encompasses any animal raised for consumption by humans, such as cattle, swine and sheep) and some small animal reproduction.

Arriving in September 1997, she initially stayed with David Pascoe, but soon moved in with Jayne. They quickly became close friends. Like Sue Hollindale, Cheryl recalled occasional personality clashes among OVH staff. Reg often argued with one particular vet, 'so there was always a lot of tension when the two of them were in the building together.' Their different approaches to clinical problems inevitably led to conflict and practice politics meant the more junior vet seemed 'pretty disgruntled all the time.' Jayne recalled these encounters as far less fraught, possibly because she'd had more time to become accustomed to it, saying, '[They] would go toe to toe a lot, which was quite funny.' But Cheryl found it a difficult environment to negotiate.

She thought the other vet resented not receiving more recognition. 'It was Reg's practice,' no matter who else held a partnership in the business. The community trusted Reg, valuing his expertise and recognising him as the nucleus around which OVH centred. 'Reg was the teacher everybody went to ... [he] was the person everybody trusted.' He had worked hard to establish that trust, and the clients extended their faith to Reg's staff, knowing that if someone worked at OVH, they had passed Reg's muster and could be relied upon. 'You'd go out on a call ... and somewhere in the background,' Jayne mused, 'they assumed that Reg was there.'

Some clients, however, were less respectful of the practice than others. While Reg might demand their courtesy, they could be snappish and intolerant of the staff – something Reg had no patience for. When one client continually antagonised the team in the late 1990s, Reg took him in hand. 'Look,' he said bluntly, 'you can't treat everybody like this. You have to sort yourself out or we're not going to be able to do your work.' It was typical of his approach, direct and clear-cut. There could be no misunderstanding how Reg expected OVH clients to deal with his people. And it was effective. 'At the end,' Cheryl remembered, 'the guy was so apologetic, he was almost hugging us. You could see him falling over himself because he didn't want to lose the vet clinic.'

Cheryl's experience at OVH was rewarding, but it was also challenging.

She arrived in Australia having just finished the American breeding season and quickly found herself in deep water, performing the work of two people. 'Everyone was working such long hours, and everyone was so tired all the time.' Reg 'was always trying to make everyone laugh and keep it fun ... if there wasn't anybody to try and lighten things up, we would have all gone crazy. He was very serious about his medicine, but he was very good at keeping everyone from being mad; he could always dissipate any kind of anger or anxiety in a room.' He seemed to be everywhere, capable of doing anything and doing it well. 'Reg was always smiling and was always willing to help in any way that he could no matter where it was in the hospital.'

In the busiest season for equine reproductive vets, a challenging workload could be intensified by shifting schedules and staffing issues. Reg and Joy did what they could. Often when Cheryl drove up to the practice late at night, they'd invite her in for supper. 'I spent a lot of time with them after long days,' she recalled. 'They really made it liveable for me.' And Reg helped with ongoing patient management that otherwise might have overwhelmed her

Still, by the end of her time at OVH, Cheryl was exhausted. 'It was a really stressful time for me,' she said. Grateful for Reg's kindness and his help, Cheryl offered no criticism of him, though she perhaps could have done so; the staffing problems that made her experience an abnormally punishing were Reg's responsibility.

Reg was as Cheryl noted 'truly the centre of the clinic.' She recalled that Reg 'had a tremendous influence on me. I could not have asked for a more intensive learning experience after just finishing my residency ... I honed tons of my skills during [those] six months and became a better veterinarian ... he was always there to answer my questions and help me push through.' Reg passed on his belief in the journey of problem solving, using what you knew to discover an answer rather than prescriptively applying rules to unknown situations. 'He always helped your thought process to get you where you needed to go. Even though he sometimes didn't know the answer, he helped you find your way to the answer.' During one of the most frenetic periods of her professional life, Cheryl credited Reg with holding her together. 'He was my stabilising force.'

Debbie Dennien, OVH client

Reg's manner was often blunt and could come across as unfeeling, but he always balanced this with kindness. He had a deep well of compassion for people, as well as the animals they brought to him for treatment, and his love of dogs like Middy and Sassy never allowed him to forget the bonds that existed between people and their animals. His was a kindness, however, that never obscured the truth and while he strove to achieve the best outcome for the animal, that wasn't always what the client wanted. But he never lost sight of his priority. His capacity for balancing these two aspects of his profession – caring for the client and caring for the animal – touched those who witnessed it and is among his greatest legacies.

Debbie Dennien was an OVH client for several years and recalled Reg as someone who 'was very straight down the line and had the reputation of being grumpy and non-caring ... [but] anyone who knew him knew he was a super vet.' She had sent a few of her horses to Reg by way of her local vet when her family decided to get one of their horses in foal. At fourteen, the mare, who the family used for pony club, was beautiful and much-loved. She had never been in foal before, but it all seemed to go smoothly. The foal was born without complication, a lovely filly that was everything Debbie and her family had been hoping for. Then, seemingly out of nowhere, the filly got sick. Frightened and distressed, Debbie rang OVH.

'[Reg] didn't pander to people because it was their baby ... He wasn't mean, by any stretch of the imagination, he was just factual. And in stressful situations with an animal that you adore, factual isn't always as well-accepted as it could be.' Candid, but never cruel. Faced with Debbie's fear, Reg listened and gave his assessment before instructing her to call back in a couple of hours. When she did, he explained the problem and prepared her for what was to come. 'He didn't give me any airs: "Oh it might live, it mightn't live." He said, "It'll die."'

As the filly lay dying with her head in Debbie's lap, the woman cradled the cordless phone to her ear and Reg helped her through the devastating loss. Still emotional at the memory years later, Debbie said, 'All those people who said he was grumpy and mean – he wasn't. He was just wonderful ... He was really caring and he was really clever.'

Reg's treatment of Debbie, a microcosm of thousands of professional relationships throughout his career, displays the fundamental equity of his relationships – his leadership was not limited to surgical techniques, clinical research efforts, nor even his personal and professional integrity. It was about treating everyone with the care and compassion they deserved.

Part VI — Winding Down

15
Retirement

The first decade of the 2000s saw Reg's gradual withdrawal from professional practice and a reduction in his industry commitments as he prepared for retirement. For half a century, he had dedicated himself to his profession. His career had been wildly successful, glittering with numerous prestigious awards. In 1986 he received the AVA's highest honour, the Gilruth Prize, but between 1987 and 1988, he was recognised at the highest levels not only by the industry, but by the nation at large.

In 1987, he received an Order of Australia. A newspaper article recorded that, 'He paid special tribute to the help and support of his wife Joy and regarded his award more as a combined effort, as without her continuous support he would not have been able to accomplish many of the tasks which have made his life in Oakey so enjoyable.' The same year, he received the AEVA's inaugural VMS Award for Excellence in Veterinary Medicine. This was replicated in 1988, which also saw the somewhat belated arrival of a letter from the University of Sydney's Post-Graduate Foundation. 'At the Annual General Meeting in 1987 the Post-Graduate Committee took the decision to make an award titled "The T. G. Hungerford Award for Excellence in Post-Graduate Education" to recognise the contributions of individuals to the field of postgraduate veterinary science. It is my great pleasure to advise you that following the evaluation of nominations received you have been awarded the inaugural T. G. Hungerford Award for 1987.' The letter went on to say, 'Your contribution to postgraduate education in Australia and overseas is unsurpassed by any veterinarian in this country and your support and guidance of the Post-Graduate Committee is deeply appreciated, not only by the Committee itself, but by the thousands of veterinarians who benefit year by year from contributions such as your own.'

A decade later, Reg was recognised with another slew of awards in a short period of time. In 1997, he received the Rural Industries Research and Development Corporation (RIRDC) annual Vetsearch Major Industry Award, which emphasised his ongoing global contribution across numerous spheres. The award drew attention to his groundbreaking work with Derek Knottenbelt, noting, 'In 1993 [Reg] published with his co-author Derek Knottenbelt the *Colour Atlas of Diseases and Disorders of the Horse*. This is the most comprehensive pictorial list of equine diseases ever produced and has become a valuable teaching resource in veterinary schools throughout the world.' Then, in 1999, Reg was named a life member and patron of the Queensland Horse Council and the first Festival of the Horse was held in the state. It is apt that, as part of the celebrations, Reg was among the inaugural inductees into the Queensland Equine Hall of Fame – alongside that other renowned Oakey son, the famous stallion Bernborough.

In 2001, the EVA once more awarded Reg the VMS Award for Excellence in Veterinary Medicine, while the Queensland division of the AVA recognised his years of tireless work with a distinguished service award. He was also honoured by the Queensland branch of the Australian Council of Professions as their Queensland Professional of the Year, an award that recognised exemplary service to the community at any level. It was a fitting conclusion to his work and timely as Reg began to farewell his beloved profession.

But it was by no means a straightforward process: retiring from active practice was one of the biggest challenges he ever faced. More than one OVH staff member struggled to define *when*, precisely, Reg quit practising – certainly, there was no official farewell like those that had been held for countless staff members over the decades. Rather, Reg's retirement was the gradual disentangling of every fibre of his being that had for so long been intertwined with the Oakey Veterinary Hospital. In 2001, he retired as principal and director, passing the shared responsibility reins to the partners ready to succeed him.

It was a decision many believed he made reluctantly, though few were privy to his deliberations. Vic Menrath recalled Reg's distress at leaving behind the organisation he had poured so much of his soul into. 'He was tough, and he was used to being in control,' Vic said. So used to it, in fact, that he had 'never been *out* of control', and handing over as director required just that: surrender. Remembering their conversations, Vic described Reg being 'pushed aside' by the new, younger partners, but while Reg may have expressed frustration and sadness about relinquishing his role as director, it's more likely that he saw it as the inevitable decline of age rather than being deliberately ousted. He dominated OVH's surgeries and this, certainly, was subject to the challenges of ageing: his hands were not as steady as they once had been, the fine motor control gradually slipping away.

Reg's resignation from surgery was tied into his transition of the hospital's directorship; if he had to leave the surgery he loved, perhaps he thought it best to also cede control of the hospital's oversight. That his staff struggled to nominate precisely when he finished practising was, then, likely due to two factors. The first was that he remained involved with the University of Queensland's Equine Teaching Unit at OVH for another two years after transferring the directorship, and this would have necessitated his ongoing presence around the hospital. The second was that living so close to OVH blurred the lines. 'He was just up the hill,' Sue Hollindale said, and 'he'd wander down whenever he sort of felt like it. It was still his property; he still owned the buildings of the vet hospital.' Reg could often be found strolling the grounds with his golden Labrador Sassy, his continued presence inescapable and undeniable, even as he slowly extricated himself.

The original OVH partnership trio had begun to dissolve with David Laws's retirement in 1998. His son Glen, who had known the Pascoes his whole life, returned from four years in the UK to buy his father's share in the business. It felt natural to Glen: much of his childhood had been spent running around OVH with Reg and Joy's second-youngest son Roess, who was his best friend. Glen had worked in the practice in the late 1980s, performing the anaesthetics for most of Reg's surgeries, and he understood Reg's temperament very well. Meanwhile, David Pascoe had been a partner since 1989 and there was a third vet, a surgeon called Steve Rayner, waiting to buy Reg out when the time came, though Paul Green remained at

OVH until 2009. These vets, it seemed, would split the management. Ostensibly, Reg was leaving the practice on solid footings for the future.

There were five different operational branches within OVH at the time of Reg's retirement. Steve managed surgeries, David oversaw equine reproduction, and Glen handled the hospital's racehorse track commitments, while the small animal practice and the general farming clients fell within the remit of other vets. Under Reg's direction, these distinct sections had functioned as a unified hospital, but there were cracks and Reg's retirement saw the entity fracture.

'After he left, there was virtually no boss,' remembered Sue Hollindale, who was at OVH during this period. With no principal director holding everyone together, the vets splintered into the various functional elements of the clinic. It was one of Reg's weaknesses that despite all his business acumen, he didn't ensure a robust enough succession plan to survive his retirement. 'He probably didn't imagine that [deterioration of OVH following his retirement] would ever happen – he built an amazing practice, an amazing reputation.' He was so central to operations that his departure was crippling. 'People didn't say: "If you've got a problem, go to Oakey." People said, "Go to *Pascoe*." That's a big difference.'[29]

Veterinary science had been Reg's life, his passion and his calling for half a century and ending the clinical chapter was difficult. Still, his mind remained sharp and for almost a decade after leaving he channelled his energies into other aspects of veterinary science.

Of course, the momentous change of life offered possibilities too. Faced with the open road and the long-awaited opportunity to travel without any real commitments, Reg and Joy pursued their desire to see more of Australia. But even in retirement, Reg didn't truly slow down – he and Joy bought a 28-foot motorhome in 2000 and planned out their adventures. Of course, his ties to his beloved profession remained strong. As they travelled, he wrote various papers that Joy typed up for him; intermittently, he flew out from one city or another to attend conferences or meetings, such as those for the NVE. On other occasions, they drove across Australia for veterinary conventions, living in the motorhome as they went.

Joy recalled travelling to the Northern Tablelands of New England in New South Wales. Here she came to grips with their new 'steed', fondly dubbed 'Swag' or 'Swaggie.' 'Our first outing was to friends on a cattle station west of Stonehenge where I thought I could get some driving experience in open country,' she recalled, 'having had to study to upgrade my licence: Reg always had a truck licence. My first lesson was when we left.' Everything was fine 'until we had to cross on a wooden bridge over a dry creek. I freaked: "I can't do this." The lord and master said, "Just line it up and drive." Swag and I managed but the adrenalin was flowing.'

A friend somewhat hyperbolically described the succession of Pascoe vehicles as: 'first up about 30 foot (minimum) and then it was 40 and then it was 50. [Joy] finally drew the line,' but Reg threw himself into the mastery of each new vehicle with unparalleled enthusiasm ... though of course, there were some incidents along the way.

Once while attending a conference in Rockhampton, Reg demonstrated the motorhome's controls to David Johnson. After putting the vehicle in reverse to show the rear camera capability, they went to look at the rest of the living quarters when David felt an unexpected shift underfoot. 'Reg, I think we're moving!' he yelled. Reg had taken the handbrake off and forgotten to put it back on. As they started rolling down the hill in the hotel carpark, Reg raced back to the driver's seat to slam his foot on the brake. 'We didn't hit anything,' David remembered, 'but it was quite funny.' On another occasion, Reg and Joy dropped in to see Reg's old friend Vic Menrath in Brisbane, but navigating the narrow backstreets was challenging and they got lost ... and accidentally collected several letterboxes on the way.

When the Bain Fallon was held in Darwin in 2004, a fellow vet coordinated a three-night 'camping' trip around Kakadu. Reg's friend Chris Johnson recalled that Reg, then in his mid-seventies, still seemed indefatigable. He was 'amazingly active': faced with waterfalls in Kakadu, he climbed to the top and took the chance to swim in a waterhole they found along the way.

Increased leisure time allowed Reg to indulge his lifelong interest in Australian flora and native birds: he loved birdwatching and identifying different species, an interest he sought to pass on to his sons during their childhood. While they were in Kakadu, Chris remembered that the group would be walking, and Reg would be pointing out all the plants he recognised, taking countless photos as he went. His loves of photography and of native wildlife colliding, his personal slide collection grew to gargantuan proportions. And, on the rare occasions when he wasn't sure about a plant or a bird, he was more than happy to ask his network for help. Chris Johnson was out on her station one night when the phone rang. 'What noise does a brolga make?' came Reg's voice. Spending the night somewhere out in the middle of Australia, he and Joy had heard a noise.

'Hang on,' Chris answered, unfazed by the strange request. Moments later, she had her husband doing his best to imitate a brolga, the hoarse cry echoing throughout their home into the darkness.

Though Reg and Joy owned the 'Swaggie' for several years, it spent much of that period sitting at the bottom of the orchard. Reg's commitment to the ETU consumed more of his time than he anticipated, and he later confided to a friend that he regretted not doing as much travel in the motorhome as he would have liked.

Reg's lifelong dedication to community service continued during this period of 'semi-retirement.' He believed that the privileged social and professional positions he had attained by dint of hard work and determination conveyed a responsibility to use those advantages for the benefit of others. This philosophy underpinned his community work throughout his life. He was actively involved in the Lions Club, the Oakey State School P&C Committee, and the Oakey chapters of the Freemasons, all of which was in support of the underprivileged and less fortunate, or the improvement of living conditions for the small rural town.

His local involvement began with his son John's entry into Oakey State School, when 'obviously recalling his own attendance there during the period in which his father, Vyvyan Pascoe was headmaster' Reg joined the P&C committee. He served for ten years, and during his term as chair, spearheaded the establishment of a volunteer-operated school tuck shop as well as numerous fancy dress balls and an annual school picnic.

Despite his many professional commitments, Reg always

supported both his sons and the community they grew up in. He was often to be found in his workshop of a weekend, building or repairing a piece of equipment for the hospital. If Reg and Joy's youngest son Andrew came looking for his dad, Reg would point him towards the other end of the bandsaw. 'Grab the other end of that timber there – no, there. Hold it still. No, still; I mean *really* still. Okay, got that? Watch your hand, you'll lose a finger.'

It was the kind of environment where there was always something going on and always something for the boys to be doing. If they ever came to him asking for an amusement or a job, and sometimes even when they didn't, Reg could find a task that required willing young hands. And, rather than being a chore, Andrew remembered these occasions fondly. The tasks Reg divvied out were usually engaging because he 'always made things seem interesting. You learnt things; he taught you jobs and skills', in much the same way as Vyvyan had sought to teach Reg when he was a boy. Sometimes Reg would supervise; other times he would detail how the job was to be done and then vanish, leaving his sons to ensure it was complete. 'Reg did play a very big part in the boys' lives,' Andrew Dart recalled. 'He was treasurer of the school and was in the local community and ... contributed in a lot of other ways too to the benefit of the boys.'

In 1964, Reg was a charter member when the Lions Club of Oakey was established. 'In those years, members came from business and farming; wives became members of the Lions Ladies for companionship and fundraising, as did the men,' Joy recalled. She shared her husband's passion for community service and became a member of the Lions Ladies around the same time. Over Reg's decades of involvement, he undertook stints as president, secretary a few times, and treasurer. He was serving in the latter role when the two Lions' branches banded together to build the Oakey kindergarten that Joy had dreamt of years earlier. Joy and two other women had recognised the need for a kindergarten and, 'with help from a retired young schoolteacher, began in a local hall with meagre equipment' in 1963. Joy remembered that when the kindy 'was officially opened in February 1966 by the Minister of Education, Sir Alan Fletcher' she was handed the keys as president. Not only that, the 'Oakey Lions Club received the District Governors Award for the project.'

All four of Reg and Joy's sons progressed through the scouting movement in Oakey, which led to Joy's involvement in committee meetings, fundraising activities and many bottle drives. It shows the power of their parents' example in leading John, David, Roess and Andrew to similarly value community service. Joy's twenty years of work with the Oakey & District Arts Council (affiliated with Queensland Arts Council), helped to bring the broader arts to regional and remote communities. She wanted to promote culture in Oakey regardless of the challenges of rural life and Reg supported her wherever he could, even selling tickets at performances 'with a reputation that patrons seldom escaped.'

The district appreciated these efforts and was proud to lay claim to Reg and his successes. In 2000, he was awarded an Oakey and District Community 'Certificate of Recognition' which acknowledged his 'attainment of a standard of excellence within the field of Veterinary Science' that had brought him international recognition. 'We are proud of you and your accomplishments!' the certificate proclaimed. The following year, for the 2001 Centenary of Federation exhibition at Parliament House, the 'People Scape' artwork created by the Oakey Art Group also celebrated Reg. It stated: 'Reg Pascoe has over the years devoted much time and effort to community organisations and projects and has demonstrated that worthwhile achievements can and do evolve in rural areas.'

Less well-known however was Reg's work with the Freemasons. He was never a particularly religious man but he found spiritual succour in the fraternal association that he first joined in 1958 at the age of twenty-nine. A diverse organisation with many different orders, the Freemasons originated in Great Britain, where the first 'grand lodge' was established in the early eighteenth century. Reg's father, Vyvyan, had been a Freemason and it's likely Reg's participation stemmed from this.

Oakey's Freemasons comprise two different branches: the Ashlar Lodge, also known as the 'Craft' or 'Blue Lodge' because members wear blue aprons; and the Oakey Royal Arch Chapter, also known as the 'Red Lodge.' Reg appears to have been involved with both – records indicate that he was initiated into the Ashlar Lodge on 13 June 1958 while he joined the Royal Arch chapter on 9 November

1959. He rapidly progressed through several Freemasonry 'degrees' over a two-year period, but struggled to continue his involvement as OVH grew increasingly busy. He eventually realised one had to cede to the other and stopped attending Red Lodge meetings in 1961, and Blue Lodge meetings sometime in 1966, the same year he was awarded, for his service to the lodge and community, 'the Life Governor Jewel.' It was not until forty years later, after he retired from OVH in 2001, that he returned to actively participating in Oakey's Freemasonry chapters. The energy that had sustained and propelled him through his career for over fifty years languished following his retirement – the Freemasons offered a path by which he could invest himself constructively and continue his contribution to the community.

In 2007, he completed his final degrees in Royal Arch Masonry and belatedly received his forty-year jewel (which he had qualified for in 1998), then his fifty-year jewel. He was invested as treasurer of the Blue Lodge, then elected as one of the three Blue Lodge trustees; two years later, he was invested as secretary, and held all three positions until his death in 2017. Besides these roles, he sought ways to develop the chapter, initiating projects including the installation of solar panels, which saved the organisation thousands of dollars.

Reg became president of the Red Lodge in 2010. The chapter's secretary, Colin Currie, recalled that he 'soon learnt that with Reg, when I was going to do something, I would do it as I said I would, not when I felt like it.' In this facet of life, however, Reg was 'a behind the scenes person', Colin noted, doing a great deal 'for Masonry in Oakey without much fuss.' Reg oversaw the lodges' ongoing operations, a job that was detailed and time-consuming. He continually appraised the lodge's condition and coordinated maintenance. When major renovations were needed, he 'was the driving force in organising architectural plans, building quotes, and numerous other details.'

Reg's love of woodworking saw him create many pieces expressly for the lodge. Joy recalled him 'building new forms for seating/storage, making shelving for members' bags' as well as 'two magnificent chairs for the master and another VIP. These are much appreciated and admired by members and visitors alike.'

Reg's sons knew little of his involvement with the Freemasons. They remembered his habitual black-tie weekend meetings, but the only time Andrew asked about the Freemasons, Reg was closemouthed. He never asked his sons to carry on his work and, much later when he approached several of his grandsons to the same end, Reg's reasoning was simple. By the time he thought to offer membership to his sons, he told his grandson, they all had young families of their own and he didn't want them to feel pressured or expected to take up his mantle, when their children were more important.

2016. Reg enjoying time with sons Roess (left) and John (right).

Jane Axon, delivering the Reg Pascoe Peroration in 2018, reminded her audience that, 'Although Dr Pascoe was an internationally renowned veterinarian, he remained devoted to his local community on Queensland's Darling Downs and family. He had a well-balanced life ... He was president and a charter member of the Oakey Lions Club and actively involved in the Oakey kindergarten and state school. In his later years, he joined the protest to protect the Downs from inappropriate mining. At the age of eighty-two, he took his place on an anti-mining protest line, in freezing mid-winter rain, placard in hand fighting to protect one of the nation's great food bowls. What a great inspiring man!'

Formed in 2011 in response to the expansion of the New Acland Coal Mine (an open-cut coal mine owned by the New Hope Group that began operating in 2002), the Oakey Coal Action Alliance (OCAA) is a group of farmers and community members from Oakey and surrounding townships. Reg joined as secretary upon the group's establishment and filled this position for several years, speaking to anyone who would listen about the horrific long-term effects of mining on Darling Downs farmland. He died before the protracted and painful legal battle between OCAA and the New Hope Group had reached any kind of satisfying conclusion, but he would have been gratified with its eventual outcome: in February 2021, the High Court ruled that there be a fresh Land Court hearing into the expansion. It was a huge victory for the OCAA and the local agricultural communities.

Reg, camera always to hand, pausing to pet some wallabies.

Reg's devotion to bettering his local environment was partially responsible for the fact that his true 'retirement' from veterinary science was both a long time in coming and drawn out, even half-hearted in execution. It was only after he turned eighty in 2009 that he began to consider signing off from some of the organisations in which he was still involved, such as the National Veterinary Exam (NVE). He'd worked with the NVE for almost three decades and had been at the helm for two-thirds of that time.

When considering his replacement, his eye fell upon Leo Jeffcott. A British expat who had been dean of the University of Sydney's Veterinary School since 2004, Leo and Reg first met in Newmarket in 1968 during Reg's international study trip. Leo's ascension to dean, however, had brought the two men into more regular contact. Though Leo recalled with amusement that they 'certainly had some fiery times', they generally worked well together, theirs a relationship characterised by mutual respect. As Reg prepared to leave the board, he contacted Leo about taking over as NVE chair, despite Leo's unabashed scepticism about the exam's legitimacy. In Leo's eyes, applying for the position of chair was last on his list of good ideas.

Reg had always been forthright in his intent for the organisation during his tenure as chair. He believed the exam's quality meant it should be a compulsory benchmark assessment for *all* Australian veterinarians, even if they'd completed their tertiary studies in Australia. Leo thought this idea was shaped by Reg's awareness of what was happening in the US, given his eldest son John Pascoe had worked since 1976 at the University of California, Davis. That every veterinarian in the US must, without exception, pass the National Veterinary Licensing Exam (the NAVLE) to practise may have influenced Reg's belief that Australia's NVE should be similarly universal. Certainly, the US provided a useful blueprint for the creation of the EVA and had informed Reg's efforts to form Australia's National Horse Council ... but it's also possible that this had little impact on his thinking, since the NAVLE is solely a computer-based MCQ without any practical component, very different to the multi-part, highly practical NVE.

Regardless of the origins of Reg's belief, Leo vehemently disagreed. As dean, he saw Reg's wish for the NVE as merely adding further administration and cost to veterinary qualification in Australia, a perception strong enough to make the idea of taking over as chair unpalatable. Leo never changed his mind about making the NVE compulsory for Australian-educated vets, but he also knew that if he *did* become chair, he wasn't honour-bound to Reg's idea. The more he considered the position, the more it appealed. He applied and was successful, succeeding Reg in 2010.

Whether Reg saw the import of this transition is unlikely – grandstanding was never his style – but his long-lasting influence on the NVE is undeniable. As of 2021, his desire for a national benchmark exam for all vets has not happened, and likely never will. Reg's reasoning was sound, Leo noted, but the time, cost and energy required made it untenable, and he didn't pursue it once he became chair. Since Reg's retirement, however, the NVE has developed to encompass New Zealand, the AVBC administering the Australasian Veterinary Examination (AVE) to assess the competencies of internationally qualified vets looking to practise in either Australia or New Zealand.

The ongoing evolution of the NVE was a communal effort by the board members, who worked hard to develop the exam to meet changing times and changing needs. Reg would have been the first to say so. Yet his contribution was critical and, like his fellow board members, given freely without expectation of recompense. Julie Strous, executive director of the AVBC, emphasised how important it was for Reg to not just contribute to, but to chair the NVE board for so long. 'Someone of his calibre, who could have been making a lot of cash – he put that into giving back. That's something quite special about Reg and it's really something that's changed significantly in the profession since we lost him.' In farewell, the AVBC recognised Reg with a special award, writing: 'The Australian Veterinary Boards Council is deeply appreciative of the time, energy, expertise, guidance and thoughtful contributions [Reg] has brought to the Board of Examiners as the foundation chair and to the running of the NVE. His expertise, experience, wit and good humour will be greatly missed on the board.' At its core, the widespread success of the NVE owes much to Reg's tireless work, a legacy that continues to maintain the standards of veterinary practice he believed were so paramount for the wellbeing of vets, clients and animals alike.

For a time, OVH carried on after Reg's retirement as it always had.

Paul Green remained until 2009 and as the senior partner, was both a valuable source of management continuity and a steadying influence among the new partners. The ETU continued until UQ opened its new Gatton Veterinary School in 2010; although all student training moved to the new facility, OVH continued to support the school with lectures and tutorials. The hospital was further expanded and in a 2010 update to his record of OVH's development, Reg recorded that stage eight in 2006 saw a sizeable addition to the 'Repro Barn' for lecture space. Two additional exam crushes were added and there were two large mare stables and several smaller adjacent holding yards. Three years later, stage nine saw further reproduction facilities added or enhanced: there was a new covered semen collection area and semen laboratory, four stallion stables and a feed and tack room. A total of thirty-three new yards were added: six stallion yards intended for isolating animals prior to semen export, and twenty-seven mare holding yards for breeding. OVH was shifting its focus – or perhaps simply time, space and money – towards equine reproduction, David Pascoe's passion.

In 2010, just after Paul Green's retirement, OVH was operating at full throttle: Reg's notes show that there were eight veterinarians and seven total vet nurses on staff, including two trainees.

Underneath this veneer, however, something was simmering.

Perhaps Paul's retirement removed the last remaining steadying hand on the tiller, or the final tangible reminder of the 'old guard' and the legacy Reg, David Laws and Paul had left the three junior partners. Perhaps some resented the clinic's move towards equine reproduction, potentially at the cost of other work ... or perhaps it was simply that Reg had been the heart and soul, the creator and driver of the Oakey Veterinary Hospital, and without him it was never going to be the same.

Regardless, tensions between David, Steve and Glen reached boiling point. Then they erupted. The details of what followed are vague: no one who was involved, either directly or peripherally, cared to discuss it. What *is* known is that the partnership crumbled; Glen and Steve left to open their own practice and in 2016, David and his wife Heather became the outright owners of OVH.

It must have been torturous for Reg. He was intensely loyal and he loved his sons deeply … but watching the gradual disintegration of the world that he had so painstakingly nurtured for decades would have been very hard. He must have felt the urge to step in and arrest the fall, but he didn't. Maybe he realised that, fundamentally, he could not. He had left and retired; he couldn't spin the hands of the clock back and return. The pieces had to be allowed to fall as they would.

In 2022, the Oakey Veterinary Hospital is a different place to what it once was. Myriad challenges have beset the Australian horse industry in the past twenty years. The early 2010s were characterised by Australian breeders, vets and horse lovers struggling with the aftershocks of the Global Financial Crisis, devastation wrought by the deadly Hendra virus, and competition from coal mining interests for prime agricultural land. More recently, fodder shortages caused by extended drought and poor crop yields have strained breeders and undercut breeding programs around the country. It's been a hard slog, and remains a harsh world in which to toil.

Still, the OVH persists – horse people in rural Queensland still 'take them to Pascoe.' And as Christmas lights bedeck houses in the fierce summer months, leggy foals in the OVH mare yards peek shyly around their mothers; sidling away from the shelter of the mares' broad backs, they cavort in the sunshine.

It's a different place but, at its heart, it's still the one Reg loved best.

16
A Lasting Legacy

Reg's legacy – and the lessons that can be learnt from a life so well-lived – extend far beyond what is readily visible. As a vet, he had a colossal impact both in Australia and abroad. As a father and husband, he helped raise four happy and successful sons. As an Oakey local, he served and shaped his community.

But he achieved so much more beyond just this.

Human beings are not single stars, but galaxies of light and space, containing vast swirling multitudes – both magnificent and humbling. In his homily to Reg, broadcaster Alan Jones described him by saying, 'This is one of the great Australians. A pioneering Australian ... [who possessed] an unyielding humanity and humility about the way in which he discharged all his responsibilities towards his community, towards his family, and towards his own profession.' Reg's life is more than just the story of a successful vet. It is the intricate and beautiful tale of a giant of a man who, as a seventeen-year-old boy opening a letter that was not meant for him, tentatively conceived an implausible dream. Despite the obstacles thrown into his path, he pursued that dream for the remainder of his life and made it a glorious triumph.

Reg came from humble beginnings. His father Vyvyan, like his father before him, was a schoolteacher, then later a dairy farmer. Like many women of the time, Reg's mother Milly had her own professional aspirations quashed and devoted herself to her family. While the Pascoes believed in education, this referred to a certain kind and a certain trajectory: a teacher, Vyvyan could understand. Teachers trained through state-funded colleges, usually a year or so of practical experience. This shifted towards a three-year university degree in the 1950s, but veterinary science was an entirely different matter. It must have seemed to Vyvyan and Milly like another universe. Although they were fortunate to inherit Reg's childhood home, Schoenberg, from his maternal grandfather, the family didn't have much money. Then there were the privations of the Great Depression and the Second World War, as well as the devastating loss of Reg's adored elder brother, Roess, when Reg was only thirteen. Such experiences were the norm – common in a way that many readers in the twenty-first century might struggle to comprehend – but that does not diminish how they shaped those who lived through them, particularly members of the 'Silent Generation' like Reg and Joy.

That Reg entered a Bachelor of Veterinary Science at the University of Queensland in 1947 was as much about luck as good management. Had that fateful, misdelivered letter not arrived in Schoenberg's mailbox; had the Toowoomba City Council chief engineer not taken the time to listen to a seventeen-year-old applicant; and had the kind-hearted official not recognised Reg could qualify for a hardship scholarship ... Reg's life would certainly have been different. But once he received that opportunity, he committed himself to it wholeheartedly. It must have been daunting, leaving the quiet open spaces of Schoenberg for Brisbane and a new path about which he had virtually no understanding – and yet Reg, as he did so often throughout his life, simply steeled himself and got on with it.

His university years, coming as they did after the Second World War and in an important period of growth for Queensland tertiary education, witnessed big changes in veterinary science. These years influenced Reg's beliefs about his profession and his own interests, as well as the importance of veterinary education; that his was the first year to remain in Brisbane for the full duration of their BVSc seems only fitting.

During this period Reg met Joy: his true and unwavering partner in every venture, and the love of his life.

Reg and Joy shared a beautiful, enduring partnership for over 65 years.

Their move back to Oakey and establishment of Reg's first small clinic in the garage of their house – to which Joy's practical support was essential – brought new challenges. Reg found himself confronted by rural communities who had no faith in his skills, didn't believe those skills were necessary, and mistrusted his presence almost on principle. At the age of twenty-two, a new professional, he was alone and yet, this too, did not sway him. Though he must have experienced doubts and frustrations, he continued to move steadfastly onwards. Leaping at the chance to take on the Department of Primary Industries' contract to test cattle for tuberculosis meant a steady income and, more importantly, it gave him an incontestable reason to work with the region's farmers and allowed him to build trust.

The 1957 addition of Reg's first equine clients was monumental. No less so was the acquisition, that same year, of a dry hilly paddock on Hamlyn Road on the outskirts of Oakey. Reg and Joy spent three years transforming that barren block: fencing and bulldozing and drilling a bore for water, and surviving the cold, draughty blue shed that provided both practice and home until their own house could be built. Managing the emerging veterinary clinic and a family of four young boys was the definition of tenacity. They found pride and fulfilment in the work which, at its core, was about creating something from nothing and serving the community. This extended to supporting UQ vet students conducting 'seeing practice', an activity that brought David Laws, then later Paul Green, into the OVH partnership trio that steered the clinic for almost sixty years. Whatever he created, Reg wanted it to be the best. He developed OVH with passion and determination, travelling overseas to observe the best equine hospitals in the world and to continually extend his own knowledge, testing new ideas and pushing the boundaries.

The pursuit of excellence was complemented by Reg's irrepressible curiosity. This resulted in remarkable scientific accomplishments: confronted by a problem or a mysterious condition, he was driven to find an answer. The upshot was an array of important equine medicine developments across a broad swathe of specialities. He investigated, often with revolutionary outcomes, equine virology, dermatology, surgery and reproduction, and his effect on how various conditions were understood and approached was profound. His inquiring mind propelled him forward and there was nothing beyond his remit or unworthy of his energies. But he didn't dabble. Rather, his hard work delivered across a range of fields at levels comparable to specialists who dedicate their entire careers to a single arena. He was, essentially, a veterinary virtuoso. His friend Patricia Ellis eloquently encapsulated this. 'Reg really was a Leonardo – clinician, academic, teacher, leader, visionary, and more.'

It was a marker of his influence that Reg was able to achieve such success and renown in such a remote location. What he created in Oakey – a small, rural Queensland town that few beyond the region had ever heard of – was a world-class hospital to which people would truck their horses from around the country. At the forefront of equine veterinary science for decades, the Oakey Veterinary Hospital was a locus of influence and esteem within the Australian industry and it provided an important contribution to Australian veterinary science.

Such an impact resulted, at least in part, from Reg's perspicacity. He had an uncanny ability to imagine new ways of doing things, ideas that he pursued with a formidable resolve until he had either exhausted all possible avenues, or proven that his plan was not only achievable, but superior. On countless occasions, he encountered extremely complex, clinically ambiguous cases. And on countless occasions, he achieved groundbreaking outcomes. Just as importantly, he propagated his methods and his ideas so that they permeated throughout the veterinary profession.

These abilities made him a legend, but he never disavowed the price of achieving success, and his honesty provided rare insight into the full scope of those costs. When one day an ETU student marvelled to Reg, 'You've done so much. You've saved a lot of horses,' Reg's reply was grave. 'Mate,' he said sombrely, 'I've killed a lot of horses as well.' Success came from repeated failures, but it only came because he accepted those failures as part of the process. He was brave enough to try things, even if they might not succeed.

Reg's participation in founding and nurturing Australian veterinary organisations is another visible example of his impact. The dedication of years of expertise, energy and expense did not always give rise to the outcomes he had envisioned; the somewhat fragmentary and ineffective final manifestation of the Australian Horse Industry Council suggests that even the most determined and committed cannot always force their desired vision to come to fruition, particularly when the stars align against them. Yet his contributions elsewhere were manifold and effective, particularly his efforts on behalf of both the AVA and the EVA. Neither would be what they are today without the ceaseless work of Reg and others like him. His efforts in cultivating the Bain Fallon memorial lecture series helped establish it around the world as a renowned equine conference and one that played a key role in the development of countless Australian vets.

There are of course organisations in which Reg was an animating force which are now either extinct, subsumed into other bodies, or mere shadows of what they were and might have been – groups like the Australian Equine Research Foundation, the Darling Downs Equine Group, and the Queensland Horse Council. Yet though they may no longer exist, it would be a disservice to relegate them to a column of inconsequence on Reg's balance sheet; his ongoing service to these bodies provided decades of value to veterinarians.

In these arenas and others, Reg deliberately set out to use his position and his knowledge to help others succeed. Examining successful careers in retrospect, it is easy to overlook the ugly when it is outshone by accolades and attainment, but Reg had encountered formidable difficulties as a newly minted graduate. Later in life, he recalled in an interview how, as a young man, people laughed when he said that one day he'd have a five-man practice. These experiences could easily have bred bitterness. There are many accomplished individuals who believe that to earn success, others must suffer as they have. Instead, his trials instilled an unwavering conviction that he could, and must, persevere – and that he should take along on that journey as many people as were willing to follow his lead.

Reg always shared his hard-won knowledge widely. He had to be secure – in himself, in his expertise, in his professional value – to do this. Anyone less sure-footed would struggle to give without the fear of being lost in the giving. And he had to believe that others deserved these benefits without having to pay for them. By virtue of his desire to do better by the profession and by the animals they treated, Reg instinctually assumed the job of guiding his fellow veterinarians. He was a natural leader. In veterinary gatherings, he could always be relied upon as a bastion of common sense, asking the sensible questions that had been overlooked, and yet somehow also providing an alternate view that sparked innovation. In discussions, his friend Bruce Pott recalled, 'Everybody waited … to hear what Reg had to say.' If knowledge and expertise were a ladder, Reg spent his life standing on the top rung, reaching down to bring others up … and then he'd push ahead again and find a way of making another rung.

Achieving this meant looking beyond what others thought was possible: that seventeen-year-old with the capacity for huge dreams lived within him, always. His contributions demonstrate this. He wasn't an egoist: the idea on the table didn't need to be his. His work with Provet, that spectacularly successful brainchild of the Menrath brothers, Vic and Bob, proves this. Nor did he conceive of the National Veterinary Exam – a process instituted by Mike Rex, the man who less than a decade earlier had secured UQ's Professor of Veterinary Surgery position that Reg so desired. Yet he supported the NVE for almost thirty years, pouring his energies and intellect into making it the best he possibly could. And, facing UQ's inability to adequately teach equine medicine for BVSc students, Reg and UQ Veterinary School dean Keith Hughes envisioned and created the Equine Teaching Unit in Oakey. To do so was a mammoth undertaking. Reg was seventy, nearing retirement, but he didn't hesitate, because what was at stake was the education and livelihood of young Queensland vets. These endeavours, which lay far beyond Reg's core role as a veterinary practitioner, share a common characteristic which always warranted his wholesale investment: serving the industry.

Reg's accomplishments in furthering veterinary science both at home and abroad cannot be underestimated. To view them as the nucleus of his life, however, repudiates an essential truth: that it was his unshakeable ethos in all facets of his existence that distinguished him and transformed those who knew him. The drive to excel; the commitment to a life lived with integrity and with honour; the devotion to serving others; and the efforts to develop and encourage people of all backgrounds to become the best they could be ... these comprised a unique constellation of character traits whose effects were unconstrained by vocation. The consequence was that beyond the transference of clinical advancements in knowledge, surgical skills and specialised techniques, his most enduring footprint remains the impression he left on the countless people he met throughout his life – whether they were vets or not.

For some, this was direct: Reg mentored those veterinarians he recruited to OVH, as well as a number who never worked for him but whom he encountered through the Australian veterinary scene. Those students who went through the ETU during his years there in the late 1990s and early 2000s were also shaped by his clinical and scientific techniques: those are easily observable, and numerous vets point to the ways in which his fingerprints resonate in their professional lives.

Less readily seen are those who *indirectly* benefited. The scores of vets he mentored represent only a tiny percentage of the full scope of his influence. He was a fearless pioneer and though he wasn't the first or the earliest, he helped pull together what we today see as the contemporary Australian veterinary industry, particularly when it comes to horses. His broader influence is harder to quantify, but includes many textbooks translated into numerous languages and sold around the globe; worldwide networks of friends and colleagues who called on him for advice and continue to disseminate his wisdom; and lectures, papers and consultancy roles in various international institutions that have seen his knowledge proliferated many times over. 'Generations of veterinarians and those they serve will benefit from his research, great stories, and his example,' Julie Strous noted.

US vet Cheryl Lopate agreed. 'Hundreds of thousands of veterinarians have been impacted by him in so many ways. Whether you're an Australian veterinarian student or American, everyone knows the Pascoe name.'

Ironically, the likelihood of Reg himself recognising his impact was low. His friend Andrew Dart said, 'I don't think Reg ever thought what he had achieved in life or what he did was anything out of the ordinary. I think he just thought that everyone should have the opportunity and you should step up and make the most of [it] ... he thought that was just a very normal thing to do.'

Yet few could lay claim to a lasting impact as extensive or meaningful as Reg Pascoe. He led by example, demanding his high standards of no one more than himself. One result of this was that mentoring others came naturally. Veterinary science was his higher calling and he inspired others to work hard and find joy in the effort. He inspired them to strive and strive to be better than they had been before. To passionately and generously mentor others as he had so generously mentored them and to foster their own thirst for knowledge alongside a respect for and love of ongoing education. To treat people equally and well, regardless of who they were, and to give your time freely. For all his reserve, even reticence, Reg's character was a force of nature: he reached people. And he changed them.

His professional mastery gave him an authority that's been felt throughout the decades and across the generations. They called him 'God' with awe and respect, for who else reached down from on high and laid his enduring mark on them? He never underestimated the power that came with this, nor his responsibility to deploy it judiciously and with integrity. Honesty was his watchword. Even when it might not be well-received, he maintained a personal code of integrity that he refused to compromise. This guidance was often brusque, delivered with a characteristic gruffness; even those who remember Reg with fondness would never deny he could be irascible.

Reg expected, even demanded, that others hold the truth in similarly high regard. Actively condemning unethical or borderline practices, he was a fierce defender of Australian equine standards. His beliefs about the quality of research and the ethics that underpinned everyday practice elevated the acceptable standard.

The lessons he'd learnt as a child during the Great Depression and the hard years following it never left him. He came from a time when people didn't have much, but what they had, they shared: the only way to survive was to pull together. That trait had been carved so deeply in his bones that it permeated everything he did.

Considering the role of the horse in Australian history, author Cameron Forbes mused, 'The tale of the horse in this country is sometimes cruel, sometimes heroic, sometimes simply a series of dull and dutiful events, but the horse's input has been an uncomplaining constant, a sentient subtext, a contribution for which we ought all feel a little tug of gratitude and wonder.' In a similar way, Reg Pascoe was a constant in the industry. He was imperfect, as all people are, and this imperfection meant there were more than a few who thought him arrogant, even unfeeling. His social reticence meant he could be terse, though more often he is remembered for his kindness and generosity. Much of his most meaningful work came about after decades of quiet, seemingly ordinary labour to reach the flashpoint of discovery or triumph. These various aspects of his character created something unique: someone whose like we will never see again.

Reg was 'the Mount Everest of Australian equine veterinarians'[30] and, in a small rural Queensland town, he built a world-class hospital. OVH, that cornerstone of Australian veterinary science has changed, but though some might mourn the passage of time as the loss of Reg's gifts to his profession, this would be a mistake. There is no doubt that Reg was the heart and soul of OVH. The hospital's lifeblood flowed from and through him, carried to every inch of the practice by a network of capillaries and blood vessels so small as to be almost invisible – but undeniable. That in 2022 OVH is quieter and less central to the wider veterinary community is not a demonstration of Reg's impermanence, or that his legacy has been lost. Buildings are only buildings, after all. What Reg gave was so much greater. For decades, he carried the Australian veterinary profession on his shoulders. He assumed this weight with humility and ease and with a quiet, unassuming pragmatism.

In the end, Reg Pascoe's life stands as a testament to his inimitable character: an unquenchable thirst for knowledge; a boundless capacity for work; an unceasing quest for excellence; and an unshakeable dedication to serving his community and his profession. Those who come after to benefit from the Australian veterinary industry's professionalism, knowledge, skill and compassion, should always be grateful for those who poured those foundations, and built those edifices high ... and Reg was there, quiet and constant, building his whole life through. It's a fitting legacy for the vet they called God.

Afterword

On 19 October 2017, Reg took Joy to the hospital to check on a lingering cough. He sat her down and walked to the reception desk to speak to the nurse, and as he waited, he collapsed on the cold tiled floor of St Vincent's Private Hospital in Toowoomba. He died instantly.

In the aftermath, more than one person asked what happened, but the truth is, the cause of Grandad's death is inconsequential. All that matters is that, in a moment, he was gone. He always gave the impression he'd simply go on forever: an institution, seemingly strong as an ox and indefatigable ... that, of course, is naive. But we were all shellshocked. Our family did the only thing we could: wherever possible, we came home.

I flew from Oklahoma to Australia for the funeral, wondering if perhaps the world had come off its axis. It was inconceivable that Grandad was gone, without warning, without any second chances; yet even amid my grief, the need to record his life remained in the back of my mind. I wrote down names amid Grandma Joy's recollections and the mounting pile of condolence cards; I took notes as various people, events and organisations cropped up in conversation and articles were published across various media.

I was single-minded in my purpose.

But more importantly, I tried to say goodbye. I wrote Grandad a letter that despite my best efforts still failed to encapsulate the world I wanted to convey to him and tucked it into the breast pocket of his suit. I stood in a black dress at the funeral home and sat among my brothers and my cousins, and I cried those sobs that feel as if they have been wrenched from your guts against your will.

That night, our family gathered around Grandma in that faithful blue house up behind the practice, those buildings that had been

Grandad's great life's work. I don't think I saw clearly then what I know now to be true: that a truly great human life isn't encapsulated by concrete footpaths, bricks and mortar, or how many horses fill the hospital paddocks.

In the weeks that followed, I began emailing and calling people around the world – England, Australia, the US, Hong Kong. In the years after that, I gathered people's stories the way a bower bird gathers beauty to feather its nest. And with every new person I spoke to, it became clearer that Reg had achieved professional and personal feats that were not only rare, but crucial to the development of both Australia's horse and veterinary industries ... But that those accomplishments were not his true legacy.

I know enough of humanity to recognise that of all the hundreds, if not thousands, of lives he had touched, each would only have taken away the tiniest fragment of who he was and what he'd done. Every new fragment revealed that to measure such a man is a herculean task, perhaps even an impossible one – not because of the effort of tallying awards, but from attempting to quantify the unquantifiable: how we change the lives of those we meet, and how we remain etched in their hearts, and their minds, and their own lives.

What did my grandfather, Reginald Roland Roessler Pascoe, leave me?

So many things. There are the deep-set eyes, and his rather distinctive ears, and various realisations: that anyone can reach above where they began; that to have a great passion upon which to centre our lives is a gift, but that it is also a responsibility; that to help others and share what we have learnt without the need for payment is easier than it sounds and more important than we might ever know.

Finally, that what matters is *who we are*, not what we do.

The people we love best are usually the ones we yearn to make proud and to honour in our lives. I owe parts of myself to Grandad and whatever mixture of pieces have created me, who I am has allowed me to perform this final service to him.

In the immediate aftermath of his death, I wrote, 'Why are words, one of the things I trust and rely on the most, deserting me now?'

I hope that they have not deserted me in trying to capture the brilliance and greatness of who he was.

Acknowledgements

When a book is published, the author's name is usually prominent on the cover, and to the author goes the credit ... but, as with any book, this biography was only made possible through the assistance of many people around the world, who gave generously of themselves so that I could bring Reg Pascoe's tale to life.

This project would not have been possible without the love, support and faith of Reg's wife, my Grandma Joy. Grandma, I came to you six years ago with a tiny kernel of an idea and a tentative suggestion for a project that I think we both thought would be somewhat smaller than it's ended up. Since that first moment, you have believed in this book. This is *your* story as much as it is Grandad's, and there is no greater act of kindness and trust than to hand that story to someone else and allow them to tell it. Thank you for your faith in me. You have been an incredible source of wonderful stories, useful documentation – and boundless patience.

I am, as always, indebted to my husband James. I am so grateful for you and everything you are; our life together is far, far better than anything I could ever have imagined – except, perhaps, getting a third cat. If two got me this far, think what I could do with another furry muse/assistant! Thanks must go to Bragi and Cicero for bringing so much laughter and joy to my life, as well as endless snuggles; happiness truly is a warm cat.

We are all a product of where we come from and I can confidently say that my stock is good. For that, and for many other reasons, I'd like to express my deepest thanks to my family, both near and far. To my dad, Roess, thank you for casually looking at any possible issue with this book and shrugging, saying, 'You can sort that out when you get there.' What I heard then and have always heard from you throughout my life is, 'You can do this, and anything else you set your mind to.' It is one of the greatest gifts anyone has ever given me.

To my uncles, John and Andrew (Rabbit!), I am grateful for your support of this project and your willingness to help me out where possible. Thanks to Uncle Rabbit for sharing wonderful memories of your childhood, and for wise and measured advice when I was stuck on a particularly tricky issue. I would like to recognise the invaluable assistance of Uncle John and Aunty Sue; your priceless support in fact-checking veterinary 'stuff' for me when I needed help figuring out a tricky technical issue is appreciated more than I can say.

I am fortunate enough to have four wonderful brothers who enrich my life – even when they drive me up the wall. Thanks to Ello, Lach and Ferg for your love, support and friendship during this project and always. I love you guys. I'd also like to pay my special regards to my younger brother, Derm, for always being willing to seek out various 'vet-y' articles for me … no matter how long it took to trawl the university archives for them! Thanks, Derm, I love you.

I cannot begin to express my love for, and gratitude to, my cousin Kelley for her support and enthusiasm. Kel, you replied to every single update with such encouragement, passion and faith. When I was wrestling with an issue or excited about something else, you were one of the first (and only) people I wanted to share it with, because doing so was a recurrent source of joy. You are a bright light in the world and in my life – thank you for being you.

Endless thanks must also go to my two closest friends, Clare Coburn and Renee Summers. For about six years, you have always asked how 'the bio' is going – even when I'm sure it seemed like it would be 'going' forever! Your quiet, ready certainty that it was all going to work out and that whatever the book needed, I had it within me, has been a balm during difficult times.

This book would be a very different beast were it not for the work and wisdom of some fantastic editors. I cannot begin to express my thanks to Bronwyn O'Reilly for her brilliant structural edit of this book in 2020 and to Rod Morrison for his precise and insightful copy-edit in 2021: between the two of you, you transformed this book in ways for which I will always be grateful. Thanks too to Tricia Dearborn for her discerning assessment of an earlier manuscript version in 2019 and to Jacqui Lipton at Raven Quill Literary Agency for her guidance on nonfiction book proposals in 2018 and 2019.

I was fortunate enough to interview many people who kindly shared their memories of Reg with me. I'm extremely grateful to Andrew Dart; David Laws; Trevor Heath; Dorraine Waldow; Bob Menrath; Jon Hill; Jayne McGhie; Alan Seawright; Vic Menrath; Jonathon Pycock; Paul Green; Derek Knottenbelt; Chris Riggs; Scott McAlpine; Dave Lovell; Cheryl Lopate; Mike Huber; Bill Howey; Twink Allen; Julie Strous; David Skerman; Glen Laws; Debbie Dennien; Glenda Sinclair-Gordon; Max Wilson; Nigel Nichols; Shirl Adamson; Hugh White; Chris Johnson; Bruce Donaldson; David Johnson; George Smyth; Eric Donaldson Snr; Patricia Ellis; Colin Curry; Doug Eckhardt; David Norgate; Ian Nielsen; Leo Jeffcott; Louise Winkel; Keith Hughes; Peter Huntington; Jim Vasey; Quentin Wallace; Malcolm McLennan; Sue Hollindale; Roger Kelly; James Gilkerson; Bruce Pott; Garth McGilvray; Tony Nicholls; Mark Benson; Barrie Grant; Murray Wise; Chris Pollitt; Sandy and Bill Harbison; Andrew Van Eps; Jane Axon; Virginia Studdert; Graham Burgess; Chris Reardon; Nick Kannegieter; Frank Low; and Jakob Malmo. Without you, this book could never have happened. Your kindness, patience and generosity allowed me to discover more about Reg than would ever have otherwise been possible. Some of you kindly sent photos or patiently answered numerous emails when I found myself struggling with minor tricky questions. Your heartfelt words of encouragement buoyed me. On days when I felt overwhelmed or unsure, you reminded me how worthwhile this task was. I am so grateful for you all, and I hope you find joy in this tribute.

Where would any author be without archivists? I'd like to extend my gratitude to the historians, archivists and library staff at the University of Queensland, the Toowoomba & Darling Downs Family History Society, the Toowoomba Historical Society and the Toowoomba Regional Council – particularly Bruce Ibsen, Susan Kotzur and Maurice French. Without your time, patience and diligent searching for supporting materials, much of my fact-checking would have been very poor, very difficult, or non-existent! I'm also grateful for the aid of Diane Taylor and Julanne Neal at the Queensland State Archives.

There were also many people who, receiving in their inbox an unexpected email from a stranger, went out of their way to help me hunt down information, raided their personal archives for content, or generously built bridges to take me to others who might be able to help. For this, I would also like to thank Dr Kerry Dowsett; Professor Nigel Perkins, the University of Queensland, and the Thoroughbred Advisory Board AgriFutures; Dr Anne Jackson; Dr Brian Sheahan; Mrs Diana Hughes; Sophie Han, the Australian Research Centre; Dr Oliver J. Ginther, the University of Wisconsin – Madison; Annelies McGaw, AgriFutures; Jeffrey Wilkinson, Equine Vets Australia; Tanya William, Victoria Racing Club; and Alex Watt, Australian Research Council.

I'd also like to acknowledge the assistance of an assorted group of UK doctors and administrators who received a request for help that must have seemed both bizarre and unreasonable, but very kindly did their best to create a chain of human connection to lead me to my goal. At the Cancer Research UK Cambridge Centre, I am indebted particularly to Dr John Griffiths for distributing my request far and wide, and appreciate the help of Professor Richard Gilbertson, Dr Davina Honess, Dr Anwar Padhani, and Dr Peter Hoskins in suggesting new avenues to try. I would like to pay my special regards to Wendy Sookram at the Paul Strickland Scanner Centre, Mount Vernon Hospital, who was vital in helping me find the person I was looking for. You all played critical parts in helping me to track down information about Reg's role in equine ultrasound.

Several friends kindly offered to be the (very!) early readers of sections of this book and offered both perceptive comments and much-needed encouragement. I'd like to acknowledge the help of Sita Norsworthy, Steve Rogers and Veronica Townley-Jones.

All writers knows that we are sometimes just a flimsy shell of humanity, hollowed out by rejection and the challenge of pursuing our craft ... but endlessly propped up on the inside by a steel framework of writer friends. Thank you to the inimitable Nancy Koziol for so readily sharing your blueprint for nonfiction book proposals and offering to help with any questions I might have. I love being a part of the brilliant, multinational Scribes United, a writers' group that continually pushes me to be better and allows me to share the at times lonely life of a writer with an awesome crew who know exactly what it's like: thank you to you all for the innumerable short stories you have read and helped me finesse! Several SU friends – Carrie Houghton, Laila Miller, Myna Chang and Jennifer Worrell – kindly read through synopsis and other section drafts at various stages; thank you for your considered commentary and encouragement. Thanks must also go to Kylie Hough for always sending me writing competitions, calls for nonfiction submissions and just general 'we'll get there, someday!' props on a regular basis.

Finally, I cannot fail to acknowledge that this book was predominantly written in Australia, and therefore was imagined, researched and created on the traditional lands of many Aboriginal nations. I would like to acknowledge and pay my respects to the peoples of the Darug, Tharawal, Eora, Yuggera and Barunggam nations, and to their elders past and present. Sovereignty was never ceded. It always was, and always will be, Aboriginal land.

About the Author

AZ Pascoe is a Queensland-born Australian writer who, despite having spent most her adult life living interstate, proclaims herself a Queenslander whenever the opportunity arises. After several years in the Australian Army, she completed both a Bachelor and a Master of Arts, majoring in Literature and Writing and currently works part-time as an adult gymnastics coach. When not pursuing some new project (writing or otherwise), she enjoys lifting weights and spending time upside down in a handstand, which considering that she also loves the topsy-turvy world of writing, makes perfect sense really.

AZ Pascoe's writing is inspired by the fragility of relationships, everything uniquely Australian, and those subtle moments in life that are so vital, but so easily missed. She currently lives in Sydney with her husband and two cheeky, demanding cat-muses who want to be involved in almost everything she does.

Visit azpascoe.com
or check out @azpascoe on Instagram to learn more.

Glossary

ACVS – Australian College of Veterinary Surgeons
AVBC – Australian Veterinary Boards Council
AERF – Australian Equine Research Foundation
AEVA – Australian Equine Veterinarians Association (see: EVA)
AVA – Australian Veterinary Association
BEVA – British Equine Veterinarians Association
BVSc – Bachelor of Veterinary Science
CVE – Centre for Veterinary Education
CEM – Contagious Equine Metritis
DVSc – Doctorate of Veterinary Science
ECE – Equine Coital Exanthema
EHV – Equine Herpesvirus
ETU – Equine Teaching Unit
EVA – Equine Veterinarians Australia (originally AEVA: Australian Equine Veterinarians Association)
ISER – International Symposium on Equine Reproduction
MCQ – Multiple Choice Quiz
NOOSR – National Office for Overseas Skills Recognition
NVE – National Veterinary Examination
OVH – Oakey Veterinary Hospital
PGF – Post-Graduate Foundation
QERF – Queensland Equine Research Foundation
RCVS – Royal College of Veterinary Surgeons
RIRDC – Rural Industries Research and Development Commission
UQ – University of Queensland
VSB – Veterinary Surgeons Board

Endnotes

[1] Interview with David Johnson, 17 Aug 2019
[2] Interview with David Laws, 17 Feb 2018
[3] Interview with Jayne McGhie, 06 Apr 2018
[4] Interview with Chris Riggs, 28 Aug 2018
[5] Alan Jones homily, Reg Pascoe Memorial Service 2017
[6] Interview with Jayne McGhie, 06 Apr 2018
[7] Interview with Chris Pollitt, 29 Jan 2020
[8] Interview with Derek Knottenbelt, 24 Aug 2018
[9] Interview with Scott McAlpine, 30 Aug 2018
[10] Interview with Shirl Adamson, 03 Jul 2019
[11] Interview with Andrew Dart, 28 Jan 2018
[12] Interview with Cheryl Lopate, 07 Oct 2018
[13] Interview with Andrew Dart, 28 Jan 2018
[14] Interview with David Skerman, 23 May 2019
[15] Interview with Bill Howey, 20 Nov 2018
[16] Interview with Trevor Heath, 01 Mar 2018
[17] Interview with Keith Hughes, 27 Oct 2019
[18] Interview with Patricia Ellis, 27 Sep 2019
[19] Interview with Bob Menrath, 13 Mar 2018
[20] Interview with Cheryl Lopate, 07 Oct 2018
[21] Interview with Andrew Dart, 28 Jan 2018
[22] Interview with Chris Riggs, 28 Aug 2018
[23] Interview with Max Wilson, 23 Jun 2019
[24] Interview with Chris Reardon, 04 Mar 2020
[25] Interview with Trevor Heath, 01 Mar 2018
[26] Interview with Dorraine Waldow, 04 Mar 2018
[27] Interview with David Johnson, 17 Aug 2019
[28] Notes from Dr Leanne Begg, 25 Feb 2019
[29] Interview with Frank Low, 28 Mar 2020
[30] Interview with Peter Huntington, 27 Oct 2019

www.ingramcontent.com/pod-product-compliance
Lightning Source LLC
Chambersburg PA
CBHW070247010526
44107CB00056B/2366